The Recollections of
Constant

NAPOLEON AT MALMAISON

The Recollections of
Constant
Valet to the Emperor Napoleon
Volume 1: 1790 - 1809

Louis Constant Wairy

The Recollections of Constant Valet to the Emperor Napoleon
Volume 1: 1790 - 1809
by Louis Constant Wairy
Translated by Walter Clark

This two volume Leonaur edition contains the complete text of the three volume edition of 1895.
The chapters in this edition have been re-numbered and follow sequentially from Volume 1 to Volume 2.

Leonaur is an imprint of Oakpast Ltd

Material original to this edition and presentation of text in this form copyright © 2009 Oakpast Ltd

ISBN: 978-1-84677-818-6 (hardcover)
ISBN: 978-1-84677-817-9 (softcover)

http://www.leonaur.com

Publisher's Notes

The views expressed in this book are not necessarily those of the publisher.

Introduction

The career of a man compelled to make his own way, who is not an artisan or in some trade, does not usually begin till he is about twenty years of age. Till then he vegetates, uncertain of his future, neither having, nor being able to have, any well-defined purpose. It is only when he has arrived at the full development of his powers, and his character and bent of mind are shown, that he can determine his profession or calling. Not till then does he know himself, and see his way open before him. In fact, it is only then that he begins to live.

Reasoning in this manner, my life from my twentieth year has been thirty years, which can be divided into equal parts, so far as days and months are counted, but very unequal parts, considering the events which transpired in each of those two periods of my life.

Attached to the person of the Emperor Napoleon for fifteen years, I have seen all the men, and witnessed all the important events, which centred around him. I have seen far more than that; for I have had under my eyes all the circumstances of his life, the least as well as the greatest, the most secret as well as those which are known to history,—I have had, I repeat, incessantly under my eyes the man whose name, solitary and alone, fills the most glorious pages of our history. Fifteen years I followed him in his travels and his campaigns, was at his court, and saw him in the privacy of his family. Whatever step he wished to take, whatever order he gave, it was necessarily very difficult for the Emperor not to admit me, even though involuntarily, into his confidence; so that without desiring it, I have more than once found myself in the possession of secrets I should have preferred not to know. What wonderful things happened during those fifteen years! Those near the Emperor lived as if in the centre of a whirlwind; and so quick was the succession of overwhelming events, that one felt dazed, as it were, and if he wished to pause and fix his attention for a moment, there instantly came, like another flood, a succession of events which carried him along with them without giving him time to fix his thoughts.

Succeeding these times of activity which made one's brain whirl, there came to me the most absolute repose in an isolated retreat where I passed another interval of fifteen years after leaving the Emperor. But what a contrast! To those who have lived, like myself, amid the conquests and wonders of the Empire, what is left today? If the strength of our manhood was passed amid the bustle of years so short, yet so fully occupied, our careers were sufficiently long and fruitful, and it is time to give ourselves up to repose. We can withdraw from the world, and close our eyes. Can it be possible to see anything equal to what we have seen? Such scenes do not come twice in the lifetime of any man; and having seen them, they suffice to occupy his memory through all his remaining years, and in retirement he can find nothing better to occupy his leisure moments than the recollections of what he has witnessed.

Thus it has been with me. The reader will readily believe that I have had no greater pleasure than that of recalling the memories of the years passed in the service of the Emperor. As far as possible, I have kept myself informed as to everything that has been written of my former master, his family, and his court; and while listening to these narrations read by my wife and sister at our fireside, the long evenings have passed like an instant! When I found in these books, some of which are truly only miserable rhapsodies, statements which were incorrect, false, or slanderous, I, took pleasure in correcting such statements, or in showing their absurdity. My wife, who lived, as I did, in the midst of these events, also made her corrections, and, without other object than our own satisfaction, made notes of our joint observations.

All who came to see us in our retreat, and took pleasure in having me narrate what I had seen, were astonished and often indignant at the falsehoods with which ignorance or malevolence had calumniated the Emperor and the Empire, and expressing their gratitude for the correct information I was able to give them, advised me also to furnish it to the public. But I attached no importance to the suggestion, and was far from dreaming that some day I should be the author of a book, until M. Ladvocat came to our hermitage, and urged me earnestly to publish my memoirs, offering himself to become the publisher.

At the very time my wife and I received this unexpected visit, we were reading together the *Memoirs of Bourrienne*, which the Ladvocat publishing-house had just issued; and we had remarked more than once how exempt these Memoirs were from both that spirit of disparagement and of adulation which we had noticed with disgust in other books on the same subject. M. Ladvocat advised me to complete the sketch of the Emperor, which, owing to his elevated position and habitual occupations, Bourrienne had been able to make only from a political point of view; and in accordance with his advice, I shall relate in simple words, and in a manner suited to my relations with the Emperor, those things which Bourrienne has necessarily omitted, and which no one could know so well as I.

I candidly admit that my objections to M. Ladvocat's advice were entirely overcome when he called my attention to this passage in the introduction to Bourrienne's memoirs:

> If every one who had any relations with Napoleon, whatever the time and place, will accurately and without prejudice record what he saw and heard, the future historian of his life will be rich in materials. I hope that whoever undertakes that difficult task will find in my notes some information which may be useful in perfecting his work.

Having re-read these lines attentively, I said to myself that I could furnish memoranda and information which would refute errors, brand falsehoods, and bring to light what I knew to be the truth. In a word, I felt that I could give in my testimony, and that it was my duty to do so, in the long trial which has been held ever since the overthrow of the Emperor; for I had been an eye-witness, had seen everything, and could say, "I was there." Others also have been close to the Emperor and his court, and I may often repeat what they have said, for the feats which they describe I had the same opportunity of witnessing; but, on the other hand, whatever I know of private matters, and whatever I may reveal which was secret and unknown, no one till this time could possibly have known, or consequently have related.

From the departure of the First Consul for the campaign of Marengo, whither I went with him, until the departure from Fontainebleau, when I was compelled to leave him, I was absent only twice, once for three days and once for seven or eight days. Excepting these short leaves of absence, the latter of which was on account of my health, I quitted the Emperor no more than his shadow.

It has been said that no one is a hero to his *valet de chambre*. I beg leave to dissent from this. The Emperor, as near as I was to him, was always a hero; and it was a great advantage also to see the man as he was. At a distance you were sensible only of the prestige of his glory and his power; but on getting closer to him you enjoyed, besides, the surprising charm of his conversation, the entire simplicity of his family life, and I do not hesitate to say, the habitual kindliness of his character.

The reader, if curious to learn beforehand in what spirit these Memoirs are written, will perhaps read with interest this passage of a letter that I wrote to my publisher:

> Bourrienne had, perhaps, reason for treating Napoleon, as a public man, with severity. But we view him from different standpoints, and I speak only of the hero in undress. He was then almost always kind, patient, and rarely unjust. He was much attached to those about him, and received with kindness and good nature the services of those whom he liked. He was a man of habit. It is as a devoted servant that I wish to speak of the Emperor, and in no wise as a critic. It is not, however, an apotheosis in several volumes that I wish to write: for I am on this point somewhat like fathers who recognize the faults of their children, and reprove them earnestly, while at the same time they are ready to make excuses for their errors.

I trust that I shall be pardoned the familiarity, or, if you will, the inappropriateness of this comparison, for the sake of the feeling which dictates it. Besides, I do not propose either to praise or blame, but simply to relate that which fell within my knowledge, without trying to prejudice the opinion of any one.

I cannot close this introduction without a few words as to myself, in reply to the calumnies which have not spared, even in his retirement, a man who should have no enemies, if, to be protected from malice, it were sufficient to have done a little good, and no harm to any one. I am reproached with having abandoned my master after his fall, and not having shared his exile. I will show that, if I did not follow the Emperor, it was because I lacked not the will but the power to do so. God knows that I do not wish to undervalue the devotion of the faithful servants who followed the fortunes of the Emperor to the end. However, it is not improper to say that, however terrible the fall of the Emperor was for him, the situation (I speak here only of the personal advantages), in the island of Elba, of those who remained in his service, and who were not detained in France by an inexorable necessity, was still not without its advantages; and it was not, therefore, my personal interests which caused me to leave him. I shall explain hereafter my reasons for quitting his service.

I shall also give the truth as to the alleged abuse of confidence, of which, according to others, I was guilty in respect to the Emperor. A simple statement of the mistake which gave rise to this falsehood, I trust, will clear me of every suspicion of indelicacy; but if it is necessary to add other proofs, I could obtain them from those who lived nearest to the Emperor, and who were in a condition to both know and understand what passed between us; and lastly, I invoke fifty years of a blameless life, and I can say: "When I was in a situation to render great services, I did so; but I never sold them. I could have derived advantages from the petitions that I made for people, who, in consequence of my solicitations, have acquired immense fortunes; but I refused even the proper acknowledgment which in, their gratitude (very deep at that time) they felt compelled to offer me, by proposing an interest in their enterprises. I did not seek to take advantage, for my own benefit, of the generosity with which the Emperor so long deigned to honour me, in order to enrich or secure places for my relatives; and I retired poor after fifteen years passed in the personal service of the richest and most powerful monarch of Europe."

Having made these statements, I shall await with confidence the judgment of my readers.

Constant

Chapter 1

I shall refer to myself very little in these memoirs, for I am aware the public will examine them only for details concerning the great man to whom fortune attached me for sixteen years, and whom I scarcely quitted during the whole of that time. Notwithstanding, I ask permission to say a few words as to my childhood, and the circumstances which made me *valet de chambre* of the Emperor.

I was born Dec. 2, 1778, at Peruelz, a town which became French on the annexation of Belgium to the Republic, and which then belonged to the Department of Jemmapes. Soon after my birth at the baths of Saint Amand, my father took charge of a small establishment called the Little Chateau, at which visitors to the waters were boarding, being aided in this enterprise by the Prince de Croi, in whose house he had been steward. Business prospered beyond my father's hopes, for a great number of invalids of rank came to his house. When I attained my eleventh year, the Count de Lure, head of one of the chief families of Valenciennes, happened to be one of the boarders at the Little Chateau; and as that excellent man had taken a great fancy to me, he asked my parents permission that I should become a companion to his son, who was about. the same age. My family had intended me for the church, to gratify one of my uncles, who was Dean of Lessine, a man of great wisdom and rigid virtue; and thinking that the offer of the Count de Lure would not affect my intended destination, my father accepted it, judging that some years passed in a family so distinguished would give me a taste for the more serious studies necessary to fit me for the priesthood. I set out, therefore, with the Count de Lure, much grieved at leaving my parents, but pleased also at the same time, as is usual with one at my age, with new scenes. The count took me to one of his estates near Tours, where I was received with the greatest kindness by the countess and her children, with whom I was placed on a footing of perfect equality.

Unfortunately I did not profit very long by the kindness of the count and the lessons. I was taught at his house, for hardly a year had passed at the chateau when we learned of the arrest of the king at Varennes. The count and his family were in despair; and child as I was, I remember that I was deeply pained at the news, without knowing why, but doubtless because it is natural to share the sentiments of those with whom you live, when they treat you with as much kindness as the count and countess had treated me. However, I continued to enjoy the happy freedom from care natural to youth, till one morning I was awakened by a loud noise, and was immediately surrounded by a great number of people, none of whom I knew, and who asked me countless questions which I could not answer. I then learned that the count and his family had emigrated. I was carried to the town hall, where the same questions were renewed, with the same fruitless result; for I knew nothing of the intentions of my late protectors, and could only reply by a flood of tears when I saw myself abandoned and left to my own resources, at a great distance from my family.

I was too young then to reflect on the conduct of the count; but I have since thought that his abandonment of me was an act of delicacy on his part, as he did not wish to make me an *émigré* without the consent of my parents. I have always believed that, before his departure, the count had committed me to the care of some one, who subsequently did not dare to claim me, lest he should compromise himself, which was then, as is well known, exceedingly dangerous. Behold me, then, at twelve years of age, left without a guide, without means of support, without any one to advise me, and without money, more than a hundred leagues from my home, and already accustomed to the comforts of a luxurious life. It is hardly credible that in this state of affairs I was regarded almost as a suspect, and was required each day to present myself before the city authorities for the greater safety of the Republic. I remember well that whenever the Emperor was pleased to make me relate these tribulations of my childhood, he never failed to repeat several times, "the fools," referring to these same city authorities. However that may be, the authorities of Tours, coming to the conclusion, at last, that a child of twelve was incapable of overthrowing the Republic, gave me a passport, with the injunction to leave the city within twenty-four hours, which I proceeded to do with a hearty good-will, but not without deep grief also at seeing myself alone, and on foot, with a long journey before me. After much privation and many hardships I arrived at last in the neighbourhood of Saint-Amand, which I found in the possession of the Austrians, and that it was impossible for me to reach the town, as the French surrounded it. In my despair I seated myself on the side of a ditch and was weeping bitterly, when I was noticed by the chief of squadron, Michau,[1] who afterwards became colonel and *aide-de-camp* to General Loison. Michau approached me, questioned me with great interest, and made me relate my sad adventures, which touched him deeply, while he did not conceal his inability to send me back to my family. He had just obtained leave of absence, which he was going to spend with his family at Chinon, and proposed to me to accompany him, which invitation I accepted with gratitude. I cannot say too much of the kindness and consideration shown me by his household during the three or four months I spent with them. At the end of that time he took me to Paris, where I was soon after placed in the house of M. Gobert, a rich merchant, who treated me with the greatest, kindness.

I lately visited M. Gobert; and he recalled to me that, when we travelled together, he gave up to me one of the seats of his carriage, upon which I was permitted to stretch myself out and sleep. I mention this circumstance, otherwise unimportant, to show the kindness he always showed me.

Some years later I made the acquaintance of Carrat, who was in the service of Madame Bonaparte while the general was absent on the Egyptian expedition. Before relating how I came to enter her household, it is proper to mention how Carrat himself came into her service, and at the same time narrate some anecdotes in regard to him, which will show what were the pastimes of the inhabitants of Malmaison at that date.

Carrat happened to be at Plombieres when Madame Bonaparte[2] went there to take the waters. Every day he brought her bouquets, and addressed to her little complimentary speeches, so singular and so droll, that Josephine was much diverted, as were also the ladies who accompanied her, among whom were Mesdames de Cambis and de Criguy, and especially her own daughter Hortense, who was convulsed at his oddities. The truth is, he was exceedingly amusing, by reason of a certain simplicity and originality of character, which, however, did not prevent him from being a person of intelligence; and his eccentricities did not displease Madame Bonaparte. A sentimen-

---

1. I afterwards had the happiness of obtaining for him, from the Emperor, a position he wished, as a place of retirement, having lost the use of his right arm.—Constant.
2. Madame Bonaparte, nee Marie Joseph Rose Tascher de la Pagerie, was born in Martinique, 1763; became the widow of Viscount Alexander de Beauharnais, 1794; married Napoleon Bonaparte March, 1796; became Empress May 18, 1804; was divorced Dec. 16, 1809; died at Malmaison, May 20, 1814.—Trans.

tal scene took place when this excellent lady left the springs. Carrat wept, bemoaned himself, and expressed his lasting grief at not being able to see Madame Bonaparte daily, as he had been accustomed; and Madame Bonaparte was so kind-hearted that she at once decided to carry him to Paris with her. She taught him to dress hair, and finally appointed him her hair-dresser and valet, at least such were the duties he had to perform when I made his acquaintance. He was permitted a most astonishing freedom of speech, sometimes even scolding her; and when Madame Bonaparte, who was extremely generous and always gracious towards every one, made presents to her women, or chatted familiarly with them, Carrat would reproach her. "Why give that?" he would say, adding, "See how you do, Madame; you allow yourself to jest with your domestics. Some day they will show you a want of respect." But if he thus endeavoured to restrain the generosity of his mistress towards those around her, he did not hesitate to stimulate her generosity towards himself; and whenever he took a fancy to anything, would simply say, "You ought to give me that."

Bravery is not always the inseparable companion of wit, and Carrat gave more than once proof of this. Being endowed with a kind of simple and uncontrollable poltroonery, which never fails in comedies to excite the laughter of the spectators, it was a great pleasure to Madame Bonaparte to play on him such pranks as would bring out his singular want of courage.

It should be stated, first of all, that one of the greatest pleasures of Madame Bonaparte, at Malmaison, was to take walks on the road just outside the walls of the park; and she always preferred this outside road, in spite of the clouds of dust which were constantly rising there, to the delightful walks inside the park. One day, accompanied by her daughter Hortense, she told Carrat to follow her in her walk; and he was delighted to be thus honoured until he saw rise suddenly out of a ditch; a great figure covered with a white sheet, in fact, a genuine ghost, such as I have seen described in the translations of some old English romances.

It is unnecessary to say, that the ghost was some one placed there by order of these ladies, in order to frighten Carrat; and certainly the comedy succeeded marvellously well, for as soon as Carrat perceived the ghost, he was very much frightened, and clutching Madame Bonaparte, said to her in a tremor, "Madame, Madame, do you see that ghost? It is the spirit of the lady who died lately at Plombieres."

"Be quiet, Carrat, you are a coward."

"Ah, but indeed it is her spirit which has come back." As Carrat

PRINCE EUGENE

thus spoke, the man in the white sheet advanced toward him, shaking it; and poor Carrat, overcome with terror, fell backwards in a faint, and it required all the attentions which were bestowed upon him to restore him to consciousness.

Another day, while the general was still in Egypt, and consequently before I was in the service of any member of his family, Madame Bonaparte wished to give some of her ladies an exhibition of Carrat's cowardice; and for this purpose there was concerted among the ladies of Malmaison a plot, in which Mademoiselle Hortense[3] was chief conspirator. This incident has been so often narrated in my presence by Madame Bonaparte, that I am familiar with the ludicrous details. Carrat slept in a room adjoining which there was a closet. A hole was made in the wall between these rooms, and a string passed through, at the end of which was tied a can filled with water, this cooling element being suspended exactly over the head of the patient's bed. This was not all, for they had also taken the precaution to remove the slats which supported the mattress; and as Carrat was in the habit of going to sleep without a light, he saw neither the preparations for his downfall, nor the can of water provided for his new baptism. All the members of the plot had been waiting for some moments in the adjoining closet; when he threw himself heavily upon his bed, it crashed in, and at the same instant the play of the string made the can of water do its effective work. The victim at the same time of a fall, and of a nocturnal shower-bath, Carrat cried out against his double misfortune. "This is horrible," he yelled at the top of his voice; while Hortense maliciously said aloud to her mother, Madame de Crigny (afterwards Madame Denon), Madame Charvet, and to several others in the room, "Oh, Mamma, those toads and frogs in the water will get on him." These words, joined to the utter darkness, served only to increase the terror of Carrat, who, becoming seriously frightened, cried out, "It is horrible, Madame, it is horrible, to amuse yourself thus at the expense of your servants."

I do not say that the complaints of Carrat were entirely wrong, but they. served only to increase the gayety of the ladies who had taken him for the object of their pleasantries.

However that may be, such was the character and position of Carrat, whom I had known for some time, when General Bonaparte returned from his expedition into Egypt, and Carrat said to me that Eugene de Beauharnais had applied to him for a confidential valet,

---

3. Hortense Beauharnais, born at Paris, 1783, was then just sixteen years of age. Married Louis Bonaparte and became Queen of Holland, 1806. Died 1837. She was the mother of Napoleon III.—Trans.

his own having been detained in Cairo by severe illness at the time of his departure. He was named Lefebvre, and was an old servant entirely devoted to his master, as was every one who knew Prince Eugene; for I do not believe that there has ever lived a better man, or one more polite, more considerate, or indeed more attentive, to those who served him.

Carrat having told me that Eugene de Beauharnais[4] desired a young man to replace Lefebvre, and having recommended me for the place, I had the good fortune to be presented to Eugene, and to give satisfaction; indeed, he was so kind as to say to me that my appearance pleased him, and he wished me to enter upon my duties immediately. I was delighted with this situation, which, I know not why, painted itself to my imagination in the brightest colours, and without loss of time, went to find my modest baggage, and behold me *valet de chambre*, ad interim, of M. de Beauharnais, not dreaming that I should one day be admitted to the personal service of General Bonaparte, and still less that I should become the chief valet of an Emperor.

---

4. Born 1781, viceroy of Italy 1805. In 1806 married the daughter of the King of Bavaria. Died 1824. Among his descendants are the present King of Sweden and the late Emperor of Brazil.—Trans.

Chapter 2

It was on Oct. 16, 1799, that Eugene de Beauharnais arrived in Paris on his return from Egypt; and almost immediately thereafter I had the good fortune to be taken into his service, M. Eugene being then twenty-one years of age. I soon after learned a few particulars, which I think are little known, relative to his former life, and the marriage of his mother with General Bonaparte.

His father, as is well known, was one of the victims of the Revolution; and when the Marquis de Beauharnais had perished on the scaffold, his widow, whose property had been confiscated, fearing that her son, although still very young, might also be in danger on account of his belonging to the nobility, placed him in the home of a carpenter on the Rue de l'Echelle where, a lady of my acquaintance, who lived on that street, has often seen him passing, carrying a plank on his shoulder. It seems a long distance from this position to the colonelcy of a regiment of the Consular guards, and the vice-royalty of Italy.

I learned, from hearing Eugene himself relate it, by what a singular circumstance he had been the cause of the first meeting between his mother and his step-father. Eugene, being then not more than fourteen or fifteen years of age, having been informed that General Bonaparte had become possessor of the sword of the Marquis de Beauharnais, took a step which seemed hazardous, but was crowned with success. The general having received him graciously, Eugene explained that he came to beg of him the restoration of his father's sword. His face, his bearing, his frank request, all made such a pleasant impression on Bonaparte, that he immediately presented him with the sword which he requested. As soon as this sword was in his hands he covered it with kisses and tears; and the whole was done in so artless a manner, that Bonaparte was delighted with him.

Madame de Beauharnais, being informed of the welcome the general had given her son, thought it her duty to make him a visit of gratitude. Bonaparte, being much pleased with Josephine in this first interview, returned her visit. They met again frequently; and as is well known, one event led to another, until she became the first Empress of the French; and I can assert from the numerous proofs that I have had of this fact, that Bonaparte never ceased to love Eugene as well as if he, had been his own son.

The qualities of Eugene were both attractive and solid. His features were not regular, and yet his countenance prepossessed every one in his favour. He had a well-proportioned figure, but did not make a distinguished appearance, on account of the habit he had of swinging himself as he walked. He was about five feet three or four inches[1] in height. He was kind, gay, amiable, full of wit, intelligent, generous; and it might well be said that his frank and open countenance was the mirror of his soul. How many services he has rendered others during the course of his life, and at the very period when in order to do so he had often to impose privations on himself.

It will soon be seen how it happened that I passed only a month with Eugene; but during this short space of time, I recall that, while fulfilling scrupulously his duties to his mother and his step-father, he was much addicted to the pleasures so natural to his age and position. One of his greatest pleasures was entertaining his friends at breakfast; which he did very often. This amused me much on account of the comical scenes of which I was often a witness. Besides the young officers of Bonaparte's staff, his most frequent guests, he had also frequently at his table the ventriloquist Thiemet, Dugazon, Dazincourt, and Michau of the Theatre Francais, and a few other persons, whose names escape me at this moment. As may be imagined, these reunions were extremely gay; these young officers especially, who had returned like Eugene from the expedition to Egypt, seemed trying to indemnify themselves for the recent privations they had had to suffer. At this time ventriloquists, among whom Thiemet held a very distinguished position, were the fashion in Paris, and were invited to private gatherings. I remember on one occasion, at one of these breakfasts of Eugene's, Thiemet called by their names several persons present, imitating the voices of their servants, as if they were just outside the door, while he remained quietly in his seat, appearing to be using his lips only to eat and drink, two duties' which he performed admirably. Each of the officers called in this manner went out, and found no one; and then Thiemet went out with them, under the pretext of assisting them in the search, and increased their perplexity by continuing to make them

---

1. About five feet six or seven inches in English measurement.—Trans.

hear some well-known voice. Most of them laughed heartily at the joke of which they had just been the victims; but there was one who, having himself less under control than his comrades, took the thing seriously, and became very angry, whereupon Eugene had to avow that he was the author of the conspiracy.

I recall still another amusing scene, the two heroes of which were this same Thiemet, of whom I have just spoken, and Dugazon. Several foreigners were present at a breakfast given by Eugene, the parts having been assigned, and learned in advance, and the two victims selected. When each had taken his place at table, Dugazon, pretending to stammer, addressed a remark to Thiemet, who, playing the same role, replied to him, stammering likewise; then each of them pretended to believe that the other was making fun of him, and there followed a stuttering quarrel between the two parties, each one finding it more and more difficult to express himself as his anger rose. Thiemet, who besides his role of stammering was also playing that of deafness, addressed his neighbour, his trumpet in his ear:

"Wha-wha-what-do-does he say?"

"Nothing," replied the officious neighbour, wishing to prevent a quarrel, and to supply facts while defending the other stammerer.—"So-so-he-he-he-he's ma-making fun of me!" Then the quarrel became more violent still; they were about to come to blows, when each of the two stammerers seizing a carafe of water, hurled it at the head of his antagonist, and a copious deluge of water from the bottles taught the officious neighbours the great danger of acting as peacemakers. The two stammerers continued to scream as is the custom of deaf persons, until the last drop of water was spilt; and I remember that Eugene, the originator of this practical joke, laughed immoderately the whole time this scene lasted. The water was wiped off; and all were soon reconciled, glass in hand. Eugene, when he had perpetrated a joke of this sort, never failed to relate it to his mother, and sometimes to his stepfather, who were much amused thereby, Josephine especially.

I had led for one month a very pleasant life with Eugene, when Lefebvre, the *valet de chambre* whom he had left sick at Cairo, returned in restored health, and asked to resume his place. Eugene, whom I suited better on account of my age and activity, proposed to him to enter his mother's service, suggesting to him that he would there have an easier time than with himself; but Lefebvre, who was extremely attached to his master, sought Madame Bonaparte, and confided to her his chagrin at this decision.

Josephine promised to assist him; and consoled him by assurances that she would suggest to her son that Lefebvre should reassume his former position, and that she would take me into her own service. This was done according to promise; and one morning Eugene announced to me, in the most gratifying manner, my change of abode. "Constant," he said to me, "I regret very much that circumstances require us to part; but you know Lefebvre followed me to Egypt, he is an old servant, and I feel compelled to give him his former position. Besides, you will not be far removed, as you will enter my mother's service, where you will be well treated, and we will see each other often. Go to her this morning; I have spoken to her of you. The matter is already arranged, and she expects you."

As may be believed, I lost no time in presenting myself to Madame Bonaparte. Knowing that she was at Malmaison, I went there immediately, and was received by her with a kindness which overwhelmed me with gratitude, as I was not then aware that she manifested this same graciousness to every one, and that it was as inseparable from her character as was grace from her person. The duties required of me, in her service, were altogether nominal; and nearly all my time was at my own disposal, of which I took advantage to visit Paris frequently. The life that I led at this time was very pleasant to a young man like myself, who could not foresee that in a short while he would be as much under subjection as he was then at liberty.

Before bidding adieu to a service in which I had found so much that was agreeable, I will relate some incidents which belong to that period, and which my situation with the stepson of General Bonaparte gave me the opportunity of learning.

M. de Bourrienne has related circumstantially in his memoirs the events of the 18th Brumaire;[2] and the account which he has given of that famous day is as correct as it is interesting, so that any one curious to know the secret causes which led to these political changes will find them faithfully pointed out in the narration of that minister of state. I am very far from intending to excite an interest of this, kind, but reading the work of M. Bourrienne put me again on the track of my own recollections. These memoirs relate to circumstances of which he was ignorant, or possibly may have omitted purposely as being of little importance; and whatever he has let fall on his road I think myself fortunate in being permitted to glean.

I was still with Eugene de Beauharnais when General Bonaparte overthrew the Directory; but I found myself in as favourable a situ-

---

2. The 18th Brumaire, Nov. 9, 1799, was the day Napoleon overthrew the Directory and made himself First Consul.—Trans.

ation to know all that was passing as if I had been in the service of Madame Bonaparte, or of the general himself, for my master, although he was very young, had the entire confidence of his stepfather, and, to an even greater degree, that of his mother, who consulted him on every occasion.

A few days before the 18th Brumaire, Eugene ordered me to make preparations for a breakfast he wished to give on that day to his friends, the number of the guests, all military men, being much larger than usual. This bachelor repast was made very gay by an officer, who amused the company by imitating in turn the manners and appearance of the directors and a few of their friends. To represent the Director Barras, he draped himself *'a la grecque'* with the tablecloth, took off his black cravat, turned down his shirt-collar, and advanced in an affected manner, resting his left arm on the shoulder of the youngest of his comrades, while with his right he pretended to caress his chin. Each person of the company understood the meaning of that kind of charade; and there were uncontrollable bursts of laughter.

He undertook then to represent the Abbe Sieyes, by placing an enormous band of paper inside of his neck cloth, and lengthening thus indefinitely a long, pale face. He made a few turns around the room, astraddle of his chair, and ended by a grand somersault, as if his steed had dismounted him. It is necessary to know, in order to understand the significance of this pantomime, that the Abbe Sieges had been recently taking lessons in horseback, riding in the garden of the Luxembourg, to the great amusement of the pedestrians, who gathered in crowds to enjoy the awkward and ungraceful exhibition made by this new master of horse.

The breakfast ended, Eugene reported for duty to General Bonaparte, whose *aide-de-camp* he was, and his friends rejoined the various commands to which they belonged.

I went out immediately behind them; for from a few words that had just been dropped at my young master's, I suspected that something grave and interesting was about to take place. M. Eugene had appointed a rendezvous with his comrades at Pont-Tournant; so I repaired to that spot, and found a considerable gathering of officers in uniform and on horseback, assembled in readiness to escort General Bonaparte to Saint-Cloud.

The commandant of each part of the army had been requested by General Bonaparte to give a breakfast to their corps of officers; and they had done so like my young master. Nevertheless, the officers, even the generals, were not all in the secret; and General Murat himself, who rushed into the Hall of the Five Hundred at the head of the grenadiers, believed that it was only a question of exemption, on account of age, that General Bonaparte intended to propose, in order that he might obtain the place of director.

I have learned from an authoritative source, that when General Jube, who was devoted to General Bonaparte, assembled in the court of the Luxembourg, the guard of the directors of which he was commander, the honest M. Gohier, president of the Directory, put his head out of the window, and cried to Jube: "Citizen General, what are you doing down there?"

"Citizen President, you can see for yourself I am mustering the guard."

"Certainly, I see that very plainly, Citizen General; but why are you mustering them?"

"Citizen President, I am going to make an inspection of them, and order a grand manoeuvre. Forward—march!" And the citizen general filed out at the head of his troop to rejoin General Bonaparte at Saint-Cloud; while the latter was awaited at the house of the citizen president, and the breakfast delayed to which General Bonaparte had been invited for that very morning.

General Marmont had also entertained at breakfast the officers of the division of the army which he commanded (it was, I think, the artillery). At the end of the repast he addressed a few words to them, urging them not to alienate their cause from that of the conqueror of Italy, and to accompany him to Saint-Cloud. "But how can we follow him?" cried one of his guests. "We have no horses."

"If that alone deters you, you will find horses in the court of this hotel. I have seized all those of the national riding-school. Let us go below and mount." All the officers present responded to the invitation except General Allix, who declared he would take no part in all this disturbance.

I was at Saint-Cloud on the two days, 18th and 19th Brumaire. I saw General Bonaparte harangue the soldiers, and read to them the decree by which he had been made commander-in-chief of all the troops at Paris, and of the whole of the Seventeenth Military Division. I saw him come out much agitated first from the Council of the Ancients, and afterwards from the Assembly of the Five Hundred. I saw Lucien Bonaparte brought out of the hall, where the latter assembly was sitting, by some grenadiers, sent in to protect him from the violence of his colleagues. Pale and furious, he threw himself on his horse and galloped straight to the troops to address them; and when he pointed his sword at his brother's breast, saying he would be the first to slay him if he dared to strike at liberty, cries of "Vive Bonaparte! down with the lawyers!" burst forth on all sides; and the soldiers, led by General Murat, rushed into the Hall of the Five Hundred. Everybody knows what then occurred, and I will not enter into details which have been so often related.

The general, now made First Consul, installed himself at the Luxembourg, though at this time he resided also at Malmaison. But he was often on the road, as was also Josephine; for their trips to Paris when they occupied this residence were very frequent, not only on Government business, which often required the presence of the First Consul, but also for the purpose of attending the theatre, of whose performances General Bonaparte, was very fond, giving the preference always to the Theatre Francais and the Italian Opera. This observation I make in passing, preferring to give hereafter the information I have obtained as to the tastes and habits of the emperor.

Malmaison, at the period of which I speak, was a place of unalloyed happiness, where all who came expressed their satisfaction with the state of affairs; everywhere also I heard blessings invoked upon the First Consul and Madame Bonaparte. There was not yet the shadow of that strict etiquette which it was necessary afterwards to observe at Saint-Cloud, at the Tuileries, and in all the palaces in which the Emperor held his court. The consular court was as yet distinguished by a simple elegance, equally removed from republican rudeness and the luxuriousness of the Empire. Talleyrand was, at this period, one of those who came most frequently to Malmaison. He sometimes dined there, but arrived generally in the evening between eight and nine o'clock, and returned at one, two, and sometimes three in the morning.

All were admitted at Madame Bonaparte's on a footing of equality, which was most gratifying. There came familiarly Murat, Duroc, Berthier, and all those who have since figured as great dignitaries, and some even as sovereigns, in the annals of the empire.

The family of General Bonaparte were assiduous in their attentions; but it was known among us that they had no love for Madame Bonaparte, of which fact I had many proofs. Mademoiselle Hortense never left her mother, and they were devotedly attached to each other.

Besides men distinguished by their posts under the government or in the army, there gathered others also who were not less distinguished by personal merit, or the position which their birth had given them before the Revolution. It was a veritable panorama, in which we saw the persons themselves pass before our eyes. The scene itself, even exclusive of the gayety which always attended the dinings of Eugene, had its attractions. Among those whom we saw most frequently were Volney, Denon, Lemercier, the Prince of Poix, de Laigle, Charles Baudin, General Beurnonville, Isabey, and a number of others, celebrated in science, literature, and art; in short, the greater part of those who composed the society of Madame de Montesson.

Madame Bonaparte and Mademoiselle Hortense often took excursions on horseback into the country. On these occasions her most constant escorts were the Prince de Poix and M. de Laigle. One day, as this party was re-entering the court-yard at Malmaison, the horse which Hortense rode became frightened, and dashed off. She was an accomplished rider, and very active, so she attempted to spring off on the grass by the roadside; but the band which fastened the end of her riding-skirt under her foot prevented her freeing herself quickly, and she was thrown, and dragged by her horse for several yards. Fortunately the gentlemen of the party, seeing her fall, sprang from their horses in time to rescue her; and, by extraordinary good fortune, she was not even bruised, and was the first to laugh at her misadventure.

During the first part of my stay at Malmaison, the First Consul always slept with his wife, like an ordinary citizen of the middle classes in Paris; and I heard no rumour of any intrigue in the chateau. The persons of this society, most of whom were young, and who were often very numerous, frequently took part in sports which recalled college days. In fact, one of the greatest diversions of the inhabitants of Malmaison was to play "prisoners' base." It was usually after dinner; and Bonaparte, Lauriston, Didelot, de Lucay, de Bourrienne, Eugene, Rapp, Isabey, Madame Bonaparte, and Mademoiselle Hortense would divide themselves into two camps, in which the prisoners taken, or exchanged, would recall to the First Consul the greater game, which he so much preferred. In these games the most active runners were Eugene, Isabey, and Hortense. As to General Bonaparte, he often fell, but rose laughing boisterously.

General Bonaparte and his family seemed to enjoy almost unexampled happiness, especially when at Malmaison, which residence, though agreeable at that time, was far from being what it has since become. This estate consisted of the chateau, which Bonaparte found in bad condition on his return from Egypt, a park already somewhat improved, and a farm, the income of which did not with any certainty exceed twelve thousand *francs* a year. Josephine directed in person all the improvements made there, and no woman ever possessed better taste.

From the first, they played amateur comedy at Malmaison, which was a relaxation the First Consul enjoyed greatly, but in which he took no part himself except that of looker-on. Every one in the house attended these representations; and I must confess we felt perhaps even more pleasure than others in seeing thus travestied on the stage those in whose service we were.

The Malmaison Troupe, if I may thus style actors of such exalted social rank, consisted principally of Eugene, Jerome, Lauriston, de Bourrienne, Isabey, de Leroy, Didelot, Mademoiselle Hortense, Madame Caroline Murat, and the two Mademoiselles Auguie, one of whom afterwards married Marshal Ney,[3] and the other M. de Broc. All four were very young and charming, and few theatres in Paris could show four actresses as pretty. In addition to which, they showed much grace in their acting, and played their parts with real talent; and were as natural on the stage as in the saloon, where they bore themselves with exquisite grace and refinement. At first the repertoire contained little variety, though the pieces were generally well selected. The first representation which I attended was the "Barber of Seville" in which Isabey played the role of Figaro, and Mademoiselle Hortense that of Rosine—and the *Spiteful Lover*. Another time I saw played the *Unexpected Wager*, and *False Consultations*. Hortense and Eugene played this last piece perfectly; and I still recall that, in the role of Madame le Blanc, Hortense appeared prettier than ever in the character of an old woman, Eugene representing Le Noir, and Lauriston the charlatan. The First Consul, as I have said, confined himself to the role of spectator; but he seemed to take in these fireside plays, so to speak, the greatest pleasure, laughed and applauded heartily, though sometimes he also criticised.

Madame Bonaparte was also highly entertained; and even if she could not always boast of the successful acting of her children, "the chiefs of the troupe," it sufficed her that it was an agreeable relaxation to her husband, and seemed to give him pleasure; for her constant study was to contribute to the happiness of the great man who had united her destiny with his own.

When the day for the presentation of a play had been appointed, there was never any postponement, but often a change of the play;

---

3. Michel Ney, Styled by Napoleon the "bravest of the brave," was born 1769, at Sarre-Louis (now in Prussia), son of a cooper. Entered the army as a private 1787, adjutant-general 1794, general of brigade 1796, general of division 1799, marshal 1804, Duke of Elchingen 1805, Prince of Moskwa 1812, and commanded the rearguard in the famous retreat from Russia. On the return from Elba he went over to Napoleon; was at Waterloo. Was afterwards taken, and in spite of the terms of the surrender of Paris was tried for treason, and shot in the gardens of the Luxembourg, Dec. 8, 1815.—Trans.

not because of the indisposition, or fit of the blues, of an actress (as often happens in the theatres of Paris), but for more serious reasons. It sometimes happened that M. d'Etieulette received orders to rejoin his regiment, or an important mission was confided to Count Almaviva, though Figaro and Rosine always remained at their posts; and the desire of pleasing the First Consul was, besides, so general among all those who surrounded him, that the substitutes did their best in the absence of the principals, and the play never failed for want of an actor.[4]

---

4. Michau, of the Comedie Francaise, was the instructor of the troupe. Wherever it happened that an actor was wanting in animation, Michau would exclaim. "Warmth! Warmth! Warmth!"—Constant.

Chapter 3

I had been only a very short time in the service of Madame Bonaparte when I made the acquaintance of Charvet, the concierge of Malmaison, and in connection with this estimable man became each day more and more intimate, till at last he gave me one of his daughters in marriage. I was eager to learn from him all that he could tell me concerning Madame Bonaparte and the First Consul prior to my entrance into the house; and in our frequent conversations he took the greatest pleasure in satisfying my curiosity. It is to him I owe the following details as to the mother and daughter.

When General Bonaparte set out for Egypt, Madame Bonaparte accompanied him as far as Toulon, and was extremely anxious to go with him to Egypt. When the general made objections, she observed that having been born a Creole, the heat of the climate would be more favourable than dangerous to her. By a singular coincidence it was on *'La Pomone'* that she wished to make the journey; that is to say, on the very same vessel which in her early youth had brought her from Martinique to France. General Bonaparte, finally yielding to the wishes of his wife, promised to send *'La Pomone'* for her, and bade her go in the meantime to take the waters at Plombieres. The matter being arranged between husband and wife, Madame Bonaparte was delighted to go to the springs of Plombieres which she had desired to visit for a long time, knowing, like every one else, the reputation these waters enjoyed for curing barrenness in women.

Madame Bonaparte had been only a short time at Plombieres, when one morning, while occupied in hemming a turban and chatting with the ladies present, Madame de Cambis, who was on the balcony, called to her to come and see a pretty little dog passing along the street. All the company hastened with Madame Bonaparte to the balcony, which caused it to fall with a frightful crash. By a most fortunate chance, no one was killed; though Madame de Cambis had her leg broken, and Madame Bonaparte was most painfully bruised, without, however, receiving any fracture. Charvet, who was in a room behind the saloon, heard the noise, and at once had a sheep killed and skinned, and Madame Bonaparte wrapped in the skin. It was a long while before she regained her health, her arms and her hands especially being so bruised that she was for a long time unable to use them; and it was necessary to cut up her food, feed her, and, in fact, perform the same offices for her as for an infant.

I related above that Josephine thought she was to rejoin her husband in Egypt, and consequently that her stay at the springs of Plombieres would be of short duration but her accident led her to think that it would be prolonged indefinitely; she therefore desired, while waiting for her complete recovery, to have with her her daughter Hortense, then about fifteen years of age, who was being educated in the boarding-school of Madame Campan. She sent for her a mulatto woman to whom she was much attached, named Euphemie, who was the foster-sister of Madame Bonaparte, and passed (I do not know if the supposition was correct) as her natural sister. Euphemie, accompanied by Charvet, made the journey in one of Madame Bonaparte's carriages. Mademoiselle Hortense, on their arrival, was delighted with the journey she was about to make, and above all with the idea of being near her mother, for whom she felt the tenderest affection. Mademoiselle Hortense was, I would not say, greedy, but she was exceedingly fond of sweets; and Charvet, in relating these details, said to me, that at each town of any size through which they passed the carriage was filled with bonbons and dainties, of which mademoiselle consumed a great quantity. One day, while Euphemie and Charvet were sound asleep, they were suddenly awakened by a report, which sounded frightful to them, and caused them intense anxiety, as they found when they awoke that they were passing through a thick forest. This ludicrous incident threw Hortense into fits of laughter; for hardly had they expressed their alarm when they found themselves deluged with an odoriferous froth, which explained the cause of the explosion. A bottle of champagne, placed in one of the pockets of the carriage, had been uncorked; and the heat, added to the motion of the carriage, or rather the malice of the young traveller, had made it explode with a loud report.

When mademoiselle arrived at Plombieres, her mother's health was almost restored; so that the pupil of Madame Campan found there all the distractions which please and delight at the age which the daughter of Madame Bonaparte had then attained.

There is truth in the saying that in all evil there is good, for had this accident not happened to Madame Bonaparte, it is very probable she would have become a prisoner of the English; in fact, she learned that 'La Pomone', the vessel on which she wished to make the voyage, had fallen into the power of the enemies of France. General Bonaparte, in all his letters, still dissuaded his wife from the plan she had of rejoining him; and, consequently, she returned to Paris.

On her arrival Josephine devoted her attention to executing a wish General Bonaparte had expressed to her before leaving. He had remarked to her that he should like, on his return, to have a country seat; and he charged his brother to attend to this, which Joseph, however, failed to do. Madame Bonaparte, who, on the contrary, was always in search of what might please her husband, charged several persons to make excursions in the environs of Paris, in order to ascertain whether a suitable dwelling could be found. After having vacillated long between Ris and Malmaison, she decided on the latter, which she bought from M. Lecoulteux-Dumoley, for, I think, four hundred thousand *francs*. Such were the particulars which Charvet was kind enough to give me when I first entered the service of Madame Bonaparte. Every one in the house loved to speak of her; and it was certainly not to speak evil, for never was woman more beloved by all who surrounded her, and never has one deserved it more. General Bonaparte was also an excellent man in the retirement of private life.

After the return of the First Consul from his campaign in Egypt, several attempts against his life had been made; and the police had warned him many times to be on his guard, and not to risk himself alone in the environs of Malmaison. The First Consul had been very careless up to this period; but the discovery of the snares which were laid for him, even in the privacy of his family circle, forced him to use precautions and prudence. It has been stated since, that these pretended plots were only fabrications of the police to render themselves necessary to the First Consul, or, perhaps, of the First Consul himself, to redouble the interest which attached to his person, through fear of the perils which menaced his life; and the absurdity of these attempts is alleged as proof of this. I could not pretend to elucidate such mysteries; but it seems to me that in such matters absurdity proves nothing, or, at least, it does not prove that such plots did not exist. The conspirators of that period set no bounds to their extravagance; for what could be more absurd, and at the same time more real, than the atrocious folly of the infernal machine?

Be that as it may, I shall relate what passed under my own eyes during the first month of my stay at Malmaison. No one there, or, at least, no one in my presence, showed the least doubt of the reality of these attempts.

In order to get rid of the First Consul, all means appeared good to his enemies: they noted everything in their calculations, even his absence of mind. The following occurrence is proof of this:

There were repairs and ornamentations to be made to the mantel in the rooms of the First Consul at Malmaison. The contractor in charge of this work had sent marble cutters, amongst whom had slipped in, it seems, a few miserable wretches employed by the conspirators. The persons attached to the First Consul were incessantly on the alert, and exercised the greatest watchfulness; and it was observed that among these workmen there were men who pretended to work, but whose air and manner contrasted strongly with their occupation. These suspicions were unfortunately only too well founded; for when the apartments had been made ready to receive the First Consul, and just as he was on the eve of occupying them, some one making a final inspection found on the desk at which he would first seat himself, a snuff-box, in every respect like one of those which he constantly used. It was thought at first that this box really belonged to him, and that it had been forgotten and left there by his valet; but doubts inspired by the suspicious manner of a few of the marble-cutters, leading to further investigation, the tobacco was examined and analyzed. It was found to be poisoned.

The authors of this perfidy had, it is said, at this time, communication with other conspirators, who engaged to attempt another means of ridding themselves of the First Consul. They promised to attack the guard of the chateau (Malmaison), and to carry off by force the chief of the government. With this intention, they had uniforms made like those of the consular guards, who then stood sentinel, day and night, over the First Consul, and followed him on horseback in his excursions. In this costume, and by the aid of signals, with their accomplices (the pretended marble-cutters) on the inside, they could easily have approached and mingled with the guard, who were fed and quartered at the chateau. They could even have reached the First Consul, and carried him off. However, this first project was abandoned as too uncertain; and the conspirators flattered themselves that they would succeed in their undertaking more surely, and with less danger, by taking advantage of the frequent journeys of the First Consul to Paris. By means of their disguise they planned to distribute themselves on the road, among the guides of the escort, and massacre them, their rallying-point being the quarries of Nanterre; but their plots were for the second time foiled. There was in the park at Malmaison a deep quarry; and fears being entertained that they would profit by it to conceal themselves therein, and exercise some violence against the First Consul on one of his solitary walks, it was decided to secure it with an iron door.

On the 19th of February, at one in the afternoon, the First Consul went in state to the Tuileries, which was then called the Government palace, to install himself there with all his household. With him were his two colleagues; one of whom, the third consul, was to occupy the same residence, and be located in the Pavilion de Flore. The carriage of the consuls was drawn by six white horses, which the Emperor of Germany had presented to the conqueror of Italy after the signature of the treaty of peace of Campo-Formio. The sabre that the First Consul wore at this ceremony was magnificent, and had also been presented to him by this monarch on the same occasion.

A remarkable thing in this formal change of residence was that the acclamations and enthusiasm of the crowd, and even of the most distinguished spectators, who filled the windows of Rue Thionville and of the Quai Voltaire, were addressed only to the First Consul, and to the young warriors of his brilliant staff, who were yet bronzed by the sun of the Pyramids or of Italy. At their head rode General Lannes and Murat; the first easy to recognize by his bold bearing and soldierly manners; the second by the same qualities, and further by a striking elegance, both of costume and equipments. His new title of brother-in-law of the First Consul contributed, also, greatly to fix upon him the attention of all. As for myself, all my attention was absorbed by the principal personage of the cortege, whom, like every one around me, I regarded with something like a religious reverence; and by his stepson, the son of my excellent mistress, himself once my master,—the brave, modest, good Prince Eugene, who at that time, however, was not yet a prince. On his arrival at the Tuileries, the First Consul took possession at once of the apartments which he afterwards occupied, and which were formerly part of the royal apartments. These apartments consisted of a bed-chamber, a bathroom, a cabinet, and a saloon, in which he gave audience in the forenoon; of a second saloon, in which were stationed his *aides-de-camp* on duty, and which he used as a dining-room; and also a very large antechamber. Madame Bonaparte had her separate apartments on the ground floor, the same which she afterwards occupied as Empress. Beneath the suite of rooms occupied by the First Consul was the room of Bourrienne, his private secretary, which communicated with the apartments of the First Consul by means of a private staircase.

Although at this period there were already courtiers, there was not, however, yet a court, and the etiquette was exceedingly simple. The First Consul, as I believe I have already said, slept in the same bed with his wife; and they lived together, sometimes at the Tuileries, sometimes at Malmaison. As yet there were neither grand marshal, nor chamberlains, nor *prefects* of the palace, nor ladies of honour, nor lady ushers, nor ladies of the wardrobe, nor pages. The household of the First Consul was composed only of M. Pfister, steward; Venard, chief cook; Galliot, and Dauger, head servants; Colin, butler. Ripeau was librarian; Vigogne, senior, in charge of the stables. Those attached to his personal service were Hambard, head valet; Herbert, ordinary valet; and Roustan, Mameluke of the First Consul. There were, beside these, fifteen persons to discharge the ordinary duties of the household. De Bourrienne superintended everything, and regulated expenses, and, although very strict, won the esteem and affection of every one.

He was kind, obliging, and above all very just; and consequently at the time of his disgrace the whole household was much distressed. As for myself, I retain a sincerely respectful recollection of him; and I believe that, though he has had the misfortune to find enemies among the great, he found among his inferiors only grateful hearts and sincere regrets.

Some days after this installation, there was at the chateau a reception of the diplomatic corps. It will be seen from the details, which I shall give, how very simple at that time was the etiquette of what they already called the Court.

At eight o'clock in the evening, the apartments of Madame Bonaparte, situated, as I have just said, on the ground floor adjoining the garden, were crowded with people. There was an incredible wealth of plumes, diamonds, and dazzling toilets. The crowd was so great that it was found necessary to throw open the bedroom of Madame Bonaparte, as the two saloons were so full there was not room to move.

When, after much embarrassment and difficulty, every one had found a place as they could, Madame Bonaparte was announced, and entered, leaning on the arm of Talleyrand. She wore a dress of white muslin with short sleeves, and a necklace of pearls. Her head was uncovered; and the beautiful braids of her hair, arranged with charming negligence, were held in place by a tortoise-shell comb. The flattering murmur which greeted her appearance was most grateful to her; and never, I believe, did she display more grace and majesty.

Talleyrand,[1] giving his hand to Madame Bonaparte, had the honour of presenting to her, one after another, the members of the Diplomatic Corps, not according to their names, but that of the courts they represented. He then made with her the tour of the two saloons, and the circuit of the second was only half finished when the First Consul entered without being announced. He was dressed in a very plain uniform, with a tricolored silk scarf, with fringes of the same around his waist. He wore close-fitting pantaloons of white cassimere, and top-boots, and held his hat in his hand. This plain dress, in the midst of the embroidered coats loaded with cordons and orders worn by the ambassadors and foreign dignitaries, presented a contrast as striking as the toilette of Madame Bonaparte compared with that of the other ladies present.

Before relating how I exchanged the service of Madame Bonaparte for that of the chief of state, and a sojourn at Malmaison for the second campaign of Italy, I think I should pause to recall one or two incidents which belong to the time spent in the service of Madame Bonaparte. She loved to sit up late, and, when almost everybody else had retired, to play a game of billiards, or more often of backgammon. It happened on one occasion that, having dismissed every one else, and not yet being sleepy, she asked if I knew how to play billiards, and upon my replying in the affirmative, requested me with charming grace to play with her; and I had often afterwards the honour of doing so. Although I had some skill, I always managed to let her beat me, which pleased her exceedingly. If this was flattery, I must admit it; but I would have done the same towards any other woman, whatever her rank and her relation to me, had she been even half as lovely as was Madame Bonaparte.

The concierge of Malmaison, who possessed the entire confidence of his employers, among other means of precaution and watchfulness conceived by him in order to protect the residence and person of the First Consul from any sudden attack, had trained for the chateau several large dogs, among which were two very handsome Newfound-

---

1. Charles Maurice de Talleyrand-Perigord, born at Paris, 1754, was descended from the counts of Perigord. Rendered lame by an accident, he entered the clergy, and in 1788 became Bishop of Autun. In the States-General he sided with the Revolution. During the Reign of Terror he visited England and the United States. Recalled in 1796, he became minister of foreign affairs under the Directory, which post he retained under the Consulate. In 1806 he was made Prince of Benevento. He soon fell into disgrace. Sided with the Bourbons in 1814, and was minister at the congress of Vienna, president of the council, and minister under the king. Died 1838.—Trans.

lands. Work on the improvements of Malmaison went on incessantly, and a large number of workmen lodged there at night, who were carefully warned not to venture out alone; but one night as some of the watchdogs were with the workmen in their lodgings, and allowed themselves to be caressed, their apparent docility encouraged one of these men to attempt the imprudence of venturing out. Believing that the surest way to avoid danger was to put himself under the protection of one of those powerful animals, he took one of them with him, and in a very friendly manner they passed out of the door together; but no sooner had they reached the outside, than the dog sprang upon his unfortunate companion and threw him down. The cries of the poor workman brought some of the guard, who ran to his aid. Just in time; for the dog was holding him fast to the ground, and had seized him by the throat. He was rescued, badly wounded. Madame Bonaparte, when she was informed of this accident, had him nursed till perfectly cured, and gave him a handsome gratuity, but recommended him to be more prudent in the future.

Every moment that the First Consul could snatch from affairs of state he passed at Malmaison. The evening of each *decadi*[2] was a time of expectation and joy at the chateau. Madame Bonaparte sent domestics on horseback and on foot to meet her husband, and often went herself, accompanied by her daughter and her Malmaison friends. When not on duty, I went myself and alone: for everybody felt for the First Consul the same affection, and experienced in regard to him the same anxiety; and such was the bitterness and boldness of his enemies that the road, though short, between Paris and Malmaison was full of dangers and snares. We knew that many plans had been laid to kidnap him on this road, and that these attempts might be renewed. The most dangerous spot was the quarries of Nanterre, of which I have already spoken; so they were carefully examined, and guarded by his followers each day on which the First Consul was to pass, and finally the depressions nearest the road were filled up. The First Consul was gratified by our devotion to him, and gave us proofs of his satisfaction, though he himself seemed always free from fear or uneasiness. Very often, indeed, he mildly ridiculed our anxiety, and would relate very seriously to the good Josephine what a narrow escape he had on the road; how men of a sinister appearance had shown themselves many times on his way; how one of them had had the boldness to aim at him, etc. And when he saw

---

2. Under the Republic, Sunday was abolished. A decade of ten days was substituted for the week; and the *decadi*, or tenth day, took the place of the Sabbath.—Trans.

her well frightened, he would burst out laughing, give her some taps or kisses on her cheek and neck, saying to her, "Have no fear, little goose; they would not dare." On these "days of furlough," as he called them, he was occupied more with his private affairs than with those of state; but never could he remain idle. He would make them pull down, put up again, build, enlarge, set out, prune, incessantly, both in the chateau and in the park, while he examined the bills of expenses, estimated receipts, and ordered economies. Time passed quickly in all these occupations; and the moment soon came when it was necessary to return, and, as he expressed it, put on again the yoke of misery.

Chapter 4

Towards the end of March, 1800, five or six months after my entrance into the service of Madame. Bonaparte, the First Consul while at dinner one day regarded me intently; and having carefully scrutinized and measured me from head to foot, "Young man," said he, "would you like to go with me on the campaign?" I replied, with much emotion, that I would ask nothing better. "Very well, then, you shall go with me!" and on rising from the table, he ordered Pfister, the steward, to place my name on the list of the persons of his household who would accompany him. My preparations did not require much time; for I was delighted with the idea of being attached to the personal service of so great a man, and in imagination saw myself already beyond the Alps. But the First Consul set out without me. Pfister, by a defect of memory, perhaps intentional, had forgotten to place my name on the list. I was in despair, and went to relate, with tears, my misfortune to my excellent mistress, who was good enough to endeavour to console me, saying, "Well, Constant, everything is not lost; you will stay with me. You can hunt in the park to pass the time; and perhaps the First Consul may yet send for you." However, Madame Bonaparte did not really believe this; for she thought, as I did, although out of kindness she did not wish to say this to me, that the First Consul having changed his mind, and no longer wishing my services on the campaign, had himself given the counter orders. However, I soon had proof to the contrary. In passing through Dijon, on his way to Mt. St. Bernard, the First Consul asked for me, and learning that they had forgotten me, expressed his dissatisfaction, and directed Bourrienne to write immediately to Madame Bonaparte, requesting her to send me on without delay.

One morning, when my chagrin was more acute than ever, Madame Bonaparte sent for me, and said, holding Bourrienne's letter in her hand, "Constant, since you have determined to quit us to make the campaign, you may rejoice, for you are now about to leave. The First Consul has sent for you. Go to the office of Maret, and ascertain if he will not soon send a courier. You will accompany him." I was inexpressibly delighted at this good news, and did not try to conceal my pleasure. "You are very well satisfied to leave us," said Madame Bonaparte with a kind smile. "It is not leaving Madame, but joining the First Consul, which delights me."

"I hope so," replied she. "Go, Constant; and take good care of him." If any incentive had been needed, this injunction of my noble mistress would have added to the zeal and fidelity with which I had determined to discharge my new duties. I hurried without delay to the office of Maret, secretary of state, who already knew me, and had shown his good-will for me. "Get ready at once," said he; "a courier will set out this evening or tomorrow morning." I returned in all haste to Malmaison, and announced to Madame Bonaparte my immediate departure. She immediately had a good post-chaise made ready for me, and Thibaut (for that was the name of the courier I was to accompany) was directed to obtain horses for me along the route. Maret gave me eight hundred *francs* for the expenses of my trip, which sum, entirely unexpected by me, filled me with wonder, for I had never been so rich. At four o'clock in the morning, having heard from Thibaut that everything was ready, I went to his house, where the post-chaise awaited me, and we set out.

I travelled very comfortably, sometimes in the post chaise, sometimes on horseback; I taking Thibaut's place, and he mine. I expected to overtake the First Consul at Martigny; but his travelling had been so rapid, that I caught up with him only at the convent of Mt. St. Bernard. Upon our route we constantly passed regiments on the march, composed of officers and soldiers who were hastening to rejoin their different corps. Their enthusiasm was irrepressible,—those who had made the campaign of Italy rejoiced at returning to so fine a country; those who had not yet done so were burning with impatience to see the battlefields immortalized by French valour, and by the genius of the hero who still marched at their head. All went as if to a festival, and singing songs they climbed the mountains of Valais. It was eight o'clock in the morning when I arrived at headquarters. Pfister announced me; and I found the general-in-chief in the great hall, in the basement of the Hospice. He was taking breakfast, standing, with his staff. As soon as he saw me, he said, "Here you are, you queer fellow! why didn't you come with me?" I excused myself by saying that to my great regret I had received a counter order, or, at least, they had left me behind at the moment of departure. "Lose no time, my friend; eat quickly; we are about to start." From this moment I was attached to the personal service of the First Consul, in the quality of ordinary valet; that is to say, in my turn. This duty gave me little to do; Hambard, the head valet of the First Consul, being in the habit of dressing him from head to foot.

Immediately after breakfast we began to descend the mountain, many sliding down on the snow, very much as they coast at the garden Beaujon, from top to bottom of the Montagnes Russes, and I followed their example. This they called "sledding." The general-in-chief also descended in this manner an almost perpendicular glacier. His guide was a young countryman, active and courageous, to whom the First Consul promised a sufficiency for the rest of his days. Some young soldiers who had wandered off into the snow were found, almost dead with cold, by the dogs sent out by the monks, and carried to the Hospice, where they received every possible attention, and their lives were saved. The First Consul gave substantial proof of his gratitude to the good fathers for a charity so useful and generous. Before leaving the Hospice, where he had found tables loaded with food already prepared awaiting the soldiers as soon as they reached the summit of the mountain, he gave to the good monks a considerable sum of money, in reward for the hospitality he and his companions in arms had received, and an order on the treasury for an annuity in support of the convent.

The same day we climbed Mount Albaredo; but as this passage was impracticable for cavalry and artillery, he ordered them to pass outside the town of Bard, under the batteries of the fort. The First Consul had ordered that they should pass it at night, and on a gallop; and he had straw tied around the wheels of the caissons and on the feet of the horses, but even these precautions were not altogether sufficient to prevent the Austrians hearing our troops. The cannon of the fort rained grape-shot incessantly; but fortunately the houses of the town sheltered our soldiers from the enemy's guns, and more than half the army passed without much loss. I was with the household of the First Consul, which under the care of General Gardanne flanked the fort.

The 23rd of May we forded a torrent which flowed between the town and the fort, with the First Consul at our head, and then, followed by General Berthier and some other officers, took the path over the Albaredo, which overlooked the fort and the town of Bard. Directing his field-glass towards the hostile batteries, from the fire of which he was protected only by a few bushes, he criticised the dispositions which had been made by the officer in charge of the siege of the fort, and ordered changes, which he said would cause the place to fall into our hands in a short time. Freed now from the anxiety which this fort had caused him, and which he said had prevented his sleeping the two days he had passed in the convent of Maurice, he stretched himself at the foot of a fir-tree and took a refreshing nap, while the army was making good its passage. Rising from this brief interval of repose, he descended the mountain and continued his march to Ivree, where we passed the night.

The brave General Lannes, who commanded the advance guard, acted somewhat in the capacity of quartermaster, taking possession of all the places which barred the road. Only a few hours before we entered he had forced the passage of Ivree.

Such was this miraculous passage of St. Bernard. Horses, cannon, caissons, and an immense quantity of army stores of all kinds, everything, in fact, was drawn or carried over glaciers which appeared inaccessible, and by paths which seemed impracticable even for a single man. The Austrian cannon were not more successful than the snow in stopping the French army. So true is it that the genius and perseverance of the First Consul were communicated, so to speak, to the humblest of his soldiers, and inspired them with a courage and a strength, the results of which will appear fabulous to posterity.

On the 2nd of June, which was the day after the passage of the Ticino, and the day of our entrance into Milan, the First Consul learned that the fort of Bard had been taken the evening before, showing that his dispositions had led to a quick result, and the road of communication by the St. Bernard was now free from all obstructions. The First Consul entered Milan without having met much resistance, the whole population turned out on his entrance, and he was received with a thousand acclamations. The confidence of the Milanese redoubled when they learned that he had promised the members of the assembled clergy to maintain the catholic worship and clergy as already established, and had compelled them to take the oath of fidelity to the cisalpine republic.

The First Consul remained several days in this capital; and I had time to form a more intimate acquaintance with my colleagues, who were, as I have said, Hambard, Roustan, and Hebert. We relieved each other every twenty-four hours, at noon precisely. As has always been my rule when thrown into association with strangers, I observed, as closely as circumstances permitted, the character and temper of my

JOSEPHINE

comrades, so that I could regulate my conduct in regard to them, and know in advance what I might have to fear or hope from association with them.

Hambard had an unbounded devotion for the First Consul, whom he had followed to Egypt, but unfortunately his temper was gloomy and misanthropic, which made him extremely sullen and disagreeable; and the favour which Roustan enjoyed perhaps contributed to increase this gloomy disposition. In a kind of mania he imagined himself to be the object of a special espionage; and when his hours of service were over, he would shut himself up in his room, and pass in mournful solitude the whole time he was not on duty. The First Consul, when in good humour, would joke with him upon this savage disposition, calling him Mademoiselle Hambard. "Ah, well, what were you doing there in your room all by yourself? Doubtless you were reading some poor romances, or some old books about princesses carried off and kept under guard by a barbarous giant." To which Hambard would sullenly reply, "General, you no doubt know better than I what I was doing," referring in this way to the spies by which he believed himself to be always surrounded. Notwithstanding this unfortunate disposition, the First Consul felt very kindly to him. When the Emperor went to camp at Boulogne, Hambard refused to accompany him; and the Emperor gave him, as a place of retreat, the charge of the palace of Meudon. There he showed unmistakable symptoms of insanity, and his end was lamentable. During the Hundred Days, after a conversation with the Emperor, he threw himself against a carving-knife with such violence that the blade came out two inches behind his back. As it was believed at this time that I had incurred the anger of the Emperor, the rumour went abroad that it was I who had committed suicide, and this tragic death was announced in several papers as mine.

Hebert, ordinary valet, was a very agreeable young fellow, but very timid, and was, like all the rest of the household, devotedly attached to the First Consul. It happened one day in Egypt that the latter, who had never been able to shave himself (it was I who taught him how to shave himself, as I shall relate elsewhere at length), called Hebert to shave him, in the absence of Hambard, who ordinarily discharged that duty. As it had sometimes happened that Hebert, on account of his great timidity, had cut his master's chin, on that day the latter, who held a pair of scissors in his hand, when Hebert approached him, holding his razor, said, "Take care, you scamp; if you cut me, I will stick my scissors into your stomach." This threat, made with an air of pretended seriousness, but which was in fact only a jest, such as I have seen the

Emperor indulge in a hundred times, produced such an impression on Hebert, that it was impossible for him to finish his work. He was seized with a convulsive trembling, the razor fell from his hand, and the general-in-chief in vain bent his neck, and said to him many times, laughing "Come, finish, you scamp." Not only was Hebert unable to complete his task that day, but from that time he had to renounce the duty of barber. The Emperor did not like this excessive timidity in the servants of his household; but this did not prevent him, when he restored the castle of Rambouillet, from giving to Hebert the place of concierge which he requested.

Roustan, so well known under the name of Mameluke, belonged to a good family of Georgia; carried off at the age of six or seven, and taken to Cairo, he was there brought up among the young slaves who attended upon the Mamelukes, until he should be of sufficient age to enter this warlike militia. The Sheik of Cairo, in making a present to General Bonaparte of a magnificent Arab horse, had given him at the same time Roustan and Ibrahim, another Mameluke, who was afterwards attached to the service of Madame Bonaparte, under the name of Ali. It is well known that Roustan became an indispensable accompaniment on all occasions when the Emperor appeared in public. He was with him in all his expeditions, in all processions, and, which was especially to his honour, in all his battles. In the brilliant staff which followed the Emperor he shone more than all others by the richness of his Oriental costume; and his appearance made a decided impression, especially upon the common people and in the provinces. He was believed to have great influence with the Emperor; because, as credulous people said, Roustan had saved his master's life by throwing himself between him and the sabre of an enemy who was about to strike him. I think that this belief was unfounded, and that the especial favour he enjoyed was due to the habitual kindness of his Majesty towards every one in his service. Besides, this favour affected in no wise his domestic relations; for when Roustan, who had married a young and pretty French girl, a certain Mademoiselle Douville, whose father was valet to the Empress Josephine, was reproached by certain journals in 1814 and 1815 with not having followed to the end of his fortunes the man for whom he had always expressed such intense devotion, Roustan replied that the family ties which he had formed prevented his leaving France, and that he could not destroy the happiness of his own household.

Ibrahim took the name of Ali when he passed into the service of Madame Bonaparte. He was of more than Arabic ugliness, and had a wicked look. I recall in this connection a little incident which took place at Malmaison, which will give an idea of his character. One day, while playing on the lawn of the chateau, I unintentionally threw him down while running; and furious at his fall, he rose up, drew his poniard, which he always wore, and dashed after me to strike me. I laughed at first, like every one else, at the accident, and amused myself by making him run; but warned by the cries of my comrades, and looking back to see how close he was, I perceived at the same time his dagger and his rage. I stopped at once, and planted my foot, with my eye fixed upon his poniard, and was fortunate enough to avoid his blow, which, however, grazed my breast. Furious in my turn, as may be imagined, I seized him by his flowing pantaloons, and pitched him ten feet into the stream of Malmaison, which was barely two feet deep. The plunge brought him at once to his senses; and besides, his poniard had gone to the bottom, which made him much less dangerous. But in his disappointment he yelled so loudly that Madame Bonaparte heard him; and as she had quite a fancy for her Mameluke, I was sharply scolded. However, this poor Ali was of such an unsocial temperament that he got into difficulties with almost every one in the household, and at last was sent away to Fontainebleau, to take the place of manservant there.

I now return to our campaign. On the 13th of June the First Consul spent the night at Torre-di-Galifolo, where he established his headquarters. From the day of our entry into Milan the advance of the army had not slackened; General Murat had passed the Po, and taken possession of Piacenza; and General Lannes, still pushing forward with his brave advance guard, had fought a bloody battle at Montebello, a name which he afterwards rendered illustrious by bearing it. The recent arrival of General Desaix, who had just returned from Egypt, completed the joy of the general-in-chief, and also added much to the confidence of the soldiers, by whom the good and modest Desaix was adored. The First Consul received him with the frankest and most cordial friendship, and they remained together three consecutive hours in private conversation. At the end of this conference, an order of the day announced to the army that General Desaix would take command of the division Boudet. I heard some persons in the suite of General Desaix say that his patience and evenness of temper were rudely tried during his voyage, by contrary winds, forced delays, the ennui of quarantine, and above all by the bad conduct of the English, who had kept him for some time a prisoner in their fleet, in sight of the shores of France, although he bore a passport, signed by the English authorities in Egypt, in consequence of the capitulation which had been mutually agreed upon. Consequently his resentment against them was very ardent; and he regretted much, he said, that the enemy he was about to fight was not the English.

In spite of the simplicity of his tastes and habits, no one was more ambitious of glory than this brave general. All his rage against the English was caused by the fear that he might not arrive in time to gather new laurels. He did indeed arrive in time, but only to find a glorious death, alas, so premature!

It was on the fourteenth that the celebrated battle of Marengo took place, which began early in the morning, and lasted throughout the day. I remained at headquarters with all the household of the First Consul, where we were almost within range of the cannon on the battlefield. Contradictory news constantly came, one report declaring the battle completely lost, the next giving us the victory. At one time the increase in the number of our wounded, and the redoubled firing of the Austrian cannon, made us believe that all was lost; and then suddenly came the news that this apparent falling back was only a bold manoeuvre of the First Consul, and that a charge of General Desaix had gained the battle. But the victory was bought at a price dear to France and to the heart of the First Consul. Desaix, struck by a bullet, fell dead on the field; and the grief of his soldiers serving only to exasperate their courage, they routed, by a bayonet charge, the enemy, who were already shaken by the brilliant cavalry charge of General Kellermann. The First Consul slept upon the field of battle, and notwithstanding the decisive victory that he had gained, was very sad, and said that evening, in the presence of Hambard and myself, many things which showed the profound grief he experienced in the death of General Desaix. He said, "France has lost one of her bravest defenders, and I one of my best friends; no one knew how much courage there was in the heart of Desaix, nor how much genius in his head." He thus solaced his grief by making to each and all a eulogy on the hero who had died on the field of honour.

"My brave Desaix," he further said, "always wished to die thus;" and then added, almost with tears in his eyes, "but ought death to have been so prompt to grant his wish?"

There was not a soldier in our victorious army who did not share so just a sorrow. Rapp and Savary, the *aides-de-camp* of Desaix, remained plunged in the most despairing grief beside the body of their chief, whom they called their father, rather to express his unfailing kindness to them than the dignity of his character. Out of respect to the memory of his friend, the general-in-chief, although his staff was full, added these two young officers in the quality of *aides-de-camp*.

Commandant Rapp (for such only was his rank at that time) was then, as he has ever been, good, full of courage, and universally beloved. His frankness, which sometimes bordered on brusqueness, pleased the Emperor; and I have many times heard him speak in praise of his *aide-de-camp*, whom he always styled, "My brave Rapp." Rapp was not lucky in battle, for he rarely escaped without a wound. While thus anticipating events, I will mention that in Russia, on the eve of the battle of La Moskwa, the Emperor said, in my presence, to General Rapp, who had just arrived from Dantzic, "See here, my brave fellow, we will beat them tomorrow, but take great care of yourself. You are not a favourite of fortune."

"That is," said the general, "the premium to be paid on the business, but I shall none the less on that account do my best."

Savary manifested for the First Consul the same fervid zeal and unbounded devotion which had attached him to General Desaix; and if he lacked any of the qualities of General Rapp, it was certainly not bravery. Of all the men who surrounded the Emperor, no one was more absolutely devoted to his slightest wishes. In the course of these memoirs, I shall doubtless have occasion to recall instances of this unparalleled enthusiasm, for which the Duke de Rovigo I was magnificently rewarded; but it is just to say that he did not bite the hand which rewarded him, and that he gave to the end, and even after the end, of his old master (for thus he loved to style the Emperor) an example of gratitude which has been imitated by few.

A government decree, in the month of June following, determined that the body of Desaix should be carried to the Hospice of St. Bernard, and that a tomb should be erected on that spot, in the country where he had covered himself with immortal glory, as a testimonial to the grief of France, and especially that of the First Consul.

Chapter 5

The victory of Marengo had rendered the conquest of Italy certain. Therefore the First Consul, thinking his presence more necessary at Paris than at the head of his army, gave the command in chief to General Massena, and made preparations to repass the mountains. On our return to Milan, the First Consul was received with even more enthusiasm than on his first visit.

The establishment of a republic was in accordance with the wishes of a large number of the Milanese; and they called the First Consul their Saviour, since he had delivered them from the yoke of the Austrians. There was, however, a party who detested equally these changes, the French army which was the instrument of them, and the young chief who was the author. In this party figured a celebrated artist, the singer Marchesi.

During our former visit, the First Consul had sent for him; and the musician had waited to be entreated, acting as if he were much inconvenienced, and at last presented himself with all the importance of a man whose dignity had been offended. The very simple costume of the First Consul, his short stature, thin visage, and poor figure were not calculated to make much of an impression on the hero of the theatre; and after the general-in-chief had welcomed him cordially, and very politely asked him to sing an air, he replied by this poor pun, uttered in a tone the impertinence of which was aggravated by his Italian accent: "Signor General, if it is a good air which you desire, you will find an excellent one in making a little tour of the garden." The Signor Marchesi was for this fine speech immediately put out of the door, and the same evening an order was sent committing the singer to prison. On our return the First Consul, whose resentment against Marchesi the cannon of Marengo had doubtless assuaged, and who thought besides that the penance of the musician for a poor joke had been sufficiently long, sent for him again, and asked him once more to sing; Marchesi this time was modest and polite, and sang in a charming manner. After the concert the First Consul approached him, pressed his hand warmly, and complimented him in the most affectionate manner; and from that moment peace was concluded between the two powers, and Marchesi sang only praises of the First Consul.

At this same concert the First Consul was struck with the beauty of a famous singer, Madame Grassini. He found her by no means cruel, and at the end of a few hours the conqueror of Italy counted one conquest more.

The following day she breakfasted with the First Consul and General Berthier in the chamber of the First Consul. General Berthier was ordered to provide for the journey of Madame Grassini, who was carried to Paris, and attached to the concert-room of the court.

The First Consul left Milan on the 24th; and we returned to France by the route of Mont Cenis, travelling as rapidly as possible. Everywhere the Consul was received with an enthusiasm difficult to describe. Arches of triumph had been erected at the entrance of each town, and in each canton a deputation of leading citizens came to make addresses to and compliment him. Long ranks of young girls, dressed in white, crowned with flowers, bearing flowers in their hands, and throwing flowers into the carriage of the First Consul, made themselves his only escort, surrounded him, followed him, and preceded him, until he had passed, or as soon as he set foot on the ground wherever he stopped.

The journey was thus, throughout the whole route, a perpetual fete; and at Lyons it amounted to an ovation, in which the whole town turned out to meet him. He entered, surrounded by an immense crowd, amid the most noisy demonstrations, and alighted at the hotel of the Celestins. In the Reign of Terror the Jacobins had spent their fury on the town of Lyons, the destruction of which they had sworn; and the handsome buildings which ornamented the Place Belcour had been levelled to the ground, the hideous cripple Couthon, at the head of the vilest mob of the clubs, striking the first blow with the hammer. The First Consul detested the Jacobins, who, on their side, hated and feared him; and his constant care was to destroy their work, or, in other words, to restore the ruins with which they had covered France. He thought then, and justly too, that he could not better respond to the affection of the people of Lyons, than by promoting with all his power the rebuilding of the houses of the Place Belcour; and before his departure he himself laid the first stone. The town of Dijon gave the First Consul a reception equally as brilliant.

Between Villeneuve-le-Roi and Sens, at the descent to the bridge of Montereau, while the eight horses, lashed to a gallop, were bearing the carriage rapidly along (the First Consul already travelled like a king), the tap of one of the front wheels came off. The inhabitants who lined the route, witnessing this accident, and foreseeing what would be the result, used every effort to stop the postilions, but did not succeed, and the carriage was violently upset. The First Consul received no injury; General Berthier had his face slightly scratched by the windows, which were broken; and the two footmen, who were on the steps, were thrown, violently to a distance, and badly wounded. The First Consul got out, or rather was pulled out, through one of the doors. This occurrence made no delay in his journey; he took his seat in another carriage immediately, and reached Paris with no other accident. The night of the 2nd of July, he alighted at the Tuileries; and the next day, as soon as the news of his return had been circulated in Paris, the entire population filled the courts and the garden. They pressed around the windows of the pavilion of Flora, in the hope of catching a glimpse of the saviour of France, the liberator of Italy.

That evening there was no one, either rich or poor, who did not take delight in illuminating his house or his garret. It was only a short time after his arrival at Paris that the First Consul learned of the death of General Kleber. The poniard of Suleyman had slain this great captain the same day that the cannon of Marengo laid low another hero of the army of Egypt. This assassination caused the First Consul the most poignant grief, of which I was an eyewitness, and to which I can testify; and, nevertheless, his calumniators have dared to say that he rejoiced at an event, which, even considered apart from its political relations, caused him to lose a conquest which had cost him so much, and France so much blood and expense. Other miserable wretches, still more stupid and more infamous, have even gone so far as to fabricate and spread abroad the report that the First Consul had himself ordered the assassination of his companion in arms, whom he had placed in his own position at the head of the army in Egypt. To these I have only one answer to make, if it is necessary to answer them at all; it is this, they never knew the Emperor.

After his return, the First Consul went often with his wife to Malmaison, where he remained sometimes for several days. At this time it was the duty of the *valet de chambre* to follow the carriage on horseback. One day the First Consul, while returning to Paris, ascertained a short distance from the chateau that he had forgotten his snuff-box, and sent me for it. I turned my bridle, set off at a gallop, and, having found the snuff-box on his desk, retraced my steps to overtake him, but did not succeed in doing so till he had reached Ruelle. Just as I drew near the carriage my horse slipped on a stone, fell, and threw me some distance into a ditch. The fall was very severe; and I remained stretched on the ground, with one shoulder dislocated, and an arm badly bruised. The First Consul ordered the horses stopped, himself gave orders to have me taken up, and cautioned them to be very careful in moving me; and I was borne, attended by-him, to the barracks of Ruelle, where he took pains before continuing his journey to satisfy himself that I was in no danger. The physician of his household was sent to Ruelle, my shoulder set, and my arm dressed; and from there I was carried as gently as possible to Malmaison, where, good Madame, Bonaparte had the kindness to come to see me, and lavished on me every attention.

The day I returned to service, after my recovery, I was in the antechamber of the First Consul as he came out of his cabinet. He drew near me, and inquired with great interest how I was. I replied that, thanks to the care taken of me, according to the orders of my excellent master and mistress, I was quite well again. "So much the better," said the First Consul. "Constant, make haste, and get your strength back. Continue to serve me well, and I will take care of you. Here," added he, placing in my hand three little crumpled papers, "these are to replenish your wardrobe;" and he passed on, without listening to the profuse thanks which, with great emotion, I was attempting to express, much more for the consideration and interest in me shown by him than for his present, for I did not then know of what it consisted. After he passed on I unrolled my papers: they were three bank-bills, each for a thousand *francs*! I was moved to tears by so great a kindness. We must remember that at this period the First Consul was not rich, although he was the first magistrate of the republic. How deeply the remembrance of this generous deed touches me, even today. I do not know if details so personal to me will be found interesting; but they seem to me proper as evidence of the true character of the Emperor, which has been so outrageously misrepresented, and also as an instance of his ordinary conduct towards the servants of his house; it shows too, at the same time, whether the severe economy that he required in his domestic management, and of which I will speak elsewhere, was the result, as has been stated, of sordid avarice, or whether it was not rather a rule of prudence, from which he departed willingly whenever his kindness of heart or his humanity urged him thereto.

I am not certain that my memory does not deceive me in leading me to put in this place a circumstance which shows the esteem in which the First Consul held the brave soldiers of his army, and how he loved to manifest it on all occasions. I was one day in his sleeping-room, at the usual hour for his toilet, and was performing that day the duties of chief valet, Hambard being temporarily absent or indisposed, there being in the room, besides the body servants, only the brave and modest Colonel Gerard Lacuee, one of the *aides-de-camp* of the First Consul. Jerome Bonaparte, then hardly seventeen years of age, was introduced. This young man gave his family frequent cause of complaint, and feared no one except his brother Napoleon, who reprimanded, lectured, and scolded him as if he had been his own son. There was a question at the time of making him a sailor, less with the object of giving him a career, than of removing him from the seductive temptations which the high position of his brother caused to spring up incessantly around his path, and which he had little strength to resist. It may be imagined what it cost him to renounce pleasures so accessible and so delightful to a young man. He did not fail to protest, on all occasions, his unfitness for sea-service, going so far, it is said, that he even caused himself to be rejected by the examining board of the navy as incompetent, though he could easily have prepared himself to answer the few questions asked. However, the will of the First Consul must be obeyed, and Jerome was compelled to embark. On the day of which I have spoken, after some moments of conversation and scolding, still on the subject of the navy, Jerome said to his brother, "Instead of sending me to perish of ennui at sea, you ought to take me for an *aide-de-camp*."

"What, take you, greenhorn," warmly replied the First Consul; "wait till a ball has furrowed your face and then I will see about it," at the same time calling his attention to Colonel Lacuee, who blushed, and dropped his eyes to the floor like a young girl, for, as is well known, he bore on his face the scar made by a bullet. This gallant colonel was killed in 1805 before Guntzbourg; and the Emperor deeply regretted his loss, for he ways one of the bravest and most skilful officers of the army.

It was, I believe, about this time that the First Consul conceived a strong passion for a very intelligent and handsome young woman, Madame D. Madame Bonaparte, suspecting this intrigue, showed jealousy; and her husband did all he could to allay her wifely suspicions. Before going to the chamber of his mistress he would wait until every one was asleep in the chateau; and he even carried his precautions so far as to go from his room to hers in his night-dress, without shoes or slippers. Once I found that day was about to break before his return; and fearing scandal, I went, as the First Consul had ordered me to do in such a case, to notify the chambermaid of Madame D. to go to her mistress and tell her the hour. It was hardly five minutes after this timely notice had been given, when I saw the First Consul returning, in great excitement, of which I soon learned the cause. He had discovered, on his return, one of Madame Bonaparte's women, lying in wait, and who had seen him through the window of a closet opening upon the corridor. The First Consul, after a vigorous outburst against the curiosity of the fair sex, sent me to the young scout from the enemy's camp to intimate to her his orders to hold her tongue, unless she wished to be discharged without hope of return. I do not know whether I added a milder argument to these threats to buy her silence; but, whether from fear or for compensation, she had the good sense not to talk. Nevertheless, the successful lover, fearing another surprise, directed me to rent in the Allee des Ireuves a little house where he and Madame D. met from time to time. Such were, and continued to be, the precautions of the First Consul towards his wife. He had the highest regard for her, and took all imaginable care to prevent his infidelities coming to her knowledge. Besides, these passing fancies did not lessen the tenderness he felt for her; and although other women inspired him with love, no other woman had his confidence and friendship to the same extent as Madame Bonaparte. There have been a thousand and one calumnies repeated of the harshness and brutality of the First Consul towards women. He was not always gallant, but I have never seen him rude; and, however singular it may seem after what I have just related, he professed the greatest veneration for a wife of exemplary conduct, speaking in admiring terms of happy households; and he did not admire cynicism, either in morals or in language. When he had any liaisons he kept them secret, and concealed them with great care.

Chapter 6

The 3rd Nivose, year IX. (Dec. 21, 1800),[1] the Opera presented, by order, The Creation of Haydn; and the First Consul had announced that he would be present, with all his household, at this magnificent oratorio. He dined on that day with Madame Bonaparte, her daughter, and Generals Rapp, Lauriston, Lannes, and Berthier. I was on duty; but as the First Consul was going to the Opera, I knew that I should not be needed at the chateau, and resolved, for my part, to go to the Feydeau, occupying the box which Madame Bonaparte allowed us, and which was situated under hers. After dinner, which the First Consul bolted with his usual rapidity, he rose from the table, followed by his officers, with the exception of General Rapp, who remained with Madame Josephine and Hortense. About seven o'clock the First Consul entered his carriage with Lannes, Berthier, and Lauriston, to go to the Opera. When they arrived in the middle of Rue Sainte-Nicaise, the escort who preceded the carriage found the road obstructed by a cart, which seemed to be abandoned, and on which a cask was found fastened strongly with ropes. The chief of the escort had this cart removed to the side of the street; and the First Consul's coachman, whom this delay had made impatient, urged on his horses vigorously, and they shot off like lightning. Scarcely two seconds had passed when the barrel which was on the cart burst with a frightful explosion. No one of the escort or of the companions of the First Consul was slain, but several were wounded; and the loss among the

---

1. Under the Republican regime the years were counted from the proclamation of the Republic, Sept. 22, 1792. The year was divided into twelve months of thirty days each, re-named from some peculiarity, as Brumaire (foggy); Nivose (snowy); Thermidor (hot); Fructidor (fruit), etc.; besides five supplementary days of festivals, called 'sans-culottides'. The months were divided into three decades of ten days instead of weeks, the tenth day (*decadi*) being in lieu of Sunday. The Republican calendar lasted till Jan 1, 1806, as to the years and months at least, though the Concordat had restored the weeks and Sabbaths.—Trans.

residents in the street and the passers-by near the horrible machine was much greater. More than twenty of these were killed, and more than sixty seriously wounded. Trepsat, the architect, had his thigh broken. The First Consul afterwards decorated him, and made him the architect of the Invalides, saying that he had long enough been the most invalid of architects. All the panes of glass at the Tuileries were broken, and many houses thrown down. All those of the Rue Sainte-Nicaise, and even some in the adjacent streets, were badly damaged, some fragments being blown into the house of the Consul Cambaceres. The glass of the First Consul's carriage was shivered to fragments. By a fortunate chance, the carriages of the suite, which should have been immediately behind that of the First Consul, were some distance in the rear, which happened in this way: Madame Bonaparte, after dinner, had a shawl brought to wear to the opera; and when it came, General Rapp jestingly criticised the colour, and begged her to choose another. Madame Bonaparte defended her shawl, and said to the general that he knew as much about criticising a toilet as she did about attacking a fort. This friendly banter continued for some moments; and in the interval, the First Consul, who never waited, set out in advance, and the miserable assassins and authors of the conspiracy set fire to the infernal machine. Had the coachman of the First Consul driven less rapidly, and thereby been two seconds later, it would have been all over with his master; while, on the other hand, if Madame Bonaparte had followed her husband promptly, it would have been certain death to her and all her suite.

It was, in fact, the delay of an instant which saved her life, as well as that of her daughter, her sister-in-law, Madame Murat, and all who were to accompany them, since the carriage of these ladies, instead of being immediately behind that of the First Consul, was just leaving the Place Carrousel, when the machine exploded. The glass was shivered; and though Madame Bonaparte received no injury except the terrible fright, Hortense was slightly wounded in the face by a piece of glass, and Madame Caroline Murat, who was then far advanced in pregnancy, was so frightened that it was necessary to carry her back to the Tuileries. This catastrophe had its influence, even on the health of her child; for I have been told that Prince Achille Muratz is subject, to this day, to frequent attacks of epilepsy. As is well known, the First Consul went on to the opera, where he was received with tumultuous acclamations, the immobility of his countenance contrasting strongly with the pallor and agitation of Madame Bonaparte's, who had feared not so much for herself as for him. The coachman who had driven the

First Consul with such good fortune was named Germain. He had followed him in Egypt, and in a skirmish had killed an Arab, with his own hand, under the eyes of the general-in-chief, who, struck with his courage, had cried out, "*Diable!* that's a brave man, he is a Caesar." The name had clung to him. It has been said that this brave man was drunk at the time of this explosion; but this is a mistake, which his conduct under the circumstances contradicts in the most positive manner. When the First Consul, after he became Emperor, went out, incognito, in Paris, it was Caesar who was his escort, without livery. It is said in the Memorial de Sainte Helene that the Emperor, in speaking of Caesar, stated that he was in a complete state of intoxication, and took the noise of the explosion for an artillery salute, nor did he know until the next day what had taken place. This is entirely untrue, and the Emperor was incorrectly informed in regard to his coachman. Caesar drove the First Consul very rapidly because he had been ordered to do so, and because he considered his honour interested in not allowing the obstacle which the infernal machine placed in his way before the explosion to delay him. The evening of the event I saw Caesar, who was perfectly sober, and he himself related to me part of the details that I have just given. A few days after, four or five hundred hackney-coachmen clubbed together to honour him, and gave him a magnificent dinner at twenty-four *francs* per head.

While the infernal plot was being executed, and costing the lies of many innocent citizens, without attaining the object the assassins proposed, I was, as I have said, at the Theatre Feydeau, where I had prepared myself to enjoy at my leisure an entire evening of freedom, amid the pleasures of the stage, for which I had all my life a great liking. Scarcely had I seated myself comfortably, however, when the box-keeper entered in the greatest excitement, crying out, "Monsieur Constant, it is said that they have just blown up the First Consul; there has been a terrible explosion, and it is asserted that he is dead." These terrible words were like a thunderbolt to me. Not knowing what I did, I plunged down-stairs, and, forgetting my hat, ran like mad to the chateau. While crossing Rue Vivienne and the Palais Royal, I saw no extraordinary disturbance; but in Rue Sainte Honore there was a very great tumult, and I saw, borne away on litters, many dead and wounded, who had been at first carried into the neighbouring houses of Rue Sainte Nicaise. Many groups had formed, and with one voice all were cursing the still unknown authors of this dastardly attempt. Some accused the Jacobins of this, because three months before they had placed the poniard in the hands of Cerrachi, of Arena, and of Topino Lebrun; whilst others, less numerous perhaps, thought the aristocrats, the Royalists, could alone be guilty of this atrocity. I could give no time to these various accusations, except as I was detained in forcing my way through an immense and closely packed crowd, and as rapidly as possible went on, and in two seconds was at the Carrousel. I threw myself against the wicket, but the two sentinels instantly crossed bayonets before my breast. It was useless to cry out that I was *valet de chambre* of the First Consul; for my bare head, my wild manner, the disorder, both of my dress and ideas, appeared to them suspicious, and they refused energetically and very obstinately to allow me to enter. I then begged them to send for the gatekeeper of the chateau; and as soon as he came, I was admitted, or rather rushed into the chateau, where I learned what had just happened. A short time after the First Consul arrived, and was immediately surrounded by his officers, and by all his household, every one present being in the greatest state of anxiety. When the First Consul alighted from his carriage he appeared calm and smiling; he even wore an air of gayety. On entering the vestibule he said to his officers, rubbing his hands, "Well, sirs, we made a fine escape!" They shuddered with indignation and anger. He then entered the grand saloon on the ground floor, where a large number of counsellors of state and dignitaries had already assembled; but hardly had they begun to express their congratulations, when he interrupted them, and in so vehement a manner that he was heard outside the saloon. We were told that after this council he had a lively altercation with Fouche, Minister of Police, whom he reproached with his ignorance of this plot, openly accusing the Jacobins of being the authors.

That evening, on retiring, the First Consul asked me laughingly if I was afraid. "More than you were, my general," I replied; and I related to him how I had heard the fatal news at the Feydeau, and had run without my hat to the very wicket of the Carrousel, where the sentinels tried to prevent my entering. He was amused at the oaths and abusive epithets with which they had accompanied their defence of the gate, and at last said to me, "After all, my dear Constant, you should not be angry with them; they were only obeying orders. They are brave men, on whom I can rely." The truth is, the Consular Guard was at this period no less devoted than it has been since as the Imperial Guard. At the first rumour of the great risk which the First Consul had run, all the soldiers of that faithful band had gathered spontaneously in the court of the Tuileries.

After this melancholy catastrophe, which carried distress into all

France, and mourning into so many families, the entire police were actively engaged in searching for the authors of the plot. The dwelling of the First Consul was first put under surveillance, and we were incessantly watched by spies, without suspecting it. All our walks, all our visits, all our goings and comings, were known; and attention was especially directed to our friends, and even our liaisons. But such was the devotion of each and all to the person of the First Consul, such was the affection that he so well knew how to inspire in those around him, that not one of the persons attached to his service was for an instant suspected of having a hand in this infamous attempt. Neither at this time, nor in any other affair of this kind, were the members of his household ever compromised; and never was the name of the lowest of his servants ever found mixed up in criminal plots against a life so valued and so glorious.

The minister of police suspected the Royalists of this attempt; but the First Consul attributed it to the Jacobins, because they were already guilty, he said, of crimes as odious. One hundred and thirty of the most noted men of this party were transported on pure suspicion, and without any form of trial. It is now known that the discovery, trial, and execution of Saint Regent and Carbon, the true criminals, proved that the conjectures of the minister were more correct than those of the chief of state.

The 4th Nivose, at noon, the First Consul held a grand review in the Place Carrousel, where an innumerable crowd of citizens were collected to behold, and also to testify their affection for his person, and their indignation against the enemies who dared attack him only by assassination. Hardly had he turned his horse towards the first line of grenadiers of the Consular Guard, when their innumerable acclamations rose on all sides. He rode along the ranks, at a walk, very slowly, showing his appreciation, and replying by a few simple and affectionate words to this effusion of popular joy; and cries of "*Vive* Bonaparte! *Vive* the First Consul!" did not cease till after he had re-entered his apartments.

The conspirators who obstinately persisted, with so much animosity, in attacking the life of the First Consul, could not have chosen a period in which circumstances would have been more adverse to their plans than in 1800 and 1801, for then the Consul was beloved not only for his military deeds, but still more for the hope of peace that he gave to France, which hope was soon realized. As soon as the first rumour spread abroad that peace had been concluded with Austria, the greater part of the inhabitants of Paris gathered under the windows of the Pavilion of Flora. Blessings and cries of gratitude and joy were heard on all sides; then musicians assembled to give a serenade to the chief of state, and proceeded to form themselves into orchestras; and there was dancing the whole night through. I have never seen a sight more striking or more joyous than the bird's-eye view of this improvised jubilee.

When in the month of October, the, peace of Amiens having been concluded with England, France found herself delivered from all the wars that she had maintained through so many years, and at the cost of so many sacrifices, it would be impossible to form an idea of the joy which burst forth on all sides. The decrees which ordered either the disarmament of vessels of war, or the placing of the forts on a peace footing, were welcomed as pledges of happiness and security. The day of the reception of Lord Cornwallis, Ambassador of England, the First Consul ordered that the greatest magnificence should be displayed. "It is necessary," he had said the evening before, "to show these proud Britons that we are not reduced to beggary." The fact is, the English, before setting foot on the French continent, had expected to find only ruins, penury, and misery. The whole of France had been described to them as being in the most distressing condition, and they thought themselves on the point of landing in a barbarous country. Their surprise was great when they saw how many evils the First Consul had already repaired in so short a time, and all the improvements that he still intended to carry out; and they spread through their own country the report of what they themselves called the prodigies of the First Consul, by which thousands of their compatriots were influenced to come and judge with their own eyes. At the moment that Lord Cornwallis entered the great hall of the Ambassadors with his suite, the eyes of all the English must have been dazzled by the sight of the First Consul, surrounded by his two colleagues, with all the diplomatic corps, and with an already brilliant military court.

In the midst of all these rich uniforms, his was remarkable for its simplicity; but the diamond called the Regent, which had been put in pawn under the Directory, and redeemed a few days since by the First Consul, sparkled on the hilt of his sword.

Chapter 7

In the month of May, 1801, there came to Paris, on his way to take possession of his new kingdom, the Prince of Tuscany, Don Louis the First, whom the First Consul had just made King of Etruria. He travelled under the name of the Count of Leghorn, with his wife, who was the *infanta* of Spain, Maria Louisa, third daughter of Charles the Fourth; but in spite of the incognito, which, from the modest title he had assumed, he seemed really anxious to preserve, especially, perhaps, on account of the poor appearance of his small court, he was, notwithstanding, received and treated at the Tuileries as a king. This prince was in feeble health, and it was said had epilepsy. They were lodged at the residence of the Spanish Embassy, formerly the Hotel Montessori; and he requested Madame de Montessori, who lived in the next house, to reopen a private communication between the houses which had long been closed. He, as well as the Queen of Etruria, greatly enjoyed the society of this lady, who was the widow of the Duke of Orleans, and spent many hours every day in her house. A Bourbon himself, he doubtless loved to hear every particular relating to the Bourbons of France, which could so well be given by one who had lived at their court, and on intimate terms with the royal family, with which she was connected by ties which, though not official, were none the less well known and recognized.

Madame de Montesson received at her house all who were most distinguished in Parisian society. She had reunited the remnants of the most select society of former times, which the Revolution had dispersed. A friend of Madame Bonaparte, she was also loved and respected by the First Consul, who was desirous that they should speak and think well of him in the most noble and elegant saloon of the capital. Besides, he relied upon the experience and exquisite refinement of this lady, to establish in the palace and its society, out of which he already dreamed of making a court, the usages and etiquette customary with sovereigns.

The King of Etruria was not fond of work, and in this respect did not please the First Consul, who could not endure idleness. I heard him one day, in conversation with his colleague, Cambaceres, score severely his royal *protégé* (in his absence, of course). "Here is a prince," said he, "who does not concern himself much with his very dear and well-beloved subjects, but passes his time cackling with old women, to whom he dilates in a loud tone on my good qualities, while he complains in a whisper of owing his elevation to the chief of this cursed French Republic. His only business is walking, hunting, balls, and theatres."

"It is asserted," remarked Cambaceres, "that you wished to disgust the French people with kings, by showing them such a specimen, as the Spartans disgusted their children with drunkenness by exhibiting to them a drunken slave."

"Not so, not so, my dear sir," replied the First Consul. "I have no desire to disgust them with royalty; but the sojourn of the King of Etruria will annoy a number of good people who are working incessantly to create a feeling favourable to the Bourbons." Don Louis, perhaps, did not merit such severity, although he was, it must be admitted, endowed with little mind, and few agreeable traits of character. When he dined at the Tuileries, he was much embarrassed in replying to the simplest questions the First Consul addressed him. Beyond the rain and the weather, horses, dogs, and other like subjects of conversation, he could not give an intelligent reply on any subject. The Queen, his wife, often made signs to put him on right road, and even whispered to him, what he should say or do; but this rendered only the more conspicuous his absolute want of presence of mind. People made themselves merry at his expense; but they took good care, however, not to do this in the presence of the First Consul, who would not have suffered any want of respect to a guest to whom he had shown so much. What gave rise to the greatest number of pleasantries, in regard to the prince, was his excessive economy, which reached a point truly incredible. Innumerable instances were quoted, which this is perhaps the most striking. The First Consul sent him frequently during his stay, magnificent presents, such as Savonnerie carpets, Lyons cloths, and Sevres porcelain; and on such occasions his Majesty would give some small gratuity to the bearers of these precious articles. One day a vase of very great value (it cost, I believe, a hundred thousand crowns) was brought him which it required a dozen workmen to place in the apartments of the king. Their work being finished, the workmen waited until his Majesty should give them some token of his satisfaction, and flattered themselves he would display a truly royal liberality. As, notwithstanding, time passed, and the expected gratuity did not arrive, they finally applied to one of his chamberlains, and asked him to lay their petition at the feet of the King of Etruria. His Majesty, who was still in ecstasy over the beauty of the present, and the munificence of the First Consul, was astounded at such a request. "It was a present," said he; "and hence it was for him to receive, not to give;" and it was only after much persistence that the chamberlain obtained six *francs* for each of these workmen, which were refused by these good people. The persons of the prince's suite asserted that to this extreme aversion to expense he added an excessive severity towards themselves; however, the first of these traits probably disposed the servants of the King of Etruria to exaggerate the second.

Masters who are too economical never fail to be deemed severe themselves, and at the same time are severely criticised by their servants. For this reason, perhaps (I would say in passing), there is current among some people a calumny which represents the Emperor as often taking a fancy to beat his servants. The economy of the Emperor Napoleon was only a desire for the most perfect order in the expenses of his household. One thing I can positively assert in regard to his Majesty, the King of Etruria, is that he did not sincerely feel either all the enthusiasm or all the gratitude which he expressed towards the First Consul, and the latter had more than one proof of this insincerity. As to the king's talent for governing and reigning, the First Consul said to Cambaceres at his levee, in the same conversation from which I have already quoted, that the Spanish Ambassador had complained of the haughtiness of this prince towards him, of his extreme ignorance, and of the disgust with which all kind of business inspired him. Such was the king who went to govern part of Italy, and was installed in his kingdom by General Murat, who apparently had little idea that a throne was in store for himself a few leagues distant from that on which he seated Don Luis.

The Queen of Etruria was, in the opinion of the First Consul, more sagacious and prudent than her august husband. This princess was remarkable neither for grace nor elegance; she dressed herself in the morning for the whole day, and walked in the garden, her head adorned with flowers or a diadem, and wearing a dress, the train of which swept up the sand of the walks; often, also, carrying in her arms one of her children, still in long dresses, from which it can be readily understood that by night the toilet of her Majesty was somewhat disarranged. She was far from pretty, and her manners were not suited to her rank. But, which fully atoned for all this, she was good-tempered, much beloved by those in her service, and fulfilled scrupulously all the duties of wife and mother; and in consequence the First Consul, who made a great point of domestic virtues, professed for her the highest and most sincere esteem.

During the entire month which their Majesties spent in Paris, there was a succession of fetes, one of which Talleyrand gave in their honour at Neuilly, of great magnificence and splendour, and to which I, being on duty, accompanied the First Consul. The chateau and park were illuminated with a brilliant profusion of coloured lights. First there was a concert, at the close of which the end of the hall was moved aside, like the curtain of a theatre, and we beheld the principal square in Florence, the ducal palace, a fountain playing, and the Tuscans giving themselves up to the games and dances of their country, and singing couplets in honour of their sovereigns. Talleyrand came forward, and requested their Majesties to mingle with their subjects; and hardly had they set foot in the garden than they found themselves in fairyland, where fireworks, rockets, and Bengal fires burst out in every direction and in every form, colonnades, arches of triumph, and palaces of fire arose, disappeared, and succeeded each other incessantly. Numerous tables were arranged in the apartments and in the garden, at which all the spectators were in turn seated, and last of all a magnificent ball closed this evening of enchantments. It was opened by the King of Etruria and Madame Le Clerc (Pauline Borghese).

Madame de Montesson also gave to their Majesties a ball, at which the whole family of the First Consul was present. But of all these entertainments, I retain the most vivid recollection of that given by Chaptal, Minister of the Interior, the day which he chose being the fourteenth of June, the anniversary of the battle of Marengo. After the concert, the theatre, the ball, and another representation of the city and inhabitants of Florence, a splendid supper was served in the garden, under military tents, draped with flags, and ornamented with groupings of arms and trophies, each lady being accompanied and served at table by an officer in uniform. When the King and Queen of Etruria came out of their tent, a balloon was released which carried into the heavens the name of Marengo in letters of fire.

Their Majesties wished to visit, before their departure, the chief public institutions, so they were taken to the Conservatory of Music, to a sitting of the Institute, of which they did not appear to comprehend much, and to the Mint, where a medal was struck in their honour. Chaptal received the thanks of the queen for the manner in which he had entertained and treated his royal guests, both as a member of the Institute, as minister at his hotel, and in the visits which they had made to the different institutions of the capital. On the eve of his departure the king had a long private interview with the First Consul; and though I do not know what passed, I observed that on coming out neither appeared to be satisfied with the other. However, their Majesties, on the whole, should have carried away a most favourable impression of the manner in which they had been received.

Chapter 8

In all the fetes given by the First Consul in honour of their Majesties, the King and Queen of Etruria, Mademoiselle Hortense shone with that brilliancy and grace which made her the pride of her mother, and the most beautiful ornament of the growing court of the First Consul.

About this time she inspired a most violent passion in a gentleman of a very good family, who was, I think, a little deranged before this mad love affected his brain. This poor unfortunate roamed incessantly around Malmaison; and as soon as Mademoiselle Hortense left the house, ran by the side of her carriage with the liveliest demonstrations of tenderness, and threw through the window flowers, locks of his hair, and verses of his own composition. When he met Mademoiselle Hortense on foot, he threw himself on his knees before her with a thousand passionate gestures, addressing her in most endearing terms, and followed her, in spite of all opposition, even into the courtyard of the chateau, and abandoned himself to all kinds of folly. At first Mademoiselle Hortense, who was young and gay, was amused by the antics of her admirer, read the verses which he addressed to her, and showed them to the ladies who accompanied her. One such poetical effusion was enough to provoke laughter (and can you blame her?); but after the first burst of laughter, Mademoiselle Hortense, good and charming as her mother, never failed to say, with a sympathetic expression and tone, "The poor man, he is much to be pitied!" At last, however, the importunities of the poor madman increased to such an extent that they became insupportable. He placed himself at the door of the theatres in Paris at which Mademoiselle Hortense was expected, and threw himself at her feet, supplicating, weeping, laughing, and gesticulating all at once. This spectacle amused the crowd too much to long amuse Mademoiselle de Beauharnais; and Carrat was ordered to remove the poor fellow, who was placed, I think, in a private asylum for the insane.

Mademoiselle Hortense would have been too happy if she could have known love only from the absurd effects which it produced on this diseased brain, as she thus saw it only in its pleasant and comic aspect. But the time came when she was forced to feel all that is painful and bitter in the experience of that passion. In January, 1802, she was married to Louis Bonaparte, brother of the First Consul, which was a most suitable alliance as regards age, Louis being twenty-four years old, and Mademoiselle de Beauharnais not more than eighteen; and nevertheless it was to both parties the beginning of long and interminable sorrows.

Louis, however, was kind and sensible, full of good feeling and intelligence, studious and fond of letters, like all his brothers (except one alone); but he was in feeble health, suffered almost incessantly, and was of a melancholy disposition. All the brothers of the First Consul resembled him more or less in their personal appearance, and Louis still more than the others, especially at the time of the Consulate, and before the Emperor Napoleon had become so stout. But none of the brothers of the Emperor possessed that imposing and majestic air and that rapid and imperious manner which came to him at first by instinct, and afterwards from the habit of command. Louis had peaceful and modest tastes. It has been asserted that at the time of his marriage he was deeply attached to a person whose name could not be ascertained, and who, I think, is still a mystery.

Mademoiselle Hortense was extremely pretty, with an expressive and mobile countenance, and in addition to this was graceful, talented, and affable. Kind-hearted and amiable like her mother, she had not that excessive desire to oblige which sometimes detracted from Madame Bonaparte's character. This is, nevertheless, the woman whom evil reports, disseminated by miserable scandal-mongers, have so outrageously slandered! My heart is stirred with disgust and indignation when I hear such revolting absurdities repeated and scattered broadcast. According to these honest fabricators, the First Consul must have seduced his wife's daughter, before giving her in marriage to his own brother. Simply to announce such a charge is to comprehend all the falsity of it. I knew better than any one the amours of the Emperor. In these clandestine liaisons he feared scandal, hated the ostentations of vice, and I can affirm on honour that the infamous desires attributed to him never entered his mind. Like every one else, who was near Mademoiselle de Beauharnais, and because he knew his step-daughter even more intimately, he felt for her the tenderest affection; but this sentiment was entirely paternal, and Mademoiselle Hortense reciprocated it by that reverence which a wellborn young girl feels towards her father. She could have obtained from her step-father anything that she wished, if her extreme timidity had not prevented her asking; but, instead of addressing herself directly to him, she first had recourse to the intercession of the secretary, and of those around the Emperor. Is it thus she would have acted if the evil reports spread by her enemies, and those of the Emperor, had had the least foundation?

Before her marriage Hortense had an attachment for General Duroc, who was hardly thirty years of age, had a fine figure, and was a favourite with the chief of state, who, knowing him to be prudent and discreet, confided to him important diplomatic missions. As *aide-de-camp* of the First Consul, general of division, and governor of the Tuileries, he lived long in familiar intimacy at Malmaison, and in the home life of the Emperor, and during necessary absences on duty, corresponded with Mademoiselle Hortense; and yet the indifference with which he allowed the marriage of the latter with Louis to proceed, proves that he reciprocated but feebly the affection which he had inspired. It is certain that he could have had. Mademoiselle de Beauharnais for his wife, if he had been willing to accept the conditions on which the First Consul offered the hand of his step-daughter; but he was expecting something better, and his ordinary prudence failed him at the time when it should have shown him a future which was easy to foresee, and calculated to satisfy the promptings of an ambition even more exalted than his. He therefore refused positively; and the entreaties of Madame Bonaparte, which had already influenced her husband, succeeded.

Madame Bonaparte, who saw herself treated with so little friendship by the brothers of the First Consul, tried to make his family a defence for herself against the plots which were gathering incessantly around her to drive her away from the heart of her husband. It was with this design she worked with all her might to bring about the marriage of her daughter with one of her brothers-in-law.

General Duroc doubtless repented immediately of his precipitate refusal when crowns began to rain in the august family to which he had had it in his power to ally himself; when he saw Naples, Spain, Westphalia, Upper Italy, the duchies of Parma, Lucca, etc., become the appendages of the new imperial dynasty; when the beautiful and graceful Hortense herself, who had loved him so devotedly, mounted in her turn a throne that she would have been only too happy to have shared with the object of her young affections. As for him, he married Mademoiselle Hervas d'Almenara, daughter of the banker of the court of Spain. She was a little woman with a very dark complexion, very thin, and without grace; but, on the other hand, of a most peevish, haughty, exacting, and capricious temper. As she was to have on her marriage an enormous dowry, the First Consul had demanded her hand in marriage for his senior *aide-de-camp*. Madame Duroc forgot herself, I have heard, so far as to beat her servants, and to bear herself in a most singular manner toward people who were in no wise her dependants. When M. Dubois came to tune her piano, unfortunately she was at home, and finding the noise required by this operation unendurable, drove the tuner off with the greatest violence. In one of these singular attacks she one day broke all the keys of his instrument. Another time Mugnier, clockmaker of the Emperor, and the head of his profession in Paris, with Breguet, having brought her a watch of very great value that *madame*, the Duchess of Friuli had herself ordered, but which did not please her, she became so enraged, that, in the presence of Mugnier, she dashed the watch on the floor, danced on it, and reduced it to atoms. She utterly refused to pay for it, and the marshal was compelled to do this himself. Thus Duroc's want of foresight in refusing the hand of Hortense, together with the interested calculations of Madame Bonaparte, caused the misery of two households.

The portrait I have sketched, and I believe faithfully, although not a flattering picture, is merely that of a young woman with all the impulsiveness of the Spanish character, spoiled as an only daughter, who had been reared in indulgence, and with the entire neglect which hinders the education of all the young ladies of her country. Time has calmed the vivacity of her youth; and *madame*, the Duchess of Friuli, has since given an example of most faithful devotion to duty, and great strength of mind in the severe trials that she has endured. In the loss of her husband, however grievous it might be, glory had at least some consolation to offer to the widow of the grand marshal. But when her young daughter, sole heiress of a great name and an illustrious title, was suddenly taken away by death from all the expectations and the devotion of her mother, who could dare to offer her consolation? If there could be any (which I do not believe), it would be found in the remembrance of the cares and tenderness lavished on her to the last by maternal love. Such recollections, in which bitterness is mingled with sweetness, were not wanting to the duchess.

The religious ceremony of marriage between Louis and Hortense took place Jan. 7, in a house in the Rue de la Victoire; and the marriage of General Murat with Caroline Bonaparte, which had been acknowledged only before the civil authorities, was consecrated on the same day. Both Louis and his bride were very sad. She wept bitterly during the whole ceremony, and her tears were not soon dried. She made no attempt to win the affection of her husband; while he, on his side, was too proud and too deeply wounded to pursue her with his wooing. The good Josephine did all she could to reconcile them; for she must have felt that this union, which had begun so badly, was her work, in which she had tried to combine her own interest, or at least that which she considered such, and the happiness of her daughter. But her efforts, as well as her advice and her prayers, availed nothing; and I have many a time seen Hortense seek the solitude of her own room, and the heart of a friend, there to pour out her tears. Tears fell from her eyes sometimes even in the midst of one of the First Consul's receptions, where we saw with sorrow this young woman, brilliant and gay, who had so often gracefully done the honours on such occasions and attended to all the details of its etiquette, retire into a corner, or into the embrasure of a window, with one of her most intimate friends, there to sadly make her the a confidante of her trials. During this conversation, from which she rose with red and swollen eyes, her husband remained thoughtful and taciturn at the opposite end of the room. Her Majesty, the Queen of Holland, has been accused of many sins; but everything said or written against this princess is marked by shameful exaggeration. So high a fortune drew all eyes to her, and excited bitter jealousy; and yet those who envied her would not have failed to bemoan themselves, if they had been put in tier place, on condition that they were to bear her griefs. The misfortunes of Queen Hortense began with life itself. Her father having been executed on a revolutionary scaffold, and her mother thrown into prison, she found herself, while still a child, alone, and with no other reliance than the faithfulness of the old servants of the family. Her brother, the noble and worthy Prince Eugene, had been compelled, it is said, to serve as an apprentice. She had a few years of happiness, or at least of repose, during the time she was under the care of Madame Campan, and just after she left boarding-school. But her evil destiny was far from quitting her; and her wishes being thwarted, an unhappy marriage opened for her a new succession of troubles. The death of her first son, whom the Emperor wished to adopt, and whom he had intended to be his successor in the Empire, the divorce of her mother, the tragic death of her best-loved friend, Madame de Brocq, who, before her eyes, slipped over a precipice; the overturning of the imperial throne, which caused her the loss of her title and rank as queen, a loss which she, however, felt less than the misfortunes of him whom she regarded as her father; and finally, the continual annoyance of domestic dissensions, of vexatious lawsuits, and the agony she suffered in beholding her oldest surviving son removed from her by order of her husband,—such were the principal catastrophes in a life which might have been thought destined for so much happiness.

The day after the marriage of Mademoiselle Hortense, the First Consul set out for Lyons, where there awaited him the deputies of the Cisalpine Republic, assembled for the election of a president. Everywhere on his route he was welcomed with fetes and congratulations, with which all were eager to overwhelm him on account of the miraculous manner in which he had escaped the plots of his enemies. This journey differed in no wise from the tours which he afterwards made as Emperor. On his arrival at Lyons, he received the visit of all the authorities, the constituent bodies, the deputations from the neighbouring departments, and the members of the Italian councils. Madame Bonaparte, who accompanied him on this journey, attended with him these public displays, and shared with him the magnificent fete given to him by the city of Lyons. The day on which the council elected and proclaimed the First Consul president of the Italian Republic he reviewed, on the Place des Brotteaux, the troops of the garrison, and recognized in the ranks many soldiers of the army of Egypt, with whom he conversed for some time. On all these occasions the First Consul wore the same costume that he had worn at Malmaison, and which I have described elsewhere. He rose early, mounted his horse, and visited the public works, among others those of the Place Belcour, of which he had laid the corner-stone on his return from Italy, passed through the Place des Brotteaux, inspected, examined everything, and, always indefatigable, worked on his return as if he had been at the Tuileries. He rarely changed his dress, except when he received at his table the authorities or the principal inhabitants of the city. He received all petitions most graciously, and before leaving presented to the mayor of the city a scarf of honour, and to the legate of the Pope a handsome snuff-box ornamented with his likeness.

The deputies of the council received presents, and were most generous in making them, presenting Madame Bonaparte with magnificent ornaments of diamonds and precious stones, and other most valuable jewellery.

The First Consul, on arriving at Lyons, had been deeply grieved at the sudden death of a worthy prelate whom he had known in his first campaign in Italy.

The Archbishop of Milan had come to Lyons, notwithstanding his great age, in order to see the First Consul, whom he loved with such tenderness that in conversation the venerable old man continually addressed the young general as "my son." The peasants of Pavia, having revolted because their fanaticism had been excited by false assertions that the French wished to destroy their religion, the Archbishop of Milan, in order to prove that their fears were groundless, often showed himself in a carriage with General Bonaparte.

This prelate had stood the journey well, and appeared in good health and fine spirits. Talleyrand, who had arrived at Lyons a few days before the First Consul, gave a dinner to the Cisalpine deputies and the principal notables of the city, at which the Archbishop of Milan sat on his right. He had scarcely taken his seat, and was in the act of leaning forward to speak to M. de Talleyrand, when he fell dead in his armchair.

On the 12th of January the town of Lyons gave, in honour of the First Consul and Madame Bonaparte, a magnificent fete, consisting of a concert, followed by a ball. At eight o'clock in the evening, the three mayors, accompanied by the superintendents of the fete, called upon their illustrious guests in the government palace. I can imagine that I see again spread out before me that immense amphitheatre, handsomely decorated, and illuminated by innumerable lustres and candles, the seats draped with the richest cloths manufactured in the city, and filled with thousands of women, some brilliant in youth and beauty, and all magnificently attired. The theatre had been chosen as the place of the fete; and on the entrance of the First Consul and Madame Bonaparte, who advanced leaning on the arm of one of the mayors, there arose a thunder of applause and acclamations. Suddenly the decorations of the theatre faded from sight, and the Place Bonaparte (the former Place Belcour) appeared, as it had been restored by order of the First Consul. In the midst rose a pyramid, surmounted by the statue of the First Consul, who was represented as resting upon a lion. Trophies of arms and bas-reliefs represented on one side, the other that of Marengo.

When the first, transports excited by this spectacle, which recalled at once the benefits and the victories of the hero of the fete, had subsided, there succeeded a deep silence, and delightful music was heard, mingled with songs, dedicated to the glory of the First Consul, to his wife, the warriors who surrounded him, and the representatives of the Italian republics. The singers and the musicians were amateurs of Lyons. Mademoiselle Longue, Gerbet, the postmaster, and Theodore, the merchant, who had each performed their parts in a charming manner, received the congratulations of the First Consul, and the most gracious thanks of Madame Bonaparte.

What struck me most forcibly in the couplets which were sung on that occasion, and which much resembled all verses written for such occasions, was that incense was offered to the First Consul in the very terms which all the poets of the Empire have since used in their turn. All the exaggerations of flattery were exhausted during the consulate; and in the years which followed, it was necessary for poets often to repeat themselves. Thus, in the couplets of Lyons, the First Consul was the God of victory, the conqueror of the Nile and of Neptune, the saviour of his country, the peacemaker of the world, the arbiter of Europe. The French soldiers were transformed into friends and companions of Alcides, etc., all of which was cutting the ground from under the feet of the singers of the future.

The fete of Lyons ended in a ball which lasted until daylight, at which the First Consul remained two hours, which he spent in conversation with the magistrates of the city. While the better class of the inhabitants gave these grand entertainments to their guests, the people, notwithstanding the cold, abandoned themselves on the public squares to pleasure and dancing, and towards midnight there was a fine display of fireworks on the Place Bonaparte.

After fifteen or eighteen days passed at Lyons, we returned to Paris, the First Consul and his wife continuing to reside by preference at Malmaison. It was, I think, a short time after the return of the First Consul that a poorly dressed man begged an audience; an order was given to admit him to the cabinet, and the First Consul inquired his name. "General," replied the petitioner, frightened by his presence, "it is I who had the honour of giving you writing lessons in the school of Brienne."

"Fine scholar you have made!" interrupted vehemently the First Consul; "I compliment you on it!" Then he began to laugh at his own vehemence, and addressed a few kind words to this good man, whose timidity such a compliment had not reassured. A few days after the master received, from the least promising, doubtless, of all his pupils at Brienne (you know how the Emperor wrote), a pension amply sufficient for his needs.

Another of the old teachers of the First Consul, the Abbe Dupuis, was appointed by him to the post of private librarian at Malmaison, and lived and died there. He was a modest man, and had the reputation of being well-educated. The First Consul visited him often in his room, and paid him every imaginable attention and respect.

Chapter 9

The day on which the First Consul promulgated the law of public worship, he rose early, and entered the dressing-room to make his toilet. While he was dressing I saw Joseph Bonaparte enter his room with Cambaceres.

"Well," said the First Consul to the latter, "we are going to mass. What do they think of that in Paris?"

"Many persons," replied M. Cambaceres, "will go to the representation with the intention of hissing the piece, if they do not find it amusing."

"If any one thinks of hissing, I will have him put out-of-doors by the grenadiers of the Consular Guard."

"But if the grenadiers begin to hiss like the others?"

"I have no fear of that. My old soldiers will go to Notre Dame exactly as they went to the mosque at Cairo. They will watch me; and seeing their general remain quiet and reverent, they will do as he does, saying to themselves, 'That is the countersign!'"

"I am afraid," said Joseph Bonaparte, "that the general officers will not be so accommodating. I have just left Augereau, who was vomiting fire and fury against what he calls your capricious proclamations. He, and. a few others, will not be easy to bring back into the pale of our holy mother, the church."

"Bah! that is like Augereau. He is a bawler, who makes a great noise; and yet if he has a little imbecile cousin, he puts him in the priests college for me to make a chaplain of him.

"That reminds me," continued the First Consul, addressing his colleague, "when is your brother going to take possession of his see of Rouen? Do you know it has the finest archiepiscopal palace in France? He will be cardinal before a year has passed; that matter is already arranged."

The second consul bowed. From that moment his manner towards the First Consul was rather that of a courtier than an equal.

The plenipotentiaries who had been appointed to examine and sign the Concordat were Joseph Bonaparte, Cruet, and the Abbe Bernier. This latter, whom I saw sometimes at the Tuileries, had been a chief of the Chouans,[1] and took a prominent part in all that occurred. The First Consul, in this same conversation, the opening of which I have just related, discussed with his two companions the subject of the conferences on the Concordat. "The Abby Bernier," said the First Consul, "inspired fear in the Italian prelates by the vehemence of his logic. It might have been said that he imagined himself living over again the days in which he led the Vendeens to the charge against the blues. Nothing could be more striking than the contrast of his rude and quarrelsome manner with the polished bearing and honeyed tones of the prelates. Cardinal Caprara came to me two days ago, with a shocked air, to ask if it is true that, during the war of the Vendee, the Abbe Bernier made an altar on which to celebrate mass out of the corpses of the Republicans. I replied that I knew nothing of it, but that it was possible. 'General, First Consul,' cried the frightened cardinal, 'it is not a red hat, but a red cap, which that man should have?'

"I am much afraid," continued the First Consul, "that that kind of cap would prevent the Abbe Bernier from getting the red hat."

These gentlemen left the First Consul when his toilet was finished, and went to make their own. The First Consul wore on that day the costume of the consuls, which consisted of a scarlet coat without facings, and with a broad embroidery of palms, in gold, on all the seams. His sword, which he had worn in Egypt, hung at his side from a belt, which, though not very wide, was of beautiful workmanship, and richly embroidered. He wore his black stock, in preference to a lace cravat, and like his colleagues, wore knee-breeches and shoes; a French hat, with floating plumes of the three colours, completed this rich costume.

The celebration of this sacrament at Notre Dame was a novel sight to the Parisians, and many attended as if it were a theatrical representation. Many, also, especially amongst the military, found it rather a matter of raillery than of edification; and those who, during the Revolution, had contributed all their strength to the overthrow of the worship which the First Consul had just re-established, could with difficulty conceal their indignation and their chagrin.

The common people saw in the *Te Deum* which was sung that day for peace and the Concordat, only an additional gratification of their curiosity; but among the middle classes there was a large number

---

1. The Chouans were Royalists in insurrection in Brittany.

of pious persons, who had deeply regretted the suppression of the forms of devotion in which they had been reared, and who were very happy in returning to the old worship. And, indeed, there was then no manifestation of superstition or of bigotry sufficient to alarm the enemies of intolerance.

The clergy were exceedingly careful not to appear too exacting; they demanded little, condemned no one; and the representative of the Holy Father, the cardinal legate, pleased all, except perhaps a few dissatisfied old priests, by his indulgence, the worldly grace of his manners, and the freedom of his conduct. This prelate was entirely in accord with the First Consul, and he took great pleasure in conversing with him.

It is also certain, that apart from all religious sentiment, the fidelity of the people to their ancient customs made them return with pleasure to the repose and celebration of Sunday. The Republican calendar was doubtless wisely computed; but every one is at first sight struck with the ridiculousness of replacing the legend of the saints of the old calendar with the days of the ass, the hog, the turnip, the onion, etc. Besides, if it was skilfully computed, it was by no means conveniently divided. I recall on this subject the remark of a man of much wit, and who, notwithstanding the disapprobation which his remark implied, nevertheless desired the establishment of the Republican system, everywhere except in the almanac. When the decree of the Convention which ordered the adoption of the Republican calendar was published, he remarked: "They have done finely; but they have to fight two enemies who never yield, the beard, and the white shirt."[2]

The truth is, the interval from one *decadi* to another was too long for the working-classes, and for all those who were constantly occupied. I do not know whether it was the effect of a deep-rooted habit, but people accustomed to working six days in succession, and resting on the seventh, found nine days of consecutive labour too long, and consequently the suppression of the *decadi* was universally approved. The decree which ordered the publication of marriage bans on Sunday was not so popular, for some persons were afraid of finding in this the revival of the former dominance of the clergy over the civil authorities.

A few days after the solemn re-establishment of the catholic worship, there arrived at the Tuileries a general officer, who would perhaps have preferred the establishment of Mahomet, and the change of Notre Dame into a mosque. He was the last general-in-chief of the army of Egypt, and was said to have turned Mussulman at Cairo,

---

[2] That is to say, the barber and the washerwoman, for whom ten days was too long an interval.—Trans.

ex-Baron de Menou. In spite of the defeat by the English which he had recently undergone in Egypt, General Abdallah-Menou was well received by the First Consul, who appointed him soon after governor-general of Piedmont. General Menou was of tried courage, and had given proof of it elsewhere, as well as on the field of battle, and amid the most trying circumstances.

After the 10th of August, although belonging to the Republican party, he had accompanied Louis Sixteenth to the Assembly, and had been denounced as a Royalist by the Jacobins. In 1795 the Faubourg Saint Antoine having risen en masse, and advanced against the Convention, General Menou had surrounded and disarmed the seditious citizens; but he had refused to obey the atrocious orders of the commissioners of the Convention, who decreed that the entire *faubourg* should be burned, in order to punish the inhabitants for their continued insurrections. Some time afterwards, having again refused to obey the order these commissioners of the Convention gave, to mow down with grapeshot the insurrectionists of Paris, he had been summoned before a commission, which would not have failed to send him to the guillotine, if General Bonaparte, who had succeeded him in the command of the army of the interior, had not used all his influence to save his life. Such repeated acts of courage and generosity are enough, and more than enough, to cause us to pardon in this brave officer, the very natural pride with which he boasted of having armed the National Guards, and having caused the *tricolor* to be substituted for the white flag. The *tricolor* he called my flag. From the government of Piedmont he passed to that of Venice; and died in 1810 for love of an actress, whom he had followed from Venice to Reggio, in spite of his sixty years.

The institution of the order of the Legion of Honour preceded by a few days the proclamation of the Consulate for life, which proclamation was the occasion of a fete, celebrated on the 15th of August. This was the anniversary of the birth of the First Consul, and the opportunity was used in order to make for the first time this anniversary a festival. On that day the First Consul was thirty-three years old.

In the month of October following I went with the First Consul on his journey into Normandy, where we stopped at Ivry, and the First Consul visited the battlefield. He said, on arriving there, "Honour to the memory of the best Frenchman who ever sat upon the throne of France," and ordered the restoration of the column, which had been formerly erected, in memory of the victory achieved by Henry the Fourth. The reader will perhaps desire to read here the inscriptions, which were engraved by his order, on the four faces of the pyramid.

First Inscription

Napoleon Bonaparte, First Consul, to the Memory Of Henry the Fourth, victorious over the enemies of the state, on the field of Ivry, 14th March, 1590.

Second Inscription

Great men love the glory of those who resemble them.

Third Inscription

The 7th Brumaire, year XI, of the French Republic, Napoleon Bonaparte, First Consul, having visited this field, ordered the rebuilding of the monument destined to perpetuate the memory of Henry IV., and the victory of Ivry.

Fourth Inscription

The woes experienced by France, at the epoch of the battle of Ivry, were the result of the appeal made by the opposing parties in France to Spain and England. Every family, every party which calls in foreign powers to its aid, has merited and will merit, to the most distant posterity the malediction of the French people.

All these inscriptions have since been effaced, and replaced by this, "On this spot Henry the Fourth stood the day of the battle of Ivry, 14th March, 1590."

Monsieur Ledier, Mayor of Ivry, accompanied the First Consul on this excursion; and the First Consul held a long conversation with him, in which he appeared to be agreeably impressed. He did not form so good an opinion of the Mayor of Evreux, and interrupted him abruptly, in the midst of a complimentary address which this worthy magistrate was trying to make him, by asking if he knew his colleague, the Mayor of Ivry. "No, general," replied the mayor. "Well, so much the worse for you; I trust you will make his acquaintance."

It was also at Evreux that an official of high rank amused Madame Bonaparte and her suite, by a *naiveté* which the First Consul alone did not find diverting, because he did not like such simplicity displayed by an official. Monsieur de Ch—— did the honours of the country town to the wife of the First Consul, and this, in spite of his age, with much zeal and activity; and Madame Bonaparte, among other questions which. her usual kindness and grace dictated to her, asked him if he was married, and if he had a family. "Indeed, Madame, I should think so," replied Monsieur de Ch——with a smile and a bow, *"j'ai cinq-z-enfants."*

"*Oh, mon Dieu,*" cried Madame Bonaparte, "what a regiment! That is extraordinary; what, sir, seize *enfants?*"

"Yes, Madame, *cinq-z-enfants, cinq-z-enfants,*" repeated the official, who did not see anything very marvellous in it, and who wondered at the astonishment shown by Madame Bonaparte. At last some one explained to her the mistake which *la liaison dangereuse* of M. de Ch had caused her to make, and added with comic seriousness, "Deign, Madame, to excuse M. de Ch——. The Revolution has interrupted the prosecution of his studies." He was more than sixty years of age.

From Evreux we set out for Rouen, where we arrived at three o'clock in the afternoon. Chaptal, Minister of the Interior, Beugnot, Prefect of the Department, and Cambaceres, Archbishop of Rouen, came to meet the First Consul at some distance from the city. The Mayor Fontenay waited at the gates, and presented the keys. The First Consul held them some time in his hands, and then returned them to the mayor, saying to him loud enough to be heard by the crowd which surrounded the carriage,

"Citizens, I cannot trust the keys of the city to any one better than the worthy magistrate who so worthily enjoys my confidence and your own;" and made Fontenay enter his carriage, saying he wished to honour Rouen in the person of its mayor.

Madame Bonaparte rode in the carriage with her husband; General Moncey, Inspector-general of the Constabulary, on horseback on the right; in the second carriage was General Soult and his *aides-de-camp*; in the third carriage, General Bessieres and M. de Lugay; in the fourth, General Lauriston; then came the carriages of the personal attendants, Hambard, Hebert, and I being in the first.

It is impossible to give an idea of the enthusiasm of the inhabitants of Rouen on the arrival of the First Consul. The market-porters and the boatmen in grand costume awaited us outside the city; and when the carriage which held the two august personages was in sight, these brave men placed themselves in line, two and two, and preceded thus the carriage to the hotel of the prefecture, where the First Consul alighted. The *prefect* and the mayor of Rouen, the archbishop, and the general commanding the division dined with the First Consul, who showed a most agreeable animation during the repast, and with much solicitude asked information as to the condition of manufactures, new discoveries in the art of manufacturing, in fact, as to everything relating to the prosperity of this city, which was essentially industrial.

In the evening, and almost the whole night, an immense crowd surrounded the hotel, and filled the gardens of the prefecture, which were illuminated and ornamented with allegorical transparencies in praise of the First Consul; and each time he showed himself on the terrace of the garden the air resounded with applause and acclamations which seemed most gratifying to him.

The next morning, after having made on horseback the tour of the city, and visited the grand sites by which it is surrounded, the First Consul heard mass, which was celebrated at eleven o'clock by the archbishop in, the chapel of the prefecture. An hour after he had to receive the general council of the department, the council of the prefecture, the municipal council, the clergy of Rouen, and the courts of justice, and was obliged to listen to a half-dozen discourses, all expressed in nearly the same terms, and to which he replied in such a manner as to give the orators the highest opinion of their own merit. All these bodies, on leaving the First Consul, were presented to Madame Bonaparte, who received them with her accustomed grace, in, the evening Madame Bonaparte held a reception for the wives of the officials, at which the First Consul was present, of which fact some availed themselves to present to him several *émigrés*, who had recently returned under the act of amnesty, and whom he received graciously.

After which followed crowds, illuminations, acclamations, all similar to those of the evening before. Every one wore an air of rejoicing which delighted me, and contrasted strangely, I thought, with the dreadful wooden houses, narrow, filthy streets, and Gothic buildings which then distinguished the town of Rouen.

Monday, Nov. 1, at seven o'clock in the morning, the First Consul mounted his horse, and, escorted by a detachment of the young men of the city, forming a volunteer guard, passed the bridge of boats, and reached the Faubourg Saint-Sever. On his return from this excursion, we found the populace awaiting him at the head of the bridge, whence they escorted him to the hotel of the prefecture, manifesting the liveliest joy.

After breakfast, there was a high mass by the archbishop, the occasion being the fete of All Saints; then came the learned societies, the chiefs of administration, and justices of the peace, with their speeches, one of which contained a remarkable sentence, in which these good magistrates, in their enthusiasm, asked the First Consul's permission to surname him the great justice of the peace of Europe.

As they left the Consul's apartment I noticed their spokesman; he had tears in his eyes, and was repeating with pride the reply he had just received.

I regret that I do not remember his name, but I was told that he was one of the most highly esteemed men in Rouen. His countenance inspired confidence, and bore an expression of frankness, which prepossessed me in his favour.

In the evening the First Consul went to the theatre, which was packed to the ceiling, and offered a charming sight. The municipal authorities had a delightful fete prepared, which the First Consul found much to his taste, and upon which he complimented the *prefect* and the mayor on several different occasions. After witnessing the opening of the ball, he made two or three turns in the hall, and retired, escorted by the staff of the National Guard.

On Tuesday much of the day was spent by the First Consul in visiting the workshops of the numerous factories of the city, accompanied by the minister of the interior, the *prefect*, the mayor, the general commanding the division, the inspector-general of police, and the staff of the Consular Guard. In a factory of the Faubourg Saint-Sever, the minister of the interior presented to him the dean of the workmen, noted as having woven the first piece of velvet in France; and the First Consul, after complimenting this honourable old man, granted him a pension. Other rewards and encouragements were likewise distributed to several parties whose useful inventions commended them to public gratitude.

Wednesday morning early we left for Elbeuf, where we arrived at ten o'clock, preceded by threescore young men of the most distinguished families of the city, who, following the example of those of Rouen, aspired to the honour of forming the guard of the First Consul.

The country around us was covered with an innumerable multitude, gathered from all the surrounding *communes*. The First Consul alighted at Elbeuf, at the house of the mayor, where he took breakfast, and then visited the town in detail, obtaining information everywhere; and knowing that one of the first wishes of the citizens was the construction of a road from Elbeuf to a small neighbouring town called Romilly, he gave orders to the minister of the interior to begin work upon it immediately.

At Elbeuf, as at Rouen, the First Consul was overwhelmed with homage and benedictions; and we returned from this last town at four o'clock in the afternoon.

The merchants of Rouen had prepared a fete in the hall of the

Stock Exchange, which the First Consul and his family attended after dinner. He remained a long time on the ground floor of this building, where there were displayed magnificent specimens from the industries of this Department. He examined everything, and made Madame Bonaparte do the same; and she also purchased several pieces of cloth.

The First Consul then ascended to the first floor, where, in the grand saloon, were gathered about a hundred ladies, married and single, and almost all pretty, the wives and daughters of the principal merchants of Rouen, who were waiting to compliment him. He seated himself in this charming circle, and remained there perhaps a quarter of an hour; then passed into another room, where awaited him the representation of a little proverb, containing couplets expressing, as may be imagined, the attachment and gratitude of the inhabitants of Rouen. This play was followed by a ball.

Thursday evening the First Consul announced that he would leave for Havre the next morning at daybreak; and exactly at five o'clock I was awakened by Hebert, who said that at six o'clock we would set out. I awoke feeling badly, was sick the whole day, and would have given much to have slept a few hours longer; but we were compelled to begin our journey. Before entering his carriage, the First Consul made a present to *Monseigneur*, the archbishop, of a snuff-box with his portrait, and also gave one to the mayor, on which was the inscription, 'Peuple Francais'.

We stopped at Caudebec for breakfast. The mayor of this town presented to the First Consul a corporal who had made the campaign of Italy (his name was, I think, Roussel), and who had received a sword of honour as a reward for his brave conduct at Marengo. He was at Caudebec on a half-year's furlough, and asked the First Consul's permission to be a sentinel at the door of the apartment of the august travellers, which was granted; and after the First Consul and Madame Bonaparte were seated at the table, Roussel was sent for, and invited to breakfast with his former general. At Havre and at Dieppe the First Consul invited thus to his table all the soldiers or sailors who had received guns, sabres, or boarding-axes of honour. The First Consul stopped an hour at Bolbec, showing much attention and interest in examining the products of the industries of the district, complimenting the guards of honour who passed before him on their fine appearance, thanking the clergy for the prayers in his behalf which they addressed to Heaven, and leaving for the poor, either in their own hands, or in the hands of the mayor, souvenirs of his stay. On the arrival of the First Consul at Havre, the city was illuminated; and the First Consul and his numerous cortege passed between two rows of illuminations and columns of fire of all kinds. The vessels in the port appeared like a forest on fire; being covered with coloured lamps to the very top of their masts. The First Consul received, the day of his arrival at Havre, only a part of the authorities of the city, and soon after retired, saying that he was fatigued; but at six o'clock in the morning of the next day he was on horseback, and until two o'clock he rode along the seacoast and low hills of Ingouville for more than a league, and the banks of the Seine as far as the cliffs of Hoc. He also made a tour outside of the citadel. About three o'clock the First Consul began to receive the authorities. He conversed with them in great detail upon the work that had, been done at this place in order that their port, which he always called the port of Paris, might reach the highest degree of prosperity, and did the sub-*prefect*, the mayor, the two presidents of the tribunals, the commandant of the place, and the chief of the tenth demi-brigade of light infantry the honour of inviting them to his table.

In the evening the First Consul went to the theatre, where they played a piece composed for the occasion, about as admirable as such pieces usually are, but on which the First Consul and Madame Bonaparte especially complimented the authors. The illuminations were more brilliant even than on the evening before; and I remember especially that the largest number of transparencies bore the inscription, 18th Brumaire, year VIII.

Sunday, at seven o'clock in the morning, after having visited the Marine Arsenal and all the docks, the weather being very fine, the First Consul embarked in a little barge, and remained in the roadstead for several hours, escorted by a large number of barges filled with men and elegantly dressed women, and musicians playing the favourite airs of the First Consul. Then a few hours were again passed in the reception of merchants, the First Consul assuring them that he had taken the greatest pleasure in conferring with them in regard to the commerce of Havre with the colonies. In the evening, there was a fete prepared by the merchants, at which the First Consul remained for half an hour; and on Monday, at five o'clock in the morning, he embarked on a lugger for Honfleur. At the time of his departure the weather was a little threatening, and the First Consul was advised not to embark. Madame Bonaparte, whose ears this rumour reached, ran after her husband, begging him not to set out; but he embraced her, laughing, calling her a coward, and entered the vessel which was awaiting him. He had hardly embarked when the wind suddenly lulled, and the weather became very fine. On his return to Havre, the First Consul held a review on the Place de la Citadelle, and visited the artillery barracks, after which he received, until the evening, a large number of public dignitaries and merchants; and the next day, at six o'clock in the morning, we set out for Dieppe.

When we arrived at Fecamp, the town presented an extremely singular spectacle. All the inhabitants of the town, and of the adjoining towns and villages, followed the clergy, chanting a *Te Deum* for the anniversary of the 18th Brumaire; and these countless voices rising to heaven for him affected the First Consul profoundly. He repeated several times during breakfast that he had felt more emotion on hearing these chants under the dome of heaven than he had ever felt while listening to the most brilliant music.

We arrived at Dieppe at six o'clock in the evening. The First Consul retired, only after having received all their felicitations, which were certainly very sincere there, as throughout all France at that time. The next day, at eight o'clock, the First Consul repaired to the harbour, where he remained a long while watching the return of the fishermen, and afterwards visited the *faubourg* of Pollet, and the work on the docks, which was then just beginning. He admitted to his table the sub-*prefect*, the mayor, and three sailors of Dieppe who had been given boarding-axes of honour for distinguishing themselves in the combat off Boulogne. He ordered the construction of a breakwater in the inner port, and the continuation of a canal for navigation, which was to be extended as far as Paris, and of which, until this present time, only a few fathoms have been made. From Dieppe we went to Gisors and to Beauvais; and finally the First Consul and his wife returned to Saint-Cloud, after an absence of two weeks, during which workmen had been busily employed in restoring the ancient royal residence, which the First Consul had decided to accept, as I have before stated.

Chapter 10

The tour of the First Consul through the wealthiest and most enlightened departments of France had removed from his mind the apprehension of many difficulties which he had feared at first in the execution of his plans. Everywhere he had been treated as a monarch, and not only he personally, but Madame Bonaparte also, had been received with all the honours usually reserved for crowned heads. There was no difference between the homage offered them at this time, and that which they received later, even during the Empire, when their Majesties made tours of their states at different times. For this reason I shall give some details; and if they should seem too long, or not very novel, the reader will remember that I am not writing only for those who lived during the Empire. The generation which witnessed such great deeds, and which, under their very eyes, and from the beginning of his career, saw the greatest man of this century, has already given place to another generation, which can judge him only by what others may narrate of him. What may be familiar to those who saw with their own eyes is not so to others, who can only take at second-hand those things which they had no opportunity of seeing for themselves. Besides, details omitted as frivolous or commonplace by history, which makes a profession of more gravity, are perfectly appropriate in simple memoirs, and often enable one to understand and judge the epoch more correctly. For instance, it seems to me that the enthusiasm displayed by the entire population and all the local authorities for the First Consul and his wife during their tour in Normandy showed clearly that the chief of the state would have no great opposition to fear, certainly none on the part of the nation, whenever it should please him to change his title, and proclaim himself Emperor.

Soon after our return, by a decree of the consuls four ladies were assigned to Madame Bonaparte to assist her in doing the honours of the palace. They were Mesdames de Remusat, de Tallouet, de Lucay, and de Lauriston. Under the Empire they became ladies-in-waiting. Madame de Lauriston often raised a smile by little exhibitions of parsimony, but she was good and obliging. Madame de Remusat possessed great merit, and had sound judgment, though she appeared somewhat haughty, which was the more remarkable as M. de Remusat was exactly the reverse. Subsequently there was another lady of honour, Madame de La Rochefoucault, of whom I shall have occasion to speak later.

The lady of the robes, Madame de Lucay, was succeeded by Madame La Vallette, so gloriously known afterwards by her devotion to her husband. There were twenty-four French ladies-in-waiting, among whom were Mesdames de Remusat, de Tallouet, de Lauriston, Ney, d'Arberg, Louise d'Arberg (afterwards the Countess of Lobau), de Walsh-Serent, de Colbert, Lannes, Savary, de Turenne, Octave de Segur, de Montalivet, de Marescot, de Bouille Solar, Lascaris, de Brignole, de Canisy, de Chevreuse, Victor de Mortemart, de Montmorency, Matignon, and Maret. There were also twelve Italian ladies-in-waiting.

These ladies served in turn one month each, there being thus two French and one Italian lady on duty together. The Emperor at first did not admit unmarried ladies among the ladies-in-waiting; but he relaxed this rule first in favour of Mademoiselle Louise d'Arberg (afterwards Countess of Lobau), and then in favour of Mademoiselle de Lucay, who has since married Count Philip de Segur, author of the excellent history of the campaign in Russia; and these two young ladies by their prudence and circumspect conduct proved themselves above criticism even at court.

There were four lady ushers, Mesdames Soustras, Ducrest-Villeneuve, Felicite Longroy, and Egle Marchery.

Two first ladies' maids, Mesdames Roy and Marco de St. Hilaire, who had under their charge the grand wardrobe and the jewel-box.

There were four ladies' maids in ordinary.

A lady reader.

The men on the staff of the Empress's household were the following: A grand equerry, Senator Harville, who discharged the duties of a chevalier of honour.

A head chamberlain, the general of division, Nansouty.

A vice-chamberlain, introducer of the ambassadors, de Beaumont.

Four chamberlains in ordinary, de Courtomer, Degrave, Galard de Bearn, Hector d'Aubusson de la Feuillade.

Four equerries, Corbineau, Berckheim, d'Audenarde, and Fouler.

A superintendent-general of her Majesty's household, Hinguerlot.

Rapp

A secretary of commands, Deschamps.
Two head valets, Frere and Douville.
Four valets in ordinary.
Four men servants.
Two head footmen, L'Esperance and d'Argens. Six ordinary footmen. The staff of the kitchen and sanitation were the same as in the household of the Emperor; and besides these, six pages of the Emperor were always in attendance upon the Empress.

The chief almoner was Ferdinand de Rohan, former archbishop of Cambray.

Another decree of the same date fixed the duties of the *prefects* of the palace. The four head *prefects* of the consular palace were de Remusat, de Crayamel (afterwards appointed introduces of ambassadors, and master of ceremonies), de Lugay, and Didelot. The latter subsequently became *prefect* of the Department of the Cher.

Malmaison was no longer sufficient for the First Consul, whose household, like that of Madame Bonaparte, became daily more numerous. A much larger building had become necessary, and the First Consul fixed his choice upon Saint-Cloud.

The inhabitants of Saint-Cloud addressed a petition to the Corps Legislatif, praying that the First Consul would make their chateau his summer residence; and this body hastened to transmit it to him, adding their prayers to the same effect, and making comparisons which they believed would be agreeable to him. The general refused formally, saying that when he should have finished and laid down the duties with which the people had charged him, he would feel honoured by any recompense which the popular will might award him; but that so long as he was the chief of the Government he would accept nothing.

Notwithstanding the determined tone of this reply, the inhabitants of the village of Saint-Cloud, who had the greatest interest in the petition being granted, renewed it when the First Consul was chosen consul for life; and he then consented to accept. The expenses of the repairs and furnishing were immense, and greatly exceeded the calculations that had been made for him; nevertheless, he was not satisfied either with the furniture or ornaments, and complained to Charvet, the concierge at Malmaison, whom he appointed to the same post in the new palace, and whom he had charged with the general supervision of the furnishing and the placing of the furniture, that he had fitted up apartments suitable only for a mistress, and that they contained only gewgaws and spangles, and nothing substantial. On this occasion, also, he gave another proof of his habitual desire to do good, in spite of prejudices which had not yet spent their force. Knowing that there were at Saint-Cloud a large number of the former servants of Queen Marie Antoinette, he charged Charvet to offer them either their old places or pensions, and most of them resumed their former posts. In 1814 the Bourbons were far from acting so generously, for they discharged all employees, even those who had served Marie Antoinette.

The First Consul had been installed at Saint-Cloud only a short while, when the chateau, which had thus again become the residence of the sovereign at enormous expense, came near falling a prey to the flames. The guard room was under the vestibule, in the centre of the palace; and one night, the soldiers having made an unusually large fire, the stove became so hot that a sofa, whose back touched one of the flues which warmed the saloon, took fire, and the games were quickly communicated to the other furniture. The officer on duty perceiving this, immediately notified the concierge, and together they ran to General Duroc's room and awoke him. The general rose in haste, and, commanding perfect silence, made a chain of men. He took his position at the pool, in company with the concierge, and thence passed buckets of water to the soldiers for two or three hours, at the end of which time the fire was extinguished, but only after devouring all the furniture; and it was not until the next morning that the First Consul, Josephine, Hortense, in short, all the other occupants of the chateau, learned of the accident, all of whom, the First Consul especially, expressed their appreciation of the consideration shown in not alarming them.

To prevent, or at least to render such accidents less likely in future, the First Consul organized a night-guard at Saint-Cloud, and subsequently did the same at all his residences; which guard was called "the watch."

During his early occupation of Saint-Cloud the First Consul slept in the same bed with his wife; afterwards etiquette forbade this; and as a result, conjugal affection was somewhat chilled, and finally the First Consul occupied an apartment at some distance from that of Madame Bonaparte. To reach her room it was necessary to cross a long corridor, on the right and left of which were the rooms of the ladies-in-waiting, the women of the service, etc. When he wished to pass the night with his wife, he undressed in his own room, and went thence in his wrapper and night-cap, I going before him with a candle. At the end of this corridor a staircase of fifteen or sixteen steps led to the apartment of Madame Bonaparte. It was a great joy to her to receive a visit from her husband, and every one was informed of it next morning. I can see her now rubbing her little hands, saying, "I rose late today; but, you see, it is because Bonaparte spent the night with me." On such days she was more amiable than ever, refused no one, and all got whatever they requested. I experienced proofs of this myself many times.

One evening as I was conducting the First Consul on one of these visits to his wife, we perceived in the corridor a handsome young fellow coming out of the apartment of one of Madame Bonaparte's women servants. He tried to steal away; but the First Consul cried in a loud voice, "Who goes there? Where are you going? What do you want? What is your name?" He was merely a valet of Madame Bonaparte, and, stupefied by these startling inquiries, replied in a frightened voice that he had just executed an errand for Madame Bonaparte. "Very well," replied the First Consul, "but do not let me catch you again." Satisfied that the gallant would profit by the lesson, the general did not seek to learn his name, nor that of his *inamorata*. This reminds me of an occasion on which he was much more severe in regard to another chambermaid of Madame Bonaparte. She was young, and very pretty, and inspired very tender sentiments in Rapp and E——, two *aides-de-camp*, who besieged her with their sighs, and sent her flowers and *billets-doux*. The young girl, at least such was the opinion of every one, gave them no encouragement, and Josephine was much attached to her; nevertheless, when the First Consul observed the gallantries of the young men, he became angry, and had the poor girl discharged, in spite of her tears and the prayers of Madame Bonaparte and of the brave and honest Colonel Rapp, who swore naively that the fault was entirely on his side, that the poor child had not listened to him, and that her conduct was worthy of all praise. Nothing availed against the resolution of the First Consul, whose only reply was, "I will have nothing improper in my household, and no scandal."

Whenever the First Consul made a distribution of arms of honour, there was always a banquet at the Tuileries, to which were admitted, without distinction, and whatever their grade, all who had a share in these rewards. At these banquets, which took place in the grand gallery of the chateau, there were sometimes two hundred guests; and General Duroc being master of ceremonies on these occasions, the First Consul took care to recommend him to intermingle the private soldiers, the colonels, the generals, etc. He ordered the domestics to show especial attention to the private soldiers, and to see that they had plenty of the best to eat and to drink. These are the longest repasts I have seen the emperor make; and on these occasions he was amiable and entirely unconstrained, making every effort to put his guests entirely at their ease, though with many of them this was a difficult task. Nothing was more amusing than to see these brave soldiers sitting two feet from-the table, not daring to approach their plates or the food, red to the ears, and with their necks stretched out towards the general, as if to receive the word of command. The First Consul made them relate the notable deeds which had brought each his national recognition, and often laughed boisterously at their singular narrations. He encouraged them to eat, and frequently drank to their health; but in spite of all this, his encouragement failed to overcome the timidity of some, and the servants removed the plates of each course without their having touched them, though this constraint did not prevent their being full of joy and enthusiasm as they left the table. "*Au revoir*, my brave men," the First Consul would say to them; "baptize for me quickly these newborn," touching with his fingers their sabres of honour. God knows whether they spared themselves!

This preference of the First Consul for the private soldier recalls an instance which took-place at Malmaison, and which furnishes, besides, a complete refutal of the charges of severity and harshness which have been brought against him.

The First Consul set out on foot one morning, dressed in his grey riding-coat, and accompanied by General Duroc, on the road to Marly. Chatting as they walked, they saw a ploughman, who turned a furrow as he came towards them.

"See here, my good man," said the First Consul, stopping him, "your furrow is not straight. You do not know your business."

"It is not you, my fine gentleman, who can teach me. You cannot do as well. No, indeed you think so; very well, just try it," replied the good man, yielding his place to the First Consul, who took the plough-handle, and making the team start, commenced to give his lesson. But he did not plough a single yard of a straight line. The whole furrow was crooked. "Come, come," said the countryman, putting his hand on that of the general to resume his plough, "your work is no good. Each one to his trade. Saunter along, that is your business." But the First Consul did not proceed without paying for the lesson he had received. General Duroc handed the labourer two or three *louis* to compensate him for the loss of time they had caused him; and the countryman, astonished by this generosity, quitted his plough to relate his adventure, and met on the way a woman whom he told that he had met two big men, judging by what he had in his hand.

The woman, better informed, asked him to describe the dress of the men, and from his description ascertained that it was the First Consul and one of his staff; the good man was overcome with astonishment. The next day he made a brave resolution, and donning his best clothes, presented himself at Malmaison, requesting to speak to the First Consul, to thank him, he said, for the fine present he had given him the day before.

I notified the First Consul of this visit, and he ordered me to bring the labourer in. While I was gone to announce him, he had, according to his own expression, taken his courage in both hands to prepare himself for this grand interview; and I found him on my return, standing in the centre of the antechamber (for he did not dare to sit upon the sofas, which though very simple seemed to him magnificent), and pondering what he should say to the First Consul in token of his gratitude. I preceded him, and he followed me, placing each foot cautiously on the carpet; and when I opened the door of the cabinet, he insisted with much civility on my going first. When the First Consul had nothing private to say or dictate, he permitted the door to stand open; and he now made me a sign not to close it, so that I was able to see and hear all that passed.

The honest labourer commenced, on entering the cabinet, by saluting the back of de Bourrienne, who could not see him, occupied as he was in writing upon a small table placed in the recess of a window. The First Consul saw him make his bows, himself reclining in his armchair, one of the arms of which, according to habit, he was pricking with the point of his knife. Finally he spoke. "Well, my brave fellow." The peasant turned, recognized him, and saluted anew. "Well," continued the First Consul, "has the harvest been fine this year?"

"No, with all respect, Citizen General, but not so very bad."

"In order that the earth should produce, it is necessary that it should be turned up, is it not so? Fine gentlemen are no good for such work."

"Meaning no offense, General, the bourgeois have hands too soft to handle a plough. There is need of a hard fist to handle these tools."

"That is so," replied the First Consul, smiling. "But big and strong as you are, you should handle something else than a plough. A good musket, for instance, or the handle of a good sabre."

The labourer drew himself up with an air of pride. "General, in my time I have done as others. I had been married six or seven years when these d—d Prussians (pardon me, General) entered Landrecies. The requisition came. They gave me a gun and a cartridge-box at the

Commune headquarters, and march! My soul, we were not equipped like those big gallants that I saw just now on entering the courtyard." He referred to the grenadiers of the Consular Guard.

"Why did you quit the service?" resumed the First Consul, who appeared to take great interest in the conversation.

"My faith, General, each one in his turn, and there are sabre strokes enough for every one. One fell on me there" (the worthy labourer bent his head and divided the locks of his hair); "and after some weeks in the field hospital, they gave me a discharge to return to my wife and my plough."

"Have you any children?"

"I have three, General, two boys and a girl."

"You must make a soldier of the oldest. If he will conduct himself well, I will take care of him. *Adieu*, my brave man. Whenever I can help you, come to see me again." The First Consul rose, made de Bourrienne give him some *louis*, which he added to those the labourer had already received from him, and directed me to show him out, and we had already reached the antechamber, when the First Consul called the peasant back to say to him, "You were at Fleurus?"

"Yes, General."

"Can you tell me the name of your general-in-chief?"

"Indeed, I should think so. It was General Jourdan."

"That is correct. *Au revoir;*" and I carried off the old soldier of the Republic, enchanted with his reception.

Chapter 11

At the beginning of this year (1803), there arrived at Paris an envoy from Tunis, who presented the First Consul, on the part of the Bey, with ten Arab horses. The Bey at that time feared the anger of England, and hoped to find in France a powerful ally, capable of protecting him; and he could not have found a better time to make the application, for everything announced the rupture of the peace of Amiens, over which all Europe had so greatly rejoiced, for England had kept none of her promises, and had executed no article of the treaty. On his side, the First Consul, shocked by such bad faith, and not wishing to be a dupe, openly prepared for war, and ordered the filling up of the ranks, and a new levy of one hundred and twenty thousand conscripts. War was officially declared in June, but hostilities had already begun before this time.

At the end of this month the First Consul made a journey to Boulogne, and visited Picardy, Flanders, and Belgium, in order to organize an expedition which he was meditating against the English, and to place the northern seacoast in a state of defence. He returned to Paris in August, but set out in November for a second visit to Boulogne.

This constant travelling was too much for Hambard, who for a long time had been in feeble health; and when the First Consul was on the point of setting out for his first tour in the North, Hambard had asked to be excused, alleging, which was only too true, the bad state of his health. "See how you are," said the First Consul, "always sick and complaining; and if you stay here, who then will shave me?"

"General," replied Hambard, "Constant knows how to shave as well as I." I was present, and occupied at that very moment in dressing the First Consul. He looked at me and said, "Well, you queer fellow, since you are so skilled, you shall make proof of it at once. We must see how you will do." I knew the misadventure of poor Hebert, which I have already related; and not wishing a like experience, I had been for some time practicing the art of shaving. I had paid a hairdresser to teach me his trade; and I had even, in my moments of leisure, served an apprenticeship in his shop, where I had shaved, without distinction, all his customers. The chins of these good people had suffered somewhat before I had acquired sufficient dexterity to lay a razor on the consular chin; but by dint of repeated experiments on the beards of the commonalty I had achieved a degree of skill which inspired me with the greatest confidence; so, in obedience to the order of the First Consul, I brought the warm water, opened the razor boldly, and began operations. Just as I was going to place the razor upon the face of the First Consul, he raised himself abruptly, turned, and fastened both eyes upon me, with an expression of severity and interrogation which I am unable to describe. Seeing that I was not at all embarrassed, he seated himself again, saying to me in a mild tone, "Proceed." This I did with sufficient skill to satisfy him; and when I had finished, he said to me, "Hereafter you are to shave me;" and, in fact, after that he was unwilling to be shaved by any one else. From that time also my duties became much more exacting, for every day I had to shave the First Consul; and I admit that it was not an easy thing to do, for while he was being shaved, he often spoke, read the papers, moved about in his chair, turned himself abruptly, and I was obliged to use the greatest precautions in order not to cut him. Happily this never occurred. When by chance he did not speak, he remained immobile and stiff as a statue, and could not be made to lower, nor raise, nor bend his head to one side, as was necessary to accomplish the task easily. He also had a singular fancy of having one half of his face lathered and shaved before beginning the other, and would not allow me to pass to the other side of his face until the first half was completely finished, as the First Consul found that plan suited him best.

 Later, when I had become his chief valet, and he deigned to give me proofs of his kindness and esteem, and I could talk with him as freely as his rank permitted, I took the liberty of persuading him to shave himself; for, as I have just said, not wishing to be shaved by any one except me, he was obliged to wait till I could be notified, especially in the army, when his hour of rising was not regular. He refused for a long time to take my advice, though I often repeated it. "Ah, ha, Mr. Idler!" he would say to me, laughing, "you are very anxious for me to do half your work;" but at last I succeeded in satisfying him of my disinterestedness and the wisdom of my advice. The fact is, I was most anxious to persuade him to this; for, considering what would necessarily happen if an unavoidable absence, an illness, or some other reason, had separated me from the First Consul, I could not reflect, without a shudder, of his life being at the mercy of the first comer. As for him, I am sure he never gave the matter a thought; for whatever tales have been related of his suspicious nature, he never took any precaution against the snares which treason might set for him. His sense of security, in this regard, amounted even to imprudence; and consequently all who loved him, especially those who surrounded him, endeavoured to make up for this want of precaution by all the vigilance of which they were capable; and it is unnecessary to assert that it was this solicitude for the precious life of my master which had caused me to insist upon the advice I had given him to shave himself.

On the first occasions on which he attempted to put my lessons into practice, it was even more alarming than laughable to watch the Emperor (for such he was then); as in spite of the lessons that I had given him with repeated illustrations, he did not yet know how to hold his razor. He would seize it by the handle, and apply it perpendicularly to his cheek, instead of laying it flat; he would make a sudden dash with the razor, never failing to give himself a cut, and then draw back his hand quickly, crying out, "See there, you scamp; you have made me cut myself." I would then take the razor and finish the operation The next day the same scene would be repeated, but with less bloodshed; and each day the skill of the Emperor improved, until at last, by dint of numberless lessons, he became sufficiently an adept to dispense with me, though he still cut himself now and then, for which he would always mildly reproach me, though jestingly and in kindness. Besides, from the manner in which he began, and which he would never change, it was impossible for him not to cut his face sometimes, for he shaved himself downward, and not upward, like every one else; and this bad method, which all my efforts could not change, added to the habitual abruptness of his movements, made me shudder every time I saw him take his razor in hand.

Madame Bonaparte accompanied the First Consul on the first of these journeys; and there was, as on that to Lyons, a continued succession of fetes and rejoicing.

The inhabitants of Boulogne had, in anticipation of the arrival of the First Consul, raised several triumphal arches, extending from the Montreuil gate as far as the great road which led to his barrack, which was situated in the camp on the right. Each arch of triumph was decorated with evergreens, and thereon could be read the names of the skirmishes and battles in which he had been victorious. These domes and arches of verdure and flowers presented an admirable *coup-d'-oeil*. One arch of triumph, higher than the others, was placed in the midst of the Rue de l'Ecu (the main street), and the elite of the citizens had assembled around it; while more than a hundred young people with garlands of flowers, children, old men, and a great number of brave men whom military duty had not detained in the camp, awaited with impatience the arrival of the First Consul. At his approach the joyful booming of cannon announced to the English, whose fleet was near by in the sea off Boulogne, the appearance of Napoleon upon the shore on which he had assembled the formidable army he had determined to hurl against England.

The First Consul was mounted upon a small grey horse, which was active as a squirrel. He dismounted, and followed by his brilliant staff, addressed these paternal words to the citizens of the town: "I come to assure the happiness of France. The sentiments which you express, and all your evidences of gratitude, touch me; I shall never forget my entrance into Boulogne, which I have chosen as the centre of the reunion of my armies. Citizens, do not be alarmed by this multitude. It is that of the defenders of your country, soon to be the conquerors of haughty England."

The First Consul proceeded on his route, surrounded by the whole populace, who accompanied him to the door of his headquarters, where more than thirty generals received him, though the firing of cannon, the ringing of bells, the cries of joy, ceased only when this great day ended.

The day after our arrival, the First Consul visited the Pont de Brique, a little village situated about half a league from Boulogne. A farmer read to him the following complimentary address:—

"General, in the name of twenty fathers we offer you a score of fine fellows who are, and always will be, at your command. Lead them, General. They can strike a good blow for you when you march into England. As to us, we will discharge another duty. We will till the earth in order that bread may not be wanting to the brave men who will crush the English."

Napoleon, smiling, thanked the patriotic countrymen, and glancing towards the little country house, built on the edge of the highway, spoke to General Berthier, saying, "This is where I wish my headquarters established." Then he spurred his horse and rode off, while a general and some officers remained to execute the order of the First Consul, who, on the very night of his arrival at Boulogne, returned to sleep at Pont de Brique.

They related to me at Boulogne the details of a naval combat which had taken place a short time before our arrival between the French fleet, commanded by Admiral Bruix, and the English squadron with which Nelson blockaded the port of Boulogne. I will relate this as told to me, deeming very unusual the comfortable mode in which the French admiral directed the operations of the sailors.

About two hundred boats, counting gunboats and mortars, barges and sloops, formed the line of defence, the shore and the forts bristling with batteries. Some frigates advanced from the hostile line, and, preceded by two or three brigs, ranged themselves in line of battle before us and in reach of the cannon of our flotilla; and the combat began. Balls flew in every direction. Nelson, who had promised the destruction of the flotilla, re-enforced his line of battle with two other lines of vessels and frigates; and thus placed en echelon, they fought with a vastly superior force. For more than seven hours the sea, covered with fire and smoke, offered to the entire population of Boulogne the superb and frightful spectacle of a naval combat in which more than eighteen hundred cannon were fired at the same time; but the genius of Nelson could not avail against our sailors or soldiers. Admiral Bruix was at his headquarters near the signal station, and from this position directed the fight against Nelson, while drinking with his staff and some ladies of Boulogne whom he had invited to dinner. The guests sang the early victories of the First Consul, while the admiral, without leaving the table, manoeuvred the flotilla by means of the signals he ordered. Nelson, eager to conquer, ordered all his naval forces to advance; but the wind being in favour of the French, he was not able to keep the promise he had made in London to burn our fleet, while on the contrary many of his own boats were so greatly damaged, that Admiral Bruix, seeing the English begin to retire, cried "Victory!" pouring out champagne for his guests. The French flotilla suffered very little, while the enemy's squadron was ruined by the steady fire, of our stationary batteries. On that day the English learned that they could not possibly approach the shore at Boulogne, which after this they named the Iron Coast (Cote de Fer).

When the First Consul left Boulogne, he made his arrangements to pass through Abbeville, and to stop twenty four hours there. The mayor of the town left nothing undone towards a suitable reception, and Abbeville was magnificent on that day. The finest trees from the neighbouring woods were taken up bodily with their roots to form avenues in all the streets through which the First Consul was to pass; and some of the citizens, who owned magnificent gardens, sent their rarest shrubs to be displayed along his route; and carpets from the factory of Hecquet-Dorval were spread on the ground, to be trodden by his horses. But unforeseen circumstances suddenly cut short the fete.

A courier, sent by the minister of police, arrived as we were approaching the town, who notified the First Consul of a plot to assassinate him two leagues farther on; the very day and hour were named. To baffle the attempt that they intended against his person, the First Consul traversed the city in a gallop, and, followed by some lancers, went to the spot where he was to be attacked, halted about half an hour, ate some Abbeville cakes, and set out. The assassins were deceived. They had not expected his arrival until the next day.

The First Consul and Madame Bonaparte continued their journey through Picardy, Flanders, and the Low Countries. Each day the First Consul received offers of vessels of war from the different council-generals, the citizens continued to offer him addresses, and the mayors to present him with the keys of the cities, as if he exercised royal power. Amiens, Dunkirk, Lille, Bruges, Ghent, Brussels, Liege, and Namur distinguished themselves by the brilliant receptions they gave to the illustrious travellers. The inhabitants of Antwerp presented the First Consul with six magnificent bay horses. Everywhere also, the First Consul left valuable souvenirs of his journey; and by his orders, works were immediately commenced to deepen and improve the port of Amiens. He visited in that city, and in all the others where he stopped, the exposition of the products of industry, encouraging manufacturers by his advice, and favouring them in his decrees. At Liege, he put at the disposal of the *prefect* of the Our the sum of three hundred thousand *francs* to repair the houses burned by the Austrians, in that department, during the early years of the Revolution. Antwerp owes to him the inner port, a basin, and the building of carpenter-shops. At Brussels, he ordered that the Rhine, the Meuse, and the Scheldt should be connected by a canal. He gave to Givet a stone bridge over the Meuse, and at Sedan the widow Madame Rousseau received from him the sum of sixty thousand *francs* for the re-establishment of the factory destroyed by fire. Indeed, I cannot begin to enumerate all the benefits, both public and private, which the First Consul and Madame Bonaparte scattered along their route.

A little while after our return to Saint-Cloud, the First Consul, while riding in the park with his wife and Cambaceres, took a fancy to drive the four horses attached to the carriage which had been given him by the inhabitants of Antwerp. He took his place on the driver's seat, and took the reins from the hands of Caesar, his coachman, who got up behind the carriage. At that instant they were in the horse-shoe alley, which leads to the road of the Pavilion Breteuil, and of Ville d'Avray. It is stated in the Memorial of St. Helena, that the *aide-de-camp*, having awkwardly frightened the horses, made them run away; but Caesar, who related to me in detail this sad disaster a few moments after the accident had taken place, said not a word to me about the *aide-de-camp*; and, in truth, there was needed, to upset the coach, nothing more than the awkwardness of a coachman with so little experience as the First Consul. Besides, the horses were young and spirited, and Caesar himself needed all his skill to guide them. Not feeling his hand on the reins, they set out at a gallop, while Caesar, seeing the new direction they were taking to the right, cried out, "To the left," in a stentorian voice. Consul Cambaceres, even paler than usual, gave himself little concern as to reassuring Madame Bonaparte, who was much alarmed, but screamed with all his might, "Stop, stop! you will break all our necks!" That might well happen, for the First Consul heard nothing, and, besides, could not control the horses; and when he reached, or rather was carried with the speed of lightning to, the very gate, he was not able to keep in the road, but ran against a post, where the carriage fell over heavily, and fortunately the horses stopped. The First Consul was thrown about ten steps, fell on his stomach, and fainted away, and did not revive until some one attempted to lift him up. Madame Bonaparte and the second consul had only slight contusions; but good Josephine had suffered horrible anxiety about her husband. However, although he was badly bruised, he would not be bled, and satisfied himself with a few rubbings with eau de Cologne, his favourite remedy. That evening, on retiring, he spoke gaily of his misadventure, and of the great fright that his colleague had shown, and ended by saying, "We must render unto Caesar that which is Caesar's; let him keep his whip, and let us each mind his own business."

He admitted, however, notwithstanding all his jokes, that he had never thought himself so near death, and that he felt as if he had been dead for a few seconds. I do not remember whether it was on this or another occasion that I heard the Emperor say, that "death was only asleep without dreams."

In the month of October of this year, the First Consul received in public audience Haled-Effendi, the ambassador of the Ottoman Porte.

The arrival of the Turkish ambassador created a sensation at the Tuileries, because he brought a large number of cashmere shawls to the First Consul, which every one was sure would be distributed, and each woman flattered herself that she would be favourably noticed.

I think that, without his foreign costume, and without his cashmere shawls, he would have produced little effect on persons accustomed to seeing sovereign princes pay court to the chief of the government at his residence and at their own. His costume even was not more remarkable than that of Roustan, to which we were accustomed; and as to his bows, they were hardly lower than those of the ordinary courtiers of the First Consul. At Paris, it is said, the enthusiasm lasted longer—"It is so odd to be a Turk!" A few ladies had the honour of seeing the bearded ambassador eat. He was polite and even gallant with them, and made them a few presents, which were highly prized; his manners were not too Mohammedan, and he was not much shocked at seeing our pretty Parisians without veils over their faces. One day, which he had spent almost entirely at Saint-Cloud, I saw him go through his prayers. It was in the court of honour, on a broad parapet bordered with a stone balustrade. The ambassador had carpets spread on the side of the apartments, which were afterwards those of the King of Rome; and there he made his genuflexions, under the eyes of many people of the house, who, out of consideration, kept themselves behind their casements. In the evening he was present at the theatre, and Zaire or Mahomet, I think, was played; but of course he understood none of it.

Chapter 12

In the month of November of this year, the First Consul returned to Boulogne to visit the fleet, and to review the troops who were already assembled in the camps provided for the army with which he proposed to descend on England. I have preserved a few notes and many recollections of my different sojourns at Boulogne. Never did the Emperor make a grander display of military power; nor has there ever been collected at one point troops better disciplined or more ready to march at the least signal of their chief; and it is not surprising that I should have retained in my recollections of this period details which no one has yet, I think, thought of publishing. Neither, if I am not mistaken, could any one be in a better position than I to know them. However, the reader will now judge for himself.

In the different reviews which the First Consul held, he seemed striving to excite the enthusiasm of the soldiers, and to increase their attachment for his person, by assiduously taking advantage of every opportunity to excite their vanity.

One day, having especially noticed the excellent bearing of the Thirty-sixth and Fifty-seventh regiments of the line, and Tenth of light infantry, he made all the officers, from corporal to colonel, come forward; and, placing himself in their midst, evinced his satisfaction by recalling to them occasions when, in the past under the fire of cannon, he had remarked the bearing of these three brave, regiments. He complimented the sub-officers on the good drilling of the soldiers, and the captains and chiefs of battalion on the harmony and precision of their evolutions. In fine, each had his share of praise.

This flattering distinction did not excite the jealousy of the other corps of the army, for each regiment had on that day its own share of compliments, whether small or great; and when the review was over, they went quietly back to their quarters. But the soldiers of the Thirty-sixth, Fifty-seventh, and Tenth, much elated by having been so specially favoured, went in the afternoon to drink to their triumph in a public house frequented by the grenadiers of the cavalry of the Guard. They began to drink quietly, speaking of campaigns, of cities taken, of the First Consul, and finally of that morning's review. It then occurred to the young men of Boulogne, who were among the drinkers, to sing couplets of very recent composition, in which were extolled to the clouds the bravery and the exploits of the three regiments, without one word of praise for the rest of the army, not even for the Guard; and it was in the favourite resort of the grenadiers of the Guard that these couplets were sung! These latter maintained at first a gloomy silence; but soon finding it unendurable, they protested loudly against these couplets, which they said were detestable. The quarrel became very bitter; they shouted, heaped insults on each other, taking care not to make too much noise; however, and appointed a meeting for the next day, at four o'clock in the morning, in the suburbs of Marquise, a little village about two leagues from Boulogne. It was very late in the evening when these soldiers left the public house.

More than two hundred grenadiers of the Guard went separately to the place of meeting, and found the ground occupied by an almost equal number of their adversaries of the Thirty-sixth, Fifty-seventh, and Tenth. Wasting no time in explanations, hardly a sound being heard, each soldier drew his sword, and for more than an hour they fought in a cool, deliberate manner which was frightful to behold. A man named Martin, grenadier of the Guard, and of gigantic stature, killed with his own hand seven or eight soldiers of the Tenth. They would probably have continued till all were massacred if General Saint-Hilaire, informed too late of this bloody quarrel, had not sent out in all haste a regiment of cavalry, who put an end to the combat. The grenadiers had lost two men, and the soldiers of the line thirteen, with a large number of wounded on both sides.

The First Consul visited the camp next day, and had brought before him those who had caused this terrible scene, and said to them in a severe tone: "I know why you fought each other; many brave men have fallen in a struggle unworthy of them and of you. You shall be punished. I have given orders that the verses which have been the cause of so much trouble shall be printed. I hope that, in learning your punishment, the ladies of Boulogne will know that you have deserved the blame of your comrades in arms."

However, the troops, and above all the officers, began to grow weary of their sojourn at Boulogne, a town less likely, perhaps, than any other to render such an inactive existence endurable. They did not murmur, however, because never where the First Consul was did murmuring find a place; but they fumed nevertheless under their breath at seeing themselves held in camp or in fort, with England just in sight, only nine or ten leagues distant. Pleasures were rare at Boulogne; the women, generally pretty, but extremely timid, did not dare to hold receptions at their own houses, for fear of displeasing their husbands, very jealous men, as are all those of Picardy. There was, however, a handsome hall in which balls and soirees could easily have been given; but, although very anxious to do this, these ladies dared not make use of it. At last a considerable number of Parisian beauties, touched by the sad fate of so many brave and handsome officers, came to Boulogne to charm away the ennui of so long a peace. The example of the Parisian women piqued those of Abbeville, Dunkirk, Amiens; and soon Boulogne was filled with strangers, male and female, who came to do the honours of the city. Among all these ladies the one most conspicuous for style, intellect, and beauty was a Dunkirk lady, named Madame F———, an excellent musician, full of gayety, grace, and youth; it was impossible for Madame F——— not to turn many heads. Colonel Joseph, brother of the First Consul, General Soult, who was afterwards Marshal, Generals Saint-Hilaire and Andre Ossy, and a few other great personages, were at her feet; though two alone, it is said, succeeded in gaining her affections, and of those two, one was Colonel Joseph, who soon had the reputation of being the preferred lover of Madame F———. The beautiful lady from Dunkirk often gave soirees, at which Colonel Joseph never failed to be present. Among all his rivals, and certainly they were very numerous, one alone bore him ill-will; this was the general-in-chief, Soult. This rivalry did no injury to the interests of Madame F———; but like a skilful tactician, she adroitly provoked the jealousy of her two suitors, while accepting from each of them compliments, bouquets, and more than that sometimes.

The First Consul, informed of the amours of his brother, concluded one evening to go and make himself merry in the little salon of Madame F———, who was very plainly domesticated in a room on the first floor in the house of a joiner, in the Rue des Minimes. In order not to be recognized, he was dressed as a citizen, and wore a wig and spectacles. He took into his confidence General Bertrand, who was already in great favour with him, and who did all in his power to render his disguise complete.

Thus disguised, the First Consul and his companion presented

Murat

themselves at Madame F——'s, and asked for Monsieur the Superintendent Arcambal. The most perfect incognito was impressed on Arcambal by the First Consul, who would not for all the world have been recognized; and M. Arcambal promising to keep the secret, the two visitors were announced under the title of commissaries of war.

They were playing *bouillotte*; gold covered the tables, and the game and punch absorbed the attention of the happy inmates to such a degree, that none of them took note of the persons who had just entered. As for the mistress of the lodging, she had never seen the First Consul except at a distance, nor General Bertrand; consequently, there was nothing to be feared from her. I myself think that Colonel Joseph recognized his brother, but he gave no evidence of this.

The First Consul, avoiding as best he could all glances, spied those of his brother and of Madame F——. Thinking signals were passing between them, he was preparing to quit the salon of the pretty Dunkirkess, when she, very anxious that the number of her guests should not yet be diminished, ran to the two false commissaries of war, and detained them gracefully, saying that all were going to play forfeits, and they must not go away without having given pledges. The First Consul having first consulted General Bertrand by a glance, found it agreeable to remain and play those innocent games.

Indeed, at the end of a few moments, at the request of Madame F——, the players deserted the *bouillotte*, and placed themselves in a circle around her. They began by dancing the Boulangere; then the young innocents kept the ball in motion. The turn of the First Consul came to give a forfeit. He was at first very much embarrassed, having with him only a piece of paper, on which he had written the names of a few colonels; he gave, however, this paper to Madame F——, begging her not to open it.

The wish of the First Consul was respected, and the paper remained folded on the lap of the beautiful woman until the time came to redeem the forfeits. Then the queer penalty was imposed on the great captain of making him doorkeeper, while Madame F——, with Colonel Joseph, made the *'voyage a Cythere'* in a neighbouring room. The First Consul acquitted himself with a good grace of the role given him; and after the forfeits had been redeemed, made a sign to General Bertrand to follow him, and they went out. The joiner who lived on the ground floor soon came up to bring a little note to Madame F——.

This was the note:

I thank you, Madame, for the kind welcome you have given

me. If you will come some day to my barracks, I will act as doorkeeper, if it seems good to you; but on that occasion I will resign to no, other the pleasure of accompanying you in the *'voyage a Cythre'*.
Bonaparte

The pretty woman did not read the note aloud; neither did she allow the givers of forfeits to remain in ignorance that she had received a visit from the First Consul. At the end of an hour the company dispersed, and Madame F—— remained alone, reflecting on the visit and the note of the great man.

It was during this same visit that there occurred a terrible combat in the roadstead of Boulogne to secure the entrance into the port of a flotilla composed of twenty or thirty vessels, which came from Ostend, from Dunkirk, and from Nieuport, loaded with arms for the national fleet.

A magnificent frigate, carrying thirty-six pounders, a cutter, and a brig, detached themselves from the English fleet, in order to intercept the route of the Dutch flotilla; but they were received in a manner which took away all desire to return.

The port of Boulogne was defended by five forts; the Fort de la Creche, the Fort en Bois, Fort Musoir, Castle Croi, and the Castle d'Ordre, all fortified with large numbers of cannon and howitzers. The line of vessels which barred the entrance was composed of two hundred and fifty gunboats and other vessels; the division of imperial gunboats formed a part of this.

Each sloop bore three pieces of cannon, twenty-four pounders,— two pieces for pursuit, and one for retreat; and five hundred mouths of fire were thus opened on the enemy, independently of all the batteries of the forts, every cannon being fired more than three times a minute.

The combat began at one o'clock in the afternoon. The weather was beautiful. At the first report of the cannon the First Consul left the headquarters at the Pont de Brique, and came at a gallop, followed by his staff, to give orders to Admiral Bruix; but soon wishing to examine for himself the operations of the defence, and to share in directing them, he threw himself, followed by the admiral and a few officers, into a launch which was rowed by sailors of the Guard. Thus the First Consul was borne into the midst of the vessels which formed the line of defence, through a thousand dangers, amid a tempest of shells, bombs, and cannon-balls. With the intention of landing at Wimereux, after having passed along the line, he ordered them to steer for the castle of Croi, saying that he must double it.

Admiral Bruix, alarmed at the danger he was about to incur, in vain represented to the First Consul the imprudence of doing this. "What shall we gain," said he, "by doubling this fort? Nothing, except to expose ourselves to the cannon-balls. General, by flanking it we will arrive as soon." The First Consul was not of the admiral's opinion, and insisted on doubling the fort. The admiral, at the risk of being reprimanded, gave contrary orders to the sailors; and the First Consul saw himself obliged to pass behind the fort, though much irritated and reproaching the admiral.

This soon ceased, however; for, hardly had the launch passed, when a transport, which had doubled the castle of Croi, was crashed into and sunk by three or four shells.

The First Consul became silent, on seeing how correct the admiral's judgment had been; and the rest of the journey, as far as the little port of Wimereux, was made without hindrance from him. Arriving there, he climbed upon the cliff to encourage the cannoneers, spoke to all of them, patted them on the shoulder, and urged them to aim well. "Courage, my friends," said he, "remember you are not fighting fellows who will hold out a long time. Drive them back with the honours of war." And noticing the fine resistance and majestic manoeuvres of a frigate, he asked, "Can you believe, my children, that captain is English? I do not think so."

The artillerymen, animated by the words of the First Consul, redoubled their zeal and the rapidity of their fire. One of them said, "Look at the frigate, General; her bowsprit is going to fall." He spoke truly, the bowsprit was cut in two by his ball. "Give twenty *francs* to that brave man," said the First Consul to the officers who were with him. Near the batteries of Wimereux there was a furnace to heat the cannon-balls; and the First Consul noticed them operating the furnaces, and gave instructions. "That is not red enough, boys; they must be sent redder than that, come, come." One of them had known him, when a lieutenant of artillery, and said to his comrades, "He understands these little matters perfectly, as well as greater ones, you see."

That day two soldiers without arms were on the cliff noticing the manoeuvres. They began a quarrel in this singular manner. "Look," said one, "do you see the Little Corporal down there?" (they were both Picards). "No; I don't see him."

"Do you not see him in his launch?"

"Oh, yes, now I do; but surely he does not remember, that if anything should strike him, it would make the whole army weep—why does he expose himself like that?"

"Indeed, it is his place!"

"No, it's not "

"It is"

"It isn't. Look here, what would you do tomorrow if the Little Corporal was killed?"

"But I tell you it is his place!" And having no other argument on either side, they commenced to fight with their fists. They were separated with much difficulty.

The battle had commenced at one o'clock in the afternoon, and about ten o'clock in the evening the Dutch flotilla entered the port under the most terrible fire that I have ever witnessed. In the darkness the bombs, which crossed each other in every direction, formed above the port and the town a vault of fire, while the constant discharge of all this artillery was repeated by echoes from the cliffs, making a frightful din; and, a most singular fact, no one in the city was alarmed. The people of Boulogne had become accustomed to danger, and expected something terrible each day. They had constantly going on, under their eyes, preparations for attack or defence, and had become soldiers by dint of seeing this so constantly. On that day the noise of cannon was heard at dinner-time; and still every one dined, the hour for the repast being neither advanced nor delayed. Men went about their business, women occupied themselves with household affairs, young girls played the piano, all saw with indifference the cannonballs pass over their heads; and the curious, whom a desire to witness the combat had attracted to the cliffs, showed hardly any more emotion than is ordinarily the case on seeing a military piece played at Franconi's.

I still ask myself how three vessels could have endured for nine hours so violent a shock; for when at length the flotilla entered the fort, the English cutter had foundered, the brig had been burnt by the red-hot cannon-balls, and there was left only the frigate, with her masts shivered and her sails torn, but she still remained there immovable as a rock, and so near to our line of defence that the sailors on either side could be seen and counted. Behind her, at a modest distance, were more than a hundred English ships.

At length, after ten o'clock, a signal from the English admiral caused the frigate to withdraw, and the firing ceased. Our line of ships was not greatly damaged in this long and terrible combat, because the broadsides from the frigate simply cut into our rigging, and did not enter the body of our vessels. The brig and the cutter, however, did more harm.

Chapter 13

The First Consul left Boulogne to return to Paris, in order to be present at the marriage of one of his sisters. Prince Camille Borghese, descendant of the noblest family of Rome, had already arrived at Paris to—marry Madame Pauline Bonaparte, widow of General Leclerc, who had died of yellow fever in San Domingo. I recollect having seen this unfortunate general at the residence of the First Consul some time before his departure on the ill-starred expedition which cost him his life, and France the loss of many brave soldiers and much treasure. General Leclerc, whose name is now almost forgotten, or held in light esteem, was a kind and good man. He was passionately in love with his wife, whose giddiness, to put it mildly, afflicted him sorely, and threw him into a deep and habitual melancholy painful to witness. Princess Pauline (who was then far from being a princess) had married him willingly, and of her own choice; but this did not prevent her tormenting her husband by her innumerable caprices, and repeating to him a hundred times a day that he was indeed a fortunate man to marry the sister of the First Consul. I am sure that with his simple tastes and quiet disposition General Leclerc would have preferred less distinction and more peace. The First Consul required his sister to accompany her husband to San Domingo. She was forced to obey, and to leave Paris, where she swayed the sceptre of fashion, and eclipsed all other women by her elegance and coquetry, as well as by her incomparable beauty, to brave a dangerous climate, and the ferocious companions of Christophe and Dessalines. At the end of the year 1801 the admiral's ship, The Ocean, sailed from Brest, carrying to the Cape (San Domingo) General Leclerc, his wife, and their son. After her arrival at the Cape, the conduct of Madame Leclerc was beyond praise. On more than one occasion, but especially that which I shall now attempt to describe, she displayed a courage worthy of her name and the position of her husband. I obtained these details from an eye-witness whom I had known at Paris in the service of Princess Pauline.

The day of the great insurrection of the blacks in September, 1802, the bands of Christophe and Dessalines, composed of more than twelve thousand negroes, exasperated by their hatred against the whites, and the certainty that if they yielded no quarter would be given, made an assault on the town of the Cape, which was defended by only one thousand soldiers; for only this small number remained of the large army which had sailed from Brest a year before, in brilliant spirits and full of hope. This handful of brave men, the most of them weakened by fever, led by the general-in-chief of the expedition, who was even then suffering from the malady which caused his death, repulsed by unheard of efforts and heroic valour the repeated attacks of the blacks.

During this combat, in which the determination, if not the number and strength, was equal on both sides, Madame Leclerc, with her son, was under the guard of a devoted friend who had subject to his orders only a weak company of artillery, which still occupied the house where her husband had fixed his residence, at the foot of the low hills which bordered the coast. The general-in-chief, fearing lest this residence might be surprised by a party of the enemy, and being unable to foresee the issue of the struggle which he was maintaining on the heights of the Cape, and against which the blacks made their most furious assaults, sent an order to convey his wife and son on board the fleet. Pauline would not consent to this. Always faithful to the pride with which her name inspired her (but this time there was in her pride as much greatness as nobility), she spoke to the ladies of the city who had taken refuge with her, and begged them to go away, giving them a frightful picture of the horrible treatment to which they would be exposed should the negroes defeat the troops. "You can leave. You are not the sisters of Bonaparte."

However, as the danger became more pressing every moment, General Leclerc sent an *aide-de-camp* to his residence, and enjoined on him, in case Pauline still persisted in her refusal, to use force, and convey her on board against her will. The officer was obliged to execute this order to the letter. Consequently Madame Leclerc was forcibly placed in an arm-chair which was borne by four soldiers, while a grenadier marched by her side, carrying in his arms the general's son. During this scene of flight and terror the child, already worthy of its mother, played with the plume of the soldier who was carrying him. Followed by her cortege of trembling, tearful women, whose only source of strength during this perilous passage was in her courage, she was thus conveyed to the seashore. Just as they were going to place her in the sloop, however, another *aide-de-camp* of her husband brought news of the defeat of the blacks. "You see now," said she, returning to her residence, "I was right in not wishing to embark." She was not yet out of danger, however; for a troop of negroes, forming part of the army which had just been so miraculously repulsed, in trying to make good their retreat to the dikes, met the small escort of Madame Leclerc. As they appeared disposed to attack, it was necessary to scatter them by shots at short range. Throughout this skirmish Pauline preserved a perfect equanimity. All these circumstances, which reflected so much honour on Madame Leclerc, were reported to the First Consul.

His self-love was flattered by it; and I believe that it was to Prince Borghese that he said one day at his levee, "Pauline is predestined to marry a Roman, for from head to foot she is every inch a Roman."

Unfortunately this courage, which a man might have envied, was not united in the Princess Pauline with those virtues which are less brilliant and more modest, and also more suitable for a woman, and which we naturally expect to find in her, rather than boldness and contempt of danger.

I do not know if it is true, as has been written somewhere, that Madame Leclerc, when she was obliged to set out for San Domingo, had a fancy for an actor of the Theatre Francais. Nor am I able to say whether it is true that Mademoiselle Duchesnois had the *naiveté* to exclaim before a hundred people in reference to this departure, "Lafon will never be consoled; it will kill him!" but what I myself know of the frailty of this princess leads me to believe that the anecdote is true.

All Paris knew the special favour with which she honoured M. Jules de Canouville, a young and brilliant colonel who was handsome and brave, with a perfect figure, and an assurance which was the cause of his innumerable successes with certain women, although he used little discretion in respect to them. The liaison of Princess Pauline[1] with this amiable officer was the most lasting that she ever

---

1. Monsieur Bousquet was called to Neuilly (residence of the Princess Pauline) in order to examine the beautiful teeth of her Imperial Highness. Presented to her, he prepared to begin work. "Monsieur," said a charming young man in a wrapper, negligently lying on a sofa, "take care, I pray, what you do. I feel a great interest in the teeth of my Paulette, and I hold you responsible for any accident." "Be tranquil, my Prince; I can assure your Imperial Highness that there is no danger." During all the time that Bousquet was engaged in working on the pretty mouth,

formed; and as, unfortunately, neither of them was discreet, their mutual tenderness acquired in a short while a scandalous publicity. I shall take occasion later to relate in its proper place the incident which caused the disgrace, banishment, and perhaps even the death, of Colonel de Canouville. A death so premature, and above all so cruel, since it was not an enemy's bullet which struck him, was deplored by the whole army.[2]

Moreover, however great may have been the frailty of Princess Pauline in regard to her lovers, and although most incredible instances of this can be related without infringing on the truth, her admirable devotion to the person of the Emperor in 1814 should cause her faults to be treated with indulgence.

On innumerable occasions the effrontery of her conduct, and especially her want of regard and respect for the Empress Marie Louise, irritated the Emperor against the Princess Borghese, though he always ended by pardoning her; notwithstanding which, at the time of the fall of her august brother she was again in disgrace, and being informed that the island of Elba had been selected as a prison for the Emperor, she hastened to shut herself up there with him, abandoning Rome and Italy, whose finest palaces were hers. Before the battle of Waterloo, his Majesty at the critical moment found the heart of his sister Pauline still faithful. Fearing lest he might be in need of money, she sent him her handsomest diamonds, the value of which

---

these recommendations continued. At length, having finished what he had to do, he passed into the waiting-room, where he found assembled the ladies of the palace, the chamberlains, etc., who were awaiting to enter the apartments of the Princess. They hastened to ask Bousquet news of the princess, "Her Imperial Highness is very well, and must be happy in the tender attachment her august husband feels for her, which he has shown in my presence in so touching a manner. His anxiety was extreme. It was only with difficulty I could reassure him as to the result of the simplest thing in the world; I shall tell everywhere what I have just witnessed. It is pleasant to be able to cite such an example of conjugal tenderness in so high a rank. I am deeply impressed with it." They did not try to stop good M. Bousquet in these expressions of his enthusiasm. The desire to laugh prevented a single word; and he left convinced that nowhere existed a better household than that of the Prince and Princess Borghese. The latter was in Italy, and the handsome young man was M. de Canouville. I borrow this curious anecdote from the *Memoirs of Josephine*, the author of which, who saw and described the Court of Navarre and Malmaison with so much truth and good judgment, is said to be a woman, and must be in truth a most intellectual one, and in a better position than any other person to know the private affairs of her Majesty, the Empress.—Constant.

2. He was slain by a ball from a French cannon, which was discharged after the close of an action in which he had shown the most brilliant courage.—Constant.

was enormous; and they were found in the carriage of the Emperor when it was captured at Waterloo, and exhibited to the curiosity of the inhabitants of London. But the diamonds have been lost; at least, to their lawful owner.

Chapter 14

On the day of General Moreau's arrest the First Consul was in a state of great excitement.[1] The morning was passed in interviews with his emissaries, the agents of police; and measures had been taken that the arrest should be made at the specified hour, either at Gros-Bois, or at the general's house in the street of the Faubourg Saint-Honore. The First Consul was anxiously walking up and down his chamber, when he sent for me, and ordered me to take position opposite General Moreau's house (the one in Paris), to see whether the arrest had taken place, and if there was any tumult, and to return promptly and make my report. I obeyed; but nothing extraordinary took place, and I saw only some police spies walking along the street, and watching the door of the house of the man whom they had marked for their prey. Thinking that my presence would probably be noticed, I retired; and, as I learned while returning to the chateau that General Moreau had been arrested on the road from his estate of Gros-Bois, which he sold a few months later to Marshal Berthier, before leaving for the United States, I quickened my pace, and hastened to announce to the First Consul the news of the arrest. He knew this already, made no response, and still continued thoughtful, and in deep reflection, as in the morning.

Since I have been led to speak of General Moreau, I will recall by what fatal circumstances he was led to tarnish his glory. Madame Bonaparte had given to him in marriage Mademoiselle Hulot, her friend, and, like herself, a native of the Isle of France. This young lady, gentle, amiable, and possessing those qualities which make a good

---

1. Jean Victor Moreau, born at Morlaix in Brittany, 1763, son of a prominent lawyer. At one time he rivalled Bonaparte in reputation. He was general-in-chief of the army of the Rhine, 1796, and again in 1800, in which latter year he gained the battle of Hohenlinden. Implicated in the conspiracy of Pichegru, he was exiled, and went to the United States. He returned to Europe in 1813, and, joining the allied armies against France, was killed by a cannon-shot in the attack on Dresden in August of that year.

wife and mother, loved her husband passionately, and was proud of that glorious name which surrounded her with respect and honour; but, unfortunately, she had the greatest deference for her mother, whose ambition was great, and who desired nothing short of seeing her daughter seated upon a throne. The influence which she exercised over Madame Moreau soon extended to the general himself, who, ruled by her counsels, became gloomy, thoughtful, melancholy, and forever lost that tranquillity of mind which had distinguished him. From that time the general's house was open to intrigues and conspiracies; and it was the rendezvous of all the discontented, of which there were many. The general assumed the task of disapproving all the acts of the First Consul; he opposed the reestablishment of public worship, and criticised as childish and ridiculous mummery the institution of the Legion of Honour. These grave imprudences, and indeed many others, came to the ears of the First Consul, who refused at first to believe them; but how could he remain deaf to reports which were repeated each day with more foundation, though doubtless exaggerated by malice?

In proportion as the imprudent speeches of the general were depriving him of the esteem of the First Consul, his mother-in-law, by a dangerous obstinacy, was encouraging him in his opposition, persuaded, she said, that the future would do justice to the present. She did not realize that she spoke so truly; and the general rushed headlong into the abyss which opened before him. How greatly his conduct was in opposition to his character! He had a pronounced aversion to the English, and he detested the Chouans, and everything pertaining to the old nobility; and besides, a man like General Moreau, who had served his country so gloriously, was not the one to bear arms against her. But he was deceived, and he deceived himself, in thinking that he was fitted to play a great political part; and he was destroyed by the flatteries of a party which excited all possible hostility against the First Consul by taking advantage of the jealousy of his former comrades in arms. I witnessed more than one proof of affection shown by the First Consul to General Moreau. In the course of a visit of the latter to the Tuileries, and during an interview with the First Consul, General Carnot arrived from Versailles with a pair of pistols of costly workmanship, which the manufactory of Versailles had sent as a gift to the First Consul. He took these handsome weapons from the hands of General Carnot, admired them a moment, and immediately offered them to General Moreau, saying to him, "Take them, truly they could not have come at a better time." All this was done quicker than I can write it; the general was highly flattered by this proof of friendship, and thanked the First Consul warmly.

The name and trial of General Moreau recall to me the story of a brave officer who was compromised in this unfortunate affair, and who after many years of disgrace was pardoned only on account of the courage with which he dared expose himself to the anger of the Emperor. The authenticity of the details which I shall relate can be attested, if necessary, by living persons, whom I shall have occasion to name in my narrative, and whose testimony no reader would dream of impeaching.

The disgrace of General Moreau extended at first to all those who surrounded him; and as the affection and devotion felt for him by all the officers and soldiers who had served under him was well known, his *aides-de-camp* were arrested, even those who were not then in Paris. One of them, Colonel Delelee, had been many months on furlough at Besancon, resting after his campaigns in the bosom of his family, and with a young wife whom he had recently married. Besides, he was at that time concerning himself very little with political matters, very much with his pleasures, and not at all with conspiracies. Comrade and brother in arms of Colonels Guilleminot, Hugo, Foy,—all three of whom became generals afterwards,—he was spending his evenings gaily with them at the garrison, or in the quiet pleasures of his family circle. Suddenly Colonel Delelee was arrested, placed in a post chaise, and it was not until he was rolling along in a gallop on the road to Paris, that he learned from the officer of the gendarmes who accompanied him, that General Moreau had conspired, and that in his quality as *aide-de-camp* he was counted among the conspirators.

Arrived at Paris, the colonel was put in close confinement, in La Force I believe. His wife, much alarmed, followed his footsteps; but it was several days before she obtained permission to communicate with the prisoner, and then could do so only by signs from the courtyard of the prison while he showed himself, for a few moments, and put his hands through the bars of the window. However, the rigor of these orders was relaxed for the colonel's young child three or four years of age, and his father obtained the favour of embracing him. He came each morning in his mother's arms, and a turnkey carried him in to the prisoner, before which inconvenient witness the poor little thing played his role with all the skill of a consummate actor. He would pretend to be lame, and complain of having sand in his shoes which hurt him and the colonel, turning his back on the jailer, and taking the child in his lap to remove the cause of the trouble, would find in his son's shoe a note from his wife, informing him in a few words of the state of the trial, and what he had to hope or fear for himself. At length, after many months of captivity, sentence having been pronounced against the conspirators, Colonel Delelee, against whom no charge had been made, was not absolved as he had a right to expect, but was struck off the army list, arbitrarily put under surveillance, and prohibited from coming within forty leagues of Paris. He was also forbidden to return to Besancon, and it was more than a year after leaving prison before he was permitted to do so.

Young and full of courage, the Colonel saw, from the depths of his retirement, his friends and comrades make their way, and gain upon the battlefield fame, rank, and glory, while he himself was condemned to inaction and obscurity, and to pass his days in following on the map the triumphant march of those armies in which he felt himself worthy to resume his rank. Innumerable applications were addressed by him and his friends to the head of the Empire, that he might be allowed to go even as a common volunteer, and rejoin his former comrades with his knapsack on his shoulder; but these petitions were refused, the will of the Emperor was inflexible, and to each new application he only replied, "Let him wait." The inhabitants of Besancon, who considered Colonel Delelee as their fellow-citizen, interested themselves warmly in the unmerited misfortunes of this brave officer; and when an occasion presented itself of recommending him anew to the clemency, or rather to the justice, of the Emperor, they availed themselves of it.

It was, I believe, on the return from Prussia and Poland that from all parts of France there came deputations charged with congratulating the Emperor upon his several victories. Colonel Delelee was unanimously elected member of the deputation of Doubs, of which the mayor and *prefect* of Besancon were also members, and of which the respectable Marshal Moncey was president, and an opportunity was thus at last offered Colonel Delelee of procuring the removal of the long sentence which had weighed him down and kept his sword idle. He could speak to the Emperor, and complain respectfully, but with dignity, of the disgrace in which he had been so long kept without reason. He could render thanks, from the bottom of his heart, for the generous affection of his fellow-citizens, whose wishes, he hoped would plead for him with his Majesty.

The deputies of Besancon, upon their arrival at Paris, presented themselves to the different ministers. The minister of police took the president of the deputation aside, and asked him the meaning of the presence among the deputies of a man publicly known to be in disgrace, and the sight of whom could not fail to be disagreeable to the chief of the Empire.

Marshal Moncey, on coming out from this private interview, pale and frightened, entered the room of Colonel Delelee:

"My friend," said he, "all is lost, for I have ascertained at the bureau that they are still hostile to you. If the Emperor sees you among us, he will take it as an open avowal of disregard for his orders, and will be furious."

"Ah, well, what have I to do with that?"

"But in order to avoid compromising the department, the deputation, and, indeed, in order to avoid compromising yourself, you would perhaps do well"—the Marshal hesitated.

"I will do well?" demanded the Colonel.

"Perhaps to withdraw without making any display—"

Here the colonel interrupted the president of the deputation: "Marshal, permit me to decline this advice; I have not come so far to be discouraged, like a child, before the first obstacle. I am weary of a disgrace which I have not deserved, and still more weary of enforced idleness. Let the Emperor be irritated or pleased, he shall see me; let him order me to be shot, if he wishes. I do not count worth having such a life as I have led for the last four years. Nevertheless, I will be satisfied with whatever my colleagues, the deputies of Besancon, shall decide."

These latter did not disapprove of the colonel's resolution, and he accompanied them to the Tuileries on the day of the solemn reception of all the deputations of the Empire. All the halls of the Tuileries were packed with a crowd in richly embroidered coats and brilliant uniforms. The military household of the Emperor, his civil household, the generals present at Paris, the diplomatic corps, ministers and chiefs of the different administrations, the deputies of the departments with their *prefects*, and mayors decorated with tricoloured scarves, were all assembled in numerous groups, and conversed in a low tone while awaiting the arrival of his Majesty.

In one of these groups was seen a tall officer dressed in a very simple uniform, cut in the fashion of several years past. He wore neither on his collar, nor even on his breast the decoration which no officer of his grade then lacked. This was Colonel Delelee. The president of the deputation of which he was a member appeared embarrassed and almost distressed. Of the former comrades of the colonel, very few dared to recognize him, and the boldest gave him a distant nod which expressed at the same time anxiety and pity, while the more prudent did not even glance at him.

As for him, he remained unconcerned and resolute.

At last the folding doors were opened, and an usher cried "The Emperor, gentlemen."

The groups separated, and a line was formed, the colonel placing himself in the first rank.

His Majesty commenced his tour of the room, welcoming the president of each delegation with a few flattering words. Arrived before the delegation from Doubs, the Emperor, having addressed a few words to the brave marshal who was president, was about to pass on to the next, when his eyes fell upon an officer he had not yet seen. He stopped in surprise, and addressed to the deputy his familiar inquiry, "Who are you?"

"Sire, I am Colonel Delelee, former *aide-de-camp* of General Moreau."

These words were pronounced in a firm voice, which resounded in the midst of the profound silence which the presence of the sovereign imposed.

The Emperor stepped back, and fastened both eyes on the colonel. The latter showed no emotion, but bowed slightly.

Marshal Moncey was pale as death.

The Emperor spoke. "What do you come to ask here?"

"That which I have asked for many years, Sire: that your Majesty will deign to tell me wherein I have been in fault, or restore to me my rank."

Among those near enough to hear these questions and replies, few could breathe freely. At last a smile half opened the firmly closed lips of the Emperor; he placed his finger on his mouth, and, approaching the colonel, said to him in a softened and almost friendly tone, "You have reason to complain a little of that, but let us say no more about it," and continued his round. He had gone ten steps from the group formed by the deputies of Bescancon, when he came back, and, stopping before the colonel, said, "Monsieur Minister of War, take the name of this officer, and be sure to remind me of him. He is tired of doing nothing, and we will give him occupation."

As soon as the audience was over, the struggle was, who should be most attentive to the colonel. He was surrounded, congratulated, embraced, and pulled about. Each of his old comrades wished to carry him off, and his hands were not enough to grasp all those extended to him. General Savary, who that very evening had added to the fright of Marshal Moncey, by being astonished that any one could have the audacity to brave the Emperor, extended his arm over the shoulders of those who pressed around the colonel, and shaking his hand in the most cordial manner possible, "Delelee," cried he, "do not forget that I expect you tomorrow to breakfast."

Two days after this scene at court, Colonel Delelee received his appointment as chief of staff of the army of Portugal, commanded by the Duke d'Abrantes. His preparations were soon made; and just before setting out he had a last interview with the Emperor, who said to him, "Colonel, I know that it is useless to urge you to make up for lost time. In a little while I hope we shall both be satisfied with each other."

On coming out from this last audience, the brave Delelee said there was nothing wanting to make him happy except a good opportunity to have himself cut to pieces for a man who knew so well how to close the wounds of a long disgrace. Such was the sway that his Majesty exercised over the minds of men.

The colonel had soon crossed the Pyrenees, passed through Spain, and been received by Junot with open arms. The army of Portugal had suffered much in the two years during which it had struggled against both the population and the English with unequal forces. Food was secured with difficulty, and the soldiers were badly clothed, and half-shod. The new chief of staff did all that was possible to remedy this disorder; and the soldiers had just begun to feel the good effects of his presence, when he fell sick from overwork and fatigue, and died before being able, according to the Emperor's expression, to "make up for lost time."

I have said elsewhere that upon each conspiracy against the life of the First Consul all the members of his household were at once subjected to a strict surveillance; their smallest actions were watched; they were followed outside the chateau; their conduct was reported even to the smallest details. At the time the conspiracy of Pichegru was discovered, there was only a single guardian of the portfolio, by the name of Landoire; and his position was very trying, for he must always be present in a little dark corridor upon which the door of the cabinet opened, and he took his meals on the run, and half-dressed. Happily for Landoire, they gave him an assistant; and this was the occasion of it.

Angel, one of the doorkeepers of the palace, was ordered by the First Consul to place himself at the barrier of Bonshommes during the trial of Pichegru, to recognize and watch the people of the household who came and went in the transaction of their business, no one being allowed to leave Paris without permission. Augel's reports having pleased the First Consul, he sent for him, was satisfied with his replies and intelligence, and appointed him assistant to Landoire in the custody of the portfolio. Thus the task of the latter became lighter by half. In 1812 Angel was in the campaign of Russia, and died on the return, when within a few leagues of Paris, in consequence of the fatigue and privations which we shared with the army.

However, it was not only those attached to the service of the First Consul, or the chateau, who were subject to this surveillance.

When Napoleon became Emperor, the custodians of all the imperial palaces were furnished with a register upon which all persons from outside, and all strangers who came to visit any one in the palace were obliged to inscribe their names, with that of the persons whom they came to see. Every evening this register was carried to the grand marshal of the palace, and in his absence to the governor, and the Emperor often consulted it. He once found there a certain name which, as a husband, he had his reasons, and perhaps good ones, to suspect. His Majesty had previously ordered the exclusion of this person; and finding this unlucky name again upon the custodian's register, he was angry beyond measure, believing that they had dared on both sides to disobey his orders. Investigation was immediately made; and it was fortunately ascertained that the visitor was a most insignificant person, whose only fault was that of bearing a name which was justly compromised.

Chapter 15

The year 1804, which was so full of glory for the Emperor, was also the year which brought him more care and anxiety than all others, except those of 1814 and 1815. It is not my province to pass judgment on such grave events, nor to determine what part was taken in them by the Emperor, or by those who surrounded and counselled him, for it is my object to relate only what I saw and heard. On the 21st of March of that year I entered the Emperor's room at an early hour, and found him awake, leaning on his elbow. He seemed gloomy and tired; but when I entered he sat up, passed his hand many times over his forehead, and said to me, "Constant, I have a headache." Then, throwing off the covering, he added, "I have slept very badly." He seemed extremely preoccupied and absorbed, and his appearance evinced melancholy and suffering to such a degree that I was surprised and somewhat anxious. While I was dressing him he did not utter a word, which never occurred except when something agitated or worried him. During this time only Roustan and I were present. His toilet being completed, just as I was handing him his snuff-box, handkerchief, and little bonbon box, the door opened suddenly, and the First Consul's wife entered, in her morning negligee, much agitated, with traces of tears on her cheeks. Her sudden appearance astonished, and even alarmed, Roustan and myself; for it was only an extraordinary circumstance which could have induced Madame Bonaparte to leave her room in this costume, before taking all necessary precautions to conceal the damage which the want of the accessories of the toilet did her. She entered, or rather rushed, into the room, crying, "The Duke d'Enghien is dead! Ah, my friend! what have you done?" Then she fell sobbing into the arms of the First Consul, who became pale as death, and said with extraordinary emotion, "The miserable wretches have been too quick!" He then left the room, supporting Madame Bonaparte, who could hardly walk, and was still weeping. The news of the prince's death spread consternation in the chateau; and the First Consul remarked this universal grief, but reprimanded no one for it. The fact is, the greatest chagrin which this mournful catastrophe caused his servants, most of whom were attached to him by affection even more than by duty, came from the belief that it would inevitably tarnish the glory and destroy the peace of mind of their master.

The First Consul probably understood our feelings perfectly; but however that may be, I have here related all that I myself saw and know of this deplorable event. I do not pretend to know what passed in the cabinet meeting, but the emotion of the First Consul appeared to me sincere and unaffected; and he remained sad and silent for many days, speaking very little at his toilet, and saying only what was necessary.

During this month and the following I noticed constantly passing, repassing, and holding frequent interviews with the First Consul, many persons whom I was told were members of the council of state, tribunes, or senators. For a long time the army and a great number of citizens, who idolized the hero of Italy and Egypt, had manifested openly their desire to see him wear a title worthy of his renown and the greatness of France. It was well known, also, that he alone performed all the duties of government, and that his nominal colleagues were really his subordinates. It was thought proper, therefore, that he should become supreme head of the state in name, as he already was in fact. I have often since his fall heard his Majesty called an usurper: but the only effect of this on me is to provoke a smile of pity; for if the Emperor usurped the throne, he had more accomplices than all the tyrants of tragedy and melodrama combined, for three-fourths of the French people were in the conspiracy. As is well known, it was on May 18 that the Empire was proclaimed, and the First Consul (whom I shall henceforward call the Emperor) received at Saint-Cloud the Senate, led by Consul Cambaceres, who became, a few hours later, arch-chancellor of the Empire; and it was by him that the Emperor heard himself for the first time saluted with the title of Sire. After this audience the Senate went to present its homage to the Empress Josephine. The rest of the day was passed in receptions, presentations, interviews, and congratulations; everybody in the chateau was drunk with joy; each one felt that he had been suddenly promoted in rank, so they embraced each other, exchanged compliments, and confided to each other hopes and plans for the future. There was no subaltern too humble to be inspired with ambition; in a word, the antechamber, saving the difference of persons, furnished an exact repetition of what passed in the saloon. Nothing could be more amusing than the embarrassment of the whole service when it was necessary to reply to his Majesty's questions. They would begin with a mistake, then would try again, and do worse, saying ten times in the same minute, "Sire, general, your Majesty, citizen, First Consul." The next morning on entering as usual the First Consul's room, to his customary questions, "What o'clock is it? What is the weather?" I replied, "Sire, seven o'clock; fine weather." As I approached his bed, he seized me by the ear, and slapped me on the cheek, calling me *"Monsieur le drole,"* which was his favourite expression when especially pleased with me. His Majesty had kept awake, and worked late into the night, and I found him serious and preoccupied, but well satisfied. How different this awakening to that of the 21st of March preceding! On this day his Majesty went to hold his first grand levee at the Tuileries, where all the civil and military authorities were presented to him. The brothers and sisters of the Emperor were made princes and princesses, with the exception of Lucien, who had quarrelled with his Majesty on the occasion of his marriage with Madame Jouberton. Eighteen generals were raised to the dignity of marshals of the empire. Dating from this day, everything around their Majesties took on the appearance of a court and royal power. Much has been said of the awkwardness of the first courtiers, not yet accustomed to the new duties imposed upon them, and to the ceremonials of etiquette; and there was, indeed, in the beginning some embarrassment experienced by those in the immediate service of the Emperor, as I have said above; but this lasted only a short while, and the chamberlains and high officials adapted themselves to the new regime almost as quickly as the valets de *chambre*. They had also as instructors many personages of the old court, who had been struck out of the list of *émigrés* by the kindness of the Emperor, and now solicited earnestly for themselves and their wives employment in the new imperial court.

His majesty had no liking for the anniversaries of the Republic; some of which had always seemed to him odious and cruel, others ridiculous; and I have heard him express his indignation that they should have dared to make an annual festival of the anniversary of the 21st of January, and smile with pity at the recollection of what he called the masquerades of the theo-philanthropists, who, he said, "would have no Jesus Christ, and yet made saints of Fenelon and Las Casas—Catholic prelates."

Bourrienne, in his Memoirs, says that it was not one of the least singular things in the policy of Napoleon, that during the first years of his reign he retained the festival of 14th July. I will observe, as to this, that if his Majesty used this annual solemnity to appear in pomp in public, on the other hand, he so changed the object of the festival that it would have been difficult to recognize in it the anniversary of the taking of the Bastille and of the First Federation. I do not think that there was one word in allusion to these two events in the whole ceremony; and to confuse still further the recollections of the Republicans, the Emperor ordered that the festival should be celebrated on the 15th, because that was Sunday, and thus there would result no loss of time to the inhabitants of the capital. Besides, there was no allusion made to honouring the, captors of the Bastille, this being made simply the occasion of a grand distribution of the cross of the Legion of Honour.

It was the first occasion on which their Majesties showed themselves to the people in all the paraphernalia of power.

The cortege crossed the grand alley of the Tuileries on their way to the Hotel des Invalides, the church of which (changed during the Revolution into a Temple of Mars) had been restored by the Emperor to the Catholic worship, and was used for the magnificent ceremonies of the day. This was also the first time that the Emperor had made use of the privilege of passing in a carriage through the garden of the Tuileries. His cortege was superb, that of the Empress Josephine not less brilliant; and the intoxication of the people reached such a height, that it was beyond expression. By order of the Emperor I mingled in the crowd, to learn in what spirit the populace would take part in the festival; and I heard not a murmur, so great was the enthusiasm of all classes for his Majesty at that time, whatever may have been said since. The Emperor and Empress were received at the door of the Hotel des Invalides by the governor and by Count de Segur, grand-master of ceremonies, and at the entrance of the church by Cardinal du Belloy at the head of a numerous clergy. After the mass, de Lacepede, grand chancellor of the Legion of Honour, delivered a speech, followed by the roll-call of the grand officers of the Legion, after which the Emperor took his seat, and putting on his hat, repeated in a firm voice the formula of the oath, at the end of which all the members of the Legion cried, *"Je le jure!"* (I swear it); and immediately shouts of "*Vive l'Empereur,*" repeated a thousand times, were heard in the church and outside.

A singular circumstance added still more to the interest which the ceremony excited. While the chevaliers of the new order were passing one by one before the Emperor, who welcomed them, a man of the people, wearing a roundabout, placed himself on the steps of the throne. His Majesty showed some astonishment, and paused an instant, whereupon the man, being interrogated, showed his warrant. The Emperor at once and with great cordiality bade him advance, and gave him the decoration, accompanied by a sharp accolade. The cortege, on its return, followed the same route, passing again through the garden of the Tuileries.

On the 18th of July, three days after this ceremony, the Emperor set out from Saint-Cloud for the camp of Boulogne. Believing that his Majesty would be willing to dispense with my presence for a few days, and as it was a number of years since I had seen my family, I felt a natural desire to meet them again, and to review with my parents the singular circumstances through which I had passed since I had left them.

I should have experienced, I confess, great joy in talking with them of my present situation and my hopes; and I felt the need of freely expressing myself, and enjoying the confidences of domestic privacy, in compensation for the repression and constraint which my position imposed on me. Therefore I requested permission to pass eight days at Perueltz. It was readily granted, and I lost no time in setting out; but my astonishment may be imagined when, the very day after my arrival, a courier brought me a letter from the Count de Remusat, ordering me to rejoin the Emperor immediately, adding that his Majesty needed me, and I should have no other thought than that of returning without delay. In spite of the disappointment induced by such orders, I felt flattered nevertheless at having become so necessary to the great man who had deigned to admit me into his service, and at once bade adieu to my family. His Majesty had hardly reached Boulogne, when he set out again immediately on a tour of several days in the departments of the north. I was at Boulogne before his return, and had organized his Majesty's service so that he found everything ready on his arrival; but this did not prevent his saying to me that I had been absent a long time.

While I am on this subject, I will narrate here, although some years in advance, one or two circumstances which will give the reader a better idea of the rigorous confinement to which I was subjected. I had contracted, in consequence of the fatigues of my continual journeyings in the suite of the Emperor, a disease of the bladder, from which I suffered horribly. For a long time I combated the disease with patience and dieting; but at last, the pain having become entirely unbearable, in 1808 I requested of his Majesty a month's leave of absence in order to be cured, Dr. Boyer having told me that a month was the shortest time absolutely necessary for my restoration, and that without it my disease would become incurable. I went to Saint-Cloud to visit my wife's family, where Yvan, surgeon of the Emperor, came to see me every day. Hardly a week had passed, when he told me that his Majesty thought I ought to be entirely well, and wished me to resume my duties. This wish was equivalent to an order; it was thus I understood it, and returned to the Emperor, who seeing me pale, and suffering excruciatingly, deigned to say to me many kind things, without, however, mentioning a new leave of absence. These two were my only absences for sixteen years; therefore, on my return from Moscow, and during the campaign of France, my disease having reached its height, I quitted the Emperor at Fontainebleau, because it was impossible for me, in spite of all my attachment to so kind a master, and all the gratitude which I felt towards him, to perform my duties longer. Even after this separation, which was exceedingly painful to me, a year hardly sufficed to cure me, and then not entirely. But I shall take occasion farther on to speak of this melancholy event. I now return to the recital of facts, which prove that I could, with more reason than many others, believe myself a person of great importance, since my humble services seemed to be indispensable to the master of Europe, and many frequenters of the Tuileries would have had more difficulty than I in proving their usefulness. Is there too much vanity in what I have just said? and would not the chamberlains have a right to be vexed by it? I am not concerned with that, so I continue my narrative. The Emperor was tenacious of old habits; he preferred, as we have already seen, being served by me in preference to all others; nevertheless, it is my duty to state that his servants were all full of zeal and devotion, though I had been with him longest, and had never left him. One day the Emperor asked for tea in the middle of the day. M. Seneschal was on duty, consequently made the tea, and presented it to his Majesty, who declared it to be detestable, and had me summoned. The Emperor complained to me that they were trying to poison him (this was his expression when he found a bad taste in anything); so going into the kitchen, I poured out of the same teapot, a cup, which I prepared and carried to his Majesty, with two silver-gilt spoons as usual, one to taste the tea in the presence of the Emperor, and the other for him. This time he said the tea was excellent, and complimented me on it with a kind familiarity which he deigned at times to use towards his servants. On returning the cup to me, he pulled my ears, and said, "You must teach them how to make tea; they know nothing about it." De Bourrienne, whose excellent

Memoirs I have read with the greatest pleasure, says somewhere, that the Emperor in his moments of good humour pinched the tip of the ears of his familiars. I myself think that he pinched the whole ear, often, indeed, both ears at once, and with the hand of a master. He also says in these same Memoirs, that the Emperor gave little friendly slaps with two fingers, in which De Bourrienne is very moderate, for I can bear witness in regard to this matter, that his Majesty, although his hand was not large, bestowed his favours much more broadly; but this kind of caress, as well as the former, was given and received as a mark of particular favour, and the recipients were far from complaining then. I have heard more than one dignitary say with pride, like the sergeant in the comedy,—

"Sir, feel there, the blow upon my cheek is still warm."

In his private apartments the Emperor was almost always cheerful and approachable, conversing freely with the persons in his service, questioning them about their families, their affairs, and even as to their pleasures. His toilet finished, his appearance suddenly changed; he became grave and thoughtful, and assumed again the bearing of an emperor. It has been said, that he often beat the people of his household, which statement is untrue. I saw him once only give himself up to a transport of this kind; and certainly the circumstances which caused it, and the reparation which followed, ought to render it, if not excusable, at least easily understood: This is the incident, of which I was a witness, and which took place in the suburbs of Vienna, the day after the death of Marshal Lannes. The Emperor was profoundly affected, and had not spoken a word during his toilet. As soon as he was dressed he asked for his horse; and as an unlucky chance would have it, Jardin, superintendent of the stables, could not be found when the horse was saddled, and the groom did not put on him his regular bridle, in consequence of which his Majesty had no sooner mounted, than the animal plunged, reared, and the rider fell heavily to the ground. Jardin arrived just as the Emperor was rising from the ground, beside himself with anger; and in his first transport of rage, he gave Jardin a blow with his riding-whip directly across his face. Jardin withdrew, overwhelmed by such cruel treatment, so unusual in his Majesty; and a few hours after, Caulaincourt, grand equerry, finding himself alone with his Majesty, described to him Jardin's grief and mortification. The Emperor expressed deep regret for his anger, sent for Jardin, and spoke to him with a kindness which effaced the remembrance of his ill treatment, and sent him a few days afterward three thousand *francs*. I have been told that a similar incident happened to Vigogne, senior, in Egypt. But although this may be true, two such instances alone in the entire life of the Emperor, which was passed amid surroundings so well calculated to make a man, even though naturally most amiable, depart from his usual character, should not be sufficient to draw down upon Napoleon the odious reproach of beating cruelly those in his service.

Chapter 16

In his headquarters at the Pont des Briques the Emperor worked as regularly as in his cabinet at the Tuileries. After his rides on horseback, his inspections, his visits, his reviews, he took his meals in haste, and retired into his cabinet, where he often worked most of the night, thus leading the same life as at Paris. In his horseback rides Roustan followed him everywhere, always taking with him a little silver flask of brandy for the use of his Majesty, who rarely asked for it.

The army of Boulogne was composed of about one hundred and fifty thousand infantry and ninety thousand cavalry, divided into four principal camps, the camp of the right wing, the camp of the left wing, the camp of Wimereux, and the camp of Ambleteuse.

His Majesty the Emperor had his headquarters at Pont de Briques; thus named, I was told, because the brick foundations of an old camp of Caesar's had been discovered there. The Pont de Briques, as I have said above, is about half a league from Boulogne; and the headquarters of his Majesty were established in the only house of the place which was then habitable, and guarded by a detachment of the cavalry of the Imperial Guard.

The four camps were on a very high cliff overlooking the sea, so situated that in fine weather the coast of England could be seen.

In the camp on the right they had established barracks for the Emperor, Admiral Bruix, Marshal Soult, and Decres, who was then minister of the navy.

The Emperor's barrack was constructed under the direction of Sordi, engineer, performing the functions of engineer-in-chief of military roads; and his nephew, Lecat de Rue, attached at that time to the staff of Marshal Soult as *aide-de-camp*, has been kind enough to furnish me with information which did not come within my province.

The Emperor's barrack was built of plank, like the booths of a country fair; with this difference, that the planks were neatly planed, and painted a greyish white. In form it was a long square, having at each end two pavilions of semicircular shape. A fence formed of wooden lattice enclosed this barrack, which was lighted on the outside by lamps placed four feet apart, and the windows were placed laterally. The pavilion next to the sea consisted of three rooms and a hall, the principal room, used as a council-chamber, being decorated with silver-grey paper. On the ceiling were painted golden clouds, in the midst of which appeared, upon the blue vault of the sky, an eagle holding the lightning, and guided towards England by a star, the guardian star of the Emperor. In the middle of this chamber was a large oval table with a plain cover of green cloth; and before this table was placed only his Majesty's armchair, which could be taken to pieces, and was made of natural wood, unpainted, and covered with green morocco stuffed with hair, while upon the table was a boxwood writing-desk. This was the entire furniture of the council-chamber, in which his Majesty alone could be seated. The generals stood before him, and had during these councils, which sometimes lasted three or four hours, no other support than the handles of their sabres.

The council-chamber was entered from a hall. On the right of this hall was his Majesty's bedroom, which had a glass door, and was lighted by a window which looked out upon the camp of the right wing, while the sea could be seen on the left. In this room was the Emperor's iron bed, with a large curtain of plain green *sarsenet* fastened to the ceiling by a gilded copper ring; and upon this bed were two mattresses, one made of hair, two bolsters, one at the head, the other at the foot, no pillow, and two coverlets, one of white cotton, the other of green *sarsenet*, wadded and quilted; by the side of the bed two very simple folding-seats, and at the window short curtains of green *sarsenet*.

This room was papered with rose-colored paper, stamped with a pattern in lace-work, with an Etruscan border.

Opposite the bedroom was a similar chamber, in which was a peculiar kind of telescope which had cost twelve thousand *francs*. This instrument was about four feet long, and about a foot in diameter, and was mounted on a mahogany support, with three feet, the box in which it was kept being almost in the shape of a piano. In the same room, upon two stools, was a little square chest, which contained three complete suits and the linen which formed the campaign wardrobe of his Majesty. Above this was a single extra hat, lined with white satin, and much the worse for wear; for the Emperor, as I shall say later in speaking of his personal peculiarities, having a very tender scalp, did not like new hats, and wore the same a long time.

The main body of the imperial barrack was divided into three rooms, a saloon, a vestibule, and a grand dining-room, which communicated with the kitchens by a passage parallel to that I have just mentioned. Outside the barrack, and connected with the kitchen, was a little shed, covered with thatch, which served as a washroom, and which was also used as a butler's pantry.

The barrack of Admiral Bruix was arranged like that of the Emperor, but on a smaller scale.

Near this barrack was the semaphore of the signals, a sort of marine telegraph by which the fleet was manoeuvred. A little farther on was the Tour d'Ordre, with a powerful battery composed of six mortars, six howitzers, and twelve twenty-four pounders.

These six mortars, the largest that had ever been made, were six inches thick, used forty-five pounds of powder at a charge, and threw bombs fifteen hundred *toises*[1] in the air, and a league and a half out to sea, each bomb thrown costing the state three hundred *francs*. To fire one of these fearful machines they used port-fires twelve feet long; and the cannoneer protected himself as best he could by bowing his head between his legs, and, not rising until after the shot was fired. The Emperor decided to fire the first bomb himself.

To the right of the headquarters battery was the barrack of Marshal Soult, which was constructed in imitation of the but of a savage, and covered with thatch down to the ground, with glass in the top, and a door through which you descended into the rooms, which were dug out like cellars. The principal chamber was round; and in it was a large work-table covered with green cloth, and surrounded with small leather folding-chairs.

The last barrack was that of Decres, minister of the navy, which was furnished like that of Marshal Soult. From his barrack the Emperor could observe all the manoeuvres at sea; and the telescope, of which I have spoken, was so good that Dover Castle, with its garrison, was, so to speak, under the very eyes of his Majesty. The camp of the right wing, situated upon the cliff, was divided into streets, each of which bore the name of some distinguished general; and this cliff bristled with batteries from Cologne to Ambleteuse, a distance of more than two leagues.

In order to go from Boulogne to the camp of the right wing, there was only one road, which began in the Rue des Vieillards, and passed over the cliff, between the barrack of his Majesty and those of Bruix,

---

1. A *toise* is six feet, and a league is three miles.

Soult, and Decres, so that if at low tide the Emperor wished to go down upon the beach, a long detour was necessary. One day when he was complaining greatly of this, it occurred to Bonnefoux, maritime *prefect* of Boulogne, to apply to Sordi, engineer of military roads, and ascertain if it was not possible to remedy this great inconvenience.

The engineer replied that it was feasible to provide a road for his Majesty directly from his barrack to the beach; but that in view of the great height of the cliff it would be necessary to moderate the rapidity of the descent by making the road zigzag. "Make it as you wish," said the Emperor, "only let it be ready for use in three days." The skilful engineer went to work, and in three days and three nights the road was constructed of stone, bound together with iron clamps; and the Emperor, charmed with so much diligence and ingenuity, had the name of Sordi placed on the list for the next distribution of the cross of the Legion of Honour, but, owing to the shameful negligence of some one, the name of this man of talent was overlooked. The port of Boulogne contained about seventeen hundred vessels, such as flat-boats, sloops, Turkish boats, gunboats, prairies, mortar-boats, etc.; and the entrance to the port was defended by an enormous chain, and by four forts, two on the right, and two on the left.

Fort Husoir, placed on the left, was armed with three formidable batteries ranged one above the other, the lower row bearing twenty-four pounders, the second and third, thirty-six pounders. On the right of this fort was the revolving bridge, and behind this bridge an old tower called Castle Croi, ornamented with batteries which were both handsome and effective. To the left, about a quarter of a league from Fort Musoir, was Fort La Creche, projecting boldly into the sea, constructed of cut stone, and crowned by a terrible battery; and finally, on the right of Fort La Creche, was the Fort en Bois, perfectly manned, and pierced by a large opening which was uncovered at low tide.

Upon the cliff to the left of the town, at nearly the same elevation as the other, was the camp of the left wing. Here was situated the barrack of Prince Joseph, at that time colonel of the Fourth Regiment of the line; this barrack was covered with thatch. Below the camp, at the foot of the cliff, the Emperor had a basin hollowed out, in which work a part of the troops were employed.

It was in this basin that one day a young soldier of the Guard, who had stuck in the mud up to his knees, tried with all his strength to pull out his wheelbarrow, which was even worse mired than himself; but he could not succeed, and covered with sweat, swore and stormed like an angry grenadier. By chance lifting his eyes, he suddenly perceived the Emperor, who was passing by the works on his way to visit his brother Joseph in the camp on the left. The soldier looked at him with a beseeching air and gesture, singing in a most sentimental tone, "Come, oh, come, to my aid." His Majesty could not help smiling, and made signs to the soldier to approach, which the poor fellow did, after extricating himself with great difficulty. "What is your regiment"

"Sire, the First of the Guard."

"How long have you been a soldier?"

"Since you have been Emperor, Sire."

"Indeed, that is not a long time! It is not long enough for me to make you an officer, is it? But conduct yourself well, and I will have you made sergeant-major. After that, the cross and epaulets on the first battlefield. Are you content?"

"Yes, Sire."

"Chief of Staff," continued the Emperor, addressing General Berthier, "take the name of this young man. You will give him three hundred *francs* to clean his pantaloons and repair his wheelbarrow." And his Majesty rode on in the midst of the acclamations of the soldiers.

At the inside extremity of the port, there was a wooden bridge which they called the Service bridge. The powder magazines were behind it, containing an immense amount of ammunition; and after nightfall no one was allowed to go upon this bridge without giving the countersign to the second sentinel, for the first always allowed him to pass. He was not allowed to pass back again, however; for if any person entering the bridge was ignorant of the countersign, or had happened to forget it, he was stopped by the second sentinel, and the first sentinel at the head of the bridge had express orders to pass his bayonet through the body of the rash man if he was unable to answer the questions of this last sentinel. These rigorous precautions were rendered necessary by the vicinity of these terrible powder magazines, which a single spark might blow up, and with it the town, the fleet, and the two camps.

At night the port was closed with the big chain I have mentioned, and the wharves were picketed by sentinels placed fifteen paces from each other. Each quarter of an hour they called, "Sentinels, look out!" And the soldiers of the marine, placed in the topsails, replied to this by, "All's well," pronounced in a drawling, mournful tone. Nothing could be more monotonous or depressing than this continual murmur, this lugubrious mingling of voices all in the same tone, especially as those making these cries endeavoured to make them as inspiring as possible.

Women not residing in Boulogne were prohibited from remaining there without a special permit from the minister of police. This measure had been judged necessary on account of the army; for otherwise each soldier perhaps would have brought a woman to Boulogne, and the disorder would have been indescribable. Strangers were admitted into the town with great difficulty.

In spite of all these precautions, spies from the English fleet each day penetrated into Boulogne. When they were discovered no quarter was given; and notwithstanding this, emissaries who had landed, no one knew where, came each evening to the theatre, and carried their imprudence so far as to write their opinion of the actors and actresses, whom they designated by name, and to post these writings on the walls of the theatre, thus defying the police. One day there were found on the shore two little boats covered with tarpaulin, which these gentry probably used in their clandestine excursions.

In June, 1804, eight Englishmen, perfectly well dressed, in white silk stockings, etc., were arrested, and on them was found sulphurated apparatus with which they had intended to burn the fleet. They were shot within an hour, without any form of trial.

There were also traitors in Boulogne. A schoolmaster, the secret agent of Lords Keith and Melville, was surprised one morning on the cliff above the camp of the right wing, making telegraphic signals with his arms; and being arrested almost in the act by the sentinels, he protested his innocence, and tried to turn the incident into a jest, but his papers were searched, and correspondence with the English found, which clearly proved his guilt. He was delivered to the council of war, and shot the next day.

One evening between eleven o'clock and midnight, a fire-ship, rigged like a French ship, flying French colours, and in every respect resembling a gunboat, advanced towards the line of battle and passed through. By unpardonable negligence the chain had not been stretched that evening. This fire-ship was followed by a second, which exploded, striking a sloop, which went down with it. This explosion gave the alarm to the whole fleet; and lights instantly shone in every direction, revealing the first fire-ship advancing between the jetties, a sight which was witnessed with inexpressible anxiety. Three or four pieces of wood connected by cables fortunately stopped her progress; but she blew up with such a shock that the glasses of all the windows in town were shattered, and a great number of the inhabitants, who for want of beds were sleeping upon tables, were thrown to the floor, and awakened by the fall without comprehending what had happened. In

Lucien Bonaparte

ten minutes everybody was stirring, as it was thought that the English were in the port; and there ensued such confusion, such a mingled tumult of noises and screams, that no one could make himself understood, until criers preceded by drums were sent through the town to reassure the inhabitants, and inform them that all danger was past.

The next day songs were composed on this nocturnal alarm, and were soon in every mouth.

Another alarm, but of an entirely different kind, upset all Boulogne in the autumn of 1804. About eight o'clock in the evening a chimney caught fire on the right of the port; and the light of this fire, shining through the masts of the flotilla, alarmed the commandant of a post on the opposite shore. At this time all the vessels had powder and ammunition on board; and the poor commandant, beside himself with terror, cried, "Boys, the fleet is on fire;" and immediately had the alarm beaten. The frightful news spread like lightning; and in less than half an hour more than sixty thousand men appeared upon the wharves, the tocsin was sounded in all the churches, the forts fired alarm guns, while drums and trumpets sounded along the streets, the whole making an infernal tumult.

The Emperor was at headquarters when this terrible cry, "The fleet is on fire," came to his ears. "It is impossible!" he immediately exclaimed, but, nevertheless, rushed out instantly.

On entering the town, what a frightful spectacle we beheld. Women in tears, holding their children in their arms, ran like lunatics, uttering cries of despair, while men abandoned their houses, carrying off whatever was most valuable, running against and knocking each other over in the darkness. On all sides was heard, "*Mauve qui peat;* we are going to be blown up, we are all lost;" and the maledictions, lamentations, blasphemies, were sufficient to make your hair stand on end.

The *aides-de-camp* of his Majesty and those of Marshal Soult galloped in every direction, forcing their way through the crowds, stopping the drummers, and asking them, "Why do you beat the alarm? Who has ordered you to beat the alarm?"

"We don't know," they replied; and the drums continued to beat, while the tumult kept on increasing, and the crowd rushed to the gates, struck by a terror which a moment's reflection would have dissipated. But, unfortunately, fear gives no time for reflection.

It is true, however, that a considerable number of inhabitants, less excitable than these I have described, remained quietly at home, well knowing that if the fleet had really been on fire, there would have been no time to give an alarm. These persons made every effort to quiet the excited crowd. Madame F——, the very pretty and very amiable wife of a clockmaker, was in her kitchen making preparations for supper, when a neighbour, thoroughly frightened, entered, and said to her, "Save yourself Madame; you have not a moment to lose!"

"What is the matter?"

"The fleet is on fire!"

"Ah-pshaw!"

"Fly then, Madame, fly! I tell you the fleet is on fire." And the neighbour took Madame F—— by the arm, and endeavoured to pull her along. Madame F—— held at the moment a frying-pan in which she was cooking some fritters. "Take care; you will make me burn my fritters," said she, laughing. And with a few half serious, half jesting words she reassured the poor fellow, who ended by laughing at himself.

At last the tumult was appeased, and to this great fright a profound calm succeeded. No explosion had been heard; and they saw that it must have been a false alarm, so each returned home, thinking no longer of the fire, but agitated by another fear. The robbers may have profited by the absence of the inhabitants to pillage the houses, but as luck would have it no mischance of this kind had taken place.

The next day the poor commandant who had so inopportunely taken and given the alarm was brought before the council of war. He was guilty of no intentional wrong; but the law was explicit, and he was condemned to death. His judges, however, recommended him to the mercy of the Emperor, who pardoned him.

Chapter 17

Many of the brave soldiers who composed the army of Boulogne had earned the cross (of the Legion of Honour) in these last campaigns, and his Majesty desired that this distribution should be made an impressive occasion, which should long be remembered. He chose the day after his fete, Aug. 16, 1804. Never has there been in the past, nor can there be in the future, a more imposing spectacle.

At six o'clock in the morning, more than eighty thousand men left the four camps,—at their head drums beating and bands playing,—and advanced by divisions towards the "Hubertmill" field, which was on the cliff beyond the camp of the right wing. On this plain an immense platform had been erected, about fifteen feet above the ground, and with its back toward the sea. It was reached by three flights of richly carpeted steps, situated in the middle and on each side. From the stage thus formed, about forty feet square, rose three other platforms, the central one bearing the imperial armchair, decorated with trophies and banners, while that on the left held seats for the brothers of the Emperor, and for the grand dignitaries, and that on the right bore a tripod of antique form, surmounted by a helmet (the helmet of Duguesclin, I think), covered with crosses and ribbons. By the side of the tripod had been placed a seat for the arch-chancellor.

About three hundred steps from the throne, the land rose in a slight and almost circular ascent; and on this ascent the troops were arranged as in an amphitheatre. To the right of the throne, on an eminence, were placed sixty or eighty tents made of naval flags; these tents were intended for the ladies of the city, and made a charming picture, but they were so far from the throne that the spectators who filled them were obliged to use glasses. Between these tents and the throne a part of the Imperial Guard was ranged in line of battle.

The weather was perfect; there was not a cloud in the sky; the

English cruisers had disappeared; and on the sea could be seen only our line of vessels handsomely decorated with flags.

At ten o'clock in the morning, a discharge of artillery announced the departure of the Emperor; and his Majesty left his barrack, surrounded by more than eighty generals and two hundred aides-decamp, all his household following him. The Emperor was dressed in the uniform of the colonel-general of the infantry of the guard. He rode at a gallop to the foot of the throne, in the midst of universal acclamations and the most deafening uproar made by drums, trumpets, and cannon, beating, blowing, and roaring all together.

His Majesty mounted the throne, followed by his brothers and the grand dignitaries; and when he was seated each one took his designated place, and the distribution of the crosses began in the following manner: An *aide-de-camp* of the Emperor called by name the soldiers to be honoured, who one by one stopped at the foot of the throne, bowed, and mounted the steps on the right. There they were received by the arch-chancellor, who delivered to them their commissions; and two pages, placed between the Emperor and the tripod, took the decoration from the helmet of Duguesclin, and handed it to his Majesty, who fastened it himself on the breast of the brave fellow. Instantly more than eight hundred drums beat a tattoo; and when the soldier thus decorated descended from the throne by the steps on the left, as he passed before the brilliant staff of the Emperor a burst of music from more than twelve hundred musicians signalled the return to his company of the Knight of the Legion of Honour. It is needless to say that the cry of '*Vive l'Empereur*' was repeated twice at each decoration.

The distribution began at ten o'clock, and ended about three. Then, according to orders borne by the aides-decamp to the divisions, a volley of artillery was heard, and eighty thousand men advanced in close columns to within twenty or thirty steps of the throne. The most profound silence succeeded the noise of drums; and, the Emperor having given his orders, the troops executed manoeuvres for about an hour, at the end of which each division defiled before the throne as they returned to the camp. Each chief, on passing, saluted by lowering the point of his sword. Specially noticeable among them was Prince Joseph, newly appointed colonel of the Fourth Regiment of the line, who made his brother a salute more graceful than military. The Emperor frowned slightly at the somewhat critical remarks which his old companions in arms seemed inclined to make on this subject; but except for this slight cloud, the countenance of his Majesty was never more radiant.

Just as the troops were filing off, the wind, which for two or three hours had been blowing violently, became a perfect gale, and an orderly officer came in haste to inform his Majesty that four or five gunboats had just been driven ashore. The Emperor at once left the plain at a gallop, followed by some of the marshals, and took his position on the shore until the crews of the gunboats were saved, and the Emperor then returned to the Pont des Briques.

This immense army could not regain its quarters before eight o'clock in the evening. The next day the camp of the left wing gave a military fete, at which the Emperor was present.

From early in the morning, launches mounted on wheels ran at full speed through the streets of the camp, driven by a favourable wind. Officers amused themselves riding after them at a gallop, and rarely overtaking them. This exercise lasted an hour or two; but, the wind having changed, the launches upset, amid shouts of laughter.

This was followed by a horseback race, the prize being twelve hundred *francs*. A lieutenant of dragoons, very popular in his company, asked as a favour to be allowed to compete; but the haughty council of superior officers refused to admit him, under the pretext that his rank was not sufficiently high, but, in reality, because he had the reputation of being a splendid horseman. Stung to the quick by this unjust refusal, the lieutenant of dragoons applied to the Emperor, who gave him permission to race with the others, after having learned that this brave officer supported by his own exertions a numerous family, and that his conduct was irreproachable.

At a given signal the races began. The lieutenant of dragoons soon passed his antagonists, and had almost reached the goal, when, by an unfortunate mischance, a little poodle ran between the legs of his horse, and threw him down. An *aide-de-camp* who came immediately after was proclaimed victor. The lieutenant picked himself up as well as he could, and was preparing, very sadly, to retire, somewhat consoled by the signs of interest which the spectators manifested, when the Emperor summoned him, and said, "You deserve the prize, and you shall have it; I make you captain." And addressing himself to the grand marshal of the palace, "You will pay twelve hundred *francs* to the Captain" (the name does not occur to me), while all cried, "*Vive l'Empereur*," and congratulated the new captain on his lucky fall.

In the evening there were fireworks, which could be seen from the coast of England. Thirty thousand soldiers executed all sorts of manoeuvres, firing sky-rockets from their guns. The crowning piece, which represented the arms of the Empire, was so fine that for five minutes Boulogne, the country, and all the coast, were lighted up as if it were broad daylight.

A few days after these fetes, as the Emperor was passing from one camp to the other, a sailor who was watching for him in order to hand him a petition was obliged, as the rain was falling in torrents, and he was afraid of spoiling the sheet of paper, to place himself under shelter in an isolated barrack on the shore, used to store rigging. He had been waiting a long time, and was wet to the skin, when he saw the Emperor coming from the camp of the left wing at a gallop. Just as his Majesty, still galloping, was about to pass before the barrack, the brave sailor, who was on the lookout, sprang suddenly from his hiding place, and threw himself before the Emperor, holding out his petition in the attitude of a fencing-master defending himself. The Emperor's horse, startled by this sudden apparition, stopped short; and his Majesty, taken by surprise, gave the sailor a disapproving glance, and passed on without taking the petition which was offered him in so unusual a manner.

It was on this day, I think, that Monsieur Decres, minister of the navy, had the misfortune to fall into the water, to the very great amusement of his Majesty. To enable the Emperor to pass from the quay to a gunboat, there had been a single plank thrown from the boat to the quay. Napoleon passed, or rather leaped, over this light bridge, and was received on board in the arms of a soldier of the guard; but M. Decres, more stout, and less active than the Emperor, advanced carefully over the plank that he found to his horror was bending under his feet, until just as he arrived in the middle, the weight of his body broke the plank, and the minister of the navy was precipitated into the water, midway between the quay and the boat. His Majesty turned at the noise that M. Decres made in falling, and leaning over the side of the boat, exclaimed, "What! Is that our minister of the navy who has allowed himself to fall in the water? Is it possible it can be he?" The Emperor during this speech laughed most uproariously. Meanwhile, two or three sailors were engaged in getting M. Decres out of his embarrassing position. He was with much difficulty hoisted on the sloop, in a sad state, as may be believed, vomiting water through his nose, mouth, and ears, and thoroughly ashamed of his accident, which the Emperor's jokes contributed to render still more exasperating.

Towards the end of our stay the generals gave a magnificent ball to the ladies of the city, at which the Emperor was present.

For this purpose a temporary hall had been erected, which was tastefully decorated with garlands, flags, and trophies.

General Bertrand was appointed master of ceremonies by his colleagues; and General Bisson. I was put in charge of the buffet, which employment suited General Bisson perfectly, for he was the greatest glutton in camp, and his enormous stomach interfered greatly with his walking. He drank not less than six or seven bottles of wine at dinner, and never alone; for it was a punishment to him not to talk while eating, consequently he usually invited his *aides-de-camp*, whom, through malice no doubt, he chose always from among the most delicate and abstemious in the army. The buffet was worthy of the one who had it in charge.

The orchestra was composed of musicians from twenty regiments, who played in turn. But on the opening of the ball the entire orchestra executed a triumphal march, during which the *aides-de-Camp*, most elegantly attired, received the ladies invited, and presented them with bouquets.

In order to be admitted to this ball, it was necessary to have at least the rank of commandant. It is, impossible to give an idea of the scene presented by this multitude of uniforms, each vying in brilliancy with the other. The fifty or sixty generals who gave the ball had ordered from Paris magnificently embroidered uniforms, and the group they formed around his Majesty as he entered glittered with gold and diamonds. The Emperor remained an hour at this fete, and danced the Boulanyere with Madame Bertrand. He wore the uniform of colonel-general of the cavalry of the guard.

The wife of Marshal Soult was queen of the ball. She wore a black velvet dress besprinkled with the kind of diamonds called rhinestones.

At midnight a splendid supper was served, the preparation of which General Bisson had superintended, which is equivalent to saying that nothing was wanting thereto.

The ladies of Boulogne, who had never attended such a fete, were filled with amazement, and when supper was served advised each other to fill up their reticules with dainties and sweets. They would have carried away, I think, the hall, with the musicians and dancers; and for more than a month this ball was the only subject of their conversation.

About this time his Majesty was riding on horseback near his barracks, when a pretty young girl of fifteen or sixteen, dressed in white, her face bathed in tears, threw herself on her knees in his path. The Emperor immediately alighted from his horse, and assisted her to rise, asking most compassionately what he could do for her. The poor girl had come to entreat the pardon of her father, a storekeeper in the commissary department, who had been condemned to the galleys for grave crimes. His Majesty could not resist the many charms of the youthful suppliant, and the pardon was granted.

Chapter 18

At Boulogne, as everywhere else, the Emperor well knew how to win all hearts by his moderation, his justice, and the generous grace with which he acknowledged the least service. All the inhabitants of Boulogne, even all the peasants of the suburbs, would have died for him, and the smallest particulars relating to him were constantly repeated. One day, however, his conduct gave rise to serious complaints, and he was unanimously blamed; for his injustice was the cause of a terrible tragedy. I will now relate this sad event, an authentic account of which I have never seen in print.

One morning, as he mounted his horse, the Emperor announced that he would that day review the naval forces, and gave orders that the boats which occupied the line of defence should leave their position, as he intended to hold the review in the open sea. He set out with Roustan for his morning ride, and expressed a wish that all should be ready on his return, the hour of which he designated. Every one knew that the slightest wish of the Emperor was law; and the order was transmitted, during his absence, to Admiral Bruix, who replied with imperturbable *'sang froid'*, that he much regretted it, but the review would not take place that day, and in consequence no boat stirred.

On his return from his ride, the Emperor asked if everything was ready, and the admiral's answer was reported to him. Astonished by its tone, so different from what he was accustomed to, he had it repeated to him twice, and then, with a violent stamp of his foot, ordered the admiral to be summoned. He obeyed instantly; but the Emperor, thinking he did not come quickly enough, met him half-way from his barracks. The staff followed his Majesty, and placed themselves silently around him, while his eyes shot lightning.

"Admiral Bruix," said the Emperor in a tone showing great excitement, "why have you not obeyed my orders?"

"Sire," responded Bruix with respectful firmness, "a terrible storm is gathering. Your Majesty can see this as well as I; are you willing to uselessly risk the lives of so many brave men?" In truth, the heaviness of the atmosphere, and the low rumbling which could be heard in the distance, justified only too well the admiral's fears. "Monsieur," replied the Emperor, more and more irritated, "I gave the orders; once again, why have you not executed them? The consequences concern me alone. Obey!"

"Sire, I will not obey!"

"Monsieur, you are insolent!" And the Emperor, who still held his riding-whip in his hand, advanced on the admiral, making a threatening gesture. Admiral Bruix retreated a step, and placed his hand on the hilt of his sword: "Sire," said he, growing pale, "take care!" All those present were paralyzed with terror. The Emperor remained for some time immovable, with his hand raised, and his eyes fixed on the admiral, who still maintained his defiant attitude. At last the Emperor threw his whip on the ground. Admiral Bruix relaxed his hold on his sword, and, with uncovered head, awaited in silence the result of this terrible scene.

"Rear-Admiral Magon!" said the Emperor, "you will see that the orders which I have given are executed instantly. As for you, sir," continued he, turning to Admiral Bruix, "you will leave Boulogne within twenty-four hours, and retire to Holland. Go!" His Majesty returned at once to headquarters; some of the officers, only a small number, however, pressed in parting the hand that the admiral held out to them.

Rear-Admiral Magon immediately ordered the fatal movement commanded by the Emperor; but hardly had the first dispositions been made when the sea became frightful to behold, the sky, covered with black clouds, was furrowed with lightning, the thunder roared incessantly, and the wind increased to a gale. In fact, what Admiral Bruix had foreseen occurred; a frightful tempest scattered the boats in every direction, and rendered their condition desperate. The Emperor, anxious and uneasy, with lowered head and crossed arms, was striding up and down the shore, when suddenly terrible cries were heard. More than twenty gunboats, filled with soldiers and sailors, had just been driven on the shore; and the poor unfortunates who manned them, struggling against furious waves, were imploring help which none could venture to render. The Emperor was deeply touched by this sight, while his heart was torn by the lamentations of an immense crowd which the tempest had collected on the shore and the adjoining cliffs. He beheld his generals and officers stand in shuddering horror around him, and wishing to set an example of self-sacrifice, in spite of all efforts made to restrain him, threw himself into a lifeboat, saying, "Let me alone; let me alone! They must be gotten out of there." In an instant the boat filled with water, the waves dashed over it, and the Emperor was submerged, one wave stronger than the others threw his Majesty on the shore, and his hat was swept off.

Electrified by such courage, officers, soldiers, sailors, and citizens now began to lend their aid, some swimming, others in boats; but, alas! they succeeded in saving—only a very small number of the unfortunate men who composed the crews of the gunboats, and the next day the sea cast upon the shore more than two hundred men, and with them the hat of the conqueror of Marengo.

The next was a day of mourning and of grief, both in Boulogne and the camp. The inhabitants and soldiers covered the beach, searching anxiously among the bodies which the waves incessantly cast upon the shore; and the Emperor groaned over this terrible calamity, which in his inmost heart he could not fail to attribute to his own obstinacy. By his orders agents entrusted with gold went through the city and camp, stopping the murmurs which were ready to break forth.

That day I saw a drummer, who had been among the crew of the shipwrecked vessels, washed upon the shore upon his drum, which lie had used as a raft. The poor fellow had his thigh broken, and had remained more than twenty hours in that horrible condition.

In order to complete in this place my recollections of the camp of Boulogne, I will relate the following, which did not take place, however, until the month of August, 1805, after the return of the Emperor from his journey to Italy, where he had been crowned.

Soldiers and sailors were burning with impatience to embark for England, but the moment so ardently desired was still delayed. Every evening they said to themselves, "Tomorrow there will be a good wind, there will also be a fog, and we shall start," and lay down with that hope, but arose each day to find either an unclouded sky or rain.

One evening, however, when a favourable wind was blowing, I heard two sailors conversing together on the wharf, and making conjectures as to the future. "The Emperor would do well to start tomorrow morning," said one; "he will never have better weather, and there will surely be a fog."

"Bah!" said the other, "only he does not think so. We have now waited more than fifteen days, and the fleet has not budged; however, all the ammunition is on board, and with one blast of the whistle we can put to sea."

The night sentinels came on, and the conversation of the old seawolves stopped there; but I soon had to acknowledge that their nautical experience had not deceived them. In fact, by three o'clock in the morning, a light fog was spread over the sea, which was somewhat stormy, the wind of the evening before began to, blow again, and at daylight the fog was so thick as to conceal the fleet from the English, while the most profound silence reigned everywhere. No hostile sails had been signalled through the night, and, as the sailors had predicted, everything favoured the descent.

At five o'clock in the morning, signals were made from the semaphore; and in the twinkling of an eye all the sailors were in motion, and the port resounded with cries of joy, for the order to depart had just been received. While the sails were being hoisted, the long roll was beaten in the four camps, and the order was given for the entire army to take arms; and they marched rapidly into the town, hardly believing what they had just heard. "We are really going to start," said all the soldiers; "we are actually going to say a few words to those Englishmen," and the joy which animated them burst forth in acclamations, which were silenced by a roll of the drums. The embarkation then took place amid profound silence, and in such perfect order that I can hardly give an idea of it. At seven o'clock two hundred thousand soldiers were on board the fleet; and when a little after midday this fine army was on the point of starting amidst the adieus and good wishes of the whole city, assembled upon the walls and upon the surrounding cliffs, and at the very moment when all the soldiers standing with uncovered heads were about to bid farewell to the soil of France, crying, "*Vive l'Empereur!*" a message arrived from the imperial barrack, ordering the troops to disembark, and return to camp. A telegraphic dispatch just then received by his Majesty had made it necessary that he should move his troops in another direction; and the soldiers returned sadly to their quarters, some expressing in a loud tone, and in a very energetic manner, the disappointment which this species of mystification caused them.

They had always regarded the success of the enterprise against England as assured, and to find themselves stopped on the eve of departure was, in their eyes, the greatest misfortune which could happen to them.

When order had again been restored, the Emperor repaired to the camp of the right wing, and made a proclamation to the troops, which was sent into the other camps, and posted everywhere. This was very nearly the tenor of it: "Brave soldiers of the camp of Boulogne! you will not go to England. English gold has seduced the Emperor of Austria, who has just declared war against France. His army has passed the line which he should have respected, and Bavaria is invaded. Soldiers! new laurels await you beyond the Rhine. Let us hasten to defeat once more enemies whom you have already conquered." This proclamation called forth unanimous acclamations of joy, and every face brightened, for it mattered little to these intrepid men whether they were to be led against Austria or England; they simply thirsted for the fray, and now that war had been declared, every desire was gratified.

Thus vanished all those grand projects of descent upon England, which had been so long matured, so wisely planned. There is no doubt now that with favourable weather and perseverance the enterprise would have been crowned with the greatest success; but this was not to be.

A few regiments remained at Boulogne; and while their brethren crushed the Austrians, they erected upon the seashore a column destined to recall for all time the memory of Napoleon and his immortal army.

Immediately after the proclamation of which I have just spoken, his Majesty gave orders that all should prepare for immediate departure; and the grand marshal of the palace was charged to audit and pay all the expenses which the Emperor had made, or which he had ordered to be made, during his several visits, not without cautioning him, according to custom, to be careful not to pay for too much of anything, nor too high a price. I believe that I have already stated that the Emperor was extremely economical in everything which concerned him personally, and that he was afraid of spending twenty *francs* unless for some directly useful purpose. Among many other accounts to be audited, the grand marshal of the palace received that of Sordi, engineer of military roads, whom he had ordered to decorate his Majesty's barrack, both inside and out. The account amounted to fifty thousand *francs*. The grand marshal exclaimed aloud at this frightful sum. He was not willing to approve the account of Sordi, and sent it back to him, saying that he could not authorize the payment without first receiving the orders of the Emperor. The engineer assured the grand marshal that he had overcharged nothing, and that he had closely followed his instructions, and added, that being the case, it was impossible for him to make the slightest reduction. The next day Sordi received instructions to attend his Majesty. The Emperor was in his barrack, which was the subject under discussion, and spread out before him was, not the account of the engineer, but a map, upon which he was tracing the intended march of his army. Sordi came, and was admitted by General

Caffarelli. The half-open door permitted the general, as well as myself, to hear the conversation which followed. "Monsieur," said his Majesty, "you have spent far too much money in decorating this miserable barrack. Yes; certainly far too much. Fifty thousand *francs*! Just think of it, *monsieur*! That is frightful; I will not pay you!" The engineer, silenced by this abrupt entrance upon business, did not at first know how to reply. Happily the Emperor, again casting his eyes on the map which lay unrolled before him, gave him time to recover himself; and he replied, "Sire, the golden clouds which ornament this ceiling" (for all this took place in the council-chamber), "and which surround the guardian star of your Majesty, cost twenty thousand *francs* in truth; but if I had consulted the hearts of your subjects, the imperial eagle which is again about to strike with a thunderbolt the enemies of France and of your throne, would have spread its wings amid the rarest diamonds."

"That is very good," replied the Emperor, laughing, "very good; but I will not have you paid at present, and since you tell me that this eagle which costs so dear will strike the Austrians with a thunderbolt, wait until he has done so, and I will then pay your account in *rix* dollars of the Emperor of Germany, and the gold *frederics* of the King of Prussia." His Majesty, resuming his compass, began to move his armies upon the map; and truth to tell, the account of the engineer was not paid until after the battle of Austerlitz, and then, as the Emperor had said, in *rix* dollars and *frederics*.

About the end of July (1804), the Emperor left Boulogne in order to make a tour through Belgium before rejoining the Empress, who had gone direct to Aix-la-Chapelle. Everywhere on this tour he was welcomed, not only with the honours reserved for crowned heads, but with hearty acclamations, addressed to him personally rather than to his official position. I will say nothing of the fetes which were given in his honour during this journey, nor of the remarkable things which occurred. Descriptions of these can easily be found elsewhere; and it is my purpose to relate only what came peculiarly under my own observation, or at least details not known to the general public. Let it suffice, then, to say that our journey through Arras, Valenciennes, Mons, Brussels, etc., resembled a triumphal progress. At the gate of each town the municipal council presented to his Majesty the wine of honour and the keys of the place. We stopped a few days at Lacken; and being only five leagues from Alost, a little town where my relatives lived, I requested the Emperor's permission to leave him for twenty-four hours, and it was granted, though reluctantly. Alost, like the remainder of Belgium at this time, professed the greatest attachment for the Emperor, and consequently I had hardly a moment to myself. I visited at the house of Monsieur D——, one of my friends, whose family had long held positions of honour in the government of Belgium. There I think all the town must have come to meet me; but I was not vain enough to appropriate to myself all the honour of this attention, for each one who came was anxious to learn even the most insignificant details concerning the great man near whom I was placed. On this account I was extraordinarily feted, and my twenty-four hours passed only too quickly. On my return, his Majesty deigned to ask innumerable questions regarding the town of Alost and its inhabitants, and as to what was thought there of his government and of himself. I was glad to be able to answer without flattery, that he was adored. He appeared gratified, and spoke to me most kindly of my family and of my own small interests.

We left the next day for Lacken, and passed through Alost; and had I known this the evening before, I might perhaps have rested a few hours longer. However, the Emperor found so much difficulty in granting me even one day, that I would not probably have dared to lose more, even had I known that the household was to pass by this town.

The Emperor was much pleased with Lacken; he ordered considerable repairs and improvements to be made there, and the palace, owing to this preference, became a charming place of sojourn.

This journey of their Majesties lasted nearly three months; and we did not return to Paris, or rather to Saint-Cloud, until November. The Emperor received at Cologne and at Coblentz the visits of several German princes and princesses; but as I know only from hearsay what passed in these interviews, I shall not undertake to describe them.

Chapter 19

Nothing is too trivial to narrate concerning great men; for posterity shows itself eager to learn even the most insignificant details concerning their manner of life, their tastes, their slightest peculiarities. When I attended the theatre, whether in my short intervals of leisure or in the suite of his Majesty, I remarked how keenly the spectators enjoyed the presentation on the stage, of some grand historic personage; whose costume, gestures, bearing, even his infirmities and faults, were delineated exactly as they have been transmitted to us by contemporaries. I myself always took the greatest pleasure in seeing these living portraits of celebrated men, and well remember that on no occasion did I ever so thoroughly enjoy the stage as when I saw for the first time the charming piece of *The Two Pages*. Fleury in the role of Frederick the Great reproduced so perfectly the slow walk, the dry tones, the sudden movements, and even the short-sightedness of this monarch, that as soon as he appeared on the stage the whole house burst into applause. It was, in the opinion of persons sufficiently well informed to judge, a most perfect and faithful presentation; and though for my own part, I was not able to say whether the resemblance was perfect or not, I felt that it must be. Michelot, whom I have since seen in the same role, gave me no less pleasure than his predecessor; and it is evident that both these talented actors must have studied the subject deeply, to have learned so thoroughly and depicted so faithfully the characteristics of their model.

I must confess a feeling of pride in the thought that these memoirs may perhaps excite in my readers some of the same pleasurable emotions which I have here attempted to describe; and that perhaps in a future, which will inevitably come, though far distant now perhaps, the artist who will attempt to restore to life, and hold up to the view of the world, the greatest man of this age, will be compelled, in order to give a faithful delineation, to take for his model the portrait which I, better than any one else, have been able to draw from fife. I think that no one has done this as yet; certainly not so much in detail.

On his return from Egypt the Emperor was very thin and sallow, his skin was copper-coloured, his eyes sunken, and his figure, though perfect, also very thin. The likeness is excellent in the portrait which Horace Vernet drew in his picture called "A Review of the First Consul on the Place du Carrousel." His forehead was very high, and bare; his hair thin, especially on the temples, but very fine and soft, and a rich brown colour; his eyes deep blue, expressing in an almost incredible manner the various emotions by which he was affected, sometimes extremely gentle and caressing, sometimes severe, and even inflexible. His mouth was very fine, his lips straight and rather firmly closed, particularly when irritated. His teeth, without being very regular, were very white and sound, and he never suffered from them. His nose of Grecian shape, was well formed, and his sense of smell perfect. His whole frame was handsomely proportioned, though at this time his extreme leanness prevented the beauty of his features being especially noticed, and had an injurious effect on his whole physiognomy.

It would be necessary to describe his features separately, one by one, in order to form a correct idea of the whole, and comprehend the perfect regularity and beauty of each. His head was very large, being twenty-two inches in circumference; it way a little longer than broad, consequently a little flattened on the temples; it was so extremely sensitive, that I had his hats padded, and took the trouble to wear them several days in my room to break them. His ears were small, perfectly formed, and well set. The Emperor's feet were also very tender; and I had his shoes broken by a boy of the wardrobe, called Joseph, who wore exactly the same size as the Emperor.

His height was five feet, two inches, three lines. He had a rather short neck, sloping shoulders, broad chest, almost free from hairs, well shaped leg and thigh, a small foot, and well formed fingers, entirely free from enlargements or abrasions; his arms were finely moulded, and well hung to his body; his hands were beautiful, and the nails did not detract from their beauty. He took the greatest care of them, as in fact of his whole person, without foppishness, however. He often bit his nails slightly, which was a sign of impatience or preoccupation.

Later on he grew much stouter, but without losing any of the beauty of his figure; on the contrary, he was handsomer under the Empire than under the Consulate; his skin had become very white, and his expression animated.

The Emperor, during his moments, or rather his long hours, of labour and of meditation, was subject to a peculiar spasmodic movement, which seemed to be a nervous affection, and which clung to him all his life. It consisted in raising his right shoulder frequently and rapidly; and persons who were not acquainted with this habit sometimes interpreted this as a gesture of disapprobation and dissatisfaction, and inquired with anxiety in what way they could have offended him. He, however, was not at all affected by it, and repeated the same movement again and again without being conscious of it.

One most remarkable peculiarity was that the Emperor never felt his heart beat. He mentioned this often to M. Corvisart, as well as to me; and more than once he made us pass our hands over his breast, in order to prove this singular exception. Never did we feel the slightest pulsation.[1]

The Emperor ate very fast, and hardly spent a dozen minutes at the table. When he had finished he arose, and passed into the family saloon; but the Empress Josephine remained, and made a sign to the guests to do the same. Sometimes, however, she followed his Majesty; and then, no doubt, the ladies of the palace indemnified themselves in their apartments, where whatever they wished was served them.

One day when Prince Eugene rose from the table immediately after the Emperor, the latter, turning to him, said, "But you have not had time to dine, Eugene."

"Pardon me," replied the Prince, "I dined in advance!" The other guests doubtless found that this was not a useless precaution. It was before the Consulate that things happened thus; for afterwards the Emperor, even when he was as yet only First Consul, dined *tete-a-tete* with the Empress, except when he invited some of the ladies of the household, sometimes one, sometimes another, all of whom appreciated highly this mark of favour. At this time there was already a court.

Most frequently the Emperor breakfasted alone, on a little mahogany candle-stand with no cover, which meal, even shorter than the other, lasted only eight or ten minutes.

I will mention, later on, the bad effects which the habit of eating too quickly often produced on the Emperor's health. Besides this, and due in a great measure to his haste, the Emperor lacked much of eating decently; and always preferred his fingers to a fork or spoon. Much care was taken to place within his reach the dish he preferred, which he drew toward him in the manner I have just described, and dipped his bread in the sauce or gravy it contained, which did not, however,

---

1. Another peculiarity was that his pulse was only forty to the minute.

prevent the dish being handed round, and those eating from it who could; and there were few guests who could not.

I have seen some who even appeared to consider this singular act of courage a means of making their court. I can easily understand also that with many their admiration for his Majesty silenced all repugnance, for the same reason that we do not scruple to eat from the plate, or drink from the glass, of a person whom we love, even though it might be considered doubtful on the score of refinement; this is never noticed because love is blind. The dish which the Emperor preferred was the kind of fried chicken to which this preference of the conqueror of Italy has given the name of *poulet a la Marengo*. He also ate with relish beans, lentils, cutlets, roast mutton, and roast chicken. The simplest dishes were those he liked best, but he was fastidious in the article of bread. It is not true, as reported, that he made an immoderate use of coffee, for he only took half a cup after breakfast, and another after dinner; though it sometimes happened when he was much preoccupied that he would take, without noticing it, two cups in succession, though coffee taken in this quantity always excited him and kept him from sleeping.

It also happened frequently that he took it cold, or without sugar, or with too much sugar. To avoid all which mischances, the Empress Josephine made it her duty to pour out the Emperor's coffee herself; and the Empress Marie Louise also adopted the same custom. When the Emperor had risen from the table and entered the little saloon, a page followed him, carrying on a silver gilt waiter a coffee-pot, sugar-dish and cup. Her Majesty the Empress poured out the coffee, put sugar in it, tried a few drops of it, and offered it to the Emperor.

The Emperor drank only Chambertin wine, and rarely without water; for he had no fondness for wine, and was a poor judge of it. This recalls that one day at the camp of Boulogne, having invited several officers to his table, his Majesty had wine poured for Marshal Augereau, and asked him with an air of satisfaction how he liked it. The Marshal tasted it, sipped it critically, and finally replied, "There is better," in a tone which was unmistakable. The Emperor, who had expected a different reply, smiled, as did all the guests, at the Marshal's candour.

Every one has heard it said that his Majesty used great precautions against being poisoned, which statement must be placed beside that concerning the cuirass proof against bullet and dagger. On the contrary, the Emperor carried his want of precaution only too far. His breakfast was brought every day into an antechamber open to all to whom had been granted a private audience, and who sometimes waited there for several hours, and his Majesty's breakfast also waited a long time. The dishes were kept as warm as possible until he came out of his cabinet, and took his seat at the table. Their Majesties' dinner was carried from the kitchen to the upper rooms in covered, hampers, and there was every opportunity of introducing poison; but in spite of all this, never did such an idea enter the minds of the people in his service, whose devotion and fidelity to the Emperor, even including the very humblest, surpassed any idea I could convey.

The habit of eating rapidly sometimes caused his Majesty violent pains in his stomach, which ended almost always in a fit of vomiting.

One day the valet on duty came in great haste to tell me that the Emperor desired my presence immediately. His dinner had caused indigestion, and he was suffering greatly. I hurried to his Majesty's room, and found him stretched at full length on the rug, which was a habit of the Emperor when he felt unwell. The Empress Josephine was seated by his side, with the sick man's head on her lap, while he groaned or stormed alternately, or did both at once: for the Emperor bore this kind of misfortune with less composure than a thousand graver mischances which the life of a soldier carries with it; and the hero of Arcola, whose life had been endangered in a hundred battles, and elsewhere also, without lessening his fortitude, showed himself unequal to the endurance of the slightest pain. Her Majesty the Empress consoled and encouraged him as best she could; and she, who was so courageous herself in enduring those headaches which, on account of their excessive violence, were a genuine disease, would, had it been possible, have taken on herself most willingly the ailment of her husband, from which she suffered almost as much as he did, in witnessing his sufferings. "Constant," said she, as I entered, "come quick; the Emperor needs you; make him some tea, and do not go out till he is better." His Majesty had scarcely taken three cups before the pain decreased, while she continued to hold his head on her knees, pressing his brow with her white, plump hands, and also rubbing his breast. "You feel better, do you not? Would you like to lie down a little while? I will stay by your bed with Constant." This tenderness was indeed touching, especially in one occupying so elevated a rank.

My intimate service often gave me the opportunity of enjoying this picture of domestic felicity. While I am on the subject of the Emperor's ailments, I will say a few words concerning the most serious which he endured, with the exception of that which caused his death.

At the siege of Toulon, in 1793, the Emperor being then only colonel of artillery, a cannoneer was killed at his gun; and Colonel

Bonaparte picked up the rammer and rammed home the charge several times. The unfortunate artilleryman had an itch of the most malignant kind, which the Emperor caught, and of which he was cured only after many years; and the doctors thought that his sallow complexion and extreme leanness, which lasted so long a time, resulted from this disease being improperly treated. At the Tuileries he took sulphur baths, and wore for some time a blister plaster, having suffered thus long because, as he said, he had not time to take care of himself. Corvisart warmly insisted on a *cautery*; but the Emperor, who wished to preserve unimpaired the shapeliness of his arm, would not agree to this remedy.

It was at this same siege that he was promoted from the rank of chief of battalion to that of colonel in consequence of a brilliant affair with the English, in which he received a bayonet wound in the left thigh, the scar of which he often showed me. The wound in the foot which he received at the battle of Ratisbonne left no trace; and yet, when the Emperor received it, the whole army became alarmed.

We were about twelve hundred yards from Ratisbonne, when the Emperor, seeing the Austrians fleeing on all sides, thought the combat was over. His dinner had been brought in a hamper to a place which the Emperor had designated; and as he was walking towards it, he turned to Marshal Berthier, and exclaimed, "I am wounded!" The shock was so great that the Emperor fell in a sitting posture, a bullet having, in fact, struck his heel. From the size of this ball it was apparent that it had been fired by a Tyrolean rifleman, whose weapon easily carried the distance we were from the town. It can well be understood that such an event troubled and frightened the whole staff.

An *aide-de-camp* summoned me; and when I arrived I found Dr. Yvan cutting his Majesty's boot, and assisted him in dressing the wound. Although the pain was still quite severe, the Emperor was not willing to take time to put on his boot again; and in order to turn the enemy, and reassure the army as to his condition, he mounted his horse, and galloped along the line accompanied by his whole staff. That day, as may be believed, no one delayed to take breakfast, but all dined at Ratisbonne.

His Majesty showed an invincible repugnance to all medicine; and when he used any, which was very rarely, it was chicken broth, chicory, or cream of tartar.

Corvisart recommended him to refuse every drink which had a bitter or disagreeable taste, which he did, I believe, in the fear that an attempt might be made to poison him.

At whatever hour the Emperor had retired, I entered his room at seven or eight o'clock in the morning; and I have already said that his first questions invariably were as to the hour and the kind of weather. Sometimes he complained to me of looking badly; and if this was true, I agreed with him, and if it were not, I told him the truth. In this case he pulled my ears, and called me, laughing, *"grosse bete,"* and asked for a mirror, sometimes saying he was trying to fool me and that he was very well. He read the daily papers, asked the names of the people in the waiting-room, named those he wished to see, and conversed with each one. When Corvisart came, he entered without waiting for orders; and the Emperor took pleasure in teasing him by speaking of medicine, which he said was only a conjectural art, that the doctors were charlatans, and cited instances in proof of it, especially in his own experience, the doctor never yielding a point when he thought he was right. During these conversations, the Emperor shaved himself; for I had prevailed on him to take this duty on himself, often forgetting that he had shaved only one side of his face, and when I called his attention to this, he laughed, and finished his work. Yvan, doctor-in-ordinary, as well as Corvisart, came in for his share in the criticisms and attacks on his profession; and these discussions were extremely amusing. The Emperor was very gay and talkative at such times, and I believe, when he had at hand no examples to cite in support of his theories, did not scruple to invent them; consequently these gentlemen did not always rely upon his statements. One day his Majesty pulled the ears of one of his physicians (Halle, I believe). The doctor abruptly drew himself away, crying, "Sire, you hurt me." Perhaps this speech was tinged with some irritation, and perhaps, also, the doctor was right. However that may be, his ears were never in danger again.

Sometimes before beginning my labours, his Majesty questioned me as to what I had done the evening before, asked me if I had dined in the city, and with whom, if I had enjoyed myself, and what we had for dinner. He often inquired also what such or such a part of my clothing cost me; and when I told him he would exclaim at the price, and tell me that when he was a sub-lieutenant everything was much cheaper, and that he had often during that time taken his meals at Roze's restaurant, and dined very well for forty cents. Several times he spoke to me of my family, and of my sister, who was a nun before the Revolution, and who had been compelled to leave her convent; and one day asked me if she had a pension, and how much it was. I told him, and added, that this not being sufficient for her wants, I myself gave an allowance to her, and also to my mother. His Majesty told me to apply to the Duke of Bassano, and report the matter to him, as he wished to treat my family handsomely. I did not avail myself of this kind intention of his Majesty; for at that time I had sufficient means to be able to assist my relatives, and did not foresee the future, which I thought would not change my condition, and felt a delicacy in putting my people, so to speak, on the charge of the state. I confess that I have been more than once tempted to repent this excessive delicacy, which I have seen few persons above or below my condition imitate. On rising, the Emperor habitually took a cup of tea or orange water; and if he desired a bath, had it immediately on getting out of bed, and while in it had his dispatches and newspapers read to him by his secretary (Bourrienne till 1804). If he did not take a bath, he seated himself by the fire, and had them read to him there, often reading them himself. He dictated to the secretary his replies, and the observations which the reading of these suggested to him; as he went through each, throwing it on the floor without any order. The secretary afterwards gathered them all up, and arranged them to be carried into the Emperor's private room. His Majesty, before making his toilet, in summer, put on pantaloons of white pique and a dressing-gown of the same, and in winter, pantaloons and dressing-gown of swanskin, while on his head was a turban tied in front, the two ends hanging down on his neck behind. When the Emperor donned this headdress, his appearance was far from elegant. When he came out of the bath, we gave him another turban; for the one he wore was always wet in the bath, where he turned and splashed himself incessantly. Having taken his bath and read his dispatches, he began his toilet, and I shaved him before he learned to shave himself. When the Emperor began this habit, he used at first, like every one, a mirror attached to the window; but he came up so close to it, and lathered himself so vigorously with soap, that the mirror, window-panes, curtains, his dressing-gown, and the Emperor himself, were all covered with it. To remedy this inconvenience, the servants assembled in council, and it was decided that Roustan should hold the looking-glass for his Majesty. When the Emperor had shaved one side, he turned the other side to view, and made Roustan pass from left to right, or from right to left, according to the side on which he commenced. After shaving, the Emperor washed his face and hands, and had his nails carefully cleaned; then I took off his flannel vest and shirt, and rubbed his whole bust with an extremely soft silk brush, afterwards rubbing him with *eau-de-cologne*, of which he used a great quantity, for every day he was rubbed and dressed thus. It was in the East he had acquired this hygienic custom, which he enjoyed greatly, and which is really excellent. All these preparations ended, I put on him light flannel or cashmere slippers, white silk stockings, the only kind he ever wore, and very fine linen or fustian drawers, sometimes knee-breeches of white cassimere, with soft riding-boots, sometimes pantaloons of the same stuff and colour, with little English half-boots which came to the middle of the leg, and were finished with small silver spurs which were never more than six lines in length. All his, boots were finished with these spurs. I then put on him his flannel vest and shirt, a neck-cloth of very fine muslin, and over all a black silk stock; finally a round vest of white pique, and either a chasseur's or grenadier's coat, usually the former. His toilet ended, he was presented with his handkerchief, his tobacco-box, and a little shell bog filled with aniseed and liquorice, ground very fine. It will be seen by the above that the Emperor had himself dressed by his attendants from head to foot. He put his hand to nothing, but let himself be dressed like an infant, his mind filled with business during the entire performance.

I had forgotten to say that he used boxwood toothpicks, and a brush dipped in some opiate. The Emperor was born, so to speak, to be waited on (*homme d'valets de chambre*). When only a general, he had as many as three valets, and had himself served with as much luxury as at the height of his fortunes, and from that time received all the attentions I have just described, and which it was almost impossible for him to do without; and in this particular the etiquette was never changed. He increased the number of his servants, and decorated them with new titles, but he could not have more services rendered him personally. He subjected himself very rarely to the grand etiquette of royalty, and never, for example, did the grand chamberlain hand him his shirt; and on one occasion only, when the city of Paris gave him a dinner at the time of his coronation, did the grand marshal hand him water to wash his hands. I shall give a description of his toilet on the day of his coronation; and it will be seen that even on that day his Majesty, the Emperor of the French, did not require any other ceremonial than that to which he had been accustomed as general and First Consul of the Republic.

The Emperor had no fixed hour for retiring: sometimes he retired at ten or eleven o'clock in the evening; oftener he stayed awake till two, three, or four o'clock in the morning. He was soon undressed; for it was his habit, on entering the room, to throw each garment right and left,—his coat on the floor, his grand cordon on the rug, his watch haphazard at the bed, his hat far off on a piece of furniture; thus with all his clothing, one piece after another. When he was in a good humour, he called me in a loud voice, with this kind of a cry: *"Ohe, oh! oh!"* at other times, when he was not in good humour, *"Monsieur, Monsieur Constant!"*

At all seasons his bed had to be warmed with a warming-pan, and it was only during the very hottest weather that he would dispense with this. His habit of undressing himself in haste rarely left me anything to do, except to hand him his night-cap. I then lighted his night-lamp, which was of gilded silver, and shaded it so that it would give less light. When he did not go to sleep at once, he had one of his secretaries called, or perhaps the Empress Josephine, to read to him; which duty no one could discharge better than her Majesty, for which reason the Emperor preferred her to all his readers, for she read with that especial charm which was natural to her in all she did. By order of the Emperor, there was burnt in his bedroom, in little silver perfume-boxes, sometimes aloes wood, and sometimes sugar or vinegar; and almost the year round it was necessary to have a fire in all his apartments, as he was habitually very sensitive to cold. When he wished to sleep, I returned to take out his lamp, and went up to my own room, my bedroom being just above that of his Majesty. Roustan and a valet on service slept in a little apartment adjoining the Emperor's bedroom; and if he needed me during the night, the boy of the wardrobe, who slept in an antechamber, came for me. Water was always kept hot for his bath, for often at any hour of the night as well as the day he might suddenly be seized with a fancy to take one.

Doctor Yvan appeared every morning and evening, at the rising and retiring of his Majesty.

It is well known that the Emperor often had his secretaries, and even his ministers, called during the night. During his stay at Warsaw, the Prince de Talleyrand once received a message after midnight; he came at once, and had a long interview with the Emperor, and work was prolonged late into the night, when his Majesty, fatigued, at last fell into a deep slumber. The Prince of Benevento, who was afraid to go out, fearing lest he might awaken the Emperor or be recalled to continue the conversation, casting his eyes around, perceived a comfortable sofa, so he stretched himself out on it, and went to sleep. Meneval, secretary to his Majesty, not wishing to retire till after the minister had left, knowing that the Emperor would probably call for him as soon as Talleyrand had retired, became impatient at such a long interview; and as for me, I was not in the best humour, since it was impossible for me to retire without taking away his Majesty's lamp.

Meneval came a dozen times to ask me if Prince Talleyrand had left. "He is there yet," said I. "I am sure of it, and yet I hear nothing." At last I begged him to place himself in the room where I then was, and on which the street-door opened, whilst I went to act as sentinel in a vestibule on which the Emperor's room had another opening; and it was arranged that the one of us who saw the prince go out would inform the other. Two o'clock sounded, then three, then four; no one appeared, and there was not the least movement in his Majesty's room. Losing patience at last, I half opened the door as gently as possible; but the Emperor, whose sleep was very light, woke with a start, and asked in a loud tone: "Who is that? Who comes there?" "What is that?" I replied, that, thinking the Prince of Benevento had gone out, I had come for his Majesty's lamp. "Talleyrand! Talleyrand!" cried out his Majesty vehemently. "Where is he, then?" and seeing him waking up, "well, I declare he is asleep! Come, you wretch; how dare you sleep in my room! ah! ah!" I left without taking out the lamp; they began talking again, and Meneval and I awaited the end of the *tete-a-tete*, until five o'clock in the morning.

The Emperor had a habit of taking, when he thus worked at night, coffee with cream, or chocolate; but he gave that up, and under the Empire no longer took anything, except from time to time, but very rarely, either punch mild and light as lemonade, or when he first awoke, an infusion of orange-leaves or tea.

The Emperor, who so magnificently endowed the most of his generals, who showed himself so liberal to his armies, and to whom, on the other hand, France owes so many and such handsome monuments, was not generous, and it must even be admitted was a little niggardly, in his domestic affairs. Perhaps he resembled those foolishly vain rich persons, who economize very closely at home, and in their own households, in order to shine more outside. He made very few, not to say no, presents to members of his household; and the first day of the year even passed without loosening his purse-strings. While I was undressing him the evening before, he said, pinching my ear, "Well, Monsieur Constant, what will you give me for my present?" The first time he asked this question I replied I would give him whatever he wished; but I must confess that I very much hoped it would not be I who would give presents next day. It seemed that the idea never occurred to him; for no one had to thank him for his gifts, and he never departed afterwards from this rule of domestic economy. Apropos of this pinching of ears, to which I have recurred so often, because his Majesty repeated it so often, it is necessary that

I should say, while I think of it, and in closing this subject, that any one would be much mistaken in supposing that he touched lightly the party exposed to his marks of favour; he pinched, on the contrary, very hard, and pinched as much stronger in proportion as he happened to be in a better humour.

Sometimes, when I entered his room to dress him, he would run at me like a mad man, and saluting me with his favourite greeting, "Well, Monsieur le drole," would pinch my ears in such a manner as to make me cry out; he often added to these gentle caresses one or two taps, also well applied. I was then sure of finding him all the rest of the day in a charming humour, and full of good-will, as I have seen him, so often. Roustan, and even Marshal Berthier, received their due proportion of these imperial tendernesses.

Chapter 20

The allowance made by his Majesty for the yearly expenses of his dress was twenty thousand *francs*; and the year of, the coronation he became very angry because that sum had been exceeded. It was never without trepidation that the various accounts of household expenses were presented to him; and he invariably retrenched and cut down, and recommended all sort of reforms. I remember after asking for some one a place of three thousand *francs*, which he granted me, I heard him exclaim, "Three thousand *francs*! but do you understand that this is the revenue of one of my *communes*? When I was sub-lieutenant I did not spend as much as that." This expression recurred incessantly in his conversations with those with whom he was familiar; and "when I had the honour of being sub-lieutenant" was often on his lips, and always in illustration of comparisons or exhortations to economy.

While on the subject of accounts, I recall a circumstance which should have a place in my memoirs, since it concerns me personally, and moreover gives an idea of the manner in which his Majesty understood economy. He set out with the idea, which was, I think, often very correct, that in private expenses as in public ones, even granting the honesty of agents (which the Emperor was always, I admit, very slow to do), the same things could have been done with much less money. Thus, when he required retrenchment, it was not in the number of objects of expense, but only in the prices charged for these articles by the furnishers; and I will elsewhere cite some examples of the effect which this idea produced on the conduct of his Majesty towards the accounting agents of his government. Now I am relating only private matters. One day when investigating various accounts, the Emperor complained much of the expenses of the stables, and cut off a considerable sum; and the grand equerry, in order to put into effect the required economy, found it necessary to deprive several persons in the household of their carriages, mine being included in this number. Some days after the execution of this measure, his Majesty charged me with a commission, which necessitated a carriage; and I was obliged to inform him that, no longer having mine, I should not be able to execute his orders. The Emperor then exclaimed that he had not intended this, and M. Caulaincourt must have a poor idea of economy. When he again saw the Duke of Vicenza, he said to him that he did not wish anything of mine to be touched.

The Emperor occasionally read in the morning the new works and romances of the day; and when a work displeased him, he threw it into the fire. This does not mean that only improper books were thus destroyed; for if the author was not among his favourites, or if he spoke too well of a foreign country, that was sufficient to condemn the volume to the flames. On this account I saw his Majesty throw into the fire a volume of the works of Madame de Stael, on Germany. If he found us in the evening enjoying a book in the little saloon, where we awaited the hour for retiring, he examined what we were reading; and if he found they were romances, they were burned without pity, his Majesty rarely failing to add a little lecture to this confiscation, and to ask the delinquent "if a man could not find better reading than that." One morning he had glanced over and thrown in the fire a book (by what author I do not know); and when Roustan stooped down to take it out the Emperor stopped him, saying, "Let that filthy thing burn; it is all that it deserves."

The Emperor mounted his horse most ungracefully, and I think would not have always been very safe when there, if so much care had not been taken to give him only those which were perfectly trained; but every precaution was taken, and horses destined for the special service of the Emperor passed through a rude novitiate before arriving at the honour of carrying him. They were habituated to endure, without making the least movement, torments of all kinds; blows with a whip over the head and ears; the drum was beaten; pistols were fired; fireworks exploded in their ears; flags were shaken before their eyes; heavy weights were thrown against their legs, sometimes even sheep and hogs. It was required that in the midst of the most rapid gallop (the Emperor liked no other pace), he should be able to stop his horse suddenly; and in short, it was absolutely necessary to have only the most perfectly trained animals.

M. Jardin, senior, equerry of his Majesty, acquitted himself of this laborious duty with much skill and ability, as the Emperor attached such importance to it; he also insisted strongly that his horses should be very handsome, and in the last years of his reign would ride only Arab horses.

There were a few of those noble animals for which the Emperor had a great affection; among others, Styria, which he rode over the St. Bernard and at Marengo. After this last campaign, he wished his favourite to end his days in the luxury of repose, for Marengo and the great St. Bernard were in themselves a well-filled career. The Emperor rode also for many years an Arab horse of rare intelligence, in which he took much pleasure. During the time he was awaiting his rider, it would have been hard to discover in him the least grace; but as soon as he heard the drums beat the tattoo which announced the presence of his Majesty, he reared his head most proudly, tossed his mane, and pawed the ground, and until the very moment the Emperor alighted, was the most magnificent animal imaginable.

His Majesty made a great point of good equerries, and nothing was neglected in order that the pages should receive in this particular the most careful education. To accustom them to mount firmly and with grace, they practiced exercises in vaulting, for which it seemed to me they would have no use except at the Olympic circus. And, in fact, one of the horsemen of Messieurs Franconi had charge of this part of the pages' education.

The Emperor, as has been said elsewhere, took no pleasure in hunting, except just so far as was necessary to conform to the usage which makes this exercise a necessary accompaniment to the throne and the crown; and yet I have seen him sometimes continue it sufficiently long to justify the belief that he did not find it altogether distasteful. He hunted one day in the forest of Rambouillet from six in the morning to eight in the evening, a stag being the object of this prolonged excursion; and I remember they returned without having taken him. In one of the imperial hunts at Rambouillet, at which the Empress Josephine was present, a stag, pursued by the hunters, threw himself under the Empress's carriage; which refuge did not fail him, for her Majesty, touched by the misery of the poor animal, begged his life of the Emperor. The stag was spared; and Josephine placed round its neck a silver collar to attest its deliverance, and protect it against the attacks of all hunters.

One of the ladies of the Empress one day showed less humanity than she, however; and the reply which she made to the Emperor displeased him exceedingly, for he loved gentleness and pity in women. When they had hunted for several hours in the Bois de Boulogne, the Emperor drew near the carriage of the Empress Josephine, and began talking with a lady who bore one of the most noble and most ancient names in all France, and who, it is said, had been placed near the Empress against her wishes. The Prince of Neuchatel (Berthier) announced that the stag was at bay. "Madame," said the Emperor gallantly to Madame de C——, "I place his fate in your hands."

"Do with him, Sire," replied she, "as you please. It is no difference to me." The Emperor gave her a glance of disapproval, and said to the master of the hounds, "Since the stag in his misery does not interest Madame C——, he does not deserve to live; have him put to death;" whereupon his Majesty turned his horse's bridle, and rode off. The Emperor was shocked by such an answer, and repeated it that evening, on his return from the hunt, in terms by no means flattering to Madame de C——.

It is stated in the Memorial of Saint-Helena that the Emperor, while hunting, was thrown and wounded by a wild boar, from which one of his fingers bore a bad scar. I never saw this, and never knew of such an accident having happened to the Emperor. The Emperor did not place his gun firmly to his shoulder, and as he always had it heavily loaded and rammed, never fired without making his arm black with bruises; but I rubbed the injured place with *eau de cologne*, and he gave it no further thought.

The ladies followed the hunt in their coaches; a table being usually arranged in the forest for breakfast, to which all persons in the hunt were invited.

The Emperor on one occasion hunted with falcons on the plain of Rambouillet, in order to make a trial of the falconry that the King of Holland (Louis) had sent as a present to his Majesty. The household made a fete of seeing this hunt, of which we had been hearing so much; but the Emperor appeared to take less pleasure in this than in the chase or shooting, and hawking was never tried again.

His Majesty was exceedingly fond of the play, preferring greatly French tragedy and the Italian opera. Corneille was his favourite author; and he had always on his table some volume of the works of this great poet. I have often heard the Emperor declaim, while walking up and down in his room, verses of Cinna, or this speech on the death of Caesar:

"Caesar, you will reign; see the august day In which the Roman people, always unjust to thee," etc.

At the theatre of Saint-Cloud, the piece for the evening was often made up of fragments and selections from different authors, one act being chosen from one opera, one from another, which was very vexatious to the spectators whom the first piece had begun to interest. Often, also, comedies were played; on which occasions there was great rejoicing in the household, and the Emperor himself took much pleasure in them. How many times have I seen him perfectly overcome with laughter, when seeing Baptiste junior in *'les Heritiers'*, and Michaut also amused him in *'la Partie de Chasse de Henry IV'*.

I cannot remember in what year, but it was during one of the sojourns of the court at Fontainebleau, that the tragedy of the Venetians was presented before the Emperor by Arnault, senior. That evening, as he was retiring, his Majesty discussed the piece with Marshal Duroc, and gave his opinion, adducing many reasons, in support of it. These praises, like the criticisms, were all explained and discussed; the grand marshal talking little, and the Emperor incessantly. Although a poor judge myself of such matters, it was very entertaining, and also very instructive, to hear the Emperor's opinion of pieces, ancient and modern, which had been played before him; and his observations and remarks could not have failed, I am sure, to be of great profit to the authors, had they been able like myself to hear them. As for me, if I gained anything from it, it is being enabled to speak of it here a little (although a very little), more appropriately than a blind man would of colours; nevertheless, for fear of saying the wrong thing, I return to matters which are in my department.

It has been said that his Majesty used a great quantity of tobacco, and that in order to take it still more frequently and quickly, he put it in a pocket of his vest, lined with skin for that purpose. This is an error. The Emperor never took tobacco except in his snuff-boxes; and although he wasted a great quantity of it, he really used very little, as he took a pinch, held it to his nose simply to smell it, and let it fall immediately. It is true that the place where he had been was covered with it; but his handkerchiefs, irreproachable witnesses in such matters, were scarcely stained, and although they were white and of very fine linen, certainly bore no marks of a snuff-taker. Sometimes he simply passed his open snuff-box under his nose in order to breathe the odour of the tobacco it contained. These boxes were of black shell, with hinges, and of a narrow, oval shape; they were lined with gold, and ornamented with antique cameos, or medallions, in gold or silver. At one time he used round tobacco-boxes; but as it took two hands to open them, and in this operation he sometimes dropped either the box or the top, he became disgusted with them. His tobacco was grated very coarse, and was usually composed of several kinds of tobacco mixed together. Frequently he amused himself by making the gazelles that he had at Saint-Cloud eat it. They were very fond of it, and although exceedingly afraid of every one else, came close to his Majesty without the slightest fear.

The Emperor took a fancy on one occasion, but only one, to try a pipe, as I shall now relate. The Persian ambassador (or perhaps it was the Turkish ambassador who came to Paris under the Consulate) had made his Majesty a present of a very handsome pipe such as is used by the Orientals. One day he was seized with a desire to try it, and had everything necessary for this purpose prepared. The fire having been applied to the bowl, the only question now was to light the tobacco; but from the manner in which his Majesty attempted this it was impossible for him to succeed, as he alternately opened and closed his lips repeatedly without drawing in his breath at all. "Why, what is the matter?" cried he; "it does not work at all." I called his attention to the fact that he was not inhaling properly, and showed him how it ought to be done; but the Emperor still continued his performances, which were like some peculiar kind of yawning. Tired out by his fruitless efforts at last, he told me to light it for him, which I did, and instantly handed it back to him. But he had hardly taken a whiff when the smoke, which he did not know how to breathe out again, filled his throat, got into his windpipe, and came out through his nose and eyes in great puffs. As soon as he could get his breath, he panted forth, "Take it away! what a pest! Oh, the wretches! it has made me sick." In fact, he felt ill for at least an hour after, and renounced forever the "pleasure of a habit, which," said he, "is only good to enable do-nothings to kill time."

The only requirements the Emperor made as to his clothing was that it should be of fine quality and perfectly comfortable; and his coats for ordinary use, dress-coats, and even the famous grey overcoat, were made of the finest cloth from Louviers. Under the Consulate he wore, as was then the fashion, the skirts of his coat extremely long; afterwards fashion changed, and they were worn shorter; but the Emperor held with singular tenacity to the length of his, and I had much trouble in inducing him to abandon this fashion, and it was only by a subterfuge that I at last succeeded. Each time I ordered a new coat for his Majesty, I directed the tailor to shorten the skirts by an inch at least, until at last, without his being aware of it, they were no longer ridiculous. He did not abandon his old habits any more readily on this point than on all others; and his greatest desire was that his clothes should not be too tight, in consequence of which there were times when he did not make a very elegant appearance. The King of Naples, the man in all France who dressed with the most care, and nearly always in good taste, sometimes took the liberty of bantering the Emperor slightly about his dress. "Sire," said he to the Emperor, "your Majesty dresses too much like a good family man. Pray, Sire, be an example to your faithful subjects of good taste in dress."

"Would you like me, in order to please you," replied the Emperor, "to dress like a scented fop, like a dandy, in fine, like the King of Naples and the Two Sicilies. As for me, I must hold on to my old habitudes."

"Yes, Sire, and to your *'habits tues'*," added the king on one occasion. "Detestable!" cried the Emperor; "that is worthy of Brunet;" and they laughed heartily over this play on words, while declaring it what the Emperor called it.

However, these discussions as to his dress being renewed at the time of his Majesty's marriage to the Empress Marie Louise, the King of Naples begged the Emperor to allow him to send him his tailor. His Majesty, who sought at that time every means of pleasing his young wife, accepted the offer of his brother-in-law; and that very day I went for Leger, King Joachim's tailor, and brought him with me to the chateau, recommending him to make the suits which would be ordered as loose as possible, certain as I was in advance, that, Monsieur Jourdain[1] to the contrary, if the Emperor could not get into them easily, he would not wear them. Leger paid no attention to my advice, but took his measure very closely. The two coats were beautifully made; but the Emperor pronounced them uncomfortable, and wore them only once, and Leger did no more work for his Majesty. At one time, long before this, he had ordered a very handsome coat of chestnut brown velvet, with diamond buttons, which he wore to a reception of her Majesty the Empress, with a black cravat, though the Empress Josephine had prepared for him an elegant lace stock, which all my entreaties could not induce him to put on.

The Emperor's vest and breeches were always of white cassimere; he changed them every morning, and they were washed only three or four times. Two hours after he had left his room, it often happened that his breeches were all stained with ink, owing to his habit of wiping his pen on them, and scattering ink all around him by knocking his pen against the table. Nevertheless, as he dressed in the morning for the whole day, he did not change his clothes on that account, and remained in that condition the remainder of the day. I have already said that he wore none but white silk stockings, his shoes, which were very light and thin,

---

1. A character in a Moliere comedy.

being lined with silk, and his boots lined throughout inside with white fustian; and when he felt an itching on one of his legs, he rubbed it with the heel of his shoe or the boot on the other leg, which added still more to the effect of the ink blotches. His shoe-buckles were oval, either plain gold or with medallions, and he also wore gold buckles on his garters. I never saw him wear pantaloons under the Empire.

Owing to the Emperor's tenacity to old customs, his shoemaker in the first days of the Empire was still the same he employed at the military school; and as his shoes had been made by the same measure, from that time, and no new one ever taken, his shoes, as well as his boots, were always badly made and ungraceful. For a long time he wore them pointed; but I persuaded him to have them *'en bec de canne'*, as that was the fashion. At last his old measure was found too small, and I got his Majesty's consent to have a new one-taken; so I summoned the shoemaker, who had succeeded his father, and was exceedingly stupid. He had never seen the Emperor, although he worked for him; and when he learned that he was expected to appear before his Majesty, his head was completely turned. How could he dare to present himself before the Emperor? What costume must he wear? I encouraged him, and told him he would need a black French coat, with breeches, and hat, etc.; and he presented himself thus adorned at the Tuileries. On entering his Majesty's chamber he made a deep bow, and stood much embarrassed. "It surely cannot be you who made shoes for me at the *l'ecole militaire?*"

"No, your Majesty, Emperor and King, it was my father."

"And why don't he do so now?"

"Sire, the Emperor and King, because he is dead."

"How much do you make me pay for my shoes?"

"Your Majesty, Emperor and King, pays eighteen *francs* for them."

"That is very dear."

"Your Majesty, Emperor and King, could pay much more for them if he would." The Emperor laughed heartily at this simplicity, and let him take his measure; but the Emperor's laughter had so completely disconcerted the poor man that, when he approached him, his hat under his arm, making a thousand bows, his sword caught between his legs, was broken in two, and made him fall on his hands and knees, not to remain there long, however, for his Majesty's roars of laughter increasing, and being at last freed from his sword, the poor shoemaker took the Emperor's measure with more ease, and withdrew amidst profuse apologies.

All his Majesty's linen was of extremely fine quality, marked with

NAPOLEON AND HIS SON

an "N" in a coronet; at first he wore no suspenders, but at last began using them, and found them very comfortable. He wore next his body vests made of English flannel, and the Empress Josephine had a dozen cashmere vests made for his use in summer.

Many persons have believed that the Emperor wore a cuirass under his clothes when walking and while in the army. This is entirely false: the Emperor never put on a cuirass, nor anything resembling one, under his coat any more than over it.

The Emperor wore no jewellery; he never had in his pockets either purse or silver, but only his handkerchief, his snuff-box, and his bonbon-box.

He wore on his coat only a star and two crosses, that of the Legion of Honour, and that of the Iron Crown. Under his uniform and on his vest he wore a red ribbon, the ends of which could just be seen.

When there was a reception at the chateau, or he held a review, he put this grand cordon outside his coat.

His hat, the shape of which it will be useless to describe while portraits of his Majesty exist, was-extremely fine and very light, lined with silk and wadded; and on it he wore neither tassels nor plumes, but simply a narrow, flat band of silk and a little tricolored cockade.

The Emperor purchased several watches from Breguet and Meunier,—very plain repeaters, without ornamentation or figures, the face covered with glass, the back gold. M. Las Casas speaks of a watch with a double gold case, marked with the cipher "B," and which never left the Emperor. I never saw anything of the sort, though I was keeper of all the jewels, and even had in my care for several days the crown diamonds. The Emperor often broke his watch by throwing it at random, as I have said before, on any piece of furniture in his bedroom. He had two alarm-clocks made by Meunier, one in his carriage, the other at the head of his bed, which he set with a little green silk cord, and also a third, but it was old and worn-out so that it would not work; it is this last which had belonged to Frederick the Great, and was brought from Berlin. The swords of his Majesty were very plain, with gold mountings, and an owl on the hilt.

The Emperor had two swords similar to the one he wore the day of the battle of Austerlitz. One of these swords was given to the Emperor Alexander, as the reader will learn later, and the other to Prince Eugene in 1814. That which the Emperor wore at Austerlitz, and on which he afterwards had engraved the name and date of that memorable battle, was to have been enclosed in the column of the Place Vendome; but his Majesty still had it, I think, while he was at St. Helena.

He had also several sabres that he had worn in his first campaigns, and on which were engraved the names of the battles in which he had used them. They were distributed among the various general officers of his Majesty the Emperor, of which distribution I will speak later.

When the Emperor was about to quit his capital to rejoin his army, or for a simple journey through the departments, we never knew the exact moment of his departure. It was necessary to send in advance on various roads a complete service for the bedroom, kitchen, and stables; this sometimes waited three weeks, or even a month, and when his Majesty at length set out, that which was waiting on the road he did not take was ordered to return. I have often thought that the Emperor acted thus in order to disconcert those who spied on his proceedings, and to baffle their schemes.

The day he was to set out no one could discover that fact from him, and everything went on as usual. After a concert, a play, or any other amusement which had collected a large number of people, his Majesty would simply remark on retiring, "I shall leave at two o'clock!" Sometimes the time was earlier, sometimes later; but he always began his journey at the designated hour. The order was instantly announced by each of the head servants; and all were ready at the appointed time, though the chateau was left topsy-turvy, as may be seen from the picture I have given elsewhere of the confusion at the chateau which preceded and followed the Emperor's departure. Wherever his Majesty lodged on the journey, before leaving he had all the expenses of himself and of his household paid, made presents to his hosts, and gave gratuities to the servants of the house. On Sunday the Emperor had mass celebrated by the curate of the place, giving always as much as twenty napoleons, sometimes more, and regulating the gift according to the needs of the poor of the parish. He asked many questions of the cures concerning their resources, that of their parishioners, the intelligence and morality of the population, etc. He rarely failed to ask the number of births, deaths, marriages, and if there were many young men and girls of a marriageable age. If the cure replied to these questions in a satisfactory manner, and if he had not been too-long in saying mass, he could count on the favour of his Majesty; his church and his poor would find themselves well provided for; and as for himself, the Emperor left on his departure, or had sent to him, a commission as chevalier of the Legion of Honour. His Majesty preferred to be answered with confidence and without timidity; he even endured contradiction; and one could without any risk reply inaccurately; this was almost always overlooked, for he paid little attention to the reply, but he never failed to turn away from those who spoke to him in a hesitating or embarrassed manner. Whenever the Emperor took up his residence at any place, there were on duty, night and day, a page and an aide-decamp, who slept on sacking beds. There was also constantly in attendance, in an antechamber, a quartermaster and sergeant of the stables prepared to order, when necessary, the equipages, which they took care to keep always in readiness to move; horses fully saddled and bridled, and carriages harnessed with two horses, left the stables on the first signal of his Majesty. These attendants were relieved every two hours, like sentinels.

I said above that his Majesty liked prompt replies, and those which showed vivacity and sprightliness. I will give two anecdotes in support of this assertion. Once, while the Emperor was holding a review on the Place du Carrousel, his horse reared, and in the efforts his Majesty made to control him, his hat fell to the ground; a lieutenant (his name, I think, was Rabusson), at whose feet the hat fell, picked it up, and came out from the front ranks to offer it to his Majesty. "Thanks, Captain," said the Emperor, still engaged in quieting his horse. "In what regiment?"

"Sire?" asked the officer. The Emperor, then regarding him more attentively, and perceiving his mistake, said to him, smiling, "Ah, that is so, *monsieur*, in the Guard."

The new captain received the commission which he owed to his presence of mind, but which he had in fact well earned by his bravery and devotion to duty.

At another review, his Majesty perceived in the ranks of a regiment of the line an old soldier, whose arms were decorated with three chevrons. He recognized him instantly as having seen him in the army of Italy, and approaching him, said, "Well, my brave fellow, why have you not the cross? You do not look like a bad fellow."

"Sire," replied the old soldier, with sorrowful gravity, "I have three times been put on the list for the cross."

"You shall not be disappointed a fourth time," replied the Emperor; and he ordered Marshal Berthier to place on the list, for the next promotion, the brave soldier, who was soon made a chevalier of the Legion of Honour.

Chapter 21

Pope Pius VII. had left Rome early in November, 1804; and his Holiness, accompanied by General Menou, administrator of Piedmont, arrived at Mont Cenis, on the morning of Nov. 15. The road of Mont Cenis had been surveyed and smoothed, and all dangerous points made secure by barriers. The Holy Father was received by M. Poitevin-Maissemy, *prefect* of Mont Blanc, and after a short visit to the hospice, crossed the mountain in a sedan chair, escorted by an immense crowd, who knelt to receive his blessing as he passed.

Nov. 17 his Holiness resumed his carriage, in which he made the remainder of the journey, accompanied in the same manner. The Emperor went to meet the Holy Father, and met him on the road to Nemours in the forest of Fontainebleau. The Emperor dismounted from his horse, and the two sovereigns returned to Fontainebleau in the same carriage. It is said that neither took precedence over the other, and that, in order to avoid this, they both entered the carriage at the same instant, his Majesty by the door on the right, and his Holiness by that on the left.

I do not know whether it is true that the Emperor used devices and stratagems in order to avoid compromising his dignity, but I do know that it would have been impossible to show more regard and attention to the venerable old man. The day after his arrival at Fontainebleau, the Pope made his entrance into Paris with all the honours usually rendered to the head of the Empire. Apartments had been prepared for him at the Tuileries in the Pavilion of Flora; and as a continuation of the delicate and affectionate consideration which his Majesty had shown from the beginning in welcoming the Holy Father, he found his apartments, in arrangement and furniture, an exact duplicate of those he occupied at Rome. He evinced much surprise and gratitude at this attention, which he himself, it is said, with his usual delicacy, called entirely filial; desiring thus to acknowledge the respect which the Emperor had shown him on every occasion, and the new title of eldest son of the Church, which his Majesty was about to assume with the imperial crown.

Every morning I went, by order of his Majesty, to inquire after the health of the Holy Father. Pius VII. had a noble and handsome countenance, an air of angelic sweetness, and a gentle, well modulated voice; he spoke little, and always slowly, but with grace; his tastes were extremely simple, and his abstemiousness incredible; he was indulgent to others and most lenient in his judgments. I must admit that on the score of good cheer the persons of his suite made no pretence of imitating the Holy Father, but, on the contrary, took most unbecoming advantage of the Emperor's orders, that everything requested should be furnished. The tables set for them were abundantly and even magnificently served; which, however, did not prevent a whole basket of Chambertin being requested each day for the Pope's private table, though he dined alone and drank only water.

The sojourn of nearly five months which the Holy Father made at Paris was a time of edification for the faithful; and his Holiness must have carried away a most flattering opinion of the populace, who, having ceased to practice, and not having witnessed for more than ten years, the ceremonies of the Catholic religion, had returned to them with irrepressible zeal. When the Pope was not detained in his apartments by his delicate health in regard to which the difference in the climate, compared with that of Italy, and the severity of the winter, required him to take great precautions, he visited the churches, the museum, and the establishments of public utility; and if the severe weather prevented his going out, the persons who requested this favour were presented to Pius VII. in the grand gallery of the Museum Napoleon. I was one day asked by some ladies of my acquaintance to accompany them to this audience of the Holy Father, and took much pleasure in doing so.

The long gallery of the museum was filled with ladies and gentlemen, arranged in double lines, the greater part of whom were mothers of families, with their children at their knees or in their arms, ready to be presented for the Holy Father's blessing; and Pius VII. gazed on these children with a sweetness and mildness truly angelic. Preceded by the governor of the museum, and followed by the cardinals and lords of his household, he advanced slowly between these two ranks of the faithful, who fell on their knees as he passed, often stopping to place his hand on the head of a child, to address a few words to the mother, or to give his ring to be kissed. His dress was a plain white cassock without ornament. Just as the Pope reached us, the director of the museum presented a lady who, like the others, was awaiting the blessing of his Holiness on her knees. I heard the director call this lady Madame, the Countess de Genlis, upon which the Holy Father held out to her his ring, raised her in the most affable manner, and said a few flattering words complimenting her on her works, and the happy influence which they had exercised in re-establishing the Catholic religion in France.

Sellers of chaplets and rosaries must have made their fortunes during this winter, for in some shops more than one hundred dozen were sold per day. During the month of January, by this branch of industry alone, one merchant of the Rue Saint-Denis made forty thousand *francs*. All those who presented themselves at the audience of the Holy Father, or who pressed around him as he went out, made him bless chaplets for themselves, for all their relations, and for their friends in Paris or in the provinces. The cardinals also distributed an incredible quantity in their visits to the various hospitals, to the Hotel des Invalides, etc., and even at private houses.

It was arranged that the coronation of their Majesties should take place on Dec. 2. On the morning of this great day all at the chateau were astir very early, especially the persons attached to the service of the wardrobe. The Emperor himself arose at eight o'clock. It was no small affair to array his Majesty in the rich costume which had been prepared for the occasion; and the whole time I was dressing him he uttered unlimited maledictions and apostrophes against embroiderers, tailors, and furnishers generally. As I passed him each article of his dress, "Now, that is something handsome, Monsieur le drole," said he (and my ears had their part in the play), "but we shall see the bills for it." This was the costume: silk stockings embroidered in gold, with the imperial coronet on the clocks; white velvet boots laced and embroidered with gold; white velvet breeches embroidered in gold on the seams; diamond buckles and buttons on his garters; his vest, also of white velvet, embroidered in gold with diamond buttons; a crimson velvet coat, with facings of white velvet, and embroidered on all the seams, the whole sparkling with gold and gems. A short cloak, also of crimson, and lined with white satin, hung from his left shoulder, and was caught on the right over his breast with a double clasp of diamonds. On such occasions it was customary for the grand chamberlain to pass the shirt; but it seems that his Majesty did not remember this law of etiquette, and it was I alone who performed that office, as I was accustomed. The shirt was one of those ordinarily worn by his Majesty, but of very beautiful cambric, for the Emperor would wear only very fine linen; but ruffles of very handsome lace had been added, and his cravat was of the most exquisite muslin, and his collar of superb lace. The black velvet cap was surmounted by two white aigrettes, and surrounded with a band of diamonds, caught together by the Regent. The Emperor set out, thus dressed, from the Tuileries; and it was not till he had reached Notre-Dame, that he placed over his shoulders the grand coronation mantle. This was of crimson velvet, studded with golden bees, lined with white satin, and fastened with a gold cord and tassel. The weight of it was at least eighty pounds, and, although it was held up by four grand dignitaries, bore him down by its weight. Therefore, on returning to the chateau, he freed himself as soon as possible from all this rich and uncomfortable apparel; and while resuming his grenadier uniform, he repeated over and over, "At last I can get my breath." He was certainly much more at his ease on the day of battle.

The jewels which were used at the coronation of her Majesty the Empress, and which consisted of a crown, a diadem, and a girdle, came from the establishment of M. Margueritte. The crown had eight branches, which supported a golden globe surmounted by a cross, each branch set with diamonds, four being in the shape of palm and four of myrtle leaves. Around the crown ran a band set with eight enormous emeralds, while the bandeau which rested on the brow shone with amethysts.

The diadem was composed of four rows of magnificent pearls entwined with leaves made of diamonds, each of which matched perfectly, and was mounted with a skill as admirable as the beauty of the material. On her brow were several large brilliants, each one alone weighing one hundred and forty-nine grains. The girdle, finally, was a golden ribbon ornamented With thirty-nine rose-colored stones. The sceptre of his Majesty the Emperor had been made by M. Odiot; it was of silver, entwined with a golden serpent, and surmounted by a globe on which Charlemagne was seated. The hand of Justice and the crown, as well as the sword, were of most exquisite workmanship, but it would take too long to describe them; they were from the establishment of M. Biennais.

At nine o'clock in the morning the Pope left the Tuileries for Notre Dame, in a carriage drawn by eight handsome grey horses. From the imperial of the coach rose a tiara surrounded by the insignia of the papacy in gilt bronze, while the first chamberlain of his Holiness, mounted on a mule, preceded the carriage, bearing a silver gilt cross.

There was an interval of about one hour between the arrival of the

Pope at Notre Dame and that of their Majesties, who left the Tuileries precisely at eleven o'clock, which fact was announced by numerous salutes of artillery. Their Majesties' carriage, glittering with gold and adorned with magnificent paintings, was drawn by eight bay horses superbly caparisoned.

Above the imperial of this coach was a crown supported by four eagles with extended wings. The panels of this carriage, which was the object of universal admiration, were of glass instead of wood; and it was so built that the back was exactly like the front, which similarity caused their Majesties, on entering it, to make the absurd mistake of placing themselves on the front seat. The Empress was first to perceive this, and both she and her husband were much amused.

I could not attempt to describe the cortege, although I still retain most vivid recollections of the scene, because 1 should have too much to say. Picture to yourself, then, ten thousand cavalry superbly mounted, defiling between two rows of infantry equally imposing, each body covering a distance of nearly half a league. Then think of the number of the equipages, of their magnificence, the splendour of the trappings of the horses, and of the uniforms of the soldiers; of the crowds of musicians playing coronation marches, added to the ringing of bells and booming of cannon; then to all this add the effect produced by this immense multitude of from four to five hundred thousand spectators; and still one would be very far from obtaining a correct idea of this astonishing magnificence.

In the month of December it is very rare that the weather is fine, but on that day the heavens seemed auspicious to the Emperor and just as he entered the archiepiscopal church, quite a heavy fog, which had lasted all the morning, was suddenly dissipated, and a brilliant flood of sunlight added its splendour to that of the cortege. This singular circumstance was remarked by the spectators, and increased the enthusiasm.

All the streets through which the cortege passed were carefully cleared and sanded; and the inhabitants decorated the fronts of their houses according to their varied taste and means, with drapery, tapestry, coloured paper, and some even with garlands of yew-leaves, almost all the shops on the Quai des Orfevres being ornamented with festoons of artificial flowers.

The religious ceremony lasted nearly four hours, and must have been extremely fatiguing to the principal actors. The personal attendants were necessarily on duty continually in the apartment prepared for the Emperor at the archiepiscopal palace; but the curious (and all were so) relieved each other from time to time, and each thus had an opportunity of witnessing the ceremony at leisure.

I have never heard before or since such imposing music: it was the composition of Messieurs Paesiello, Rose, and Lesueur, *precentors* of their Majesties; and the orchestra and choruses comprised the finest musicians of Paris. Two orchestras with four choruses, including more than three hundred musicians, were led, the one by M. Persuis, the other by M. Rey, both leaders of the Emperor's bands. M. Lais, first singer to his Majesty, M. Kreutzer, and M. Baillot, first violinists of the same rank, had gathered the finest talent which the imperial chapel, the opera, and the grand lyric theatres possessed, either as instrumental players or male and female singers. Innumerable military bands, under the direction of M. Lesuem, executed heroic marches, one of which, ordered by the Emperor from M. Lesueur for the army of Boulogne, is still today, according to the judgment of connoisseurs, worthy to stand in the first rank of the most beautiful and most imposing musical compositions. As for me, this music affected me to such an extent that I became pale and trembling, and convulsive tremors ran through all my body while listening to it.

His Majesty would not allow the Pope to touch the crown, but placed it on his head himself. It was a golden diadem, formed of oak and laurel leaves. His Majesty then took the crown intended for the Empress, and, having donned it himself for a few moments, placed it on the brow of his august wife, who knelt before him. Her agitation was so great that she shed tears, and, rising, fixed on the Emperor a look of tenderness and gratitude; and the Emperor returned her glance without abating in the least degree the dignity required by such an imposing ceremony before so many witnesses.

In spite of this constraint their hearts understood each other in the midst of the brilliancy and applause of the assembly, and assuredly no idea of divorce entered the Emperor's mind at that moment; and, for my part, I am very sure that this cruel separation would never have taken place if her Majesty the Empress could have borne children, or even if the young Napoleon, son of the King of Holland and Queen Hortense, had not died just at the time the Emperor had decided to adopt him. Yet I must admit that the fear, or rather the certainty, of Josephine not bearing him an heir to the throne, drove the Emperor to despair; and I have many times heard him pause suddenly in the midst of his work, and exclaim with chagrin, "To whom shall I leave all this?"

After the mass, His Excellency, Cardinal Fesch, grand almoner of

France, bore the Book of the Gospels to the Emperor, who thereupon, from his throne, pronounced the imperial oath in a voice so firm and distinct that it was heard by all present. Then, for the twentieth time perhaps, the cry of '*Vive l'Empereur*' sprang to the lips of all, the *Te Deum* was chanted, and their Majesties left the church in the same manner as they had entered. The Pope remained in the church about a quarter of an hour after the sovereigns; and, when he rose to withdraw, universal acclamations accompanied him from the choir to the portal.

Their Majesties did not return to the chateau until half-past six, and the Pope not till nearly seven. On their entrance to the church, their Majesties passed through the archbishop's palace, the buildings of which, as I have said, communicated with Notre Dame by means of a wooden gallery. This gallery, covered with slate, and hung with magnificent tapestry, ended in a platform, also of wood, erected before the principal entrance, and made to harmonize perfectly with the gothic architecture of this handsome metropolitan church. This platform rested upon four columns, decorated with inscriptions in letters of gold, enumerating the names of the principal towns of France, whose mayors had been deputized to attend the coronation. Above these columns was a painting in relief, representing Clovis and Charlemagne seated on their thrones, sceptre in hand; and in the centre of this frontispiece were presented the arms of the Empire, draped with the banners of the sixteen cohorts of the Legion of Honour, while on each side were towers, surmounted by golden eagles. The inside of this portico, as well as the gallery, was shaped like a roof, painted sky-blue, and sown with stars.

The throne of their Majesties was erected on a stage in the shape of a semicircle, and covered with a bluff carpet studded with bees, and was reached by twenty-two steps. The throne, draped in red velvet, was also covered by a pavilion of the same colour, the left wing of which extended over the Empress, the princesses, and their maids of honour, and the right over the two brothers of the Emperor, with the arch-chancellor and the arch-treasurer.

Nothing could be grander than the bird's-eye view of the garden of the Tuileries on the evening of this auspicious day, the grand parterre, encircled by illuminated colonnades from arch to arch of which were festooned garlands of rose-colored lights; the grand promenade outlined by columns, above which stars glittered; the terraces on each side filled with orange-trees, the branches of which were covered with innumerable lights; while every tree on the adjoining walks presented as brilliant a spectacle; and finally, to crown all this magnificent blaze of light, an immense star was suspended above the Place de la Concorde, and outshone all else. This might in truth be called a palace of fire.

On the occasion of the coronation his Majesty made magnificent presents to the metropolitan church. I remarked, among other things, a chalice ornamented with bas-reliefs, designed by the celebrated Germain, a *pyx*, two flagons with the waiter, a holy-water vessel, and a plate for offerings, the whole in silver gilt, and beautifully engraved. By the orders of his Majesty, transmitted through the minister of the interior, there was also presented to M. d'Astros, canon of Notre Dame, a box containing the crown of thorns, a nail, and a piece of the wood of the true cross, and a small vial, containing, it was said, some of the blood of our Lord, with an iron scourge which Saint Louis had used, and a tunic which had also belonged to that king.

In the morning Marshal Murat, Governor of Paris, had given a magnificent breakfast to the princes of Germany who had come to Paris in order to be present at the coronation; and after breakfast the marshal-governor conveyed them to Notre Dame in four carriages, each drawn by six horses, accompanied by an escort of a hundred men on horseback, and commanded by one of his *aides-de-camp*. This escort was especially noticeable for the elegance and richness of its uniforms.

The day after this grand and memorable solemnity was one of public rejoicing. From the early morning an immense crowd of the populace, enjoying the magnificent weather, spread itself over the boulevards, the quays, and the public squares, on which were prepared an infinite variety of amusements.

The heralds-at-arms went at an early hour through all the public places, throwing to the crowd, which pressed around them, medals struck in memory of the coronation. These medals represented on one side the likeness of the Emperor, his brow encircled with the crown of the Caesars, with this motto: *Napoleon, Empereur*. On the reverse side was the figure of a magistrate, with the attributes of his office around him, and that of an ancient warrior, bearing on a shield a hero crowned, and covered with the imperial mantle. Above was written: The Senate and the People. Soon after the passage of the heralds-at-arms the rejoicings commenced, and were prolonged far into the evening.

There had been erected on the Place Louis XV., which was called then the Place de la Concorde, four large square rooms of temporary woodwork, for dancing and waltzing. Stages for the presentation of pantomimes and farces were placed on the boulevards here and there;

groups of singers and musicians executed national airs and warlike marches; greased poles, rope-dancers, sports of all kinds, attracted the attention of promenaders at every step, and enabled them to await without impatience the illuminations and the fireworks.

The display of fireworks was most admirable. From the Place Louis XV. to the extreme end of the Boulevard Saint-Antoine, ran a double line of coloured lights in festoons. The palace of the Corps-Legislatif, formerly the Garde-Meuble, was resplendent with lights, and the gates of Saint-Denis and Saint-Martin were covered with lamps from top to bottom.

In the evening all those interested betook themselves to the quays and bridges, in order to witness the fireworks which were set off from the Bridge de la Concorde (now called Bridge Louis XVI.), and which far surpassed in magnificence all that had ever been seen.

Chapter 22

Wednesday, Dec. 5, three days after the coronation, the Emperor made a distribution of the colours on the Champ-de-Mars.

In front of *ecole-militaire* a balcony was erected, covered with awnings, and placed on a level with the apartments on the first floor. The middle awning, supported by four columns, each one of which was a gilded figure representing Victory, covered the throne on which their Majesties were seated. A most fortunate precaution, for on that day the weather was dreadful; the thaw had come suddenly, and every one knows what a Paris thaw is.

Around the throne were ranged princes and princesses, grand dignitaries, ministers, marshals of the Empire, grand officers of the crown, the ladies of the court, and the council of state.

This balcony was divided on the right and left into sixteen compartments, decorated with banners, and crowned with eagles, these divisions representing the sixteen cohorts of the Legion of Honour. Those on the right were occupied by the Senate, the officers of the Legion of Honour, the court of appeals, and the chiefs of the national treasury, and those on the left by the Tribunate and the Corps-Legislatif. At each end of the balcony was a pavilion. That on the side next the city was styled the imperial tribune, and intended for foreign princes, while the diplomatic corps and foreign personages of distinction filled the other pavilion.

From this gallery an immense staircase descended into the Champ-de-Mars, the first step of which formed a bench below the tribunes, and was occupied by the presidents of the cantons, the *prefects*, the sub-*prefects*, and the members of the municipal council. On each side of this staircase were placed the colossal figures of France making peace and France making war. Upon the steps were seated the colonels of regiments, and the presidents of the electoral colleges of the department, holding aloft the imperial eagles.

The cortege of their Majesties set out at noon from the chateau of the Tuileries, in the same order adopted at the coronation: the chasseurs of the guard and the squadrons of Mamelukes marching in front, the Legion d' Elite and the mounted grenadiers following the municipal guard; while the grenadiers of the guard closed up the line. Their Majesties having entered *l'ecole-militaire*, received the homage of the diplomatic corps, who were stationed for this purpose in the reception-rooms. Then the Emperor and Empress, having donned their insignia of royalty, took their seats upon the throne, while the air was rent with reiterated discharges of artillery and universal acclamations. At a given signal the deputations of the army, scattered over the Champ-de-Mars, placed themselves in solid column, and approached the throne amid a flourish of trumpets. The Emperor then rose, and immediately a deep silence ensued, while in a loud, clear tone he pronounced these words, "Soldiers, behold your standards! These eagles will serve you always as a rallying point. They will go wherever your Emperor may judge their presence necessary for the defence of his throne and of his people. Will you swear to sacrifice even your lives in their defence, and to keep them always by your valour in the path to victory? Do you swear it?"

"We swear it," repeated all the colonels in chorus, while the presidents of the colleges waved the flags they bore. "We swear it," said in its turn the whole army, while the bands played the celebrated march known as "The March of the Standards."

This intense enthusiasm was communicated to the spectators, who, in spite of the rain, pressed in crowds upon the terraces which surrounded the enclosure of the Champ-de-Mars. Soon the eagles took their designated places, and the army defiled in divisions before the throne of their Majesties.

Although nothing had been spared to give this ceremony every possible magnificence, it was by no means brilliant. It is true, the object of the occasion was imposing; but how could an impressive ceremony be held in a deluge of melted snow, and amid a sea of mud, which was the appearance the Champ-de-Mars presented that day? The troops were under arms from six in the morning, exposed to rain, and forced to endure it with no apparent necessity so at least they regarded it. The distribution of standards was to these men nothing more than a review; and surely it must strike a soldier as a very different matter to brave the weather on the field of battle, from what it is to stand idle, exposed to it for hours, with shining gun and empty cartridge-box, on a parade-day.

The cortege returned to the Tuileries at five o'clock, after which there was a grand banquet in the gallery of Diana, at which the Pope, the sovereign elector of Ratisbonne, the princes and princesses, the grand dignitaries, the diplomatic corps, and many other persons were guests. Their Majesties' table was placed in the midst of the gallery, upon a platform, and covered with a magnificent canopy, under which the Emperor seated himself on the right of the Empress, and the Pope on her left. The serving was done by the pages. The grand chamberlain, the grand equerry, and the colonel-general of the guard stood before his Majesty; the grand marshal of the palace on his right, and in front of the table, and lower down, the *prefect* of the palace; on the left, and opposite the grand marshal, was the grand master of ceremonies; all these also standing. On either side of their Majesties' table were those of their imperial highnesses, of the diplomatic corps, of the ministers and grand officers, and lastly that of the ladies of honour. At night there was given a reception, concert, and ball. The day after the distribution of the eagles, his imperial highness Prince Joseph presented to his Majesty the presidents of the electoral colleges of the departments; and the presidents of the colleges of the *arrondissements* and their *prefects* were next introduced, and received by his Majesty.

The Emperor conversed with the greater part of these officials on the needs of each department, and thanked them for their zeal in assisting him. Then he recommended to them especially the execution of the conscript law. "Without conscription," said his Majesty, "we should have neither power nor national independence. All Europe is subject to conscription. Our success and the strength of our position depend on our having a national army, and it is necessary to maintain this advantage with the greatest care."

These presentations occupied several days, during which his Majesty received in turn, and always with the same ceremonial, the presidents of the high courts of justice, the presidents of the councils-general of departments, the sub-*prefects*, the deputies of the colonies, the mayors of the thirty-six principal cities, the presidents of the cantons, the vice-presidents of the chambers of commerce, and the presidents of the consistories.

Some days later the city of Paris gave, in honour of their Majesties, a fete whose brilliance and magnificence surpassed any description that could possibly be given. On this occasion the Emperor, the Empress, and the princes Joseph and Louis, rode together in the coronation carriage; and batteries placed upon the Pont-Neuf announced the moment at which their Majesties began to ascend the steps of the Hotel de Ville. At the same time, buffets with pieces of fowl and fountains of wine attracted an immense crowd to the chief squares of each of the twelve municipalities of Paris, almost every individual of which had his share in the distribution of eatables, thanks to the precaution which the authorities took of distributing to none except those who presented tickets. The front of the Hotel de Ville was brilliant with coloured lamps; but what seemed to me the finest part of the whole display was a vessel pierced for eighty cannon, whose decks, masts, sails, and cordage were distinctly outlined in coloured lights. The crowning piece of all, which the Emperor himself set off, represented the Saint-Bernard as a volcano in eruption, in the midst of glaciers covered with snow. In it appeared the Emperor, glorious in the light, seated on his horse at the head of his army, climbing the steep summit of the mountain. More than seven hundred persons attended the ball, and yet there was no confusion. Their Majesties withdrew early. The Empress, on entering the apartment prepared for her at the Hotel de Ville, had found there a most magnificent toilets-service, all in gold. After it was brought to the Tuileries it was for many days her Majesty's chief source of entertainment and subject of conversation. She wished every one to see and admire it; and, in truth, no one who saw it could fail to do so. Their Majesties gave permission that this, with a service which the city had presented to the Emperor, should be placed on exhibition for several days, for the gratification of the public.

After the fireworks a superb balloon was sent up, the whole circumference of which, with the basket, and the ropes which attached it to the balloon, were decorated with countless festoons of coloured lights. This enormous body of coloured fire rising slowly and majestically into the air was a magnificent spectacle. It remained suspended for a while exactly over the city of Paris, as if to wait till public curiosity was fully satisfied, then, having reached a height at which it encountered a more rapid current of air, it suddenly disappeared, driven by the wind towards the south. After its disappearance it was thought of no more, but fifteen days later a very singular incident recalled it to public attention.

While I was dressing the Emperor the first day of the year, or the day before, one of his ministers was introduced; and the Emperor having inquired the news in Paris, as he always did of those whom he saw early in the morning, the minister replied, "I saw Cardinal Caprara late yesterday evening, and I learned from him a very singular circumstance."

"What was it? about what?" and his Majesty, imagining doubtless that it was some political incident, was preparing to carry off his minister into his cabinet, before having completed his toilet, when His

Excellency hastened to add, "Oh, it is nothing very serious, Sire! Your Majesty doubtless remembers that they have been discussing lately in the circle of her Majesty the Empress the chagrin of poor Garnerin, who has not succeeded up to this time in finding the balloon which he sent up on the day of the fete given to your Majesty by the city of Paris. He has at last received news of his balloon."

"Where did it fall?" asked the Emperor. "At Rome, Sire!"

"Ah, that is really very singular."

"Yes, Sire; Garnerin's balloon has thus, in twenty-four hours, shown your imperial crown in the two capitals of the world." Then the minister related to his Majesty the following details, which were published at the time, but which I think sufficiently interesting to be repeated here.

Garnerin had attached to his balloon the following notice: "The balloon carrying this letter was sent up at Paris on the evening of the 25th Frimaire (Dec. 16) by Monsieur Garnerin, special aeronaut of his Majesty the Emperor of Russia, and ordinary aeronaut of the French government, on the occasion of a fete given by the city of Paris to the Emperor Napoleon, celebrating his coronation. Whoever finds this balloon will please inform M. Garnerin, who will go to the spot."

The aeronaut expected, doubtless, to receive notice next day that his balloon had fallen in the plain of Saint-Denis, or in that of Grenelle; for it is to be presumed that he hardly dreamed of going to Rome when he engaged to go to the spot. More than fifteen days passed before he received the expected notice; and he had probably given up his balloon as lost, when there came the following letter from the nuncio of his Holiness:

> Cardinal Caprara is charged by His Excellency Cardinal Gonsalvi, Secretary of State of His Holiness, to remit to M. Garnerin a copy of a letter dated Dec. 18. He hastens to send it, and also to add a copy of the note which accompanied it. The cardinal also takes this occasion to assure Monsieur Garnerin of his highest esteem."

To this letter was added a translation of the report made to the cardinal, secretary of state at Rome, by the Duke of Mondragone, and dated from Anguillora, near Rome, Dec. 18:

> Yesterday evening about twenty-four o'clock there passed through the air a globe of astonishing size, which fell upon Lake Bracciano, and had the appearance of a house. Boatmen

were sent to bring it to land; but they were not able to do so, as a high wind prevailed, accompanied by snow. This morning early they succeeded in bringing it ashore. This globe is of oiled silk, covered with netting, and the wire gallery is a little broken. It seems to have been lighted by lamps and coloured lanterns, of which much debris remains. Attached to the globe was found the following notice. (Which is given above).

Thus we see that this balloon, which left Paris at seven o'clock on the evening of Dec. 16, had fallen next day, the 17th, near Rome, at twenty-four o'clock, that is to say, at sunset. It had crossed France, the Alps, etc., and passed over a space of more than three hundred leagues in twenty-two hours, its rate of speed being then fifteen leagues (45 miles) per hour; and, what renders this still more remarkable, is the fact that its weight was increased by decorations weighing five hundred pounds.

An account of the former trips of this balloon will not be without interest. Its first ascension was made in the presence of their Prussian Majesties and the whole court, upon which occasion it carried M. Garnerin, his wife, and M. Gaertner, and descended upon the frontiers of Saxony.

The second ascension was at St. Petersburg, in the presence of the Emperor, the two Empresses, and the court, carrying Monsieur and Madame Garnerin; and it fell a short distance off in a marsh. This was the first balloon ascension ever seen in Russia.

The third trial was also at St. Petersburg, in the presence of the imperial family. M. Garnerin ascended, accompanied by General Suolf; and the two travellers were transported across the Gulf of Friedland in three-quarters of an hour, and descended at Krasnoe-selo, twenty-five *versts* from St. Petersburg. The fourth trial took place at Moscow, and Garnerin ascended more than four thousand *toises*[1] He had many harrowing experiences, and at the end of seven hours descended three hundred and thirty *versts*[2] from Moscow, in the neighbourhood of the old frontiers of Russia. This same balloon was again used at the ascension which Madame Garnerin made at Moscow with Madame Toucheninolf, in the midst of a frightful storm, and amid flashes of lightning which killed three men within three hundred paces of the balloon, at the very instant of the ascension. These ladies descended without accident twenty-one *versts* from Moscow.

---

1. 24,000 ft.
2. 200 miles.

Soult

The city of Paris gave a gratuity of six hundred *francs* to the boatmen who had drawn out of Lake Bracciano the balloon, which was brought back to Paris, and placed in the museum of the Hotel de Ville.

I was a witness that same day of the kindness with which the Emperor received the petition of a poor woman, a notary's wife, I believe, whose husband had been condemned on account of some crime, I know not what, to a long imprisonment. As the carriage of their Imperial Majesties passed before the Palais-Royal, two women, one already old, the other sixteen or seventeen years of age, sprang to the door, crying, "Pardon for my husband, pardon for my father."

The Emperor immediately, in a loud tone, gave the order to stop his carriage, and held out his hand for the petition which the older of the two women would give to no one but him, at the same time consoling her with kind words, and showing a most touching interest lest she might be hurt by the horses of the marshals of the empire, who were on each side of the carriage. While this kindness of his august brother was exciting to the highest pitch the enthusiasm and sensibilities of the witnesses of this scene, Prince Louis, seated on the front seat of the carriage, also leaned out, trying to reassure the trembling young girl, and urging her to comfort her mother, and count with certainty on the Emperor's favourable consideration. The mother and daughter, overcome by their emotion, could make no reply; and as the cortege passed on, I saw the former on the point of falling in a swoon. She was carried into a neighbouring house, where she revived, and with her daughter shed tears of gratitude and joy.

The Corps Legislatif had decreed that a statue, in white marble, should be erected to the Emperor in their assembly hall, to commemorate the completion of the Civil Code. On the day of the unveiling of this monument, her Majesty the Empress, the princes Joseph, Louis, Borghese, Bacciochi, and their wives, with other members of the imperial family, deputations of the principal orders of the state, the diplomatic corps, and many foreigners of distinction, the marshals of the empire, and a considerable number of general officers, assembled at seven o'clock in the evening at the palace of the Legislative Corps.

As the Empress appeared in the hall, the entire assembly rose, and a band of music, stationed in the neighbouring stand, rendered the well-known chorus from Gluck, "How many charms! What majesty!" Scarcely had the first strains of this chorus been heard than each one was struck with the happy coincidence, and applause burst forth from all sides.

By invitation of the president, Marshals Murat and Massena unveiled the statue; and all eyes were fixed on this image of the Emperor, his brows encircled with a crown of laurel, and entwined with oak and olive leaves. When silence had succeeded to the acclamations excited by this sight, M. de Vaublanc mounted the tribune, and pronounced a discourse, which was loudly applauded in the assembly, whose sentiments it faithfully expressed.

"Gentlemen," said the orator, "you have celebrated the completion of the Civil Code of France by an act of admiration and of gratitude; you have awarded a statue to the illustrious prince whose firmness and perseverance have led to the completion of that grand work, while at the same time his vast intelligence has shed a most glorious light over this noble department of human institutions. First Consul then, Emperor of the French today, he appears in the temple of the laws, his head adorned with a triumphal crown as victory has so often adorned it, while foretelling that this should change to the diadem of kings, and covered with the imperial mantle, noble attribute of the highest of dignities.

"Doubtless, on this solemn day, in presence of the princes and the great of the state, before the august person whom the Empire honours for her beautiful character even more than for the high rank of which her virtues render her so worthy, in this glorious fete in which we would reunite all France, you will permit my feeble voice to be raised a moment, and to recall to you by what immortal actions Napoleon entered upon this wonderful career of power and honour.

"If praise corrupts weak minds, it is the nourishment of great souls; and the grand deeds of heroes are ties which bind them to their country. To recapitulate them is to say that we expect from them a combination of those grand thoughts, those generous sentiments, those glorious deeds, so nobly rewarded by the admiration and gratitude of the public.

"Victorious in the three quarters of the world, peacemaker of Europe, legislator of France, having bestowed and added provinces to the Empire, does not this glorious record suffice to render him worthy at one and the same time both of this august title of Emperor of the French, and this monument erected in the temple of the laws? And yet I would wish to make you forget these brilliant recollections which I have just recalled. With a stronger voice than that which sounded his praises, I would say to you: erase from your minds this glory of the legislator, this glory of the warrior, and say to yourselves, before the 18th Brumaire, when fatal laws were promulgated, and when the destructive principles proclaimed anew were already dragging along men and things with a rapidity which it would soon have been impossible to arrest—who appeared suddenly like a beneficent star, who came to abrogate these laws, who filled up the half-open abyss? You have survived, each one of you, through those threatening scenes; you live, and you owe it to him whose image you now behold. You, who were miserable outlaws, have returned, you breathe again the gentle air of your native land, you embrace your children, your wives, your friends; and you owe it to this great man. I speak no longer of his glory, I no longer bear witness to that; but I invoke humanity on the one side, gratitude on the other; and I demand of you, to whom do you owe a happiness so great so extraordinary, so unexpected? . . . And you, each and all, reply with me—to the great man whose image we behold."

The president repeated in his turn a similar eulogium, in very similar terms; and few persons then dreamed of thinking these praises exaggerated, though their opinions have perhaps changed since.

After the ceremony the Empress, on the arm of the president, passed into the hall of conference, where her Majesty's table had been prepared under a magnificent dais of crimson silk, and covers for nearly three hundred guests had been laid by the caterer Robert, in the different halls of the palace. To the dinner succeeded a brilliant ball. The most remarkable thing in this fete was the indescribable luxury of flowers and shrubs, which must doubtless have been collected at great expense, owing to the severity of the winter. The halls of Lucrece and of La Reunion, in which the dancing quadrilles were formed, resembled an immense parterre of roses, laurel, lilac, jonquils, lilies, and jessamine.

Chapter 23

It was the 2nd of January, 1805, exactly a month after the coronation, that I formed with the eldest daughter of M. Charvet a union which has been, and will I trust ever be, the greatest happiness of my life. I promised the reader to say very little of myself; and, in fact, how could he be interested in any details of my own private life which did not throw additional light upon the character of the great man about whom I have undertaken to write? Nevertheless, I will ask permission to return for a little while to this, the most interesting of all periods to me, and which exerted such an influence upon my whole life. Surely he who recalls and relates his souvenirs is not forbidden to attach some importance to those which most nearly concern himself. Moreover, even in the most personal events of my life, there were instances in which their Majesties took a part, and which, from that fact, are of importance in enabling the reader to form a correct estimate of the characters of both the Emperor and the Empress.

My wife's mother had been presented to Madame Bonaparte during the first campaign in Italy, and she had been pleased with her; for Madame Bonaparte, who was so perfectly good, had, in her own experience, also endured trials, and knew how to sympathize with the sorrows of others.

She promised to interest the General in the fate of my father-in-law, who had just lost his place in the treasury. During this time Madame Charvet was in correspondence with a friend of her husband, who was, I think, the courier of General Bonaparte; and the latter having opened and read these letters addressed to his courier, inquired who was this young woman that wrote such interesting and intelligent letters, and Madame Charvet well deserved this double praise. My father-in-law's friend, while replying to the question of the General-in-chief, took occasion to relate the misfortunes of the family, and the General remarked that, on his return to Paris, he wished to meet M. and Madame Charvet; in consequence of which they were presented to him, and Madame Bonaparte rejoiced to learn that her *protégées* had also become those of her husband. It had been decided that M. Charvet should follow the General to Egypt; but when my father-in-law arrived at Toulon, Madame Bonaparte requested that he should accompany her to the waters of Plombieres. I have previously related the accident which occurred at Plombieres, and that M. Charvet was sent to Saint-Germain to bring Mademoiselle Hortense from the boarding-school to her mother. On his return to Paris, M. Charvet searched through all the suburbs to find a country-seat, as the General had charged his wife to purchase one during his absence.

When Madame Bonaparte decided on Malmaison, M. Charvet, his wife, and their three children were installed in this charming residence.

My father-in-law was very faithful to the interests of these benefactors of his family, and Madame Charvet often acted as private secretary to Madame Bonaparte.

Mademoiselle Louise, who became my wife, and Mademoiselle Zoe, her younger sister, were favourites of Madame Bonaparte, especially the latter, who passed more time than Louise at Malmaison. The condescension of their noble protectress had rendered this child so familiar, that she said thou habitually to Madame Bonaparte. One day she said to her, "Thou art happy. Thou hast no mamma to scold thee when thou tearest thy dresses."

During one of the campaigns that I made while in the service of the Emperor, I wrote to my wife, inquiring about the life that her sister led at Malmaison. In her answer, among other things, she said (I copy a passage from one of her letters):

> Sometimes we take part in performances such as I had never dreamed of. For instance, one evening the saloon was divided in half by a gauze curtain, behind which was a bed arranged in Greek style, on which a man lay asleep, clothed in long white drapery. Near the sleeper Madame Bonaparte and the other ladies beat in unison (not in perfect accord, however) on bronze vases, making, as you may imagine, a terrible kind of music. During this charivari, one of the gentlemen held me around the waist, and raised me from the ground, while I shook my arms and legs in time to the music. The concert of these ladies awoke the sleeper, who stared wildly at me, frightened at my gestures, then sprang up and ran with all his might, followed by my brother, who crept

on all fours, representing a dog, I think, which belonged to this strange person. As I was then a mere child, I have only a confused idea of all this; but the society of Madame Bonaparte seemed to be much occupied with similar amusements.

When the First Consul went to live at Saint-Cloud, he expressed his high opinion of my father-in-law in the most flattering manner, and made him concierge of the chateau, which was a confidential position, the duties and responsibilities of which were considerable.

M. Charvet was charged with organizing the household; and, by orders of the First Consul, he selected from among the old servants of the queen those to whom he gave places as porters, scrubbers, and grooms of the chateau, and he gave pensions to those unable to work.

When the chateau took fire in 1802, as I have related previously, Madame Charvet, being several months pregnant, was terribly frightened; and as it was not thought best to bleed her, she became very ill, and died at the age of thirty years. Louise had been at a boarding-school for several years; but her father now brought her home to keep house for him, though she was then only twelve years old. One of her friends has kindly allowed me to see a letter which Louise addressed to her a short time after our marriage, and from which I have made the following extracts:

> On my return from boarding-school I went to see her Majesty the Empress (then Madame Bonaparte) at the Tuileries. I was in deep mourning. She took me on her knee, and tried to console me, saying that she would be a mother to me, and would find me a husband. I wept, and said that I did not wish to marry. 'Not at present,' replied her Majesty, but that will come; be sure of it. I was, however, by no means persuaded that this would be the case. She caressed me a while longer, and I withdrew. When the First Consul was at Saint-Cloud, all the chiefs of the different departments of the household service assembled in the apartments of my father, who was the most popular, as well as the eldest, member of the household. M. Constant, who had seen me as a child at Malmaison, found me sufficiently attractive at Saint-Cloud to ask me of my father, subject to the approval of their Majesties; and it was decided that we should be married after the coronation. I was fourteen years old fifteen days after our marriage.
>
> Both my sister and I are always received with extreme kindness by her Majesty the Empress; and whenever, for fear of annoying her, we let some time pass without going to see her, she com-

plains of it to my father. She sometimes admits us to her morning toilet, which is conducted in our presence, and to which are admitted in her apartments only her women; and a few persons of her household, who, like us, count among their happiest moments those in which they can thus behold this adored princess. The conversations are almost always delightful, and her Majesty frequently relates anecdotes which a word from one or another of us recalls to her.

Her Majesty the Empress had promised Louise a dowry; but the money which she intended for that she spent otherwise, and consequently my wife had only a few jewels of little value and two or three pieces of stuff.

M. Charvet was too refined to recall this promise to her Majesty's recollection. However, that was the only way to get anything from her; for she knew no better how to economize than how to refuse. The Emperor asked me a short time after my marriage what the Empress had given my wife, and on my reply showed the greatest possible vexation; no doubt because the sum that had been demanded of him for Louise's dowry had been spent otherwise. His Majesty the Emperor had the goodness, while on this subject, to assure me that he himself would hereafter look after my interests, and that he was well satisfied with my services, and would prove it to me.

I have said above that my wife's younger sister was the favourite of her Majesty the Empress; and yet she received on her marriage no richer dowry than Louise, nevertheless, the Empress asked to have my sister-in-law's husband presented to her, and said to him in the most maternal tone, "Monsieur, I recommend my daughter to you, and I entreat you to make her happy. She deserves it, and I earnestly hope that you know how to appreciate her!" When my sister-in-law, fleeing from Compiegne, in 1814, went with her husband's mother to Evreux for her confinement, the Empress sent by her first *valet de chambre* every thing necessary for a young woman in that condition, and, even reproached her with not having come to Navarre.

My sister-in-law had been reared in the same boarding-school as Mademoiselle Josephine Tallien, god-daughter of the Empress, who has since married M. Pelet de la Lozere, and another daughter of Madame Tallien, Mademoiselle Clemence Cabarus. The school was conducted by Madame Vigogne, widow of the colonel of that name, and an old friend of the Empress, who had advised her to take a boarding-school, and promised to procure for her as many pupils as she could. This institution prospered under the direction of this lady, who was distinguished for her intelligence and culture; and she frequently brought to the Empress these *protégées*, with other young persons who by good conduct had earned this reward; and this was made a powerful means of exciting the emulation of these children, whom her Majesty overwhelmed with caresses, and presented with little gifts.

One morning just as Madame Vigogne was about to visit the Empress, and was descending the staircase to enter her carriage, she heard piercing cries in one of the schoolrooms, and, hastening to the spot, saw a young girl with her clothing on fire. With a presence of mind worthy of a mother, Madame Vigogne wrapped her pupil in the long train of her dress, and thus extinguished the flames, not, however, until the hands of the courageous instructress had been most painfully burned. She made the visit to her Majesty in this condition, and related to her the sad accident which had occurred; while her Majesty, who was easily moved by everything noble and generous, overwhelmed her with praises for her courage, and was so deeply touched that she wept with admiration, and ordered, her private physician to give his best services to Madame Vigogne and her young pupil.

Chapter 24

The Empress Josephine was of medium height, with an exquisite figure; and in all her movements there was an airiness and grace which gave to her walk something ethereal, without detracting from the majesty of the sovereign. Her expressive countenance portrayed all the emotions of her soul, while retaining the charming sweetness which was its ruling expression. In pleasure, as in grief, she was beautiful, and even against your will you would smile when she smiled; if she was sad, you would be also. Never did a woman justify better than she the expression that the eyes are the mirror of the soul. Hers were of a deep blue, and nearly always half closed by her long lids, which were slightly arched, and fringed with the most beautiful lashes in the world; in regarding her you felt yourself drawn to her by an irresistible power. It must have been difficult for the Empress to give severity to that seductive look; but she could do this, and well knew how to render it imposing when necessary. Her hair was very beautiful, long and silken, its nut-brown tint contrasting exquisitely with the dazzling whiteness of her fine fresh complexion. At the commencement of her supreme power, the Empress still liked to adorn her head in the morning with a red madras handkerchief, which gave her a most piquant Creole air, and rendered her still more charming.

But what more than all else constituted the inexpressible charm of the Empress's presence were the ravishing tones of her voice. How many times have I, like many others, stopped suddenly on hearing that voice; simply to enjoy the pleasure of listening to it. It cannot perhaps be said that the Empress was a strictly beautiful woman; but her lovely countenance, expressing sweetness and good nature, and the angelic grace diffused around her person, made her the most attractive of women.

During her stay at Saint-Cloud, the Empress rose habitually at nine o'clock, and made her first toilet, which lasted till ten; then she passed into a saloon, where she found assembled those persons who had solicited and obtained the favour of an audience; and sometimes also at this hour, and in the same saloon, her Majesty received her trades people; and at eleven o'clock, when the Emperor was absent, she breakfasted with her first lady of honour and a few others. Madame de la Rochefoucauld, first lady of honour to the Empress, was a hunchback, and so small that it was necessary, when she was to have a place at the table, to heighten the seat of her chair by another very thick cushion made of violet satin. Madame de la Rochefoucauld knew well how to efface, by means of her bright and sparkling, though somewhat caustic wit, her striking elegance, and her exquisite court manners, any unpleasant impression which might be made by her physical deformity.

Before breakfast the Empress had a game of billiards; or, when the weather was good, she walked in the gardens or in the enclosed park, which recreation lasted only a short while, and her Majesty soon returned to her apartments, and occupied herself with embroidery, while talking with her ladies, like herself, occupied with some kind of needlework. When it happened that they were not interrupted by visits, between two and three o'clock in the afternoon the Empress took a drive in an open *barouche*; and on her return from this the grand toilet took place, at which the Emperor was sometimes present.

Now and then, also, his Majesty surprised the Empress in her saloon; and we were sure to find him, on those occasions, amusing, amiable, and in fine spirits.

At six o'clock dinner was served; this the Emperor frequently forgot, and delayed it indefinitely, in consequence of which dinner was more than once eaten at nine or ten o'clock in the evening. Their Majesties dined together alone, or in the company of a few invited guests, princes of the imperial family, or ministers, after which there was a concert, reception, or the theatre; and at midnight every one retired except the Empress, who greatly enjoyed sitting up late, and then played backgammon with one of the chamberlains. The Count de Beaumont was thus honoured most frequently.

On the days of the chase the Empress and her ladies followed in the coach. They had a special costume for this occasion, consisting of a kind of green riding-habit, and a hat ornamented with white plumes. All the ladies who followed the chase dined with their Majesties.

When the Empress spent the night in the Emperor's apartment, I entered in the morning, as usual, between seven and eight o'clock, and nearly always found the august spouses awake. The Emperor usually ordered tea, or an infusion of orange flowers, and rose immediately, the Empress saying to him, with a laugh, "What, rising already? Rest a little longer."

"Well, you are not asleep, then?" replied his Majesty, rolling her over in the covering, giving her little slaps on her cheeks and shoulders, laughing, and kissing her.

At the end of a few moments the Empress rose also, put on a wrapper, and read the journals, or descended by the little communicating stairway to her own apartment, never leaving the Emperor without a few words expressing the most touching affection and good-will.

Elegant and simple in her dress, the Empress submitted with regret to the necessity of toilets of state. Jewels, however, were much to her taste; and, as she had always been fond of them; the Emperor presented her with them often and in great quantities; and she greatly enjoyed adorning herself with them, and still more exhibiting them to the admiration of others.

One morning, when my wife was present at her toilet, her Majesty related that, being newly married to M. de Beauharnais, and much delighted with the ornaments he had given her, she was in the habit of carrying them around in her reticule (reticules were then an essential part of a woman's dress), and showing them to her young friends.

As the Empress spoke of her reticule, she ordered one of her ladies to hunt for one to show my wife. The lady whom the Empress addressed could scarcely repress a laugh at this singular request, and assured her Majesty that there was nothing similar to that now in her wardrobe; to which the Empress replied, with an air of regret, that she would have really liked to see again one of her old reticules, and that the years hall brought great changes. The jewels of the Empress Josephine could hardly have been contained in the reticule of Madame de Beauharnais, however long or deep it might have been; for the jewel case which had belonged to Queen Marie Antoinette, and which had never been quite full, was too small for the Empress. One day, when she wished to exhibit all her ornaments to several ladies who expressed a desire to see them, it was necessary to prepare a large table on which to place the caskets; and, as this table was not sufficient, several other pieces of furniture were also covered with them.

Good to excess, as everyone knows, sympathetic beyond all expression, generous even to prodigality, the Empress made the happiness of all who surrounded her; loving her husband with a devotion which nothing ever changed, and which was as deep in her last moments as at the period when Madame Beauharnais and General Bonaparte made to each other a mutual avowal of their love. Josephine was long the only woman loved by the Emperor, as she well deserved to have ever been; and for several years the harmony of this imperial household was most touching. Attentive, loving, and entirely devoted to Josephine, the Emperor took pleasure in embracing her neck, her figure, giving her taps, and calling her *'ma grosse bete'*; all of which did not prevent, it is true, his being guilty of some infidelities, but without failing otherwise in his conjugal duties. On her side the Empress adored him, sought by every means to please him, to divine his wishes, and to forestall his least desires.

At first she gave her husband cause for jealousy. Having been strongly prejudiced against her by indiscreet reports, during the campaign of Egypt, the Emperor on his return had explanations with her, which did not always end without lamentations and violent scenes; but peace was soon restored, and was thereafter very rarely broken, for the Emperor could not fail to feel the influence of so many attractions and such loveliness.

The Empress had a remarkable memory, of which the Emperor often availed himself; she was also an excellent musician, played well on the harp, and sang with taste. She had perfect tact, an exquisite perception of what was suitable, the soundest, most infallible judgment imaginable, and, with a disposition always lovely, always the same, indulgent to her enemies as to her friends, she restored peace wherever there was quarrel or discord. When the Emperor was vexed with his brothers or other persons, which often happened, the Empress spoke a few words, and everything was settled. If she demanded a pardon, it was very rare that the Emperor did not grant it, however grave the crime committed; and I could cite a thousand examples of pardons thus solicited and obtained. One occurrence which is almost personal to me will sufficiently prove how all-powerful was the intercession of this good Empress.

Her Majesty's head valet being one day a little affected by the wine he had taken at a breakfast with some friends, was obliged, from the nature of his duties, to be present at the time of their Majesties' dinner, and to stand behind the Empress in order to take and hand her the plates. Excited by the fumes of the champagne, he had the misfortune to utter some improper words, which, though pronounced in a low tone, the Emperor unfortunately overheard. His Majesty cast lightning glances at M. Frere, who thus perceived the gravity of his fault; and, when dinner was over, gave orders to discharge the impudent valet, in a tone which left no hope and permitted no reply.

Monsieur Frere was an excellent servant, a gentle, good, and honest man; it was the first fault of this kind of which he could be accused, and consequently he deserved indulgence. Application was made to the grand marshal, who refused to intercede, well knowing the inflexibility of the Emperor; and many other persons whom the poor man begged to intercede for him having replied as the grand marshal had done, M. Frere came in despair to bid us *adieu*. I dared to take his cause in hand, with the hope that by seizing a favourable moment I might succeed in appeasing his Majesty. The order of discharge required M. Frere to leave the palace in twenty-four hours; but I advised him not to obey it, but to keep himself, however, constantly concealed in his room, which he did. That evening on retiring, his Majesty spoke to me of what had passed, showing much anger, so I judged that silence was the best course to take; and therefore waited; but the next day the Empress had the kindness to tell me that she would be present at her husband's toilet, and that, if I thought proper to open the matter, she would sustain me with all her influence. Consequently, finding the Emperor in a good humour, I spoke of M. Frere; and depicting to his Majesty the despair of this poor man, I pointed out to him the reasons which might excuse the impropriety of his conduct. "Sire," said I, "he is a good man, who has no fortune, and supports a numerous family; and if he has to quit the service of her Majesty the Empress, it will not be believed that it was on account of a fault for which the wine was more to be blamed than he, and he will be utterly ruined." To these words, as well as to many other suggestions, the Emperor only replied by interruptions, made with every appearance of a decided opposition to the pardon which I had requested. Fortunately the Empress was good enough to come to my assistance, and said to her husband in her own gentle tones, always so touching and full of expression, *"Mon ami,* if you are willing to pardon him, you will be doing me a favour." Emboldened by this powerful patronage, I renewed my solicitations; to which the Emperor at last replied abruptly, addressing himself to both the Empress and myself, "In short, you wish it; well, let him stay then."

Monsieur Frere thanked me with his whole heart, and could hardly believe the good news which I brought him; and as for the Empress, she was made happy by the joy of this faithful servant, who gave her during the remainder of his life every proof of his entire devotion. I have been assured that, in 1814, on the departure of the Emperor for the Island of Elba, Monsieur Frere was by no means the last to blame my conduct, the motive of which he could not possibly know; but I am not willing to believe this, for it seems to me that in his place, if I thought I could not defend an absent friend, I should at least have kept silence.

As I have said, the Empress was extremely generous, and bestowed much in alms, and was most ingenious in finding occasions for their bestowal. Many *émigrés* lived solely on her benefactions; she also kept up a very active correspondence with the Sisters of Charity who nursed the sick, and sent them a multitude of things. Her valets were ordered to go in every direction, carrying to the needy the assistance of her inexhaustible benevolence, while numerous other persons also received each day similar commissions; and all these alms, all these multiplied gifts which were so widely diffused, received an inestimable value from the grace with which they were offered, and the good judgment with which they were distributed. I could cite a thousand instances of this delicate generosity.

Monsieur de Beauharnais had at the time of his marriage to Josephine a natural daughter named Adele. The Empress reared her as if she had been her own daughter, had her carefully educated, gave her a generous dowry, and married her to a *prefect* of the Empire.

If the Empress showed so much tenderness for a daughter who was not her own, it is impossible to give an idea of her love and devotion to Queen Hortense and Prince Eugene, which devotion her children fully returned; and there was never a better or happier mother. She was very proud of her children, and spoke of them always with an enthusiasm which seemed very natural to all who knew the Queen of Holland and the Vice-King of Italy. I have related how, having been left an orphan at a very early age by the Revolutionary scaffold, young Beauharnais had gained the heart of General Bonaparte by an interview in which he requested of him his father's sword, and that this action inspired in the General a wish to become acquainted with Josephine, and the result of that interview, all of which events are matters of history. When Madame de Beauharnais had become the wife of General Bonaparte, Eugene entered on a military career, and attached himself immediately to the fortunes of his step-father, whom he accompanied to Italy in the capacity of *aide-de-camp*. He was chief of squadron in the chasseurs of the Consular Guard, and at the immortal battle of Marengo shared all the dangers of the one who took so much pleasure in calling him his son. A few years later the chief of squadron had become Vice-King of Italy, the presumptive heir of the imperial crown (a title which, in truth, he did not long preserve), and husband of the daughter of a king.

The vice-queen (Augusta Amelia of Bavaria) was handsome and good as an angel. I happened to be at Malmaison on the day the Empress received the portrait of her daughter-in-law, surrounded by three or four children, one upon her shoulder, another at her feet, and a third in her arms, all of whom had most lovely faces. The Empress, seeing me, deigned to call me to admire with her this collection of charming heads; and I perceived that, while speaking, her eyes were full of tears. The portraits were well painted, and I had occasion later to find that they were perfect likenesses. From this time the only question was playthings and rare articles of all sorts to be bought for these dear children, the Empress going in person to select the presents she desired for them, and having them packed under her own eyes.

The prince's valet has assured me that, at the time of the divorce, Prince Eugene wrote his wife a very desponding letter, and perhaps expressed in it some regret at not being an adopted son of the Emperor, to which the Princess replied most tenderly, saying, among other things, "It is not the heir of the Emperor whom I married and whom I love, but it is Eugene de Beauharnais." The Prince read this sentence and some others in the presence of the person from whom I have these facts, and who was touched even to tears. Such a woman deserved more than a throne.

After that event, so grievous to the heart of the Empress, and for which she never found consolation, she left Malmaison no more, except to make a few visits to Navarre.

Each time that I returned to Paris with the Emperor, I had no sooner arrived than my first duty was to go to Malmaison, though I was rarely the bearer of a letter from the Emperor, as he wrote to Josephine only on extraordinary occasions. "Tell the Empress I am well, and that I wish her to be happy," were almost invariably the parting words of the Emperor as I set out. The moment I arrived the Empress quitted everything to speak to me; and I frequently remained an hour and often two hours with her; during which time there was no question of anything save the Emperor. I must tell her all that he had suffered on the journey, if he had been sad or gay, sick or well; while she wept over the details as I repeated them, and gave me a thousand directions regarding his health, and the cares with which she desired I should surround him. After this she deigned to question me about myself, my prospects, the health of my wife, her former *protégée*; and at last dismissed me, with a letter for his Majesty, begging me to say to the Emperor how happy she would be if he would come to see her.

Before his departure for Russia, the Empress, distressed at this war, of which she entirely disapproved, again redoubled her recommendations concerning the Emperor, and made me a present of her portrait, saying to me, "My good Constant, I rely on you; if the Emperor were sick, you would inform me of it, would you not? Conceal nothing from me, I love him so much."

Certainly the Empress had innumerable means of hearing news of his Majesty; but I am persuaded that, had she received each day one hundred letters from those near the Emperor, she would have read and reread them with the same avidity.

When I had returned from Saint-Cloud to the Tuileries, the Emperor asked me how Josephine was, and if I found her in good spirits; he received with pleasure the letters I brought, and hastened to open them. All the time I was travelling, or on the campaign in the suite of his Majesty, in writing to my wife, I spoke of the Emperor, and the good princess was delighted that she showed my letters to her. In fact, everything having the least connection with her husband interested the Empress to a degree which proved well the singular devotion that she still felt for him after, as before, their separation. Too generous, and unable to keep her expenses within her income, it often happened that the Empress was obliged to send away her furnishers unpaid the very day she had herself fixed for the settlement of their bills; and as this reached the ears of the Emperor on one occasion, there ensued a very unpleasant scene between the Empress and himself, ending in a decision, that in future no merchant or furnisher should come to the chateau without a letter from the lady of attire or secretary of orders; and this plan, once decided upon, was followed very closely until the divorce. During this explanation the Empress wept freely, and promised to be more economical, upon which the Emperor pardoned and embraced her, and peace was made, this being, I think, the last quarrel of this nature which disturbed the imperial household.

I have heard that after the divorce, the allowance of the Empress having been exceeded, the Emperor reproached the superintendent of Malmaison with this fact, who in turn informed Josephine. His kind-hearted mistress, much distressed at the annoyance which her steward had experienced, and not knowing how to establish a better order of things, assembled a council of her household, over which she presided in a linen dress without ornament; this dress had been made in great haste, and was used only this once. The Empress, whom the necessity for a refusal always reduced to despair, was continually besieged by merchants, who assured her that they had made such or such a thing expressly for her own use, begging her not to return it because they would not be able to dispose of it; in consequence of which the Empress kept everything they brought, though they afterwards had to be paid for.

The Empress was always extremely polite in her intercourse with the ladies of her household; and a reproach never came from those lips which seemed formed to say only pleasant things; and if any of her ladies gave her cause of dissatisfaction, the only punishment she inflicted was an absolute silence on her part, which lasted one, two, three, or even eight days, the time being longer or shorter according to the gravity of the fault. And indeed this penalty, apparently so mild, was really very cruel to many, so well did the Empress know how to make herself adored by those around her.

In the time of the Consulate, Madame Bonaparte often received from cities which had been conquered by her husband, or from those persons who desired to obtain her intercession with the First Consul, quantities of valuable furniture, curiosities of all kinds, pictures, stuffs, etc. At first these presents delighted Madame Bonaparte greatly; and she took a childish pleasure in having the cases opened to find what was inside, personally assisting in unpacking them, and rummaging through all these pretty things. But soon these consignments became so considerable, and were so often repeated, that it was found necessary to place them in an apartment, of which my father-in-law kept the key, and where the boxes remained untouched until it pleased Madame Bonaparte to have them opened.

When the First. Consul decided that he would take up his residence at Saint-Cloud, my father-in-law was obliged to leave Malmaison, and install himself in the new palace, as the master wished him to take charge there.

Before leaving Malmaison, my father-in-law rendered an account to Madame Bonaparte of everything committed to his care, and all the cases which were piled up from floor to ceiling in two rooms were opened in her presence. Madame Bonaparte was astonished at such marvellous riches, comprising marbles, bronzes, and magnificent pictures, of which Eugene, Hortense, and the sisters of the First Consul received a large part, and the remainder was used in decorating the apartments of Malmaison.

The Empress's love of ornaments included for a while antique curiosities, cut stones, and medals. M. Denon flattered this whim, and ended by persuading the good Josephine that she was a perfect connoisseur in antiques, and that she should have at Malmaison a cabinet, a keeper for it, etc. This proposition, which flattered the self-love of the Empress, was favourably received; the room was selected, M. de M—— made keeper, and the new cabinet enriched by diminishing in the same proportion the rich furniture of the apartments of the chateau. M. Denon, who had originated this idea, took upon himself to make a collection of medals; but this idea, which came so suddenly, vanished as suddenly; the cabinet was changed into a saloon for guests, and the antiques relegated to the antechamber of the bathing hall, while M. de M——, having no longer anything to keep, remained constantly in Paris.

A short time after this, two ladies of the palace took a fancy to persuade the Empress that nothing could be handsomer or more worthy of her than a necklace of Greek and Roman antique stones perfectly matched. Several chamberlains approved the idea, which, of course, pleased the Empress, for she was very fond of anything unique; and consequently one morning, as I was dressing the Emperor, the Empress entered, and, after a little conversation, said, "Bonaparte, some ladies have advised me to have a necklace made of antique stones, and I came to ask you to urge M. Denon to select only very handsome ones." The Emperor burst out laughing, and refused flatly at first; but just then the grand marshal of the palace arrived, and the Emperor informed him of this request of the Empress, asking his opinion. M. le duc de Frioul thought it very reasonable, and joined his entreaties to those of the Empress. "It is an egregious folly," said the Emperor; "but we are obliged to grant it, because the women wish it, so, Duroc, go to the cabinet of antiques, and choose whatever is necessary."

M. le duc de Frioul soon returned with the finest stones in the collection, which the crown jeweller mounted magnificently; but this ornament was of such enormous weight that the Empress never wore it.

Though I may be accused of making tiresome repetitions, I must say that the Empress seized, with an eagerness which cannot be described, on all occasions of making benefactions. For instance, one morning when she was breakfasting alone with his Majesty, the cries of an infant were suddenly heard proceeding from a private staircase. The Emperor was annoyed at this, and with a frown, asked sharply what that meant. I went to investigate, and found a new-born child, carefully and neatly dressed, asleep in a kind of cradle, with a ribbon around its body from which hung a folded paper. I returned to tell what I had seen; and the Empress at once exclaimed, "O Constant! bring me the cradle." The Emperor would not permit this at first, and expressed his surprise and disapprobation that it should have been thus introduced into the interior of his apartments, whereupon her Majesty, having pointed out to him that it must have been done by some one of the household, he turned towards me, and gave me a searching look, as if to ask if it was I who had originated this idea. I shook my head in denial. At that moment the baby began to cry, and the Emperor could not keep from smiling, still growling, and saying, "Josephine, send away that monkey!"

The Empress, wishing to profit by this return of good humour, sent me for the cradle, which I brought to her. She caressed the little new-born babe, quieted it, and read the paper attached to which was a petition from its parents. Then she approached the Emperor, insisting on his caressing the infant himself, and pinching its fat little cheeks; which he did without much urging, for the Emperor himself loved to play with children. At last her Majesty the Empress, having placed a roll of napoleons in the cradle, had the little bundle in swaddling clothes carried to the concierge of the palace, in order that he might restore it to its parents.

I will now give another instance of the kindness of heart of her Majesty the Empress, of which I had the honour to be a witness, as well as of the preceding.

A few days before the coronation, a little girl four and a half years old had been rescued from the Seine; and a charitable lady, Madame Fabien Pillet, was much interested in providing a home for the poor orphan. At the time of the coronation, the Empress, who had been informed of this occurrence, asked to see this child, and having regarded it a few moments with much emotion, offered her protection most gracefully and sincerely to Madame Pillet and her husband, and announced to them that she would take upon herself the care of the little girl's future; then, with her usual delicacy and in the affectionate tone which was so natural to her, the Empress added, "Your good action has given you too many claims over the poor little girl for me to deprive you of the pleasure of completing your work, I therefore beg your permission to furnish the expenses of her education. You have the privilege of putting her in boarding-school, and watching over her; and I wish to take only a secondary position, as her benefactress." It was the most touching sight imaginable to see her Majesty, while uttering these delicate and generous words, pass her hands through the hair of the poor little girl, as she had just called her, and kiss her brow with the tenderness of a mother. M. and Madame Pillet withdrew, for they could no longer bear this touching scene.

Chapter 25

The appointment of General Junot as ambassador to Portugal recalled to my recollection a laughable anecdote concerning him, which greatly amused the Emperor. While in camp at Boulogne, the Emperor had published in the order of the day that every soldier should discard powder, and arrange his hair *'a la Titus'*, on which there was much murmuring; but at last all submitted to the order of the chief, except one old grenadier belonging to the corps commanded by General Junot. Not being able to decide on the sacrifice of his oily tresses or his queue, the old soldier swore he would submit to it only in case his general would himself cut off the first lock; and all the officers interested in this affair having succeeded in getting no other reply, at last reported him to the general. "That can be managed; bring the idiot to me!" replied he. The grenadier was called, and General Junot himself applied the scissors to an oiled and powdered lock; after which he gave twenty *francs* to the grumbler, who went away satisfied to let the barber of the regiment finish the operation.

The Emperor having been informed of this adventure, laughed most heartily, and praised Junot, complimenting him on his condescension.

I could cite a thousand similar instances of the kindness of heart joined to military brusqueness which characterized General Junot, and could also cite those of another kind, which would do less honour to his name. The slight control he had over himself often threw him into transports of rage, the most ordinary effect of which was forgetfulness of his rank and the dignity of demeanour which it demanded of him. Every one has heard the adventure of the gambling-house, when he tore up the cards, upset the furniture, and beat both bankers and croupiers, to indemnify himself for the loss of his money; and the worst of it was, he was at that very time Governor of Paris. The Emperor, informed of this scandal, sent for him, and demanded of him (he was still very angry), if he had sworn to live and die mad.

This might have been, from the sequel, taken as a prediction; for the unfortunate general died at last in a fit of mental aberration. He replied in such improper terms to the reprimands of the Emperor that he was sent, perhaps in order that he might have time to calm himself, to the army of England. It was not only in gaming-houses, however, that the governor thus compromised his dignity; for I have heard other stories about him of a still more shocking character, which I will not allow myself to repeat. The truth is, General Junot prided himself much less on respecting the proprieties than on being one of the best pistol-shots in the army. While riding in the country, he would often put his horse into a gallop, and with a pistol in each hand, never fail to cut off, in passing, the heads of the ducks or chickens which he took as his target. He could cut off a small twig from a tree at twenty-five paces; and I have even heard it said (I am far from guaranteeing the truth of this) that on one occasion, with the consent of the party whose imprudence thus put his life in peril, he cut half in two the stem of a clay pipe, hardly three inches long, which a soldier held between his teeth.

In the first journey which Madame Bonaparte made into Italy to rejoin her husband, she remained some time at Milan. She had at that time in her service a *femme de chambre* named Louise, a large and very beautiful woman, and who showed favours, well remunerated however, to the brave Junot. As soon as her duties were ended, Louise, far more gorgeously attired than Madame Bonaparte, entered an elegant carriage, and rode through the city and the principal promenades, often eclipsing the wife of the General-in-chief. On his return to Paris, the latter obliged his wife to dismiss the beautiful Louise, who, abandoned by her inconstant lover, fell into great destitution; and I often saw her afterwards at the residence of Josephine begging aid, which was always most kindly granted. This young woman, who had dared to rival Madame Bonaparte in elegance, ended by marrying, I think, an English jockey, led a most unhappy life, and died in a miserable condition.

The First Consul of the French Republic, now become Emperor of the French, could no longer be satisfied with the title of President of Italy. Therefore, when new deputies of the Cisalpine Republic passed over the mountains, and gathered at Paris for consultation, they conferred on his Majesty the title of King of Italy, which he accepted, and a few days after his acceptance he set out for Milan, where he was to be crowned.

I returned with the greatest pleasure to that beautiful country, of which, notwithstanding the fatigues and dangers of war, I retained the most delightful recollections. How different the circumstances now! As a sovereign the Emperor was now about to cross the Alps, Piedmont, and Lombardy, each gorge, each stream, each defile of which we had been obliged in a former visit to carry by force of arms. In 1800 the escort of the First Consul was a warlike army; in 1805 it was a peaceful procession of chamberlains, pages, maids of honour, and officers of the palace.

Before his departure the Emperor held in his arms at the baptismal font, in company with Madame his mother, Prince Napoleon Louis, second son of his brother Prince Louis.[1] The three sons of Queen Hortense had, if I am not much mistaken, the Emperor as godfather; but he loved most tenderly the eldest of the three, Prince Napoleon Charles, who died at the age of five years, Prince Royal of Holland. I shall speak afterwards of this lovely child, whose death threw his father and mother into the most overwhelming grief, was the cause of great sorrow to the Emperor, and may be considered as the source of the gravest events.

After the baptismal fetes we set out for Italy, accompanied by the Empress Josephine. Whenever it was convenient the Emperor liked to take her with him; but she always desired to accompany her husband, whether or not this was the case.

The Emperor usually kept his journey a profound secret up to the moment of his departure, and ordered at midnight horses for his departure to Mayence or Milan, exactly as if a hunt at Saint-Cloud or Rambouillet was in question.

On one of his journeys (I do not remember which), his Majesty had decided not to take the Empress Josephine. The Emperor was less disturbed by this company of ladies and women who formed her Majesty's suite, than he was by the annoyance of the bandboxes and bundles with which they were usually encumbered, and wished on this occasion to travel rapidly, and without ostentation, and spare the towns on his route an enormous increase of expense.

He therefore ordered everything to be in readiness for his departure, at one o'clock in the morning, at which hour the Empress was generally asleep; but, in spite of all precautions, some slight noise warned the Empress of what was taking place. The Emperor had promised her that she should accompany him on his first journey; but he had deceived her, nevertheless, and was about to set out without her! She instantly called her women; but vexed at their slowness, her Majesty

---

1. The third son lived to become Napoleon III.

sprang out of bed, threw on the first clothing she found at hand, and ran out of her room in slippers and without stockings. Weeping like a little child that is being taken back to boarding-school, she crossed the apartments, flew down the staircase, and threw herself into the arms of the Emperor, as he was entering his carriage, barely in time, however, for a moment later he set out. As almost always happened at the sight of his wife's tears, the Emperor's heart was softened; and she, seeing this, had already entered the carriage, and was cowering down in the foot, for the Empress was scantily clad. The Emperor covered her with his cloak, and before starting gave the order in person that, with the first relay, his wife should receive all she needed.

The Emperor, leaving his wife at Fontainebleau, repaired to Brienne, where he arrived at six o'clock in the evening, and found Mesdames de Brienne and Lomenie, with several ladies of the city, awaiting him at the foot of the staircase to the chateau. He entered the saloon, and received most graciously all persons who were presented to him, and then passed into the garden, conversing familiarly with Mesdames Brienne and Lomenie, and recalling with surprising accuracy the smallest particulars of the stay which he made during his childhood at the military school of Brienne.

His Majesty invited to his table at dinner his hostesses and a few of their friends, and afterwards made a party at a game of whist with Mesdames de Brienne, de Vandeuvre, and de Nolivres. During this game, as also at the table, his conversation was animated and most interesting, and he displayed such liveliness and affability that every one was delighted.

His Majesty passed the night at the chateau of Brienne, and rose early to visit the field of la Rothiere, one of his favourite walks in former days. He revisited with the greatest pleasure those spots where his early youth had been passed, and pointed them out with a kind of pride, all his movements, all his reflections, seeming to say, "See whence I set out, and where I have arrived."

His Majesty walked in advance of the persons who accompanied him, and took much pleasure in being first to call by their names the various localities he passed. A peasant, seeing him thus some distance from his suite, cried out to him familiarly, "Oh, citizen, is the Emperor going to pass soon?"

"Yes," replied the Emperor, "have patience."

The Emperor had inquired the evening before, of Madame Brienne, news of Mother Marguerite. Thus was styled a good woman who dwelt in a cottage, in the midst of the forest, and on whom the pupils of the military academy were accustomed to make frequent visits. He had not forgotten her name, and learning, with as much joy as surprise, that she still lived, the Emperor, extended his morning ride, and galloping up to the door of the cottage, alighted from his horse, and entered the home of the good old peasant. Her sight was impaired by age; and besides, the Emperor had changed so much since she had seen him that it would have been difficult even for the best eyes to recognize him. "Good-day, Mother Marguerite," said his Majesty, saluting the old woman; "so you are not curious to see the Emperor?"

"Yes, indeed, my good sir; I am very curious to see him; so much so, that here is a little basket of fresh eggs that I am going to carry to Madame; and I shall then remain at the chateau, and endeavour to see the Emperor. But the trouble is, I shall not be able to see him so well today as formerly, when he came with his comrades to drink milk at Mother Marguerite's. He was not Emperor then; but that was nothing, he made the others step around! Indeed, you should have seen him! The milk, the eggs, the brown bread, the broken dishes though he took care to have me paid for everything, and began by paying his own bill."

"What! Mother Marguerite," replied his Majesty, smiling, "you have not forgotten Bonaparte!"

"Forgotten! my good sir; you think that any one would forget such a young man as he, who was wise, serious, and sometimes even sad, but always good to poor people? I am only a poor peasant woman, but I could have predicted that this young man would make his way. He has not done it very badly, has he? Ah, no, indeed!"

During this short dialogue, the Emperor had at first turned his back to the door, and consequently to the light, which entered the cottage only by that means. But, by degrees; the Emperor approached the good woman; and when he was quite near her, with the light shining full on his face from the door, he began to rub his hands and say, trying to recall the tone and manner of the days of his early youth, when he came to the peasant's house, "Come, Mother Marguerite, some milk and fresh eggs; we are famishing." The good old woman seemed trying to revive her memories, and began to observe the Emperor with the closest attention. "Oh, yes, Mother, you were so sure a while ago of knowing Bonaparte again. Are we not old acquaintances, we two?" The peasant, while the Emperor was addressing these last words to her, had fallen at his feet; but he raised her with the most touching kindness, and said to her, "The truth is, Mother Marguerite, I have still a schoolboy's appetite. Have you nothing to give me?" The good woman, almost beside herself with happiness, served his Majesty with eggs and milk; and when this simple repast was ended, his Majesty gave his aged hostess a purse full of gold, saying to her, "You know, Mother Marguerite, that I believe in paying my bills. *Adieu*, I shall not forget you." And while the Emperor remounted his horse, the good old woman, standing on the threshold of her door, promised him, with tears of joy, to pray to the good God for him.

One morning, when he awoke, his Majesty was speaking of the possibility of finding some of his old acquaintances; and an anecdote concerning General Junot was related to him, which amused him greatly. The General finding himself, on his return from Egypt, at Montbard, where he had passed several years of his childhood, had sought with the greatest care for his companions in school and mischief, and had found several, with whom he had talked gaily and freely of his early frolics and his schoolboy excursions. As they went together to revisit the different localities, each of which awakened in them some memory of their youth, the general saw an old man majestically promenading on the public square with a large cane in his hand. He immediately ran up to him, threw his arms around him, and embraced him many times, almost suffocating him. The promenader disengaged himself with great difficulty from his warm embraces, regarded General Junot with an amazed air, and remarked that he was ignorant to what he could attribute such excessive tenderness from a soldier wearing the uniform of a superior officer, and all the indications of high rank. "What," cried he, "do you not recognize me?"

"Citizen General, I pray you to excuse me, but I have no idea"

"Ah, Morbleu, my dear master, have you forgotten the most idle, the most lawless, the most incorrigible of your scholars?"

"A thousand pardons, you are Monsieur Junot."

"Himself!" replied Junot, renewing his embrace, and laughing with his friends at the singular characteristics by which he had caused himself to be recognized. As for his Majesty the Emperor, if any of his old masters had failed to recognize him, it could not be by reminiscences of this kind that he could have recalled himself to them; for every one knows that he was distinguished at the military school for his application to work, and the regularity and sobriety of his life.

A meeting of the same nature, saving the difference in recollections, awaited the Emperor at Brienne. While he was visiting the old military school, now falling to ruin, and pointing out to the persons who surrounded him the situation of the study halls, dormitories, refectories, etc., an ecclesiastic who had been tutor of one of the classes in the school was presented to him. The Emperor recognized him immediately; and, uttering an exclamation of surprise, his Majesty conversed more than twenty minutes with this gentleman, leaving him full of gratitude.

The Emperor, before leaving Brienne to return to Fontainebleau, required the mayor to give him a written account of the most pressing needs of the *commune*, and left on his departure a considerable sum for the poor and the hospitals.

Passing through Troyes, the Emperor left there, as everywhere else, souvenirs of his generosity. The widow of a general officer, living in retirement at Joinville (I regret that I have forgotten the name of this venerable lady, who was more than an octogenarian), came to Troyes, notwithstanding her great age, to ask aid from his Majesty. Her husband having served only before the Revolution, the pension which she had enjoyed had been taken from her under the Republic, and she was in the greatest destitution. The brother of General Vouittemont, mayor of a *commune* in the suburbs of Troyes, was kind enough to consult me as to what should be done in order to present this lady to the Emperor; and I advised him to have her name placed on the list of his Majesty's private audiences. I myself took the liberty of speaking of Madame de to the Emperor; and the audience was granted, though I do not pretend to attribute the merit of it to myself, for in travelling the Emperor was always very accessible.

When the good lady came to attend the audience with M. de Vouittemont, to whom his municipal scarf gave the right of entrance, I happened to meet them, and she stopped to thank me for the little service which she insisted I had rendered her, and mentioned that she had been obliged to pawn the six silver plates which alone remained to her, in order to pay the expenses of her journey; that, having arrived at Troyes in a poor farm wagon, covered with a cloth thrown over a hoop, and which had shaken her terribly, she could find no place in the inns, all of which were filled on account of the arrival of their Majesties; and she would have been obliged to sleep in her wagon had it not been for the kind consideration of M. de Vouittemont, who had given up his room to her, and offered his services. In spite of her more than eighty years, and her distress, this respectable lady related her story with an air of gentle gayety, and at the close threw a grateful glance at her guide, on whose arm she was leaning.

At that moment the usher came to announce that her turn had come, and she entered the saloon of audience. M. de Vouittemont awaited her return while conversing with me; and on her return she related to us, scarcely able to control her emotion, that the Emperor had in the kindest manner received the memorial she presented to him, had read it attentively, and passed it to a minister who was near him, with the order to do her justice this very day.

The next day she received the warrant for a pension of three thousand *francs*, the first year's pay being handed her at once.

At Lyons, of which Cardinal Fesch was archbishop, the Emperor lodged in the archiepiscopal palace.[2]

During the stay of their Majesties the cardinal exerted himself to the utmost to gratify every wish of his nephew; and in his eagerness to please, *monseigneur* applied to me many times each day to be assured that nothing was lacking; so everything passed off admirably. The zeal of the cardinal was remarked by all the household; but for my part I thought I perceived that the zeal displayed by *monseigneur* in the reception of their Majesties took on an added strength whenever there was a question of all the expenses incurred by this visit, which were considerable, being paid by them. His eminence, I thought, drew very fine interest on his investment, and his generous hospitality was handsomely compensated by the liberality of his guests.

The passage of Mont Cenis was by no means so difficult as had been that of Mont St. Bernard; although the road, which has since been made by the Emperor's orders, was not then commenced. At the foot of the mountain they were obliged to take the carriage to pieces, and transport it on the backs of mules; and their Majesties crossed the mountain partly on foot, partly in very handsome sedan chairs which had been made at Turin, that of the Emperor lined with crimson satin, and ornamented with gold lace and fringes, and that of the Empress in blue satin, with silver lace and fringes. The snow had been carefully swept off and removed. On their arrival at the convent they were most warmly received by the good monks; and the Emperor, who had a singular affection for them, held a long conversation with them, and did not depart without leaving rich and numerous tokens of his liberality. As soon as he arrived at Turin he gave orders for the improvement of their hospice, which he continued to support till his fall.

Their Majesties remained several days at Turin, where they occupied the former palace of the kings of Sardinia, constituted the imperial residence by a decree of the Emperor during our stay, as was also the castle of Stupinigi, situated a short distance from the town.

The Pope rejoined their Majesties at Stupinigi; the Holy Father

---

2. Joseph Fesch, born in Corsica, 1763, was half-brother to Napoleon's mother. Archbishop of Lyons 1801, cardinal 1803, died 1839.

had left Paris almost at the same time as ourselves, and before his departure had received from the Emperor magnificent presents. Among these was a golden altar with chandeliers, and holy vessels of the richest workmanship, a superb tiara, Gobelin tapestries, and carpets from the Savonnerie, with a statue of the Emperor in Sevres porcelain. The Empress also made to his Holiness a present of a vase of the same manufacture, adorned with paintings by the best artists. This masterpiece was at least four feet in height, and two feet and a half in diameter at the mouth, and was made expressly to be offered to the Holy Father, the painting representing, if my memory is correct, the ceremony of the coronation.

Each of the cardinals in the suite of the Pope had received a box of beautiful workmanship, with the portrait of the Emperor set in diamonds; and all the persons attached to the service of Pius VII. had presents more or less considerable, all these various articles being brought by the furnishers to the apartments of his Majesty, where I took a list of them, by order of his Majesty, as they arrived.

The Holy Father also made in return very handsome presents to the officers of the Emperor's household whose duties had brought them near his person during his stay at Paris.

From Stupinigi we went to Alexandria. The Emperor, the next day after his arrival, rose early, visited the fortifications of the town, reviewed all the positions of the battlefield of Marengo, and returned only at seven o'clock, and after having broken down five horses. A few days after he wished the Empress to see this famous plain, and by his orders an army of twenty-five or thirty thousand men was assembled. The morning of the day fixed for the review of these troops, the Emperor left his apartment dressed in a blue coat with long skirts, much worn, and even with holes in some places. These holes were the work of moths and not of balls, as has been said in certain memoirs. On his head his Majesty wore an old hat edged with gold lace, tarnished and frayed, and at his side a cavalry sabre, such as the generals of the Republic wore; this was the coat, hat, and sword that he had worn on the day of the battle of Marengo. I afterwards lent these articles to Monsieur David, first painter to his Majesty, for his picture of the passage of Mont St. Bernard. A vast amphitheatre had been raised on this plain for the Empress and the suite of their Majesties; the day was perfect, as is each day of the month of May in Italy. After riding along the ranks, the Emperor took his seat by the side of the Empress, and made to the troops a distribution of the cross of the Legion of Honour, after which he laid the corner stone of a monument, which he had directed to be raised on the plain to the memory of the soldiers who had fallen on the battlefield. When his Majesty, in the short address which he made to the army on this occasion, pronounced in a strong voice, vibrating with emotion, the name of Desaix, who here died gloriously for his country, a murmur of grief ran through the ranks of the soldiers. As for me, I was moved to tears; and as my eyes fell on this army, on its banners, on the costume of the Emperor, I was obliged to turn from time to time towards the throne of her Majesty the Empress, to realize that this was not the 14th of June in the year 1800.

I think it was during this stay at Alexandria, that Prince Jerome Bonaparte had an interview with the Emperor, in which the latter seriously and earnestly remonstrated with his brother, and Prince Jerome left the cabinet visibly agitated. This displeasure of the Emperor arose from the marriage contracted by his brother, at the age of nineteen, with the daughter of an American merchant.

His Majesty had this union annulled on the plea of minority, and made a decree forbidding the officers of the civil state to receive, on their registers, the record of the certificate of the celebration of the marriage of Monsieur Jerome with Mademoiselle Patterson. For some time the Emperor treated him with great coolness, and kept him at a distance; but a few days after the interview at Alexandria, he sent him to Algiers to claim as subjects of the Empire two hundred Genoese held as slaves. The young prince acquitted himself handsomely of this mission of humanity, and returned in the month of August to the port of Genoa, with the captives whom he had just released. The Emperor was well satisfied with the manner in which his brother had carried out his instructions, and said on this occasion, that "Prince Jerome was very young and very thoughtless, that he needed more weight in his head, but that, nevertheless, he hoped to make something of him."

This brother of his Majesty was one among the few persons whom he really loved, although he had often given him just cause for anger.

Chapter 26

Their Majesties remained more than a month at Milan, and I had ample leisure to acquaint myself with this beautiful capital of Lombardy. This visit was a continual succession of fetes and gayeties; and it seemed that the Emperor alone had time to give to work, for he shut himself up, as was his custom, with his ministers, while all the persons of his suite and of his household, whose duties did not detain them near his Majesty, were eagerly taking part in the sports and diversions of the Milanese. I will enter into no details of the coronation, as it was almost a repetition of what had taken place at Paris a few months before; and as all solemnities of this sort are alike, every one is familiar with the least details. Amid all these fete days there was one day of real happiness to me: it was that on which Prince Eugene, whose kindness to me I have never forgotten, was proclaimed viceroy of Italy. Truly, no one could be more worthy than he of a rank so elevated, if to attain it only nobility, generosity, courage, and skill in the art of governing, were needed; for never did prince more sincerely desire the prosperity of the people confided to his care. I have often observed how truly happy he was, and what genuine delight beamed from his countenance when he had shed happiness around him.

The Emperor and Empress went one day to breakfast in the environs of Milan, on a little island called Olona. While walking over it, the Emperor met a poor woman, whose cottage was near the place where their Majesties' table had been set, and he addressed to her a number of questions. "*Monsieur*," replied she (not knowing the Emperor), "I am very poor, and the mother of three children, whom I have great difficulty in supporting, because my husband, who is a day labourer, has not always work."

"How much would it take," replied his Majesty, "to make you perfectly happy?"

"O Sire, it would take a great deal of money."

"But how much, my good woman, how much would be necessary?"

"Ah, Monsieur, unless we had twenty *louis*, we would not be above want; but what chance is there of our ever having twenty *louis*?"

The Emperor gave her, on the spot, the sum of three thousand *francs* in gold, and ordered me to untie the rolls and pour them all into the good woman's lap.

At the sight of so much gold the latter grew pale, reeled, and I saw she was fainting. "All, that is too much, Monsieur, that is indeed too much. Surely you could not be making sport of a poor woman!"

The Emperor assured her that it was indeed all hers, and that with this money she could buy a little field, a flock of goats, and raise her children well.

His Majesty did not make himself known; for he liked, in dispensing his benefits, to preserve his incognito, and I knew, during his life, a large number of instances similar to the foregoing. It seems that historians have made it a point to pass them over in silence; and yet it is, I think, by the rehearsal of just such deeds that a correct idea of the Emperor's character can and should be formed.

Deputations from the Ligurian Republic, with the Doge at their head, had come to Milan to entreat the Emperor to annex Genoa and its territory to the Empire, which demand his Majesty took care not to refuse, and by a decree formed of the Genoese states three departments of his Italian kingdom. The Emperor and Empress set out from Milan to visit these departments and some others.

We had been at Mantua a short time, when one evening, about six o'clock, Grand Marshal Duroc gave me an order to remain alone in a little room adjoining that of the Emperor, and informed me that Count Lucien Bonaparte would arrive soon. He came in a few moments; and as soon as he announced himself, I introduced him into, the Emperor's bedroom, and then knocked at the door of the Emperor's cabinet, to inform him of his arrival. After saluting each other, the two brothers shut themselves up in the room, and there soon arose between them a very animated discussion; and being compelled to remain in the little saloon, much against my will, I overheard a great part of the conversation. The Emperor was urging his brother to get a divorce, and promised him a crown if he would do this; but Lucien replied that he would never abandon the mother of his children, which refusal irritated the Emperor so greatly, that his expressions became harsh and even insulting. When this altercation had lasted more than an hour, M. Lucien came out from it in a deplorable condition, pale and dishevelled, his eyes red and filled with tears; and we did not see him again, for, on quitting his brother, he returned to Rome.

The Emperor was greatly troubled by this refusal of his brother, and did not open his mouth on retiring. It has been maintained that the disagreement between the brothers was caused by the elevation of the First Consul to the Empire, and Lucien's disapproval of this step; but that is a mistake. It is indeed true that the latter had proposed to continue the Republic under the government of two consuls, who were to be Napoleon and Lucien, one to be at the head of the department of war and foreign relations, the other of everything connected with the affairs of the interior; but although the failure of this plan must have disappointed Lucien, the avidity with which he accepted the titles of senator and count of the Empire proved that he cared very little for a republic of which he was not to be one of the heads. I am sure that the marriage of Monsieur Lucien to Madame Jouberthon was the only cause of this disagreement. The Emperor disapproved of this union because the lady's reputation was somewhat doubtful, and she was also divorced from her husband, who had become insolvent, and had fled to America. This insolvency, and the divorce especially, offended Napoleon deeply, who always felt a great repugnance for divorced people.

Before this, the Emperor had wished to raise his brother to the rank of sovereign, by making him marry the Queen of Etruria, who had lost her husband. Lucien had refused this alliance on several different occasions; and at last the Emperor became angry, and said to him, "You see how far you are carrying your infatuation and your foolish love for a *femme galante*."

"At least," replied Lucien, "mine is young and pretty," alluding to the Empress Josephine, who had been both the one and the other.

The boldness of this reply excited the Emperor's anger beyond all bounds. At that moment he held in his hands his watch, which he dashed with all his might on the floor, crying out, "Since you will listen to nothing, see, I will break you like this watch."

Differences had arisen between the brothers before the establishment of the Empire; and among the acts which caused the disgrace of Lucien, I have often heard the following cited.

Lucien, being minister of the interior, received the order of the First Consul to let no wheat go out of the territory of the Republic. Our warehouses were filled, and France abundantly supplied; but this was not the case in England, and the scarcity of it was beginning to be felt there. It was never known how it happened; but the larger part of this grain passed the Strait of Calais, and it was stated positively that the sum of twenty millions was received for it. On learning this, the First Consul took away the portfolio of the interior from his brother, and appointed him ambassador to Spain.

At Madrid, Monsieur Lucien was well received by the king and the royal family, and became the intimate friend of Don Manuel Godoy, Prince de la Paix. It was during this mission, and by agreement with the Prince de la Paix, that the treaty of Badajos was concluded, in order to procure which it is said that Portugal gave thirty millions. It has been also declared that more than this sum, paid in gold and diamonds, was divided between the two plenipotentiaries, who did not think it necessary to render an account of this transaction to their respective courts.

Charles IV. loved Lucien tenderly, and felt for the First Consul the greatest veneration. After examining carefully several Spanish horses which he intended for the First Consul, he said to his head groom: "How fortunate you are, and how I envy your happiness! you are going to see the great man, and you will speak to him; how I should like to take your place!"

During his *embassage* Lucien had paid his court to a person of most elevated rank, and had received her portrait in a medallion surrounded with very fine brilliants. I have seen a hundred times this portrait which he wore suspended from his neck by a chain of most beautiful black hair; and far from making a mystery of it, he endeavoured, on the contrary, to show it, and bent over so that the rich medallion could be seen hanging on his breast.

Before his departure from Madrid, the king likewise made him a present of his own portrait in miniature, also set in diamonds.

These stones, remounted and set in the form of a hat buckle, passed to the second wife of Lucien. I will now give an account of his marriage with Madame Jouberthon, as related to me by a person who resided in the same house.

The First Consul was informed each day, and very promptly, of all that took place in the interior of the homes of his brothers, a circumstantial account being rendered, even as to the smallest particulars and the slightest details. Lucien, wishing to marry Madame Jouberthon, whom he had met at the house of the Count de L——, an intimate friend of his, wrote between two and three o'clock in the afternoon to Duquesnoy, mayor of the tenth *arrondissement*, requesting him to come to his residence, Rue Saint Dominique, about eight o'clock in the evening, and bring the marriage register.

Between five and six o'clock Monsieur Duquesnoy, mayor of the tenth *arrondissement*, received from the chateau of the Tuileries an order not to take the register out of the municipality, and above all not to celebrate any marriage whatever, unless, in accordance with the law, the names of the parties thereto had been published for eight days.

At the hour indicated Duquesnoy arrived at the residence, and asked to speak in private to the count, to whom he communicated the order emanating from the chateau.

Beside himself with anger, Lucien immediately hired a hundred post-horses for himself and friends; and without delay he and Madame Jouberthon, with these friends and the people of his household, took carriages for the chateau of Plessis-Chamant, a pleasure-house half a league beyond Senlis. The cure of the place, who was also associate mayor, was summoned, and at midnight pronounced the civil marriage; then, putting on his sacerdotal robes over the scarf he wore as an officer of the civil state, he bestowed on the fugitives the nuptial benediction. A good supper was then served, at which the assistant and cure were present; but, as he returned to his vicarage about six o'clock in the morning, he saw at his gate a post-chaise, guarded by two soldiers, and on entering his house, found there an officer of the armed police, who invited him politely to be kind enough to accompany him to Paris. The poor curate thought himself lost; but he was compelled to obey, under penalty of being carried to Paris from one guard-house to another by the police.

Nothing was left for him but to enter the fatal chaise, which was drawn at a gallop by two good horses, and soon arrived at the Tuileries, where he was brought into the cabinet of the First Consul, who said to him in a voice of thunder, "It is you, then, Monsieur, who marry members of my family without my consent, and without having published the bans, as is your duty in your double character of cure and assistant mayor. You well know that you deserve to be deprived of your office, excommunicated, and tried before the courts." The unfortunate priest believed himself already in prison; but after a severe lecture he was sent back to his curacy, and the two brothers were never reconciled.

In spite of all these differences, Lucien always counted on the affection of his brother to obtain him a kingdom. I guarantee the authenticity of the following incident, which was related to me by a reliable person: Lucien had in charge of his establishment a friend of his early youth, the same age as himself, and like him born in Corsica, who was named Campi, and enjoyed the most confidential relations in the count's household. On the day that the '*Moniteur*' gave a list of the new French princes, Campi was promenading in the handsome gallery of pictures collected by Lucien, with the latter's young secretary, when the following conversation occurred between them. "You have no doubt read the *'Moniteur'* of today?"

"Yes."

"You have seen that all the members of the family have had the title of French princes bestowed on them, and the name of *monsieur* le count alone is wanting to the list."

"What matters that? There are kingdoms."

"Considering the care that sovereigns take to keep them, there will hardly be any vacancy."

"Ah, well, they will be made. All the royal families of Europe are worn out, and we must have new ones." Thereupon Campi was silent, and advised the young man to hold his tongue, if he wished to preserve the favour of the count. However, it was not long after this before the young secretary repeated this confidential conversation, which, without being singularly striking, gives, however, an idea of the amount of confidence which should be placed in the pretended moderation of Count Lucien, and in the epigrams against his brother and his family which have been attributed to him.

No one in the chateau was ignorant of the hostility which existed between Lucien Bonaparte and the Empress Josephine; and to make their court to the latter the former *habitués* of Malmaison, now become the courtiers of the Tuileries; were in the habit of relating to her the most piquant anecdotes they could collect relative to the younger brother of the Emperor. Thus it happened that by chance one day I heard a dignified person and a senator of the Empire give the Empress, in the gayest manner imaginable, very minute details as to one of the temporary liaisons of Count Lucien. I do not guarantee the authenticity of the anecdote, and I experience in writing it more embarrassment than the senator displayed in relating it, and omit, indeed, a mass of details which the narrator gave without blushing, and without driving off his audience; for my object is to throw light upon the family secrets of the imperial household, and on the habits of the persons who were nearest the Emperor, and not to publish scandal, though I could justify myself by the example of a dignitary of the Empire.

Count Lucien (I do not know in what year) established himself in the good graces of Mademoiselle Meserai, an actress of the Theatre Francais, who was both pretty and sprightly. The conquest was not difficult, in the first place, because this had never been her character towards any one, and, secondly, because the artiste knew the great wealth of the count, and believed him to be prodigal. The first attentions of her lover confirmed her in this opinion, and she demanded a house. He at once presented her with one richly and elegantly furnished, the deed being put in her hands on the day she took possession; and each visit of the count added to the actress's wardrobe or jewel-case some new gifts. This lasted some months, at the end of which Lucien became disgusted with his bargain, and began to consider by what means to break it without losing too much. Among other things, he had made mademoiselle a present of a pair of girandoles, containing diamonds of great value. In one of the last interviews, before the count had allowed any signs of coldness to be seen, he perceived the girandoles on the toilet-table of his mistress, and, taking them in his hands, said, "Really, my dear, you do me injustice; why do you not show more confidence in me? I do not wish you to wear jewellery so much out of date as these."

"Why, it has been only six months since you gave them to me."

"I know it; but a woman of good taste, a woman who respects herself, should never wear anything six months old. I will take the ear-rings and send them to de Villiers[1] with orders to mount them as I wish." The count was tenderly thanked for so delicate an attention, and put the girandoles in his pocket, with one or two necklaces which had also been his gift, and which did not appear to him sufficiently new in style, and the breach took place before any of these had been returned.

Notwithstanding this, Mademoiselle believed herself well provided for with her furniture and her house, until one morning the true proprietor came to ask her wishes as to making a new lease. She ran to examine her deed, which she had not yet thought to do, and found that it was simply a description of the property, at the end of which was a receipt for two years' rent.

During our stay at Genoa the heat was insupportable; from this the Emperor suffered greatly, saying he had never experienced the like in Egypt, and undressed many times a day. His bed was covered with a mosquito netting, for the insects were numerous and worrying. The windows of the bedroom looked out upon a grand terrace on the margin of the sea, and from them could be seen the gulf and all the surrounding country. The fetes given by the city were superb. An immense number of vessels were fastened together, and filled with orange and citron trees and shrubs, some covered with flowers, some with fruits, and all combined formed a most exquisite floating garden which their Majesties visited on a magnificent yacht.

---

1. He was the count's jeweller.

On his return to France, the Emperor made no halt between Turin and Fontainebleau. He travelled incognito, in the name of the minister of the interior, and went at such speed that at each relay they were obliged to throw water on the wheels; but in spite of this his Majesty complained of the slowness of the postilions, and cried continually, "Hurry up! hurry up! we are hardly moving." Many of the servants' carriages were, left in the rear; though mine experienced no delay, and I arrived at each relay at the same time as the Emperor.

In ascending the steep hill of Tarare, the Emperor alighted from the carriage, as did also Berthier, who accompanied him; the carriages of the suite being some distance behind, as the drivers had stopped to breathe their horses.

His Majesty saw, climbing the hill a few steps before him, an old, decrepit woman, who hobbled along with great difficulty. As the Emperor approached her he inquired why, infirm as she was, and apparently so fatigued, she should attempt to travel so difficult a road.

"Sir," replied she, "they tell me the Emperor is to pass along here, and I wish to see him before I die." His Majesty, who liked to be amused, said to her, "Ah, but why trouble yourself about him? He is a tyrant, like all the rest." The good woman, indignant at this remark, angrily replied, "At least, Sir, he is our choice; and since we must have a master, it is at least right that we should choose him." I was not an eye-witness of this incident; but I heard the Emperor himself relate it to Dr. Corvisart, with some remarks upon the good sense of the masses, who, according to the opinion of his Majesty and his chief doctor, had generally formed very correct opinions.

Chapter 27

His Majesty the Emperor passed the month of January, 1806, at Munich and Stuttgard, during which, in the first of these two capitals, the marriage of the vice-king and the Princess of Bavaria was celebrated. On this occasion there was a succession of magnificent fetes, of which the Emperor was always the hero, and at which his hosts tried, by every variety of homage, to express to this great man the admiration with which his military genius inspired them.

The vice-king and vice-queen had never met before their marriage, but were soon as much attached to each other as if they had been acquainted for years, for never were two persons more perfectly congenial. No princess, and indeed no mother, could have manifested more affection and care for her children than the vice-queen; and she might well serve as a model for all women. I have been told an incident concerning this admirable princess which I take pleasure in relating here. One of her daughters, who was quite young, having spoken in a very harsh tone to her maid, her most serene highness the vice-queen was informed of it, and in order to give her daughter a lesson, forbade the servants to render the young princess any service, or to reply to any of her demands, from that time. The child at once complained to her mother, who told her gravely that when any one received, like her, the care and attention of all around them, it was necessary to merit this, and to show her appreciation by consideration and an obliging politeness. Then she required her to ask pardon of the 'femme de chambre', and henceforward to speak to her politely, assuring her that by this means she would always obtain compliance with all reasonable and just requests she might make.

The child obeyed; and the lesson was of such benefit to her that she became, if general report is to be believed, one of the most accomplished princesses of Europe. The report of her perfections spread abroad even to the New World, which contended for her with the

Old, and has been fortunate enough to obtain her. She is at this time, I think, Empress of Brazil.

His Majesty the King of Bavaria, Maximilian Joseph, then about fifty years of age, was very tall, with a noble and attractive physiognomy and fascinating manners. Before the Revolution he had been colonel of an Alsatian regiment in the service of France, under the name of Prince Maximilian, or Prince Max as the soldiers called him, and stationed at Strasburg, where he left a reputation for elegance and chivalrous gallantry. His subjects, his family, his servants, everybody, adored him. He often took long walks through the city of Munich in the morning, went to the market, inquired the price of grain, entered the shops, spoke to every one, especially the children, whom he persuaded to go to school. This excellent prince did not fear to compromise his dignity by the simplicity of his manners; and he was right, for I do not think any one ever failed to show him respect, and the love which he inspired lessened in no wise the veneration which was felt for him. Such was his devotion to the Emperor, that his kindly feelings extended even to the persons who by their functions approached nearest to his Majesty, and were in the best position to know his needs and wishes. Thus (I do not relate it out of vanity, but in proof of what I have just said) his Majesty the King of Bavaria never came to see the Emperor, that he did not take my hand and inquire first after the health of his Imperial Majesty, then after my own, adding many things which plainly showed his attachment for the Emperor and his natural goodness.

His Majesty the King of Bavaria is now in the tomb, like him who gave him a throne; but this tomb is still a royal tomb, and the loyal Bavarians can come to kneel and weep over it. The Emperor, on the contrary[1]—

The virtuous Maximilian was able to leave to a worthy son the sceptre which he had received from him who perished an exile at St. Helena. Prince Louis, the present King of Bavaria, and today perhaps the best king in Europe, was not so tall as his august father, neither was his face so handsome; and, unfortunately, he was afflicted with an extreme deafness, which made him raise his voice without knowing it, and in addition to this his utterance was impeded by a slight stammer-

---

1. Constant wrote this before the return, in 1840, of the ashes of Napoleon to rest on "the banks of the Seine, amid the French people whom he loved so well," where in a massive urn of porphyry, and beneath the gilded dome of the Invalides, in the most splendid tomb of the centuries, sleeps now the soldier of Lodi, Marengo, Austerlitz, Wagram, and Waterloo.—Trans.

ing. This prince was grave and studious; and the Emperor recognized his merit, but did not rely upon his friendship. This was not because he thought him wanting in loyalty, for the prince royal was above such suspicion; but the Emperor was aware that he belonged to a party which feared the subjection of Germany, and who suspected that the French, although they had so far attacked only Austria, had ideas of conquest over all the German powers.

However, what I have just stated in regard to the prince royal relates only to the years subsequent to 1806; for I am certain that at that epoch his sentiments did not differ from those of the good Maximilian, who was, as I have said, full of gratitude to the Emperor. Prince Louis came to Paris at the beginning of this year; and I saw him many times at the court theatre in the box of the prince arch-chancellor, where they both slept in company and very profoundly. This was also such a habit with Cambaceres, that when the Emperor asked for him, and was told that *monseigneur* was at the theatre, he replied, "Very well, very well; he is taking his siesta; let us not disturb him!"

The King of Wurtemburg was large, and so fat that it was said of him God had put him in the world to prove how far the skin of a man could be stretched. His stomach was of such dimensions that it was found necessary to make a broad, round incision in front of his seat at the table; and yet, notwithstanding this precaution, he was obliged to hold his plate on a level with his chin to drink his soup. He was very fond of hunting, either on horseback, or in a little Russian carriage drawn by four horses, which he often drove himself. He was fond of horseback riding, but it was no easy task to find a mount of size and strength sufficient to carry so heavy a burden. It was necessary that the poor animal should be progressively trained; and in order to accomplish this the king's equerry fastened round the horse a girth loaded with pieces of lead, increasing the weight daily till it equalled that of his Majesty. The king was despotic, hard, and even cruel, ever ready to sign the sentence of the condemned, and in almost all cases, if what is said at Stuttgart be true, increased the penalty inflicted by the judges. Hard to please, and brutal, he often struck the people of his household; and it is even said that he did not spare her Majesty the queen, his wife, who was a sister of the present King of England. Notwithstanding all this, he was a prince whose knowledge and brilliant mind the Emperor esteemed; for they had a mutual affection for each other, and he found him faithful to his alliance to the very end. King Frederic of Wurtemburg had a brilliant and numerous court, at which he displayed great magnificence.

The hereditary prince was much beloved; he was less haughty and more humane than his father, and was said to be just and liberal.

Besides those crowned by his hand, the Emperor, while in Bavaria, received a great number of the princes of the Confederation; and they usually dined with his Majesty. In this crowd of royal courtiers the prince primate was noticeable, who differed in nothing as to manners, bearing, and dress from the most fashionable gentlemen of Paris. The Emperor paid him special attention. I cannot pay the same eulogy to the toilet of the princesses, duchesses, and other noble ladies; for most of them dressed in exceedingly bad taste, and, displaying neither art nor grace, covered their heads with plumes, bits of gold, and silver gauze, fastened with a great quantity of diamond-headed pins.

The equipages the German nobility used were all very large coaches, which were a necessity from the enormous hoops still worn by those ladies; and this adherence to antiquated fashions was all the more surprising, because at that time Germany enjoyed the great advantage of possessing two fashion journals. One was the translation of the magazine published by Mesangere; and the other, also edited at Paris, was translated and printed at Mannheim. These ridiculous carriages, which much resembled our ancient diligences, were drawn by very inferior horses, harnessed with ropes, and placed so far apart that an immense space was needed to turn the carriage.

The Prince of Saxe-Gotha was long and thin. In spite of his great age, he was enough of a dandy to order at Paris, from our hairdresser Michalon, some pretty little wigs of youthful blonde, curled like the hair of Cupid; but, apart from this, he was an excellent man. I recollect, a propos of the noble German ladies, to have seen at the court theatre at Fontainebleau a princess of the Confederation who was being presented to their Majesties. The toilet of her Highness announced an immense progress in the elegance of civilization beyond the Rhine; for, renouncing the Gothic hoops, the princess had adopted the very latest fashions, and, though nearly seventy years of age, wore a dress of black lace over red satin, and her coiffure consisted of a white muslin veil, fastened by a wreath of roses, in the style of the vestals of the opera. She had with her a granddaughter, brilliant with the charm of youth, and admired by the whole court, although her costume was less stylish than that of her grandmother.

I heard her Majesty, the Empress Josephine, relate one day that she had much difficulty in repressing a smile when, among a number of

NEY

German princesses presented to her, one was announced under the name of Cunegonde[2] Her Majesty added that, when she saw the princess take her seat, she imagined she saw her lean to one side. Assuredly the Empress had read the adventures of *Candide* and the daughter of the very noble baron of Thunder-Ten-Trunck.

At Paris, in the spring of 1806, I saw almost as many members of the Confederation as I had seen in the capitals of Bavaria and Wurtemburg. A French name had the precedence among these names of foreign princes. It was that of Prince Murat, who in the month of March was made Grand-duke of Berg and Cleves. After Prince Louis of Bavaria, arrived the hereditary prince of Baden, who came to Paris to marry a niece of the Empress.

At the beginning this union was not happy. The Princess Stephanie (de Beauharnais) was a very pretty woman, graceful and witty; and the Emperor had wished to make a great lady of her, and had married her without consulting her wishes. Prince Charles-Louis-Frederic was then twenty years of age, and though exceedingly good, brave, and generous, and possessing many admirable traits, was heavy and phlegmatic, ever maintaining an icy gravity, and entirely destitute of the qualities which would attract a young princess accustomed to the brilliant elegance of the imperial court.

The marriage took place in April, to the great satisfaction of the prince, who that day appeared to do violence to his usual gravity, and even allowed a smile to approach his lips. The day passed off very well; but, when the time came for retiring, the princess refused to let him share her room, and for eight days was inexorable.

He was told that the princess did not like the arrangement of his hair, and that nothing inspired her with more aversion than a queue; upon which the good prince hastened to have his hair cut close, but when she saw him thus shorn, she laughed immoderately, and exclaimed that he was more ugly *a la Titus* than he was before. It was impossible that the intelligence and the kind heart of the princess could fail to appreciate the good and solid qualities of her husband; she learned to love him as tenderly as she was loved, and I am assured that the august couple lived on excellent terms.

Three months after this marriage, the prince left his wife to follow the Emperor, first on the campaign in Prussia, and afterwards in Poland. The death of his grandfather, which happened some time after the Austrian campaign of 1809, put him in possession of the

---

2. Cunegonde was the mistress of *Candide* in Voltaire's novel of *Candide*.

grand duchy, whereupon he resigned the command of his troops to his uncle the Count of Hochberg, and returned to his government, never more to leave it.

I saw him again with the princess at Erfurt, where they told me he had become jealous of the Emperor Alexander, who paid assiduous court to his wife; at which the prince took alarm and abruptly left Erfurt, carrying with him the princess, of whom it must in justice be said that there had been on her part not the slightest imprudence to arouse this jealousy, which seems very pardonable, however, in the husband of so charming a woman.

The prince's health was always delicate, and from his earliest youth alarming symptoms had been noticed in him; and this physical condition was no doubt, in a great measure, the main source of the melancholy which marked his character. He died in 1818, after a very long and painful illness, during which his wife nursed him with the most affectionate care, leaving four children, two sons and two daughters. The two sons died young, and would have left the grand duchy of Baden without heirs, if the Counts Hochberg had not been recognized as members of the ducal family. The grand-duchess is today devoting her life to the education of her daughters, who promise to equal her in graces and virtues. The nuptials of the Prince and Princess of Baden were celebrated by brilliant fetes; at Rambouillet took place a great hunting-party, in which their Majesties, with many members of their family, and all the princes of Baden, Cleves, etc., traversed on foot the forests of Rambouillet.

I recollect another hunting-party, which took place about the same time in the forest of Saint-Germain, to which the Emperor invited the ambassador of the Sublime Porte, then just arrived at Paris. His Turkish Excellency followed the chase with ardour, but without moving a muscle of his austere countenance. The animal having been brought to bay, his Majesty had a gun handed to the Turkish ambassador, that he might have, the honour of firing the first shot; but he refused, not conceiving, doubtless, that any pleasure could be found in slaying at short range a poor, exhausted animal, who no longer had the power to protect itself, even by flight.

Chapter 28

The Emperor remained only a few days at Paris, after our return from Italy, before setting out again for the camp of Boulogne. The fetes of Milan had not prevented him from maturing his political plans, and it was suspected that not without good reason had he broken down his horses between Turin and Paris. These reasons were plainly evident, when it was learned that Austria had entered secretly into the coalition of Russia and England against the Emperor. The army collected in the camp of Boulogne received orders to march on the Rhine, and his Majesty departed to rejoin his troops about the end of September. As was his custom, he informed us only an hour in advance of his departure; and it was curious to observe the contrast of the confusion which preceded this moment with the silence that followed it. Hardly was the order given, than each one busied himself hastily with his own wants and those of his Majesty; and nothing could be heard in the corridors but the sound of domestics coming and going, the noise of cases being nailed down, and boxes being carried out. In the courts appeared a great number of carriages and wagons, with men harnessing them, the scene lighted by torches, and everywhere oaths and cries of impatience; while the women, each in her own room, were sadly occupied with the departure of husband, son, or brother. During all these preparations the Emperor was making his *adieux* to her Majesty the Empress, or taking a few moments of repose; but at the appointed hour he rose, was dressed, and entered his carriage. Soon after everything was silent in the chateau, and only a few isolated persons could be seen flitting about like shadows; silence had succeeded to noise, solitude to the bustle of a brilliant and numerous court. Next morning this deep silence was broken only by a few scattered women who sought each other with pale faces and eyes full of tears, to communicate their grief and share their apprehensions. Many courtiers, who were not of the party, arrived to make their court, and were stupefied on learning of his Majesty's absence, feeling as if the sun could not have risen that day.

The Emperor went without halting as far as Strasburg; and the day after his arrival in this town, the army began to file out over the bridge of Kehl.

On the evening before this march, the Emperor had ordered the general officers to be on the banks of the Rhine on the following day, at exactly six in the morning. An hour before that set for the rendezvous, his Majesty, notwithstanding the rain which fell in torrents, went alone to the head of the bridge, to assure himself of the execution of the orders he had given, and stood exposed to this rain without moving, till the first divisions commenced to file out over the bridge. He was so drenched that the drops which fell from his clothing ran down under his horse, and there formed a little waterfall; and his cocked hat was so wet that the back of it drooped over his shoulders, like the large felt hats of the coal-burners of Paris. The generals whom he was awaiting gathered around him; and when he saw them assembled, he said, "All goes well, messieurs; this is a new step taken in the direction of our enemies; but where is Vandamme? Why is he not here? Can he be dead?" No one said a word. "Answer me, what has become of Vandamme?"

General Chardon, general of the vanguard, much loved by the Emperor, replied, "I think, Sire, that General Vandamme is still asleep; we drank together last evening a dozen bottles of Rhine wine, and doubtless—"

"He does very well to drink, sir; but he is wrong to sleep when I am waiting for him." General Chardon prepared to send an *aide-de-camp* to his companion in arms; but the Emperor prevented him, saying, "Let Vandamme sleep; I will speak to him later." At this moment General Vandamme appeared. "Well, here you are, sir; you seem to have forgotten the order that I gave yesterday."

"Sire, this is the first time this has happened, and—"

"And to avoid a repetition of it, you will go and fight under the banner of the King of Wurtemburg; I hope you will give them lessons in sobriety."

General Vandamme withdrew, not without great chagrin, and repaired to the army of Wurtemburg, where he performed prodigies of valour. After the campaign he returned to the Emperor, his breast covered with decorations, bearing a letter from the King of Wurtemburg to his Majesty, who, after reading it, said to Vandamme: "General, never forget that, if I admire the brave, I do not admire those who sleep while I await them." He pressed the general's hand, and invited him to breakfast, in company with General Chardon, who was as much gratified by this return to favour as was his friend.

On the journey to Augsburg, the Emperor, who had set out in advance, made such speed that his household could not keep up with him; and consequently he passed the night, without attendants or baggage, in the best house of a very poor village. When we reached his Majesty next day, he received us laughing, and threatened to have us taken up as stragglers by the provost guard.

From Augsburg the Emperor went to the camp before Ulm, and made preparations to besiege that place.

A short distance from the town a fierce and obstinate engagement took place between the French and Austrians, and had lasted two hours, when cries of '*Vive l'Empereur!*' were suddenly heard. This name, which invariably carried terror into the enemy's ranks, and always imparted fresh courage to our soldiers, now electrified them to such an extent that they put the Austrians to flight, while the Emperor showed himself in the front ranks, crying "Forward," and making signs to the soldiers to advance, his Majesty's horse disappearing from time to time in the smoke of the cannon. During this furious charge, the Emperor found himself near a grenadier who was terribly wounded; and yet this brave fellow still shouted with the others, "Forward! forward!"

The Emperor drew near him, and threw his military cloak over him, saying, "Try to bring it back to me, and I will give you in exchange the cross that you have just won." The grenadier, who knew that he was mortally wounded, replied that the shroud he had just received was worth as much as the decoration, and expired, wrapped in the imperial mantle.

At the close of the battle, the Emperor had this grenadier, who was also a veteran of the army of Egypt, borne from the field, and ordered that he should be interred in the cloak.

Another soldier, not less courageous than the one of whom I have just spoken, also received from his Majesty marks of distinction. The day after the combat before Ulm, the Emperor, in visiting the ambulances, had his attention attracted by a cannoneer of light artillery, who had lost one leg, but in spite of this was still shouting with all his might, '*Vive l'Empereur!*' He approached the soldier and said to him, "Is this, then, all that you have to say to me?"

"No, Sire, I can also tell you that I, I alone, have dismounted four pieces of the Austrian cannon; and it is the pleasure of seeing them silenced which makes me forget that I must soon close my eyes forever." The Emperor, moved by such fortitude, gave his cross to the cannoneer, noted the names of his parents, and said to him, "If you recover, the Hotel des Invalides is at your service." "Thanks, Sire, but the loss of blood has been too great; my pension will not cost you very dear; I know well that I must soon be off duty, but long live the Emperor all the same!" Unfortunately this brave man realized his real condition only too well, for he did not survive the amputation of his leg.

We followed the Emperor into Ulm after the occupation of that place, and saw a hostile army of more than thirty thousand men lay down their arms at the feet of his Majesty, as they defiled before him; and I have never beheld a more imposing sight. The Emperor was seated on his horse, a few steps in front of his staff, his countenance wearing a calm and grave expression, in spite of which the joy which filled his heart was apparent in his glance.

He raised his hat every moment to return the salutes of the superior officers of the Austrian troops. When the Imperial Guard entered Augsburg, eighty grenadiers marched at the head of the columns, each bearing a banner of the enemy.

The Emperor, on his arrival at Munich, was welcomed with the greatest respect by his ally, the Elector of Bavaria. His Majesty went several times to the theatre and the hunt, and gave a concert to the ladies of the court. It was, as has been since ascertained, during this stay of the Emperor at Munich that the Emperor Alexander and the King of Prussia pledged themselves at Potsdam, on the tomb of Frederick the Great, to unite their efforts against his Majesty.

A year later Napoleon also made a visit to the tomb of the great Frederick.

The taking of Ulm had finished the conquest of the Austrians, and opened to the Emperor the gates of Vienna: but meanwhile the Russians were advancing by forced marches to the help of their allies; his Majesty hastened to meet them, and the 1st of December the two hostile armies found themselves face to face. By one of those happy coincidences made only for the Emperor, the day of the battle of Austerlitz was also the anniversary of the coronation.

I do not remember why there was no tent for the Emperor at Austerlitz; but the soldiers made a kind of barrack of limbs of trees, with an opening in the top for the passage of the smoke. His Majesty, though he had only straw for his bed, was so exhausted after having passed the day on horseback on the heights of Santon, that on the eve of the battle he was sleeping soundly, when General Savary, one of his *aides-de-camp*, entered, to give an account of the mission with which he had been charged; and the general was obliged to touch his shoulder, and shake him, in order to rouse him. He then rose, and mounted his horse to visit his advance posts. The night was dark; but the whole camp was lighted up as if by enchantment, for each soldier put a bundle of straw on the end of his bayonet, and all these firebrands were kindled in less time than it takes to describe it. The Emperor rode along the whole line, speaking to those soldiers whom he recognized. "Be tomorrow what you have always been, my brave fellows," said he, "and the Russians are ours; we have them!" The air resounded with cries of '*Vive l'Empereur*', and there was neither officer nor soldier who did not count on a victory next day.

His Majesty, on visiting the line of battle, where there had been no provisions for forty-eight hours (for that day there had been distributed only one loaf of ammunition bread for every eight men), saw, while passing from bivouac to bivouac, soldiers roasting potatoes in the ashes. Finding himself before the Fourth Regiment of the line, of which his brother was colonel, the Emperor said to a grenadier of the second battalion, as he took from the fire and ate one of the potatoes of the squad, "Are you satisfied with these pigeons?"

"Humph! They are at least better than nothing; though they are very much like Lenten food."

"Well, old fellow," replied his Majesty to the soldier, pointing to the fires of the enemy, "help me to dislodge those rascals over there, and we will have a Mardi Gras at Vienna."

The Emperor returned to his quarters, went to bed again, and slept until three o'clock in the morning, while his suite collected around a bivouac fire near his Majesty's barracks, and slept on the ground, wrapped in their cloaks, for the night was extremely cold. For four days I had not closed my eyes, and I was just falling asleep, when about three o'clock the Emperor asked me for punch. I would have given the whole empire of Austria to have rested another hour; but notwithstanding this, I carried his Majesty the punch, which I made by the bivouac fire, and the Emperor insisted that Marshal Berthier should also partake of it; the remainder I divided with the attendants. Between four and five o'clock the Emperor ordered the first movements of his army, and all were on foot in a few moments, and each at his post; *aides-de-camp* and orderly officers were seen galloping in all directions, and the battle was begun.

I will not enter into the details of this glorious day, which, according to the expression of the Emperor himself, terminated the campaign by a thunderbolt. Not one of the plans of the Emperor failed in execution, and in a few hours the French were masters of the field of battle and of the whole of Germany.

The brave General Rapp was wounded at Austerlitz, as he was in every battle in which he took part, and was carried to the chateau of Austerlitz, where the Emperor visited him in the evening, and returned to pass the night in the chateau.

Two days after, the Emperor Francis sought an audience of his Majesty, to demand peace; and before the end of December a treaty was concluded, by which, the Elector of Bavaria and the Duke of Wurtemburg, faithful allies of the Emperor Napoleon, were made kings. In return for this elevation, of which he alone was the author, his Majesty demanded and obtained for Prince Eugene, viceroy of Italy, the hand of the Princess Augusta Amelia of Bavaria.

During his sojourn at Vienna, the Emperor had established his headquarters at Schoenbrunn, the name of which has become celebrated by the numerous sojourns of his Majesty there, and is today, by a singular coincidence, the residence of his son.[1]

I am not certain whether it was during this first sojourn at Schoenbrunn that his Majesty had the extraordinary encounter that I shall now relate. His Majesty, in the uniform of colonel of the *chasseurs* of the guard, rode every day on horseback, and one morning, while on the road to Vienna, saw approaching a clergyman, accompanied by a woman weeping bitterly, who did not recognize him. Napoleon approached the carriage, and inquired the cause of her grief, and the object and end of her journey. "Monsieur," replied she, "I live at a village two leagues from here, in a house which has been pillaged by soldiers, and my gardener has been killed. I am now on my way to demand a safeguard from your Emperor, who knew my family well, and is under great obligations to them."

"What is your name, Madame?"

"De Bunny. I am the daughter of Monsieur de Marbeuf, former governor of Corsica."

"I am charmed, Madame," replied Napoleon, "to find an opportunity of serving you. I am the Emperor." Madame de Bunny remained speechless with astonishment; but Napoleon reassured her, and continuing his route, requested her to go on and await him at his head-

---

1. The Duke de Reichstadt, born King of Rome, died July, 1832, soon after Constant wrote.

quarters. On his return he received her, and treated her with remarkable kindness, gave her an escort of the chasseurs of the guard, and dismissed her happy and satisfied.

As soon as the day of Austerlitz was gained, the Emperor hastened to send the courier Moustache to France to announce the news to the Empress, who was then at the chateau of Saint-Cloud. It was nine o'clock in the evening when loud cries of joy were suddenly heard, and the galloping of a horse at full speed, accompanied by the sound of bells, and repeated blows of the whip which announced a courier. The Empress, who was awaiting with the greatest impatience news from the army, rushed to the window, opened it hurriedly, and the words victory and Austerlitz fell on her ears. Eager to know the details, she ran down the steps, followed by her ladies; and Moustache in the most excited manner related the marvellous news, and handed her Majesty the Emperor's letter, which Josephine read, and then drawing a handsome diamond ring from her finger, gave it to the courier. Poor Moustache had galloped more than fifty leagues that day, and was so exhausted that he had to be lifted from his horse and placed in bed, which it required four persons to accomplish. His last horse, which he had doubtless spared less than the others, fell dead in the court of the chateau.

Chapter 29

The Emperor having left Stuttgard, stopped only twenty-four hours at Carlsruhe, and forty-eight hours at Strasburg, and between that place and Paris made only short halts, without manifesting his customary haste, however, or requiring of the postilions the breakneck speed he usually demanded.

As we were ascending the hill of Meaux, and while the Emperor was so engrossed in reading a book that he paid no attention to what was passing on the road, a young girl threw herself against the door of his Majesty's carriage, and clung there in spite of the efforts to remove her, not very vigorous in truth, made by the cavaliers of the escort. At last she succeeded in opening the door, and threw herself at the Emperor's feet. The Emperor, much surprised, exclaimed, "What the devil does this foolish creature want with me?" Then recognizing the young lady, after having scrutinized her features more closely, he added in very evident anger, "Ah, is it you again? will you never let me alone?" The young girl, without being intimidated by this rude welcome, said through her sobs that the only favour she now came to ask for her father was that his prison might be changed, and that he might be removed from the Chateau d'If, the dampness of which was ruining his health, to the citadel of Strasburg. "No, no," cried the Emperor, "don't count on that. I have many other things to do beside receiving visits from you. If I granted you this demand, in eight days you would think of something else you wished." The poor girl insisted, with a firmness worthy of better success; but the Emperor was inflexible, and on arriving at the top of the hill he said to her, "I hope you will now alight and let me proceed on my journey. I regret it exceedingly, but what you demand of me is impossible." And he thus dismissed her, refusing to listen longer.

While this was occurring I was ascending the hill on foot, a few paces from his Majesty's carriage; and when this disagreeable scene was over, the young lady, being forced to leave without having obtained what she desired, passed on before me sobbing, and I recognized Mademoiselle Lajolais, whom I had already seen in similar circumstances, but where her courageous devotion to her parents had met with better success.

General Lajolais had been arrested, as well as all his family, on the 18th Fructidor. After being confined for twenty-eight months, he had been tried at Strasburg by a council of war, held by order of the First Consul, and acquitted unanimously.

Later, when the conspiracy of Generals Pichegru, Moreau, George Cadoudal, and of Messieurs de Polignac, de Riviere, etc., were discovered, General Lajolais, who was also concerned therein, was condemned to death. His daughter and his wife were transferred from Strasburg to Paris by the police, and Madame Lajolais was placed in the most rigorous close confinement, while her daughter, now separated from her, took refuge with friends of her family. It was then that this young person, barely fourteen years old, displayed a courage and strength of character unusual at her age; and on learning that her father was condemned to death, she set out at four o'clock in the morning, without confiding her resolution to any one, alone, on foot, and without a guide, with no one to introduce her, and presented herself weeping at the chateau of Saint-Cloud, where the Emperor then was.

She succeeded in gaining an entrance into the chateau only after much opposition; but not allowing herself to be rebuffed by any obstacle, she finally presented herself before me, saying, "Monsieur, I have been promised that you would conduct me instantly to the Emperor" (I do not know who had told her this). "I ask of you only this favour; do not refuse it, I beg!" and moved by her confidence and her despair, I went to inform her Majesty the Empress.

She was deeply touched by the resolution and the tears of one so young, but did not dare, nevertheless, to promise her support at once, for fear of awakening the anger of the Emperor, who was very much incensed against those who were concerned in this conspiracy, and ordered me to say to the young daughter of Lajolais that she was grieved to be able to do nothing for her just then; but that she might return to Saint-Cloud the next day at five o'clock in the morning, and meanwhile she and Queen Hortense would consult together as to the best means of placing her in the Emperor's way. The young girl returned next day at the appointed hour; and her Majesty the Empress had her stationed in the green saloon, and there she awaited ten hours, the moment when the Emperor, coming out from the council-chamber, would cross this room to enter his cabinet.

The Empress and her august daughter gave orders that breakfast, and then dinner, should be served to her, and came in person to beg her to take some nourishment; but their entreaties were all in vain, for the poor girl had no other thought, no other desire, than that of obtaining her father's life. At last, at five o'clock in the afternoon, the Emperor appeared; and a sign being made to Mademoiselle Lajolais by which she could designate the Emperor, who was surrounded by several councillors of state and officers of his household, she sprang towards him; and there followed a touching scene, which lasted a long while. The young girl, prostrating herself at the feet of the Emperor, supplicated him with clasped hands, and in the most touching terms, to grant her father's pardon. The Emperor at first repulsed her, and said in a tone of great severity, "Your father is a traitor; this is the second time he has committed a crime against the state; I can grant you nothing." Mademoiselle Lajolais replied to this outburst of the Emperor, "The first time my father was tried and found innocent; this time it is his pardon I implore!" Finally the Emperor, conquered by so much courage and devotion, and a little fatigued besides by an interview which the perseverance of the young girl would doubtless have prolonged indefinitely, yielded to her prayers, and the life of General Lajolais was spared.[1]

Exhausted by fatigue and hunger, the daughter fell unconscious at the Emperor's feet; he himself raised her, gave her every attention, and presenting her to the persons who witnessed this scene, praised her filial piety in unmeasured terms.

His Majesty at once gave orders that she should be reconducted to Paris, and several superior officers disputed with each other the pleasure of accompanying her. Generals Wolff, *aide-de-camp* of Prince Louis, and Lavalette were charged with this duty, and conducted her to the *conciergerie* where her father was confined. On entering his cell, she threw herself on his neck and tried to tell him of the pardon she had just obtained; but overcome by so many emotions, she was unable to utter a word, and it was General Lavalette[2] who announced to the prisoner what he owed to the brave persistence of his daughter. The

---

1. It is well known that the sentence of General Lajolais was commuted to four years detention in a prison of state, that his property was confiscated and sold, and that he died in the Chateau d'If much beyond the time set for the expiration of his captivity.—Constant.
2. Marie Chamans, Count de Lavalette, was born in Paris, 1769. Entered the army 1792, made Captain at Arcola 1796, and served in Egyptian campaign. Married Emilie de Beauharnais, a niece of Josephine. Postmaster-general, 1800-1814. Condemned to death during the Hundred Days, he escaped from prison in his wife's dress. His wife was tried, but became insane from excitement. He was pardoned 1822, and died 1830, leaving two volumes of Memoirs.

next day she obtained, through the favour of the Empress Josephine, the liberty of her mother, who was to have been transported.

Having obtained the life of her father and the liberty of her mother, as I have just related, she still further exerted herself to save their companions in misfortune, who had been condemned to death, and for this purpose joined the ladies of Brittany, who had been led to seek her cooperation by the success of her former petitions, and went with them to Malmaison to beg these additional pardons.

These ladies had succeeded in getting the execution of the condemned delayed for two hours, with the hope that the Empress Josephine would be able to influence the Emperor; but he remained inflexible, and their generous attempt met with no success, whereupon Mademoiselle Lajolais returned to Paris, much grieved that she had not been able to snatch a few more unfortunates from the rigor of the law.

I have already said two things which I am compelled to repeat here: the first is, that, not feeling obliged to relate events in their chronological order, I shall narrate them as they present themselves to my memory; the second is, that I deem it both an obligation and a duty which I owe to the Emperor to relate every event which may serve to make his true character better known, and which has been omitted, whether involuntarily or by design, by those who have written his life. I care little if I am accused of monotony on this subject, or of writing only a panegyric; but, if this should be done, I would reply: So much the worse for him who grows weary of the recital of good deeds! I have undertaken to tell the truth concerning the Emperor, be it good or bad; and every reader who expects to find in my memoirs of the Emperor only evil, as well as he who expects to find only good, will be wise to go no farther, for I have firmly resolved to relate all that I know; and it is not my fault if the kind acts performed by the Emperor are so numerous that my recitals should often turn to praises.

I thought it best to make these short observations before giving an account of another pardon granted by his Majesty at the time of the coronation, and which the story of Mademoiselle Lajolais has recalled to my recollection.

On the day of the last distribution of the decoration of the Legion of Honour in the Church of the Invalides, as the Emperor was about to retire at the conclusion of this imposing ceremony, a very young man threw himself on his knees on the steps of the throne, crying out, "Pardon, pardon for my father." His Majesty, touched by his interesting countenance and deep emotion, approached him and attempted to raise him; but the young man still retained his beseeching posture, repeating his demand in moving tones. "What is your father's name?" demanded the Emperor. "Sire," replied the young man, hardly able to make himself heard, "it is well known, and has been only too often calumniated by the enemies of my father before your Majesty; but I swear that he is innocent. I am the son of Hugues Destrem."

"Your father, sir, is gravely compromised by his connection with incorrigible revolutionists; but I will consider your application. Monsieur Destrem is happy in having so devoted a son." The Emperor added a few consoling words, and the young man retired with the certainty that his father would be pardoned; but unfortunately this pardon which was granted by the Emperor came too late, and Hugues Destrem, who had been transported to the Island of Oleron after the attempt of the 3rd Nivose,[3] in which he had taken no part, died in his exile before he had even learned that the solicitations of his son had met with such complete success.

On our return from the glorious campaign of Austerlitz, the *commune* of Saint-Cloud, so favoured by the sojourn of the court, had decided that it would distinguish itself on this occasion, and take the opportunity of manifesting its great affection for the Emperor.

The mayor of Saint-Cloud was Monsieur Barre, a well informed man, with a very kind heart. Napoleon esteemed him highly, and took much pleasure in his conversation, and he was sincerely regretted by his subordinates when death removed him.

M. Barre had erected an arch of triumph, of simple but noble design, in excellent taste, at the foot of the avenue leading to the palace, which was adorned with the following inscription:

> *To Her Beloved Sovereign,*
> *The Most Fortunate of the Communes.*

The evening on which the Emperor was expected, the mayor and his associates, armed with the necessary harangue, passed a part of the night at the foot of the monument. M. Barre, who was old and feeble, then retired, after having placed as sentinel one of his associates, whose duty it was to inform him of the arrival of the first courier; and a ladder was placed across the entrance of the arch of triumph, so that no one might pass under it before his Majesty. Unfortunately, the municipal *argus* went to sleep; and the Emperor arrived in the early morning, and passed by the side of the arch of triumph, much amused at the obstacle which prevented his enjoying the distinguished honour which the good inhabitants of Saint-Cloud had prepared for him.

---

3. The affair of the infernal machine in the Rue Sainte Nicaise.

On the day succeeding this event, a little drawing was circulated in the palace representing the authorities asleep near the monument, a prominent place being accorded the ladder, which barred the passage, and underneath was written the *arch barre*, alluding to the name of the mayor. As for the inscription, they had travestied it in this manner:

To her beloved Sovereign; the sleepiest of the communes.

Their Majesties were much amused by this episode.

While the court was at Saint-Cloud, the Emperor, who had worked very late one evening with Monsieur de Talleyrand, invited the latter to sleep at the chateau; but the prince, who preferred returning to Paris, refused, giving as an excuse that the beds had a very disagreeable odour. There was no truth whatever in this statement, for there was, as may be believed, the greatest care taken of the furniture, even in the store-rooms of the different imperial palaces; and the reason assigned by M. de Talleyrand being given at random, he could just as well have given any other; but, nevertheless, the remark struck the Emperor's attention, and that evening on entering his bedroom he complained that his bed had an unpleasant odour. I assured him to the contrary, and told his Majesty that he would next day be convinced of his error; but, far from being persuaded, the Emperor, when he rose next morning, repeated the assertion that his bed had a very disagreeable odour, and that it was absolutely necessary to change it. M. Charvet, concierge of the palace, was at once summoned; his Majesty complained of his bed, and ordered another to be brought.

M. Desmasis, keeper of the furniture-room, was also called, who examined mattress, feather-beds, and covering, turned and returned them in every direction; other persons did the same, and each was convinced that there was no odour about his Majesty's bed. In spite of so many witnesses to the contrary, the Emperor, not because he made it a point of honour not to have what he had asserted proved false, but merely from a caprice to which he was very subject, persisted in his first idea, and required his bed to be changed. Seeing that it was necessary to obey, I sent this bed to the Tuileries, and had the one which was there brought to the chateau of Saint-Cloud. The Emperor was now satisfied, and, on his return to the Tuileries, did not notice the exchange, and thought his bed in that chateau very good; and the most amusing part of all was that the ladies of the palace, having learned that the Emperor had complained of his bed, all found an unbearable odour in theirs, and insisted that everything must be overhauled, which created a small revolution. The caprices of sovereigns are sometimes epidemic.

Chapter 30

His Majesty was accustomed to say that one could always tell an honourable man by his conduct to his wife, his children, and his servants; and I hope it will appear from these memoirs that the Emperor conducted himself as an honourable man, according to his own definition. He said, moreover, that immorality was the most dangerous vice of a sovereign, because of the evil example it set to his subjects.

What he meant by immorality was doubtless a scandalous publicity given to liaisons which might otherwise have remained secret; for, as regards these liaisons themselves, he withstood women no more than any other man when they threw themselves at his head. Perhaps another man, surrounded by seductions, attacks, and advances of all kinds, would have resisted these temptations still less. Nevertheless, please God, I do not propose to defend his Majesty in this respect. I will even admit, if you wish, that his conduct did not offer an example in the most perfect accord with the morality of his discourses; but it must be admitted also that it was somewhat to the credit of a sovereign that he concealed, with the most scrupulous care, his frailties from the public, lest they should be a subject of scandal, or, what is worse, of imitation; and from his wife, to whom it would have been a source of the deepest grief.

On this delicate subject I recall two or three occurrences which took place, I think, about the period which my narrative has now reached.

The Empress Josephine was jealous, and, notwithstanding the prudence which the Emperor exercised in his secret liaisons, could not remain in entire ignorance of what was passing.

The Emperor had known at Genoa Madame Gazani, the daughter of an Italian dancer, whom he continued to receive at Paris; and one day, having an appointment with her in his private apartments, ordered me to remain in his room, and to reply to whoever asked for him, even if it was her Majesty the Empress herself, that he was engaged in his cabinet with a minister.

The place of the interview was the apartment formerly occupied by Bourrienne, communicating by a staircase which opened on his Majesty's bedroom. This room had been arranged and decorated very plainly, and had a second exit on the staircase called the black staircase, because it was dark and badly lighted, and it was through this that Madame Gazani entered, while the Emperor came in by the other door. They had been together only a few moments when the Empress entered the Emperor's room, and asked me what her husband was doing. "Madame, the Emperor is very busy just now; he is working in his cabinet with a minister."

"Constant, I wish to enter."

"That is impossible, Madame. I have received a formal order not to disturb his Majesty, not even for her Majesty the Empress;" whereupon she went away dissatisfied and somewhat irritated, and at the end of half an hour returned; and, renewing her demand, I was obliged to repeat my reply, and, though much distressed in witnessing the chagrin of her Majesty the Empress, I could not disobey my orders. That evening on retiring the Emperor said to me, in a very severe tone, that the Empress had informed him she had learned from me, that, at the time she came to question me in regard to him, he was closeted with a lady. Not at all disturbed, I replied to the Emperor, that of course he could not believe that.

"No," replied the Emperor, returning to the friendly tone with which he habitually honoured me, "I know you well enough to be assured of your discretion; but woe to the idiots who are gossiping, if I can get hold of them."

The next night the Empress entered, as the Emperor was retiring, and his Majesty said to her in my presence, "It is very bad to impute falsehood to poor Monsieur Constant; he is not the man to make up such a tale as that you told me." The Empress, seated on the edge of the bed, began to laugh, and put her pretty little hand over her husband's mouth; and, as it was a matter concerning myself, I withdrew. For a few days the Empress was cool and distant to me; but, as this was foreign to her nature, she soon resumed the gracious manner which attached all hearts to her.

The Emperor's liaison with Madame Gazani lasted nearly a year, but they met only at long intervals.

The following instance of jealousy is not as personal to me as that which I have just related.

Madame de Remusat,[1] wife of one of the *prefects* of the palace, and one of the ladies of honour to whom the Empress was most attached, found her one evening in tears and despair, and waited in silence till her Majesty should condescend to tell her the cause of this deep trouble. She had not long to wait, however; for hardly had she entered the apartment than her Majesty exclaimed, "I am sure that he is now with some woman. My dear friend," added she, continuing to weep, "take this candle and let us go and listen at his door. We will hear much." Madame de Remusat did all in her power to dissuade her from this project, representing to her the lateness of the hour, the darkness of the passage, and the danger they would run of being surprised; but all in vain, her Majesty put the candle in her hand, saying, "It is absolutely necessary that you should go with me, but, if you are afraid, I will go in front." Madame de Remusat obeyed; and behold the two ladies advancing on their tiptoes along the corridor, by the light of a single candle flickering in the air. Having reached the door of the Emperor's antechamber, they stopped, hardly daring to breathe, and the Empress softly turned the knob; but, just as she put her foot into the apartment, Roustan, who slept there and was then sleeping soundly, gave a formidable and prolonged snore. These ladies had not apparently remembered that they would find him there; and Madame de Remusat, imagining that she already saw him leaping out of bed sabre and pistol in hand, turned and ran as fast as she could, still holding the candle in her hand, and leaving the Empress in complete darkness, and did not stop to take breath until she reached the Empress's bedroom, when she remembered that the latter had been left in the corridor with no light. Madame de Remusat went back to meet her, and saw her returning, holding her sides with laughter, and forgetting her chagrin in the amusement caused by this adventure. Madame de Remusat attempted to excuse herself. "My dear friend," said her Majesty, "you only anticipated me, for that pigheaded Roustan frightened me so that I should have run first, if you had not been a greater coward than I."

I do not know what these ladies would have discovered if their courage had not failed them before reaching the end of their expedition, but probably nothing at all, for the Emperor rarely received at the Tuileries any one for whom he had a temporary fancy. I have already stated that, under the consulate, he had his meetings in a small house in the Allee des Veuves; and after he became Emperor, such

---

1. Authoress of the well-known *Memoirs*. Born in Paris, 1780, died 1821. Her husband was first chamberlain to the Emperor.

meetings still took place outside the chateau; and to these rendezvous he went incognito at night, exposing himself to all the chances that a man runs in such adventures.

One evening, between eleven o'clock and midnight, the Emperor called me, asked for a black frock coat and round hat, and ordered me to follow him; and with Prince Murat as the third party, we entered a close carriage with Caesar as driver, and only a single footman, both without livery.

After a short ride, the Emperor stopped in the Rue de——, alighted, went a few steps farther, and entered a house alone, while the prince and I remained in the carriage. Some hours passed, and we began to be uneasy; for the life of the Emperor had been so often menaced, that it was very natural to fear some snare or surprise, and imagination takes the reins when beset by such fears. Prince Murat swore and cursed with all his might, sometimes the imprudence of his Majesty, then his gallantry, then the lady and her complaisance. I was not any better satisfied than he, but being calmer I tried to quiet him; and at last, unable longer to restrain his impatience, the prince sprang out of the carriage, and I followed; but, just as his hand was on the knocker of the door, the Emperor came out. It was then already broad daylight, and the Prince informed him of our anxiety, and the reflections we had made upon his rashness. "What childishness!" said his Majesty; "what is there to fear? Wherever I am, am I not in my own house?"

It was as volunteers that any courtiers mentioned to the Emperor any young and pretty persons who wished to make his acquaintance, for it was in no wise in keeping with his character to give such commissions. I was not enough of a courtier to think such an employment honourable, and never voluntarily took part in any business of the kind.

It was not, however, for want of having been indirectly sounded, or even openly solicited, by certain ladies who were ambitious of the title of favourites, although this title would have given very few rights and privileges with the Emperor; but I would never enter into such bargains, restricting myself to the duties which my position imposed on me, and not going beyond them; and, although his Majesty took pleasure in reviving the usages of the old monarchy, the secret duties of the first *valet de chambre* were not re-established, and I took care not to claim them.

Many others (not *valets de chambre*) were less scrupulous than I. General L—— spoke to the Emperor one day of a very pretty girl whose mother kept a gambling-house, and who desired to be presented to him; but the Emperor received her once only, and a few days afterwards she was married. Some time later his Majesty wished to see her again, and asked for her; but the young woman replied that she did not belong to herself any longer, and refused all the invitations and offers made to her. The Emperor seemed in no wise dissatisfied, but on the contrary praised Madame D——for her fidelity to duty, and approved her conduct highly.

In 1804 her imperial highness Princess Murat had in her household a young reader named Mademoiselle E——, seventeen or eighteen years of age, tall, slender, well made, a brunette, with beautiful black eyes, sprightly, and very coquettish. Some persons who thought it to their interest to create differences between his Majesty and the Empress, his wife, noticed with pleasure the inclination of this young reader to try the power of her glances upon the Emperor, and his disposition to encourage her; so they stirred up the fire adroitly, and one of them took upon himself all the diplomacy of this affair. Propositions made through a third party were at once accepted; and the beautiful E—— came to the chateau secretly, but rarely, and remained there only two or three, hours. When she became *enceinte*, the Emperor had a house rented for her in the Rue Chantereine, where she bore a fine boy, upon whom was settled at his birth an income of thirty thousand *francs*. He was confided at first to the care of Madame I——, nurse of Prince Achille Murat, who kept him three or four years, and then Monsieur de Meneval, his Majesty's secretary, was ordered to provide for the education of this child; and when the Emperor returned from the Island of Elba; the son of Mademoiselle E—— was placed in the care of her Majesty, the Empress-mother.

The liaison of the Emperor with Mademoiselle E——did not last long. She came one day with her mother to Fontainebleau, where the court then happened to be, went up to his Majesty's apartment, and asked me to announce her; and the Emperor, being exceedingly displeased by this step, directed me to say to Mademoiselle E—— that he forbade her to present herself before him again without his permission, and not to remain a moment longer at Fontainebleau. In spite of this harshness to the mother, the Emperor loved the son tenderly; and I brought him to him often, on which occasions he caressed the child, gave him a great many dainties, and was much amused by his vivacity and repartees, which showed remarkable intelligence for his age.

This child and that of the Polish beauty, of whom I will speak later, and the King of Rome, were the only children of the Emperor. He never had a daughter, and I believe he desired none.[2]

I have seen it stated, I know not where, that the Emperor, during the long stay we made at Boulogne, indemnified himself at night for the labours of the day with a beautiful Italian, and I will now relate what I know of this adventure. His Majesty complained one morning, while I was dressing him, in the presence of Prince Murat, that he saw none but moustached faces, which he said was very tiresome; and the prince, ever ready on occasions of this kind to offer his services to his brother-in-law, spoke to him of a handsome and attractive Genoese lady, who had the greatest desire to see his Majesty. The Emperor laughingly granted a *tete-a-tete*, the prince himself offering to send the message; and two days later, by his kind assistance, the lady arrived, and was installed in the upper town. The Emperor, who lodged at Pont des Briques, ordered me one evening to take a carriage, and find this *protégée* of Prince Murat. I obeyed, and brought the beautiful Genoese, who, to avoid scandal, although it was a dark night, was introduced through a little garden behind his Majesty's apartments. The poor woman was much excited, and shed tears, but controlled herself quickly on finding that she was kindly received, and the interview was prolonged until three o'clock in the morning, when I was called to carry her back. She returned afterwards four or five times, and was with the Emperor afterwards at Rambouillet. She was gentle, simple, credulous, and not at all intriguing, and did not try to draw any benefit from a liaison which at best was only temporary.

Another of these favourites of the moment, who threw themselves so to speak into the arms of the Emperor without giving him time to make his court to them, was Mademoiselle L. B———, a very pretty girl. She was intelligent, and possessed a kind heart, and, had she received a less frivolous education, would doubtless have been an estimable woman; but I have reason to believe that her mother had from the first the design of acquiring a protector for her second husband, by utilizing the youth and attractions of the daughter of her first. I do not now recall her name, but she was of a noble family, of which fact the mother and daughter were very proud, and the young girl was a good musician, and sang agreeably; but, which appeared to me as ridiculous as indecent, she danced the ballet before a large company in her

---

2. This son of Countess Walewska became Count Walewski, a leading statesman of the Second Empire, ambassador to London, 1852, minister of foreign affairs, 1855, minister of state, 1860, president of Corps Legislatif, 1865. Born 1810, died 1868.—Trans.

mother's house, in a costume almost as light as those of the opera, with castanets or tambourines, and ended her dance with a multiplicity of attitudes and graces. With such an education she naturally thought her position not at all unusual, and was very much chagrined at the short duration of her liaison with the Emperor; while the mother was in despair, and said to me with disgusting simplicity, "See my poor Lise, how she has ruined her complexion in her vexation at seeing herself neglected, poor child. How good you will be, if you can manage to have her sent for." To secure an interview for which the mother and daughter were both so desirous, they came together to the chapel at Saint-Cloud, and during mass the poor Lise threw glances at the Emperor which made the young ladies blush who witnessed them, and were, nevertheless, all in vain, for the Emperor remained unmoved.

Colonel L. B—— was *aide-de-camp* to General L——, the governor of Saint-Cloud; and the general was a widower, which facts alone furnish an excuse for the intimacy of his only daughter with the family of L. B——, which astonished me greatly. One day, when I was dining at the house of the colonel, with his wife, his step-daughter, and Mademoiselle L——, the general sent for his *aides-de-camp*, and I was left alone, with the ladies; who so earnestly begged me to accompany them on a visit to Mademoiselle le Normand, that it would have been impolite to refuse, consequently we ordered a carriage and went to the Rue de Tournon. Mademoiselle L. B—— was first to enter the Sybil's cave, where she remained a long while, but on her return was very reserved as to any communications made to her, though Mademoiselle L—— told us very frankly that she had good news, and would soon marry the man she loved, which event soon occurred. These ladies having urged me to consult the prophetess in my turn, I perceived plainly that I was recognized; for Mademoiselle le Normand at once discovered in my hand that I had the happiness of being near a great man and being highly esteemed by him, adding much other nonsense of the same kind, which was so tiresome that I thanked her, and made my adieux as quickly as possible.

Chapter 31

While the Emperor was giving crowns to his brothers and sisters,—to Prince Louis, the throne of Holland; Naples to Prince Joseph; the Duchy of Berg to Prince Murat; to the Princess Eliza, Lucca and Massa-Carrara; and Guastalla to the Princess Pauline Borghese; and while, by means of treaties and family alliances, he was assuring still more the co-operation of the different states which had entered into the Confederation of the Rhine,—war was renewed between France and Prussia. It is not my province to investigate the causes of this war, nor to decide which first gave cause of offense.

All I can certify is this, frequently at the Tuileries, and on the campaign, I heard the Emperor, in conversation with his intimate friends, accuse the old Duke of Brunswick, whose name had been so odious in France since 1792, and also the young and beautiful Queen of Prussia, of having influenced King Frederic William to break the treaty of peace. The Queen was, according to the Emperor, more disposed to war than General Blucher himself. She wore the uniform of the regiment to which she had given her name, appeared at all reviews, and commanded the manoeuvres.

We left Paris at the end of September. I will not enter into the details of this wonderful campaign, in which the Emperor in an incredibly short time crushed to pieces an army of one hundred and fifty thousand men, perfectly disciplined, full of enthusiasm and courage, and fighting in defence of their country. In one of the first battles, the young Prince Louis of Prussia, brother of the king, was killed at the head of his troops by Guinde, quartermaster of the Tenth Hussars. The prince fought hand to hand with this brave sub-officer, who said to him, "Surrender, Colonel, or you are a dead man," to which Prince Louis replied only by a sabre stroke, whereupon Guinde plunged his own into the body of his opponent, and he fell dead on the spot.

On this campaign, as the roads had become very rough from the continual passage of artillery, my carriage was one day upset, and one of the Emperor's hats fell out of the door; but a regiment which happened to pass along the same road having recognized the hat from its peculiar shape, my carriage was immediately set up again, "For," said these brave soldiers, "we cannot leave the first valet of the little corporal in trouble;" and the hat, after passing through many hands, was at last restored to me before my departure.

On the Emperor's arrival at the plateau of Weimar, he arranged his army in line of battle, and bivouacked in the midst of his guard. About two o'clock in the morning he arose and went on foot to examine the work on a road that was being cut in the rock for the transportation of artillery, and after remaining nearly an hour with the workmen, decided to take a look at the nearest advance posts before returning to his bivouac.

This round, which the Emperor insisted on making alone and with no escort, came near costing him his life. The night was so dark that the sentinels of the camp could not see ten steps in front of them; and the first, hearing some one in the darkness approaching our line, called out *"Qui vive?"* and prepared to fire. The Emperor being lost in thought, as he himself told me afterwards, did not notice the sentinel's challenge, and made no reply until a ball, whistling by his ears, woke him from his reverie, when immediately perceiving his danger, he threw himself face downwards on the ground, which was a very wise precaution; for hardly had his Majesty placed himself in this position, than other balls passed over his head, the discharge of the first sentinel having been repeated by the whole line. This first fire over, the Emperor rose, walked towards the nearest post, and made himself known.

His Majesty was still there when the soldier who had fired on him joined them, being just relieved at his post; he was a young grenadier of the line. The Emperor ordered him to approach, and, pinching his cheeks hard, exclaimed, "What, you scamp, you took me for a Prussian! This rascal does not throw away his powder on sparrows; he shoots only at emperors." The poor soldier was completely overcome with the idea that he might have killed the little corporal, whom he adored as much as did the rest of the army; and it was with great difficulty he could say, "Pardon, Sire, but I was obeying orders; and if you did not answer, it was not my fault. I was compelled to have the countersign, and you would not give it." The Emperor reassured him with a smile, and said, as he left the post, "My brave boy, I do not reproach you. That was pretty well aimed for a shot fired in the dark; but after awhile it will be daylight; take better aim, and I will remember you."

The results of the Battle of Jena, fought on the 14th of October (1806), are well known. Almost all the Prussian generals, at least the bravest among them, were there taken prisoners, or rendered unable to continue the campaign.

The king and queen took flight, and did not halt till they had reached Koenigsberg.

A few moments before the attack, the Queen of Prussia, mounted on a noble, graceful steed, had appeared in the midst of the soldiers; and, followed by the elite of the youth of Berlin, this royal Amazon had galloped down the front rank of the line of battle. The numerous banners which her own hands had embroidered to encourage her troops, with those of the great Frederick, blackened by the smoke of many battles, were lowered at her approach, amid shouts of enthusiasm which rang through the entire ranks of the Prussian army. The atmosphere was so clear, and the two armies so near each other, that the French could easily distinguish the costume of the queen.

This striking costume was, in fact, one great cause of the danger she encountered in her flight. Her head was covered with a helmet of polished steel, above which waved a magnificent plume, her cuirass glittered with gold and silver, while a tunic of silver cloth completed her costume and fell to her feet, which were shod in red boots with gold spurs. This dress heightened the charms of the beautiful queen.

When the Prussian army was put to flight, the queen was left alone with three or four young men of Berlin, who defended her until two hussars, who had covered themselves with glory during the battle, rushed at a gallop with drawn sabres on this little group, and they were instantly dispersed. Frightened by this sudden onset, the horse which her Majesty rode fled with all the strength of his limbs; and well was it for the fugitive queen that he was swift as a stag, else the two hussars would infallibly have made her a prisoner, for more than once they pressed so close that she heard their rude speeches and coarse jests, which were of such a nature as to shock her ears.

The queen, thus pursued, had arrived in sight of the gate of Weimar, when a strong detachment of Klein's dragoons were perceived coming at full speed, the chief having orders to capture the queen at any cost; but, the instant she entered the city, the gates swung to behind her, and the hussars and the detachment of dragoons returned disappointed to the battle-field.

The particulars of this singular pursuit soon reached the Emperor's

DAVOUST

ears, and he summoned the hussars to his presence, and having in strong terms testified his disapproval of the improper jests that they had dared to make regarding the queen; at a time when her misfortunes should have increased the respect due both to her rank and her sex, the Emperor then performed the duty of rewarding these two brave fellows for the manner in which they had borne themselves on the field of battle. Knowing that they had dons prodigies of valour, his Majesty gave them the cross, and ordered three hundred *francs* to be given each one as gratuity.

The Emperor exercised his clemency toward the Duke of Weimar, who had commanded a Prussian division. The day after the battle of Jena, his Majesty, having reached Weimar, lodged at the ducal palace, where he was received by the duchess regent, to whom he said, "Madame, I owe you something for having awaited me; and in appreciation of the confidence you have manifested in me, I pardon your husband."

While we were in the army I slept in the Emperor's tent, either on a little rug, or on the bearskin which he used in his carriage; or when it happened that I could not make use of these articles, I tried to procure a bed-of straw, and remember one evening having rendered a great service to the King of Naples, by sharing with him the bundle of straw which was to have served as my bed.

I here give a few details from which the reader can form an idea of the manner in which I passed the nights on the campaign.

The Emperor slept on his little iron bedstead, and I slept where I could. Hardly did I fall asleep before the Emperor called me, "Constant."

"Sire."

"See who is on duty" (it was the *aides-de-camp* to whom he referred).—"Sire, it is M.——"

"Tell him to come to me." I then went out of the tent to summon the officer, and brought him back with me. On his entrance the Emperor said to him, "Report to such a corps, commanded by such a marshal; you will request him to send such a regiment to such a position; you will ascertain the position of the enemy, then you will return to report." The *aide-de-camp*, having left on horseback to execute these orders, I lay down again, and the Emperor now seemed to be going to sleep; but, at the end of a few moments, I heard him call again, "Constant."

"Sire."

"Have the Prince de Neuchatel summoned." I sent for the prince, who came at once; and during the conversation I must remain at the door of the tent, until the prince wrote several orders and withdrew. These interruptions took place many times during the night, and at last towards morning his Majesty slept, when I also had a few moments of repose.

When *aides-de-camp* arrived, bringing any news to the Emperor, I awoke him, by shaking him gently.

"What is it?" said his Majesty, waking with a start; "what o'clock is it? Let him enter." The *aide-de-camp* made his report; and if it was necessary, his Majesty rose immediately, and left the tent, his toilet never occupying much time. If a battle was in contemplation the Emperor scanned the sky and the horizon carefully, and often remarked, "We are going to have a beautiful day."

Breakfast was prepared and served in five minutes, and at the end of a quarter of an hour the cloth was removed. The Prince de Neuchatel breakfasted and dined every day with his Majesty; and, in eight or ten minutes, the longest meal was over. "To horse," then exclaimed the Emperor, and set out, accompanied by the Prince de Neuchatel, and an *aide-de-camp* or two, with Roustan, who always carried a silver flask of brandy, which, however, the Emperor rarely ever used. His Majesty passed from one corps to the other, spoke to the officers and soldiers, questioned them, and saw with his own eyes all that it was possible to see.

If a battle was on hand, dinner was forgotten, and the Emperor ate only after his return; but, if the engagement lasted too long, there was carried to him, without his ordering it, a crust of bread and a little wine.

M. Colin, chief of the culinary department, many times braved the cannon to carry a light repast to the Emperor.

At the close of the combat, his Majesty never failed to visit the battle-field, where he had aid given the wounded, and encouraged them with cheering words.

The Emperor sometimes returned overcome by fatigue; he then took a light repast, and lay down again to begin his interrupted sleep.

It was remarkable, that, each time that unexpected circumstances forced the *aides-de-camp* to have the Emperor waked, he was as ready for work as he would have been at the beginning or in the middle of the day, and his awaking was as amiable as his manner was pleasant. The report of an *aide-de-camp* being finished, Napoleon went to sleep again as easily as if his sleep had not been interrupted.

During the three or four hours preceding an engagement, the Emperor spent most of the time with large maps spread out before him, the places on which he marked with pins with heads of different coloured wax.

I have already said that all the persons of the Emperor's household emulated each other in seeking the surest and promptest means of carrying out his wishes; and everywhere, whether in travelling or on the campaign, his table, his coffee, his bed, or even his bath could be prepared in five minutes. How many times were we obliged to remove, in still less time, corpses of men and horses, to set up his Majesty's tent.

In one of the campaigns beyond the Rhine we were delayed in a poor village, and, in order to prepare the Emperor's lodging, were obliged to use a peasant's hut, which had served as a field hospital; and we began preparations by carrying away the dismembered limbs, and washing up the stains of blood, this labour being finished, and everything almost in order, in less than-half an hour.

The Emperor, sometimes slept a quarter or half an hour on the field of battle when he was fatigued, or wished to await more patiently the result of the orders he had given.

While on the road to Potsdam, we were overtaken by a violent storm, which became so severe, and the rain so heavy, that we were obliged to stop and take refuge in a neighbouring house on the road. Well wrapped in his grey overcoat, and not thinking that he could be recognized, the Emperor was much surprised to see, as he entered the house, a young woman who seemed to tremble at his presence. He ascertained that she was an Egyptian, who had retained for my master the religious veneration which all the Arabs bore him, and was the widow of an officer of the army of Egypt, whom chance had led to the same house in Saxony where he had been welcomed. The Emperor granted her a pension of twelve hundred *francs*, and took upon himself the education of her son, the only legacy left her by her husband. "This is the first time," said Napoleon, "that I have alighted to avoid a storm; I had a presentiment that an opportunity of doing good awaited me here."

The loss of the battle of Jena had struck the Prussians with such terror, and the court had fled with such precipitation, that everything had been left in the royal residences; and, consequently, on his arrival at Potsdam, the Emperor found there the sword of the great Frederick, his gorget, the grand cordon of his order, and his alarm-clock, and had them carried to Paris, to be preserved at the Hotel des Invalides. "I prefer these trophies," said his Majesty, "to all the treasures of the King of Prussia; I will send them to my old soldiers of the campaign of Hanover, who will guard them as a trophy of the victories of the grand army, and of the revenge that it has taken for the disaster of Rosbach."

The Emperor the same day ordered the removal to his capital of the column raised by the great Frederick to perpetuate the remembrance of the defeat of the French at Rosbach.[1] He might have contented himself with changing the inscription.

Napoleon remained at the chateau of Charlottenburg, where he had established his headquarters, until the regiments of the guard had arrived from all points; and as soon as they were assembled, orders were given to put themselves in full uniform, which was done in the little wood before the town. The Emperor made his entry into the capital of Prussia between ten and eleven o'clock in the morning, surrounded by his *aides-de-camp*, and the officers of his staff, all the regiments filing before him in the most perfect order, drums and music at their head; and the fine appearance of the troops excited the admiration of the Prussians.

Having entered Berlin in the suite of the Emperor, we arrived at the town square, in the midst of which a bust of the great Frederick had been placed. The name of this monarch is so popular at Berlin, and, in fact, throughout all Prussia, that on many occasions, when any one by chance pronounced it, either in a cafe or in any other public place, or even in private assemblies, I have seen every one present rise, and lift his hat with an air of the most profound respect and genuine adoration.

When the Emperor arrived in front of the bust, he described a semicircle at a gallop, followed by his staff, and lowering the point of his sword, while uncovering his head, was the first to salute the image of Frederick II. His staff followed his example; and all the general and other officers who composed it ranged themselves in a semicircle around the bust, with the Emperor in the centre. His Majesty gave orders that each regiment should present arms in defiling before the bust, which manoeuvre was not to the taste of some grumblers of the first regiment of the Guard, who, with moustaches scorched, and faces still blackened with the powder of Jena, would have better liked an order for lodgings with the bourgeois than all this parade, and took no pains to conceal their ill-humour. There was one, among others, who, as he passed in front of the bust and before the Emperor, exclaimed between his teeth, without moving a muscle of his face, but still loud enough to be heard by his Majesty, "Damn the bust." His Majesty pretended not to hear, but that evening he repeated with a laugh the words of the old soldier.

---

1. At Rosbach, November, 1757, the French, under Prince de Soubise, had been shamefully defeated by Frederick the Great.

His Majesty alighted at the chateau, where his lodging was prepared, and the officers of his household had preceded him. Having learned that the electoral princess of Hesse-Cassel, sister of the king, was still ill at the end of her confinement, the Emperor ascended to the apartment of this princess, and, after quite a long visit, gave orders that she should be treated with all the deference due to her rank and unfortunate situation.

Chapter 32

I left the Emperor at Berlin, where each day, and each hour of the day, he received news of some victory gained, or some success obtained by his generals. General Beaumont presented to him eighty flags captured from the enemy by his division, and Colonel Gerard also presented sixty taken from Blucher at the battle of Wismar. Madgeburg had capitulated, and a garrison of sixty thousand men had marched out under the eyes of General Savary. Marshal Mortier occupied Hanover in the name of France, and Prince Murat was on the point of entering Warsaw after driving out the Russians.

War was about to recommence, or rather to be continued, against the latter; and since the Prussian army could now be regarded as entirely vanquished, the Emperor left Berlin in order to personally conduct operations against the Russians.

We travelled in the little coaches of the country; and as was the rule always on our journeys, the carriage of the grand marshal preceded that of the Emperor. The season, and the passage of such large numbers of artillery, had rendered the roads frightful; but notwithstanding this we travelled very rapidly, until at last between Kutow and Warsaw, the grand marshal's carriage was upset, and his collarbone broken. The Emperor arrived a short time after this unfortunate accident, and had him borne under his own eyes into the nearest post-house. We always carried with us a portable medicine-chest in order that needed help might be promptly given to the wounded. His Majesty placed him in the hands of the surgeon, and did not leave him till he had seen the first bandage applied.

At Warsaw, where his Majesty passed the entire month of January, 1807, he occupied the grand palace. The Polish nobility, eager to pay their court to him, gave in his honour magnificent fetes and brilliant balls, at which were present all the wealthiest and most distinguished inhabitants of Warsaw.

At one of these reunions the Emperor's attention was drawn to a young Polish lady named Madame Valevska, twenty-two years of age, who had just married an old noble of exacting temper and extremely harsh manners, more in love with his titles than with his wife, whom, however, he loved devotedly, and by whom he was more respected than loved. The Emperor experienced much pleasure at the sight of this lady, who attracted his attention at the first glance. She was a blonde, with blue eyes, and skin of dazzling whiteness; of medium height, with a charming and beautifully proportioned figure. The Emperor having approached her, immediately began a conversation, which she sustained with much grace and intelligence, showing that she had received a fine education, and the slight shade of melancholy diffused over her whole person rendered her still more seductive.

His Majesty thought he beheld in her a woman who had been sacrificed, and was unhappy in her domestic relations; and the interest with which this idea inspired him caused him to be more interested in her than he had ever been in any woman, a fact of which she could not fail to be conscious. The day after the ball, the Emperor seemed to me unusually agitated; he rose from his chair, paced to and fro, took his seat and rose again, until I thought I should never finish dressing him. Immediately after breakfast he ordered a person, whose name I shall not give, to pay a visit to Madame Valevska, and inform her of his subjugation and his wishes. She proudly refused propositions which were perhaps too brusque, or which perhaps the coquetry natural to all women led her to repulse; and though the hero pleased her, and the idea of a lover resplendent with power and glory revolved doubtless over and over in her brain, she had no idea of surrendering thus without a struggle. The great personage returned in confusion, much astonished that he had not succeeded in his mission; and the next day when the Emperor rose I found him still preoccupied, and he did not utter a word, although he was in the habit of talking to me at this time. He had written to Madame Valevska several times, but she had not replied; and his vanity was much piqued by such unaccustomed indifference. At last his affecting appeals having touched Madame Valevska's heart, she consented to an interview between ten and eleven o'clock that evening, which took place at the appointed time. She returned a few days after at the same hour, and her visits continued until the Emperor's departure.

Two months after the Emperor sent for her; and she joined him at his headquarters in Finkenstein, where she remained from this time, leaving at Warsaw her old husband, who, deeply wounded both in his honour and his affections, wished never to see again the wife who had abandoned him. Madame Valevska remained with the Emperor until his departure, and then returned to her family, constantly evincing the most devoted and, at the same time, disinterested affection. The Emperor seemed to appreciate perfectly the charms of this angelic woman, whose gentle and self-abnegating character made a profound impression on me. As they took their meals together, and I served them alone, I was thus in a position to enjoy their conversation, which was always amiable, gay, and animated on the Emperor's part; tender, impassioned, and melancholy on that of Madame Valevska. When his Majesty was absent, Madame Valevska passed all her time, either in reading, or viewing through the lattice blinds of the Emperor's rooms the parades and evolutions which took place in the court of honour of the chateau, and which he often commanded in person. Such was her life, like her disposition, ever calm and equable; and this loveliness of character charmed the Emperor, and made him each day more and more her slave.

After the battle of Wagram, in 1809, the Emperor took up his residence at the palace of Schoenbrunn, and sent immediately for Madame Valevska, for whom a charming house had been rented and furnished in one of the *faubourgs* of Vienna, a short distance from Schoenbrunn. I went mysteriously to bring her every evening in a close carriage, with a single servant, without livery; she entered by a secret door, and was introduced into the Emperor's apartments. The road, although very short, was not without danger, especially in rainy weather, on account of ruts and holes which were encountered at every step; and the Emperor said to me almost every day, "Be very careful, Constant, it has rained today; the road will be bad. Are you sure you have a good driver? Is the carriage in good condition?" and other questions of the same kind, which evidenced the deep and sincere affection he felt for Madame Valevska. The Emperor was not wrong, besides, in urging me to be careful; for one evening, when we had left Madame Valevska's residence a little later than usual, the coachman upset us, and in trying to avoid a rut, drove the carriage over the edge of the road. I was on the right of Madame Valevska and the carriage fell on that side, in such a position that I alone felt the shock of the fall, since Madame Valevska falling on me, received no injury. I was glad to be the means of saving her, and when I said this she expressed her gratitude with a grace peculiarly her own. My injuries were slight; and I began to laugh the first, in which Madame Valevska soon joined, and she related our accident to his Majesty immediately on our arrival.

I could not undertake to describe all the care and attentions which the Emperor lavished upon her. He had her brought to Paris, accompanied by her brother, a very distinguished officer, and her maid, and gave the grand marshal orders to purchase for her a pretty residence in the Chaussee-d'Antin. Madame Valevska was very happy, and often said to me, "All my thoughts, all my inspirations, come from him, and return to him; he is all my happiness, my future, my life!" She never left her house except to come to the private apartments at the Tuileries, and when this happiness could not be granted, went neither to the theatre, the promenade, nor in society, but remained at home, seeing only very few persons, and writing to the Emperor every day. At length she gave birth to a son,[1] who bore a striking resemblance to the Emperor, to whom this event was a source of great joy; and he hastened to her as soon as it was possible to escape from the chateau, and taking the child in his arms, and caressing him, as he had just caressed the mother, said to him, "I make you a count." Later we shall see this son receiving at Fontainebleau a final proof of affection.

Madame Valevska reared her son at her residence, never leaving him, and carried him often to the chateau, where I admitted them by the dark staircase, and when either was sick the Emperor sent to them Monsieur Corvisart. This skilful physician had on one occasion the happiness of saving the life of the young count in a dangerous illness.

Madame Valevska had a gold ring made for the Emperor, around which she twined her beautiful blonde hair, and on the inside of the ring were engraved these words:

"When you cease to love me, do not forget that I love you."

The Emperor gave her no other name but Marie.

I have perhaps devoted too much space to this liaison of the Emperor: but Madame Valevska was entirely different from the other women whose favour his Majesty obtained; and she was worthy to be named the La Valliere of the Emperor, who, however, did not show himself ungrateful towards her, as did Louis XIV. towards the only woman by whom he was beloved. Those who had, like myself, the happiness of knowing and seeing her intimately must have preserved memories of her which will enable them to comprehend why in my opinion there exists so great a distance between Madame Valevska, the tender and modest woman, rearing in retirement the son she bore to the Emperor, and the favourites of the conqueror of Austerlitz.

---

1. Count Walewski, born 1810; minister to England, 1852; minister of foreign affairs, 1855-1860; died 1868.

Chapter 33

The Russians, being incited to this campaign by the remembrance of the defeat of Austerlitz, and by the fear of seeing Poland snatched from their grasp, were not deterred by the winter season, and resolved to open the attack on the Emperor at once; and as the latter was not the man to allow himself to be forestalled, he consequently abandoned his winter quarters, and quitted Warsaw at the end of January. On the 8th of February the two armies met at Eylau; and there took place, as is well known, a bloody battle, in which both sides showed equal courage, and nearly fifteen thousand were left dead on the field of battle, equally divided in number between the French and Russians. The gain, or rather the loss, was the same to both armies; and a *'Te Deum'* was chanted at St. Petersburg as well as at Paris, instead of the *'De Profundis'*, which would have been much more appropriate. His Majesty complained bitterly on returning to his headquarters that the order he had sent to General Bernadotte had not been executed, and in consequence of this his corps had taken no part in the battle, and expressed his firm conviction that the victory, which remained in doubt between the Emperor and General Benningsen, would have been decided in favour of the former had a fresh army-corps arrived during the battle, according to the Emperor's calculations. Most unfortunately the *aide-de-camp* bearing the Emperor's orders to the Prince of Ponte-Corvo had fallen into the hands of a party of Cossacks; and when the Emperor was informed of this circumstance the day after the battle, his resentment was appeased, though not his disappointment. Our troops bivouacked on the field of battle, which his Majesty visited three times, for the purpose of directing the assistance of the wounded, and removal of the dead.

Generals d'Hautpoult, Corbineau, and Boursier were mortally wounded at Eylau; and it seems to me I can still hear the brave d'Hautpoult saying to his Majesty, just as he dashed off at a gallop to charge the enemy: "Sire, you will now see my great claws; they will pierce through the enemy's squares as if they were butter" An hour after he was no more.

One of his regiments, being engaged in the interval with the Russian army, was mowed down with grape-shot, and hacked to pieces by the Cossacks, only eighteen men being left. General d'Hautpoult, forced to fall back three times with his division, led it back twice to the charge; and as he threw himself against the enemy the third time shouted loudly, "Forward, cuirassiers, in God's name! forward, my brave cuirassiers?" But the grapeshot had mowed down too many of these brave fellows; very few were left to follow their chief, and he soon fell pierced with wounds in the midst of a square of Russians into which he had rushed almost alone.

I think it was in this battle also that General Ordenerl killed with his own hands a general officer of the enemy. The Emperor asked if he could not have taken him alive. "Sire," replied the general with his strong German accent, "I gave him only one blow, but I tried to make it a good one." On the very morning of the battle, General Corbineau, the Emperor's *aide-de-camp*, while at breakfast with the officers on duty, declared to them that he was oppressed by the saddest presentiments; but these gentlemen, attempting to divert his mind, turned the affair into a joke. General Corbineau a few moments after received an order from his Majesty, and not finding some money he wished at Monsieur de Meneval's quarters, came to me, and I gave it to him from the Emperor's private purse; at the end of a few hours I met Monsieur de Meneval, to whom I rendered an account of General Corbineau's request, and the sum I had lent him. I was still speaking to Monsieur de Meneval, when an officer passing at a gallop gave us the sad news of the general's death. I have never forgotten the impression made on me by this sad news, and I still find no explanation of the strange mental distress which gave warning to this brave soldier of his approaching end.

Poland was relying upon the Emperor to re-establish her independence, and consequently the Poles were filled with hope and enthusiasm on witnessing the arrival of the French army. As for our soldiers, this winter campaign was most distasteful to them; for cold and wretchedness, bad weather and bad roads, had inspired them with an extreme aversion to this country.

In a review at Warsaw, at which the inhabitants crowded around our troops, a soldier began to swear roundly against the snow and mud, and, as a consequence, against Poland and the Poles. "You are wrong, Monsieur soldier," replied a young lady of a good bourgeois family of the town, "not to love our country, for we love the French very much."

"You are doubtless very lovable, mademoiselle," replied the soldier; "but if you wish to persuade me of the truth of what you say, you will prepare us a good dinner, my comrade and I."

"Come, then, messieurs," said the parents of the young Pole now advancing, "and we will drink together to the health of your Emperor." And they really carried off with them the two soldiers, who partook of the best dinner the country afforded.

The soldiers were accustomed to say that four words formed the basis of the Polish language,—*kleba? niema*; "bread? there is none;" *voia? sara*; "water? they have gone to draw it."

As the Emperor was one day passing through a column of infantry in the suburbs of Mysigniez, where the troops endured great privations since the bad roads prevented the arrival of supplies, *"Papa, kleba,"* cried a soldier. *"Niema,"* immediately replied the Emperor. The whole column burst into shouts of laughter, and no further request was made.

During the Emperor's somewhat extended stay at Finkenstein, he received a visit from the Persian ambassador, and a few grand reviews were held in his honour. His Majesty sent in return an embassy to the Shah, at the head of which he placed General Gardanne, who it was then said had an especial reason for wishing to visit Persia. It was rumoured that one of his relations, after a long residence at Teheran, had been compelled, having taken part in an insurrection against the Franks, to quit this capital, and before his flight had buried a considerable treasure in a certain spot, the description of which he had carried to France. I will add, as a finale to this story, some facts which I have since learned. General Gardanne found the capital in a state of confusion; and being able neither to locate the spot nor discover the treasure, returned from his embassy with empty hands.

Our stay at Finkenstein became very tiresome; and in order to while away the time, his Majesty sometimes played with his generals and *aides-de-camp*. The game was usually *vingt-et-un*; and the Great Captain took much pleasure in cheating, holding through several deals the cards necessary to complete the required number, and was much amused when he won the game by this finesse. I furnished the sum necessary for his game, and as soon as he returned to his quarters received orders to make out his account. He always gave me half of his gains, and I divided the remainder between the ordinary *valets de chambre*.

I have no intention, in this journal, of conforming to a very exact order of dates; and whenever there recurs to my memory a fact or an anecdote which seems to me deserving of mention, I shall jot it down, at whatever point of my narrative I may have then reached, fearing lest, should I defer it to its proper epoch, it might be forgotten. In pursuance of this plan I shall here relate, in passing, some souvenirs of Saint-Cloud or the Tuileries, although we are now in camp at Finkenstein. The pastimes in which his Majesty and his general officers indulged recalled these anecdotes to my recollection. These gentlemen often made wagers or bets among themselves; and I heard the Duke of Vicenza one day bet that Monsieur Jardin, junior, equerry of his Majesty, mounted backwards on his horse, could reach the end of the avenue in front of the chateau in the space of a few moments; which bet the equerry won.

Messieurs Fain, Meneval, and Ivan once played a singular joke on Monsieur B. d'A———, who, they knew, was subject to frequent attacks of gallantry. They dressed a young man in woman's clothes, and sent him to promenade, thus disguised, in an avenue near the chateau. Monsieur B. d'A——— was very near-sighted, and generally used an eyeglass. These gentlemen invited him to take a walk; and as soon as he was outside the door, he perceived the beautiful promenader, and could not restrain an exclamation of surprise and joy at the sight.

His friends feigned to share his delight, and urged him, as the most enterprising, to make the first advances, whereupon, in great excitement, he hastened after the pretended young lady, whom they had taught his role perfectly. Monsieur d'A——— outdid himself in politeness, in attentions, in offers of service, insisting eagerly on doing the honours of the chateau to his new conquest. The other acted his part perfectly; and after many coquettish airs on his side, and many protestations on the part of Monsieur d'A, a rendezvous was made for that very evening; and the lover, radiant with hope, returned to his friends, maintaining much discretion and reserve as to his good fortune, while he really would have liked to devour the time which must pass before the day was over. At last the evening arrived which was to put an end to his impatience, and bring the time of his interview; and his disappointment and rage may be imagined when he discovered the deception which had been practiced on him. Monsieur d'A——— wished at first to challenge the authors and actors in this hoax, and could with great difficulty be appeased.

It was, I think, on the return from this campaign, that Prince Jerome saw at Breslau, at the theatre of that town, a young and very pretty actress, who played her part badly, but sang very well. He made advances, which she received coolly: but kings do not sigh long in vain; they place too heavy a weight in the balance against discretion. His Majesty, the King of Westphalia, carried off his conquest to Cassel, and at the end of a short time she was married to his first *valet de chambre*, Albertoni, whose Italian morals were not shocked by this marriage. Some disagreement, the cause, of which I do not know, having caused Albertoni to quit the king, he returned to Paris with his wife, and engaged in speculations, in which he lost all that he had gained, and I have been told that he returned to Italy. One thing that always appeared to me extraordinary was the jealousy of Albertoni towards his wife—an exacting jealousy which kept his eyes open towards all men except the king; for I am well convinced that the liaison continued after their marriage.

The brothers of the Emperor, although kings, were sometimes kept waiting in the Emperor's antechamber. King Jerome came one morning by order of the Emperor, who, having not yet risen, told me to beg the King of Westphalia to wait. As the Emperor wished to sleep a little longer, I remained with the other servants in the saloon which was used as an antechamber, and the king waited with us; I do not say in patience, for he constantly moved from chair to chair, promenaded back and forth between the window and the fireplace, manifesting much annoyance, and speaking now and then to me, whom he always treated with great kindness. Thus more than half an hour passed; and at last I entered the Emperor's room, and when he had put on his dressing-gown, informed him that his Majesty was waiting, and after introducing him, I withdrew. The Emperor gave him a cool reception, and lectured him severely, and as he spoke very loud, I heard him against my will; but the king made his excuses in so low a tone that I could not hear a word of his justification. Such scenes were often repeated, for the prince was dissipated and prodigal, which displeased the Emperor above all things else, and for which he reproved him severely, although he loved him, or rather because he loved him so much; for it is remarkable, that notwithstanding the frequent causes of displeasure which his family gave him, the Emperor still felt for all his relations the warmest affection.

A short time after the taking of Dantzig (May 24, 1807), the Emperor, wishing to reward Marshal Lefebvre for the recent services which he had rendered, had him summoned at six o'clock in the morning. His Majesty was in consultation with the chief-of-staff of the army when the arrival of the marshal was announced. "Ah!" said he to Berthier, "the duke does not delay." Then, turning to the officer on duty, "Say to the Duke of Dantzig that I have summoned him so early in order that he may breakfast with me." The officer, thinking that the Emperor had misunderstood the name, remarked to him, that the person who awaited his orders was not the Duke of Dantzig, but Marshal Lefebvre. "It seems, *monsieur*, that you think me more capable of making a count than a duke."

The officer was somewhat disconcerted by this reply; but the Emperor reassured him with a smile, and said, "Go, give the duke my invitation, and say to him that in a quarter of an hour breakfast will be served." The officer returned to the marshal, who was, of course, very anxious to know why the Emperor had summoned him. "Monsieur le Duc, the Emperor invites you to breakfast with him, and begs you to wait a quarter of an hour." The marshal, not having noticed the new title which the officer gave him, replied by a nod, and seated himself on a folding chair on the back of which hung the Emperor's sword, which the marshal inspected and touched with admiration and respect. The quarter of an hour passed, when another ordnance officer came to summon the marshal to the Emperor, who was already at table with the chief-of-staff; and as he entered, the Emperor saluted him with, "Good-day, Monsieur le Duc; be seated next to me."

The marshal, astonished at being addressed by this title, thought at first that his Majesty was jesting; but seeing that he made a point of calling him Monsieur le, Duc he was overcome with astonishment. The Emperor, to increase his embarrassment, said to him, "Do you like chocolate, Monsieur le Duc?"

"But—yes, Sire."

"Well, we have none for breakfast, but I will give you a pound from the very town of Dantzig; for since you have conquered it, it is but just that it should make you some return." Thereupon the Emperor left the table, opened a little casket, took therefrom a package in the shape of a long square, and handed it to Marshal Lefebvre, saying to him, "Duke of Dantzig, accept this chocolate; little gifts preserve friendship." The marshal thanked his Majesty, put the chocolate in his pocket, and took his seat again at table with the Emperor and Marshal Berthier. A 'pate' in the shape of the town of Dantzig was in the midst of the table; and when this was to be served the Emperor said to the new duke, "They could not have given this dish a form which would have pleased me more. Make the attack, Monsieur le Duc; behold your conquest; it is yours to do the honours." The duke obeyed; and the three guests ate of the pie, which they found much to their taste.

On his return, the marshal, Duke of Dantzig, suspecting a surprise in the little package which the Emperor had given him, hastened to open it, and found a hundred thousand crowns in bank-notes. In imitation of this magnificent present, the custom was established in the army of calling money, whether in pieces or in bank-notes, Dantzig chocolate; and when the soldiers wished to be treated by any comrade who happened to have a little money in his pocket, would say to him, "Come, now, have you no Dantzig chocolate in your pocket?"

The almost superstitious fancy of his Majesty the Emperor in regard to coincidences in dates and anniversaries was strengthened still more by the victory of Friedland, which was gained on June 14, 1807, seven years to the very day after the battle of Marengo. The severity of the winter, the difficulty in furnishing supplies (for which the Emperor had however made every possible provision and arrangement), added to the obstinate courage of the Russians, had made this a severe campaign, especially to conquerors whom the incredible rapidity of their successes in Prussia had accustomed to sudden conquests. The division of glory which he had been compelled to make with the Russians was a new experience in the Emperor's military career, but at Friedland he regained his advantage and his former superiority. His Majesty, by a feigned retreat, in which he let the enemy see only a part of his forces, drew the Russians into a decoy on the Elbe, so complete that they found themselves shut in between that river and our army. This victory was gained by troops of the line and cavalry; and the Emperor did not even find it necessary to use his Guards, while those of the Emperor Alexander was almost entirely destroyed in protecting the retreat, or rather the flight, of the Russians, who could escape from the pursuit of our soldiers only by the bridge of Friedland, a few narrow pontoons, and an almost impassable ford.

The regiments of the line in the French army covered the plain; and the Emperor, occupying a post of observation on a height whence he could overlook the whole field of battle, was seated in an armchair near a mill, surrounded by his staff. I never saw him in a gayer mood, as he conversed with the generals who awaited his orders, and seemed to enjoy eating the black Russian bread which was baked in the shape of bricks. This bread, made from inferior rye flour and full of long straws, was the food of all the soldiers; and they knew that his Majesty ate it as well as themselves. The beautiful weather favoured the skilful manoeuvres of the army, and they performed prodigies of valour. The cavalry charges especially were executed with so much precision that the Emperor sent his congratulations to the regiments.

About four o'clock in the afternoon, when the two armies were pressing each other on every side, and thousands of cannon caused the earth to tremble, the Emperor exclaimed, "If this continues two hours longer, the French army will be left standing on the plain alone." A few moments after he gave orders to the Count Dorsenne, general of the foot grenadiers of the Old Guard, to fire on a brick-yard, behind which masses of Russians and Prussians were entrenched; and in the twinkling of an eye they were compelled to abandon this position, and a horde of sharpshooters set out in pursuit of the fugitives.

The Guard made this movement at five o'clock, and at six the battle was entirely won. The Emperor said to those who were near him, while admiring the splendid behaviour of the Guard, "Look at those brave fellows, with a good-will they would run over the stone-slingers and pop-guns of the line, in order to teach them to charge without waiting for them; but it would have been useless, as the work has been well done without them."

His Majesty went in person to compliment several regiments which had fought the whole day. A few words, a smile, a salute of the hand, even a nod, was sufficient recompense to these brave fellows who had just been crowned with victory.

The number of the dead and prisoners was enormous; and seventy banners, with all the equipments of the Russian army, were left in the hands of the French.

After this decisive day, the Emperor of Russia, who had rejected the proposals made by his Majesty after the battle of Eylau, found himself much disposed to make the game on his own account; and General Bennigsen consequently demanded an armistice in the name of his Emperor, which his Majesty granted; and a short time after a treaty of peace was signed, and the famous interview between the two sovereigns held on the banks of the Niemen. I shall pass over rapidly the details of this meeting, which have been published and repeated innumerable times. His Majesty and the young Czar conceived a mutual affection from the first moment of their meeting, and each gave fetes and amusements in honour of the other. They were inseparable in public and private, and passed hours together in meetings for pleasure only, from which all intruders were carefully excluded. The town of Tilsit was declared neutral; and French, Russians, and Prussians followed the example set them by their sovereigns, and lived together in the most intimate brotherhood.

The King and Queen of Prussia soon after joined their Imperial Majesties at Tilsit; though this unfortunate monarch, to whom there remained hardly one town of the whole kingdom he had possessed, was naturally little disposed to take part in so much festivity. The queen was beautiful and graceful, though perhaps somewhat haughty and severe, which did not prevent her being adored by all who surrounded her. The Emperor sought to please her, and she neglected none of the innocent coquetries of her sex in order to soften the heart of the conqueror of her husband. The queen several times dined with the sovereigns, seated between the two Emperors, who vied with each other in overwhelming her with attentions and gallantries. It is well known that the Emperor Napoleon offered her one day a splendid rose, which after some hesitation she accepted, saying to his Majesty with a most charming smile, "With Magdeburg, at least." And it is well known also that the Emperor did not accept the condition.

The princess had among her ladies of honour a very old woman, who was most highly esteemed. One evening as the queen was being escorted into the dining-hall by the two Emperors, followed by the King of Prussia, Prince Murat, and the Grand Duke Constantine, this old lady of honour gave way to the two latter princes. Grand Duke Constantine would not take precedence of her, but entirely spoiled this act of politeness by exclaiming in a rude tone, "Pass, *madame*, pass on!" And turning towards the King of Naples, added, loud enough to be heard, this disgraceful exclamation, "The old woodcock!"

One may judge from this that Prince Constantine was far from exhibiting towards ladies that exquisite politeness and refined gallantry which distinguished his august brother.

The French Imperial Guard on one occasion gave a dinner to the guard of the Emperor Alexander. At the end of this exceedingly gay and fraternal banquet, each French soldier exchanged uniforms with a Russian, and promenaded thus before the eyes of the Emperors, who were much amused by this impromptu disguise.

Among the numerous attentions paid by the Russian Emperor to our own, I would mention a concert by a troop of Baskir musicians, whom their sovereign brought over the Niemen for this purpose, and never certainly did more barbarous music resound in the ears of his Majesty; and this strange harmony, accompanied by gestures equally as savage, furnished one of the most amusing spectacles that can be imagined. A few days after this concert, I obtained permission to make the musicians a visit, and went to their camp, accompanied by Roustan, who was to serve as interpreter. We enjoyed the pleasure of being present at a repast of the Baskirs, where around immense wooden tubs were seated groups consisting of ten men, each holding in his hand a piece of black bread which he moistened with a ladleful of water, in which had been diluted something resembling red clay. After the repast, they gave us an exhibition of shooting with the bow; and Roustan, to whom this exercise recalled the scenes of his youth, attempted to shoot an arrow, but it fell at a few paces, and I saw a smile of scorn curl the thick lips of our Baskirs. I then tried the bow in my turn, and acquitted myself in such a manner as to do me honour in the eyes of our hosts, who instantly surrounded me, congratulating me by their gestures on my strength and skill; and one of them, even more enthusiastic and more amicable than the others, gave me a pat on the shoulder which I long remembered.

The day succeeding this famous concert, the treaty of peace between the three sovereigns was signed, and his Majesty made a visit to the Emperor Alexander, who received him at the head of his guard. The Emperor Napoleon asked his illustrious ally to show him the bravest grenadier of this handsome and valiant troop; and when he was presented to his Majesty, he took from his breast his own cross of the Legion of Honour, and fastened it on the breast of the Muscovite soldier, amid the acclamations and hurrahs of all his comrades. The two Emperors embraced each other a last time on the banks of the Niemen, and his Majesty set out on the road to Koenigsberg.

At Bautzen the King of Saxony came out to meet him, and their Majesties entered Dresden together. King Frederick Augustus gave a most magnificent reception to the sovereign who, not content with giving him a sceptre, had also considerably increased the hereditary estates of the elector of Saxony. The good people of Dresden, during the week we passed there, treated the French more as brothers and compatriots than as allies.

But it was nearly ten months since we had left Paris; and in spite of all the charms of the simple and cordial hospitality of the Germans, I was very eager to see again France and my own family.

Chapter 34

It was during the glorious campaign of Prussia and Poland that the imperial family was plunged in the deepest sorrow by the death of the young Napoleon, eldest son of King Louis of Holland. This child bore a striking resemblance to his father, and consequently to his uncle. His hair was blond, but would probably have darkened as he grew older. His eyes, which were large and blue, shone with extraordinary brilliancy when a deep impression was made on his young mind. Gentle, lovable, and full of candour and gayety, he was the delight of the Emperor, especially on account of the firmness of his character, which was so remarkable that, notwithstanding his extreme youth, nothing could make him break his word. The following anecdote which I recall furnishes an instance of this.

He was very fond of strawberries; but they caused him such long and frequent attacks of vomiting that his mother became alarmed, and positively forbade his eating them, expressing a wish that every precaution should be taken to keep out of the young prince's sight a fruit which was so injurious to him. The little Napoleon, whom the injurious effects of the strawberries had not disgusted with them, was surprised to no more see his favourite dish; but bore the deprivation patiently, until one day he questioned his nurse, and very seriously demanded an explanation on this subject, which the good woman was unable to give, for she indulged him even to the point of spoiling him. He knew her weakness, and often took advantage of it, as in this instance for example. He became angry, and said to his nurse in a tone which had as much and even more effect on her than the Emperor or the King of Holland could have had, "I will have the strawberries. Give them to me at once." The poor nurse begged him to be quiet, and said that she would give them to him, but she was afraid that if anything happened he would tell the queen who had done this. "Is that all?" replied Napoleon eagerly. "Have no fear; I promise not to tell."

The nurse yielded, and the strawberries had their usual effect. The queen entered while he was undergoing the punishment for his self-indulgence; and he could not deny that he had eaten the forbidden fruit, as the proofs were too evident. The queen was much incensed, and wished to know who had disobeyed her; she alternately entreated and threatened the child, who still continued to reply with the greatest composure, "I promised not to tell." And in spite of the great influence she had over him, she could not force him to tell her the name of the guilty person.

Young Napoleon was devoted to his uncle, and manifested in his presence a patience and self-control very foreign to his usual character. The Emperor often took him on his knee during breakfast, and amused himself making him eat lentils one by one. The pretty face of the child became crimson, his whole countenance manifested disgust and impatience; but his Majesty could prolong this sport without fearing that his nephew would become angry, which he would have infallibly done with any one else.

At such a tender age could he have been conscious of his uncle's superiority to all those who surrounded him? King Louis, his father, gave him each day a new plaything, chosen exactly to suit his fancy: but the child preferred those he received from his uncle; and when his father said to him, "But, see here, Napoleon, those are ugly things; mine are prettier."

"No," said the young prince, "they are very nice; my uncle gave them to me."

One morning when he visited his Majesty, he crossed a saloon where amid many great personages was Prince Murat, at that time, I think, Grand Duke of Berg. The child passed through without saluting any one, when the prince stopped him and said, "Will you not tell me good morning?"

"No," replied Napoleon, disengaging himself from the arms of the Grand Duke; "not before my uncle the Emperor."

At the end of a review which had taken place in the court of the Tuileries, and on the Place du Carrousel, the Emperor went up to his apartments, and threw his hat on one sofa, his sword on another. Little Napoleon entered, took his uncle's sword, passed the belt round his neck, put the hat on his head, and then kept step gravely, humming a march behind the Emperor and Empress. Her Majesty, turning round, saw him, and caught him in her arms, exclaiming, "What a pretty picture!" Ingenious in seizing every occasion to please her husband, the Empress summoned M. Gerard, and ordered a portrait of the young prince in this costume; and the picture was brought to the palace of Saint-Cloud the very day on which the Empress heard of the death of this beloved child.

He was hardly three years old when, seeing his shoemaker's bill paid with five-franc pieces, he screamed loudly, not wishing that they should give away the picture of his Uncle Bibiche. The name of Bibiche thus given by the young prince to his Majesty originated in this manner. The Empress had several gazelles placed in the park of Saint-Cloud, which were very much afraid of all the inhabitants of the palace except the Emperor, who allowed them to eat tobacco out of his snuff-box, and thus induced them to follow him, and took much pleasure in giving them the tobacco by the hands of the little Napoleon, whom he also put on the back of one of them. The latter designated these pretty animals by no other name than that of Bibiche, and amused himself by giving the same name to his uncle.

This charming child, who was adored by both father and mother, used his almost magical influence over each in order to reconcile them to each other. He took his father by the hand, who allowed himself to be thus conducted by this angel of peace to Queen Hortense, and then said to him, "Kiss her, papa, I beg you;" and was perfectly overjoyed when he had thus succeeded in reconciling these two beings whom he loved with an equal affection.

How could such a beautiful character fail to make this angel beloved by all who knew him? How could the Emperor, who loved all children, fail to be devoted to him, even had he not been his nephew, and the godson of that good Josephine whom he never ceased to love for a single instant? At the age of seven years, when that malady, the croup, so dangerous to children, snatched him from his heart-broken family, he already gave evidence of remarkable traits of character, which were the foundation of most brilliant hopes. His proud and haughty character, while rendering him susceptible of the noblest impressions, was not incompatible with obedience and docility. The idea of injustice was revolting to him; but he readily submitted to reasonable advice and rightful authority.

First-born of the new dynasty, it was fitting he should attract as he did the deepest tenderness and solicitude of the chief. Malignity and envy, which ever seek to defame and vilify the great, gave slanderous explanations of this almost paternal attachment; but wise and thoughtful men saw in this adoptive tenderness only what it plainly evinced,—the desire and hope of transmitting his immense power, and the grandest name in the universe, to an heir, indirect it is true, but of imperial blood, and who, reared under the eyes, and by the direction of the Emperor, would have been to him all that a son could be. The death of the young Napoleon appeared as a forerunner of misfortunes in the midst of his glorious career, disarranging all the plans which the monarch had conceived, and decided him to concentrate all his hopes on an heir in a direct line.

It was then that the first thoughts of divorce arose in his mind, though it did not take place until two years later, and only began to be the subject of private conversation during the stay at Fontainebleau. The Empress readily saw the fatal results to her of the death of this godson, and from that time she dwelt upon the idea of this terrible event which ruined her life. This premature death was to her an inconsolable grief; and she shut herself up for three days, weeping bitterly, seeing no one except her women, and taking almost no nourishment. It even seemed that she feared to be distracted from her grief, as she surrounded herself with a sort of avidity with all that could recall her irreparable loss. She obtained with some difficulty from Queen Hortense some of the young prince's hair, which his heart-broken mother religiously preserved; and the Empress had this hair framed on a cushion of black velvet, and kept it always near her. I often saw it at Malmaison, and never without deep emotion.

But how can I attempt to describe the despair of Queen Hortense, of that woman who became as perfect a mother as she had been a daughter. She never left her son a moment during his illness; and when he expired in her arms, still wishing to remain near his lifeless body, she fastened her arms through those of her chair, in order that she might not be torn from this heartrending scene. At last nature succumbed to such poignant grief: the unhappy mother fainted; and the opportunity was taken to remove her to her own apartment, still in the chair which she had not left, and which her arms clasped convulsively. On awaking, the queen uttered piercing screams, and her dry and staring eyes and white lips gave reason to fear that she was near her end. Nothing could bring tears to her eyes, until at last a chamberlain conceived the idea of bringing the young prince's body, and placing it on his mother's knees; and this had such an effect on her that her tears burst forth and saved her life, while she covered with kisses the cold and adored remains. All France shared the grief of the Queen of Holland.

BERTHIER

Chapter 35

We arrived at Saint-Cloud on the 27th of July; and the Emperor passed the summer partly in this residence, and partly at Fontainebleau, returning to Paris only on special occasions, and never remaining longer than twenty-four hours. During his Majesty's absence, the chateau of Rambouillet was restored and furnished anew, and the Emperor spent a few days there. The first time he entered the bathroom, he stopped short at the door and glanced around with every appearance of surprise and dissatisfaction; and when I sought the cause of this, following the direction of his Majesty's eyes, I saw that they rested on various family portraits which the architect had painted on the walls of the room. They were those of *madame* his mother, his sisters, Queen Hortense, etc.; and the sight of such a gallery, in such a place, excited the extreme displeasure of the Emperor. "What nonsense!" he cried. "Constant, summon Marshal Duroc!" And when the grand marshal appeared, his Majesty inquired, "Who is the idiot that could have conceived such an idea? Order the painter to come and efface all that. He must have little respect for women to be guilty of such an indecency."

When the court sojourned at Fontainebleau, the inhabitants indemnified themselves amply for his Majesty's long absences by the high price at which they sold all articles of food. Their extortions became scandalous impositions, and more than one foreigner making an excursion to Fontainebleau thought himself held for ransom by a troop of Bedouins. During the stay of the court; a wretched sacking-bed in a miserable inn cost twelve *francs* for a single night; the smallest meal cost an incredible price, and was, notwithstanding, detestable; in fact, it amounted to a genuine pillage of travellers. Cardinal Caprara,[1] whose rigid economy was known to all Paris, went

---

1. Giovanni Battista Caprara, born of a noble family at Bologna, 1733; count and archbishop of Milan; cardinal, 1792; Negotiated the Concordat, 1801; died 1810.

one day to Fontainebleau to pay his court to the Emperor, and at the hotel where he alighted took only a single cup of bouillon, and the six persons of his suite partook only of a very light repast, as the cardinal had arranged to return in three hours; but notwithstanding this, as he was entering his carriage, the landlord had the audacity to present him with a bill for six hundred *francs*! The prince of the church indignantly protested, flew into a rage, threatened, etc., but all in vain; and the bill was paid.

Such an outrageous imposition could not fail to reach the Emperor's ears, and excited his anger to such a degree that he at once ordered a fixed schedule of prices, which it was forbidden the innkeepers to exceed. This put an end to the exactions of the bloodsuckers of Fontainebleau.

On the 21st of August, there arrived at Paris the Princess Catharine of Wurtemberg, future wife of Prince Jerome Napoleon, King of Westphalia. This princess was about twenty-four years of age, and very beautiful, with a most noble and gracious bearing; and though policy alone had made this marriage, never could love or voluntary choice have made one that was happier.

The courageous conduct of her Majesty the Queen of Westphalia in 1814, her devotion to her dethroned husband, and her admirable letters to her father, who wished to tear her from the arms of King Jerome, are matters of history. I have seen it stated that this prince never ceased, even after this marriage, which was so flattering to his ambition, to correspond with his first wife, Mademoiselle Patterson, and that he often sent to America his *valet de chambre*, Rico, to inquire after this lady and their child. If this is true, it is no less so that these attentions to his first wife, which were not only very excusable, but even, according to my opinion, praiseworthy in Prince Jerome, and of which her Majesty the Queen of Westphalia was probably well aware, did not necessarily prevent her being happy with her husband.

No testimony more reliable than that of the queen her self can be given; and she expresses herself as follows in her second letter to his Majesty, the King of Wurtemburg:—

"Forced by policy to marry the king, my husband, fate has willed that I should find myself the happiest woman in the universe. I feel towards my husband the united sentiments of love, tenderness, and esteem. In this painful moment can the best of fathers wish to destroy my domestic happiness, the only kind which now remains to me? I dare to say that you, my dear father, you and all my family, do great injustice to the king, my husband; and I trust the time will come when you will be convinced that you have done him injustice, and then you will ever find in him, as well as in myself, the most respectful and affectionate of children."

Her Majesty then spoke of a terrible misfortune to which she had been exposed. This event, which was indeed terrible, was nothing less than violence and robbery committed on a fugitive woman defenceless and alone, by a band at the head of which was the famous Marquis de Maubreuil,[2] who had been equerry of the King of Westphalia. I will recur in treating of the events of 1814 to this disgraceful affair, and will give some particulars, which I think are not generally known, in regard to the principal authors and participants in this daring act of brigandage.

In the following month of September, a courier from the Russian cabinet arrived from St. Petersburg, bearing a letter to his Majesty from the Emperor Alexander; and among other magnificent gifts were two very handsome fur pelisses of black fox and sable martin.

During their Majesties residence at Fontainebleau, the Emperor often went out in his carriage with the Empress in the streets of the city with neither escort nor guards. One day, while passing before the hospital of Mont Pierreux, her Majesty the Empress saw at a window a very aged clergyman, who saluted their Majesties. The Empress, having returned the old man's salutation with her habitual grace, pointed him out to the Emperor, who himself saluted him, and ordering his coachman to stop, sent one of the footmen with a request to the old priest to come and speak to them a moment, if it were not too great an exertion. The old man, who still walked with ease, hastened to descend; and in order to save him a few steps the Emperor had his carriage driven very close to the door of the hospital.

His Majesty conversed for some time with the good ecclesiastic, manifesting the greatest kindness and respect. He informed their Majesties that he had been, previous to the Revolution, the regular priest of one of the parishes of Fontainebleau, and had done everything possible to avoid emigrating; but that terror had at length forced him to leave his native land, although he was then more than seventy-five years old; that he had returned to France at the time of the proclamation of the Concordat, and now lived on a modest pension hardly sufficient to pay his board in the hospital. "*Monsieur l'Abbe,*" said his Majesty after listening to the old priest attentively, "I will order your pension to be doubled; and if that is not sufficient I

---

2. A French political adventurer, born in Brittany, 1782; died 1855.

hope you will apply to the Empress or to me." The good ecclesiastic thanked the Emperor with tears in his eyes. "Unfortunately, Sire," said he among other things, "I am too old to long enjoy your Majesty's reign or profit by your kindness."

"*You?*" replied the Emperor, smiling, "why, you are a young man. Look at M. de Belloy; he is much your senior, and we hope to keep him with us for a long time yet." Their Majesties then took leave of the old man, who was much affected, leaving him in the midst of a crowd of the inhabitants who had collected before the hospital during this conversation, and who were much impressed by this interesting scene and the generous kindness of the Emperor.

M. de Belloy, cardinal and archbishop of Paris, whose name the Emperor mentioned in the conversation I have just related, was then ninety-eight years of age, though his health was excellent; and I have never seen an old man who had as venerable an air as this worthy prelate. The Emperor had the profoundest respect for him, and never failed to give evidence of it on every occasion. During this same month of September, a large number of the faithful having assembled according to custom on Mount Valerien, the archbishop likewise repaired to the spot to hear mass. As he was about to withdraw, seeing that many pious persons were awaiting his benediction, he addressed them before bestowing it in a few words which showed his kindness of heart and his evangelical simplicity: "My children, I know that I must be very old from the loss of my strength, but not of my zeal and my tenderness for you. Pray God, my children, for your old archbishop, who never fails to intercede on your behalf each day."

During his stay at Fontainebleau, the Emperor enjoyed more frequently than ever before the pleasures of the chase. The costume necessary was a French coat of green dragon colour, decorated with buttons and gold lace, white cashmere breeches, and Hessian boots without facings; this was the costume for the grand hunt which was always a stag hunt; that for a hunt with guns being a plain, green French coat with no other ornament than white buttons, on which were cut suitable inscriptions. This costume was the same for all persons taking part in this hunt, with no distinguishing marks, even for his Majesty himself.

The princesses set out for the rendezvous in a Spanish carriage with either or four six horses, and thus followed the chase, their costume being an elegant riding-habit, and a hat with white or black plumes.

One of the Emperor's sisters (I do not now recall which) never failed to follow the hunt, accompanied by many charming ladies who were always invited to breakfast at the rendezvous, as was always the custom on similar occasions with the persons of the court. One of these ladies, who was both beautiful and intelligent, attracted the attention of the Emperor, a short correspondence ensued, and at last the Emperor again ordered me to carry a letter.

In the palace of Fontainebleau is a private garden called the garden of Diana, to which their Majesties alone had access. This garden is surrounded on four sides by buildings; on the left was the chapel with its gloomy gallery and Gothic architecture; on the right the grand gallery (as well as I can remember); in the middle the building which contained their Majesties' apartments; finally, in front of and facing the square were broad arcades, and behind them the buildings intended for the various persons attached to household of the princes or the Emperor. Madame de B——, the lady whom the Emperor had remarked, lodged in an apartment situated behind these arcades on the ground floor; and his Majesty informed me that I would find a window open, through which I must enter cautiously, in the darkness, and give his note to a person who would ask for it. This darkness was necessary, because this window opened on the garden, and though behind the arcades, would have been noticed had there been a light. Not knowing the interior of these apartments, I entered through the window, thinking I could then walk on a level, but had a terrible fall over a high step which was in the embrasure of the window. I heard some one scream as I fell, and a door was suddenly closed. I had received severe bruises on my knee, elbow, and head, and rising with difficulty, at once began a search around the apartment, groping in the dark; but hearing nothing more, and fearing to make some fresh noise which might be heard by persons who should not know of my presence there, I decided to return to the Emperor, and report to him my adventures.

Finding that none of my injuries were serious, the Emperor laughed most heartily, and then added, "Oh, oh, so there is a step; it is well to know that. Wait till Madame B—— is over her fright; I will go to her, and you will accompany me." At the end of an hour, the Emperor emerged with me from the door of his cabinet which opened on the garden. I conducted him in silence towards the window which was still open and assisted him to enter, and having obtained to my cost a correct idea of the spot, directed him how to avoid a fall.

His Majesty, having entered the chamber without accident, told me to retire. I was not without some anxiety as I informed the Emperor; but he replied that I was a child, and there could be no danger.

It appeared that his Majesty succeeded better than I had done,—as he did not return until daybreak, and then jested about my awkwardness, admitting, however, that if he had not been warned, a similar accident would have befallen him.

Although Madame de B—— was worthy of a genuine attachment, her liaison with the Emperor lasted only a short while, and was only a passing fancy. I think that the difficulties surrounding his nocturnal visits cooled his Majesty's ardour greatly; for the Emperor was not enough in love to be willing to brave everything in order to see his beautiful mistress. His Majesty informed me of the fright which my fall had caused her, and how anxious this amiable lady had been on my account, and how he had reassured her; this did not, however, prevent her sending next day to know how I was, by a confidential person, who told me again how interested Madame de B—— had been in my accident.

Often at Fontainebleau there was a court representation, in which the actors of the first theatres received orders to play before their Majesties scenes selected from their various repertoires. Mademoiselle Mars was to play the evening of her arrival; but at Essonne, where she was obliged to stop a moment on account of the road being filled with cattle going or returning from Fontainebleau, her trunk had been stolen, a fact of which she was not aware until she had gone some distance from the spot. Not only were her costumes missing, but she had no other clothing except what she wore; and it would be at least twelve hours before she could get from Paris what she needed. It was then two o'clock in the afternoon, and that very evening she must appear in the brilliant role of Celimene. Although much disturbed by this accident, Mademoiselle Mars did not lose her presence of mind, but visited all the shops of the town, and in a few hours had cut and made a complete costume in most excellent taste, and her loss was entirely repaired.

Chapter 36

In the month of November of this year I followed their Majesties to Italy. We knew a few days in advance that the Emperor would make this journey; but as happened on all other occasions, neither the day nor the hour was fixed, until we were told on the evening of the 15th that we would set out early on the morning of the 16th. I passed the night like all the household of his Majesty; for in order to carry out the incredible perfection of comfort with which the Emperor surrounded himself on his journeys, it was necessary that everybody should be on foot as soon as the hour of departure was known; consequently I passed the night arranging the service of his Majesty, while my wife packed my own baggage, and had but just finished when the Emperor asked for me, which meant that ten minutes after we would be on the road. At four o'clock in the morning his Majesty entered his carriage.

As we never knew at what hour or in what direction the Emperor would begin his journey, the grand marshal, the grand equerry, and the grand chamberlain sent forward a complete service on all the different roads which they thought his Majesty might take. The bedroom service comprised a *valet de chambre* and a wardrobe boy. As for me, I never left his Majesty's person, and my carriage always followed immediately behind his. The conveyance belonging to this service contained an iron bed with its accessories, a dressing-case with linen, coats, etc. I know little of the service of the stables, but that of the kitchen was organized as follows: There was a conveyance almost in the shape of the *coucous* on the Place Louis XV. at Paris, with a deep bottom and an enormous body. The bottom contained wines for the Emperor's table and that of the high officers, the ordinary wine being bought at the places where we stopped. In the body of the wagon were the kitchen utensils and a portable furnace, followed by a carriage containing a steward, two cooks, and a furnace-boy. There was besides this, a baggage-wagon full of provisions and wine to fill up the other as it was emptied; and all these conveyances set out a few hours in advance of the Emperor. It was the duty of the grand marshal to designate the place at which breakfast should be taken. We alighted sometimes at the archbishop's, sometimes at the *hotel de ville*, sometimes at the residence of the sub-*prefect*, or even at that of the mayor, in the absence of any other dignitaries. Having arrived at the designated house, the steward gave orders for the provisions, the furnaces were lighted, and spits turned; and if the Emperor alighted and partook of the repast prepared, the provisions which had been consumed were immediately replaced as far as possible, and the carriages filled again with poultry, pastry, etc.; before leaving all expenses were paid by the controller, presents were made to the master of the house, and everything which was not necessary for the service left for the use of their servants. It sometimes happened that the Emperor, finding that it was too soon for breakfast, or wishing to make a longer journey, gave orders to pass on, and everything was packed up again and the service continued its route. Sometimes also the Emperor, halting in the open field, alighted, took his seat under a tree, and ordered his breakfast, upon which Roustan and the footmen obtained provisions from his Majesty's carriage, which was furnished with small cooking utensils with silver covers, holding chickens, partridges, etc., while the other carriages furnished their proportion. M. Pfister served the Emperor, and every one ate a hasty morsel. Fires were lighted to heat the coffee; and in less than half an hour everything had disappeared, and the carriages rolled on in the same order as before.

The Emperor's steward and cooks had nearly all been trained in the household of the king and the princes. These were Messieurs Dunau, Leonard, Rouff, and Gerard. M. Colin was chief in command, and became steward-controller after the sad affliction of M. Pfister, who became insane during the campaign of 1809. All were capable and zealous servants; and, as is the case in the household of all sovereigns, each department of the domestic affairs had its chief. Messieurs Soupe and Pierrugues were in charge of the wines, and the sons of these gentleman continued to hold the same office with the Emperor.

We travelled with great speed as far as Mont-Cenis, but were compelled to go more slowly after reaching this pass, as the weather had been very bad for several days, and the road was washed out by the rain, which still fell in torrents. The Emperor arrived at Milan at noon on the 22nd; and, notwithstanding our delay at Mont-Cenis, the rest of the journey had been so rapid that no one was expecting the Emperor.

The vice-king only learned of the arrival of his step-father when he was half a league from the town, but came in haste to meet us escorted only by a few persons. The Emperor gave orders to halt, and, as soon as the door was opened, held out his hand to Prince Eugene, saying in the most affectionate manner: "Come, get up with us, my fine prince; we will enter together."

Notwithstanding the surprise which this unexpected arrival caused, we had hardly entered the town before all the houses were illuminated, and the beautiful palaces, Litta, Casani, Melzi, and many others, shone with a thousand lights. The magnificent cupola of the cathedral dome was covered with garlands of coloured lights; and in the centre of the Forum-Bonaparte, the walks of which were also illuminated, could be seen the colossal equestrian statue of the Emperor, on both sides of which transparencies had been arranged, in the shape of stars, bearing the initials S M I and R. By eight o'clock all the populace had collected around the chateau, where superb fireworks were discharged, while spirited and warlike music was performed. All the town authorities were admitted to the Emperor's presence.

On the morning of the next day there was held at the chateau a council of ministers, over which the Emperor presided; and at noon he mounted his horse to take part in the mass celebrated by the grand chaplain of the kingdom. The square of the cathedral was covered by an immense crowd, through which the Emperor advanced on horseback, accompanied by his imperial Highness, the vice-king, and his staff. The noble countenance of Prince Eugene expressed the great joy he felt in the presence of his step-father, for whom he had always so much respect and filial affection, and in hearing the incessant acclamations of the people, which grew more vociferous every moment.

After the *Te Deum*, the Emperor held a review of the troops on the square, and immediately after set out with the viceroy for Monza, the palace at which the queen resided. For no woman did the Emperor manifest more sincere regard and respect than for Princess Amelia; but, indeed there has never been a more beautiful or purer woman. It was impossible to speak of beauty or virtue in the Emperor's presence without his giving the vice-queen as an example. Prince Eugene was very worthy of so accomplished a wife, and justly appreciated her exalted character; and I was glad to see in the countenance of the excellent prince the reflection of the happiness he enjoyed. Amidst all the care he took to anticipate every wish of his step-father, I was much gratified that he found time to address a few words to me, expressing the great pleasure he felt at my promotion in the service and esteem of the Emperor. Nothing could have been more grateful to me than these marks of remembrance from a prince for whom I had always retained a most sincere, and, I made bold to say, most tender, attachment.

The Emperor remained a long while with the vice-queen, whose intelligence equalled her amiability and her beauty, but returned to Milan to dine; and immediately afterwards the ladies who were received at court were presented to him. In the evening, I followed his Majesty to the theatre of La Scala. The Emperor did not remain throughout the play, but retired early to his apartment, and worked the greater part of the night; which did not, however, prevent our being on the road to Verona before eight o'clock in the morning.

His Majesty made no stop at Brescia and Verona. I would have been very glad to have had time on the route to examine the curiosities of Italy; but that was not an easy thing to do in the Emperor's suite, as he halted only for the purpose of reviewing troops, and preferred visiting fortifications to ruins.

At Verona his Majesty dined, or rather supped (for it was very late), with their Majesties, the King and Queen of Bavaria, who arrived at almost exactly the same time as ourselves; and very early the next day we set out for Vicenza.

Although the season was already advanced, I found great pleasure in the scene which awaits the traveller on' the road from Verona to Vicenza. Imagine to yourself an immense plain, divided into innumerable fields, each bordered with different kinds of trees with slender trunks,—mostly elms and poplars,—which form avenues as far as the eye can reach. Vines twine around their trunks, climb each tree, and droop from each limb; while other branches of these vines, loosening their hold on the tree which serves as their support, droop clear to the ground, and hang in graceful festoons from tree to tree. Beyond these, lovely natural bowers could be seen far and wide, splendid fields of wheat; or, at least, this had been the case on my former journey, but at this time the harvest had been gathered for several months.

At the end of a day which I passed most delightfully amid these fertile plains, I entered Vicenza, where the authorities of the town, together with almost the entire population, awaited the Emperor under a superb arch of triumph at the entrance of the town. We were exceedingly hungry; and his Majesty himself said, that evening as he retired, that he felt very much like sitting down to the table when he entered Vicenza. I trembled, then, at the idea of those long Italian addresses, which I had found even longer than those of France, doubtless because

I did not understand a single word; but, fortunately, the magistrates of Vicenza were sufficiently well-informed not to take advantage of our position, and their speeches occupied only a few moments.

That evening his Majesty went to the theatre; and I was so much fatigued that I would have gladly profited by the Emperor's absence to take some repose, had not an acquaintance invited me to accompany him to the convent of the Servites, in order to witness the effect of the illumination of the town, which I did, and was repaid by the magnificent spectacle which met my eyes. The whole town seemed one blaze of light. On returning to the palace occupied by his Majesty, I learned that he had given orders that everything should be in readiness for departure two hours after midnight; consequently I had one hour to sleep, and I enjoyed it to the utmost.

At the appointed moment, the Emperor entered his carriage; and we were soon rolling along with the rapidity of lightning over the road to Stra, where we passed the night. Very early next morning we set out, following a long causeway raised through marshes. The landscape is almost the same, and yet not so beautiful, as that we passed before reaching Vicenza. We still saw groves of mulberry and olive trees, from which the finest oil is obtained, and fields of maize and hemp, interspersed with meadows. Beyond Stra the cultivation of rice commences; and, although the rice-fields must render the country unhealthy, still it has not the reputation of being more so than any other. On the right and left of the road are seen elegant houses, and cabins which, though covered with thatch, are very comfortable, and present a charming appearance. The vine is little cultivated in this part of the country, where it would hardly succeed, as the land is too low and damp; but there are, nevertheless, a few small vineyards on the slopes, and the vegetation in the whole country is incredibly rich and luxuriant. The late wars have left traces which only a long peace can efface.

Chapter 37

On his arrival at Fusina the Emperor found the Venetian authorities awaiting him, embarked on the *'peote'* or *gondola* of the village, and advanced towards Venice, accompanied by a numerous floating cortege. We followed, the Emperor in little black gondolas, which looked like floating coffins, with which the Brenta was covered; and nothing could be stranger than to hear, proceeding from these coffins of such gloomy aspect, delicious vocal concerts. The boat which carried his Majesty, and the gondolas of the principal persons of his suite, were handsomely ornamented.

When we arrived at the mouth of the river we were obliged to wait nearly half an hour until the locks were opened, which was done by degrees, and with every precaution; without which the waters of the Brenta, held in their canal and raised considerably above the level of the sea, would have rushed out suddenly, and in their violent descent have driven our gondolas along before them, or sunk them. Released at last from the Brenta, we found ourselves in the gulf, and saw at a distance, rising from the midst of the sea, the wonderful city of Venice. Barks, gondolas, and vessels of considerable size, filled with all the wealthy population, and all the boatmen of Venice in gala dress, appeared on every side, passing, repassing, and crossing each other, in every direction, with the most remarkable skill and speed.

The Emperor was standing at the back of the *peote*, and, as each *gondola* passed near his own, replied to the acclamations and cries of "*Viva Napoleone imperatore e re!*" by one of those profound bows which he made with so much grace and dignity, taking off his hat without bending his head, and carrying it along his body almost to his knees.

Escorted by this innumerable flotilla, of which the *peote* of the city seemed to be the admirals vessel, his Majesty entered at last the Grand Canal, which flowed between magnificent palaces, hung with banners and filled with spectators. The Emperor alighted before the palace of the procurators, where he was received by a deputation of members of the Senate and the Venetian nobility. He stopped a moment in the square of St. Mark, passed through some interior streets, chose the site for a garden, the plans for which the architect of the city then presented to him, and which were carried out as if it had been in the midst of the country. It was a novel sight to the Venetians to see trees planted in the open air, while hedges and lawns appeared as if by magic. The entire absence of verdure and vegetation, and the silence which reigns in the streets of Venice, where is never heard the hoof of a horse nor the wheels of a carriage, horses and carriages being things entirely unknown in this truly marine city, must give it usually a sad and abandoned air; but this gloom entirely disappeared during his Majesty's visit.

The prince viceroy and the grand marshal were present in the evening when the Emperor retired; and, while undressing him, I heard a part of their conversation, which turned on the government of Venice before the union of this republic with the French Empire. His Majesty was almost the only spokesman, Prince Eugene and Marshal Duroc contenting themselves with throwing a few words into the conversation, as if to furnish a new text for the Emperor, and prevent his pausing, and thus ending too soon his discourse; a genuine discourse, in fact, since his Majesty took the lead, and left the others but little to say. Such was often his habit; but no one thought of complaining of this, so interesting were nearly always the Emperor's ideas, and so original and brilliantly expressed. His Majesty did not converse, as had been truthfully said in the journal which I have added to my memoirs, but he spoke with an inexpressible charm; and on this point it seems to me that the author of the "Journal of Aix-la-Chapelle" has done the Emperor injustice.

As I said just now, his Majesty spoke of the ancient State of Venice, and from what he said on this occasion I learned more than I could have done from the most interesting book. The viceroy having remarked that a few patricians regretted their former liberty, the Emperor exclaimed, "Liberty, what nonsense! liberty no longer existed in Venice, and had, indeed, never existed except for a few families of the nobility, who oppressed the rest of the population. Liberty, with a Council of Ten! Liberty, with the inquisitors of state! Liberty, with the very lions as informers, and Venetian dungeons and bullets!" Marshal Duroc remarked that towards the end these severe regulations were much modified. "Yes, no doubt,"—replied the Emperor. "The lion of St. Mark had gotten old; he had no longer either teeth or nails! Venice was only the shadow of her former self, and her last doge found that he rose to a higher rank in becoming a senator of the French Empire." His Majesty, seeing that this idea made the vice-king smile, added very gravely, "I am not jesting, gentlemen. A Roman senator prided himself on being more than a king; a French senator is at least the equal of a doge. I desire that foreigners shall accustom themselves to show the greatest respect towards the constituted authorities of the Empire, and to treat with great consideration even the simple title of French citizen. I will take care to insure this. Good-night, Eugene. Duroc, take care to have the reception tomorrow all that it should be. After the ceremony we will visit the arsenal. Adieu, Messieurs. Constant, come back in ten minutes to put out my light; I feel sleepy. One is cradled like an infant on these gondolas."

The next day his Majesty, after receiving the homage of the Venetian authorities, repaired to the arsenal. This is an immense building, fortified so carefully that it was practically impregnable. The appearance of the interior is singular on account of several small islands which it encloses, joined together by bridges. The magazines and numerous buildings of the fortress thus appear to be floating on the surface of the water. The entrance on the land side, by which we were introduced, is over a very handsome bridge of marble, ornamented with columns and statues. On the side next the sea, there are numerous rocks and sandbanks, the presence of which is indicated by long piles. It is said that in time of war these piles were taken up, which exposed the foreign vessels, imprudent enough to entangle themselves among these shoals, to certain destruction. The arsenal could formerly equip eighty thousand men, both infantry and cavalry, independent of complete armaments for war vessels.

The arsenal is bordered with raised towers, from which the view extends in all directions. On the tallest of these towers, which is placed in the centre of the building, as well as all the others, sentinels were stationed, both day and night, to signal the arrival of vessels, which they could see at a very great distance. Nothing can be finer than the dockyards for building vessels, in which ten thousand men can work with ease. The sails are made by women, over whom other elderly women exercise an active surveillance.

The Emperor delayed only a short time to look at the *'Bucentaure'*; which is the title of the magnificent vessel in which the Doge of Venice was accustomed to celebrate his marriage with the sea; and a Venetian never sees without deep chagrin this old monument of the former glory of his country. I, in company with some persons of the Emperor's suite, had as our guide an old mariner, whose eyes filled with tears as he related to us in bad French that the last time he witnessed the marriage of the Doge with the Adriatic Sea was in 1796, a year before the capture of Venice. He also told us that he was at that time in the service of the last Doge of the republic, Lord Louis Manini, and that the following year (1797), the French entered Venice at the exact time when the marriage of the Doge to the sea, which took place on Ascension Day, was usually celebrated, and ever since the sea had remained a widow. Our good sailor paid a most touching tribute of praise to his old master, who he said had never succeeded in forcing himself, to take the oath of allegiance to the Austrians, and had swooned away while resigning to them the keys of the city.

The gondoliers are at the same time servants, errand boys, confidants, and companions in adventures to the person who takes them into his service; and nothing can equal the courage, fidelity, and gayety of these brave seamen. They expose themselves fearlessly in their slender gondolas to tempests; and their skill is so great that they turn with incredible rapidity in the narrowest canals, cross each other, follow, and pass each other incessantly, without ever having an accident.

I found myself in a position to judge of the skill of these hardy mariners the day after our visit to the arsenal. His Majesty was conducted through the lagoons as far as the fortified gate of Mala-Mocca, and the gondoliers gave as he returned a boat-race and tournament on the water. On that day there was also a special representation at the grand theatre, and the whole city was illuminated. In fact, one might think that there is a continual fete and general illumination in Venice; the custom being to spend the greater part of the night in business or pleasure, and the streets are as brilliant and as full of people as in Paris at four o'clock in the afternoon. The shops, especially those of the square of Saint Mark, are brilliantly lighted, and crowds fill the small decorated pavilions where coffee, ices, and refreshments of all kinds are sold.

The Emperor did not adopt the Venetian mode of life, however, and retired at the same hour as in Paris; and when he did not pass the day working with his ministers, rode in a *gondola* through the lagoons, or visited the principal establishments and public buildings of Venice; and I thus saw, in company with his Majesty, the church of Saint Mark, and the ancient palace of the Doge.

The church of Saint Mark has five entrances, superbly decorated with marble columns; the gates are of bronze and beautifully carved. Above the middle door were formerly the four famous bronze horses, which the Emperor carried to Paris to ornament the Arch of Triumph on the Place du Carrousel. The tower is separated from the church by a small square, from the midst of which it rises to a height of more than three hundred feet. It is ascended by an inclined platform without steps, which is very convenient; and on arriving at the summit the most magnificent panorama is spread out before you, Venice with its innumerable islands covered with palaces, churches, and buildings, and extending at a distance into the sea; also the immense dike, sixty feet broad, several fathoms deep, and built of great blocks of stone, which enormous work surrounds Venice and all its islands, and defends it against the rising of the sea.

The Venetians have the greatest admiration for the clock placed in the tower bearing its name, and the mechanism of which shows the progress of the sun and moon through the twelve signs of the zodiac. In a niche above the dial plate is an image of the Virgin, which is gilded and life-size; and it is said that on certain fete days, each blow of the pendulum makes two angels appear, trumpet in hand, followed by the Three Wise Men, who prostrate themselves at the feet of the Virgin Mary. I saw nothing of all that, but only two large black figures striking the hour on the clock with iron clubs.

The Doge's palace is a gloomy building; and the prisons, which are separated from it only by a narrow canal, render the aspect still more depressing.

At Venice one finds merchants from every nation, Jews and Greeks being very numerous. Roustan, who understood the language of the latter, was sought after by the most distinguished among them; and the heads of a Greek family came one day to invite him to visit them at their residence on one of the islands which lie around Venice. Roustan confided to me his desire to accept this invitation, and I was delighted with his proposition that I should accompany him. On our arrival at their island, we were received by our hosts, who were very wealthy merchants, as if we had been old friends. The apartment, a kind of parlour into which we were ushered, not only evinced cultivation and refinement, but great elegance; a large divan extended around the hall, the inlaid floor of which was covered with artistically woven mats. Our hosts were six men who were associated in the same trade. I would have been somewhat embarrassed had not one of them who spoke French conversed with me, while the others talked to Roustan in their native tongue. We were offered coffee, fruits, ices, and pipes; and as I was never fond of smoking, and knew besides the disgust inspired in the Emperor by odours in general, and especially that of tobacco, I refused the pipe, and expressed a fear that my clothes might be scented by being so near the smokers. I thought I perceived that this delicacy lowered me considerably in the esteem of my hosts, notwithstanding which, as we left, they gave us most urgent invitations to repeat our visit, which it was impossible to do, as the Emperor soon after left Venice.

On my return, the Emperor asked me if I had been through the city, what I thought of it, and if I had entered any residences; in fact, what seemed to me worthy of notice. I replied as well as I could; and as his Majesty was just then in a mood for light conversation, spoke to him of our excursion, and visit to the Greek family. The Emperor asked me what these Greeks thought of him. "Sire," replied I, "the one who spoke French seemed entirely devoted to your Majesty, and expressed to me the hope which he and also his brothers entertained, that the Emperor of the French, who had successfully combated the Mamelukes in Egypt, might also some day make himself the liberator of Greece."

"Ah, Monsieur Constant," said the Emperor to me, pinching me sharply, "you are meddling with politics."

"Pardon me, Sire, I only repeated what I heard, and it is not astonishing that all the oppressed count on your Majesty's aid. These poor Greeks seem to love their country passionately, and, above all, detest the Turks most cordially."

"That is good," said his Majesty; "but I must first of all attend to my own business. Constant!" continued his Majesty suddenly changing the subject of this conversation with which he had deigned to honour me, and smiling with an ironical air, "what do you think of the appearance of the beautiful Greek women? How many models have you seen worthy of Canova or of David?" I was obliged to admit to his Majesty that what had influenced me most in accepting Roustan's proposition was the hope of seeing a few of these much vaunted beauties, and that I had been cruelly disappointed in not having seen the shadow of a woman. At this frank avowal the Emperor, who had expected it in advance, laughed heartily, and took his revenge on my ears, calling me a libertine: "You do not know then, Monsieur le Drole, that your good friends the Greeks have adopted the customs of those Turks whom they detest so cordially, and like them seclude their wives and daughters in order that they may never appear before bad men like yourself."

Although the Greek ladies of Venice may be carefully watched by their husbands, they are neither secluded nor guarded in a seraglio like the Turkish women; for during our stay at Venice, a great person spoke to his Majesty of a young and beautiful Greek, who was an enthusiastic admirer of the Emperor of the French. This lady was very ambitious of being received by his Majesty in his private rooms, and although carefully watched by a jealous husband, had found means to send to the Emperor a letter in which she depicted the intensity of her love and admiration. This letter, written with real passion and in an exalted strain, inspired in his Majesty a desire to see and know the author, but it was necessary he should use precautions, for the Emperor was not the man to abuse his power to snatch a woman from her husband; and yet all the care that he took in keeping the affair secret did not prevent her husband from suspecting the plans of his wife, and before it was possible for her to see the Emperor, she was carried away far from Venice, and her prudent husband carefully covered her steps and concealed her flight. When her disappearance was announced to the Emperor: "He is an old fool," said his Majesty, laughing, "who thinks he is strong enough to struggle against his destiny." His Majesty formed no other liaison during our stay at Venice.

Before leaving this city, the Emperor rendered a decree which was received with inexpressible enthusiasm, and added much to the regret which his Majesty's departure caused the inhabitants of Venice. The department of the Adriatic, of which Venice was the chief city, was enlarged in all its maritime coasts, from the town of Aquila as far as Adria. The decree ordered, moreover, that the port should be repaired, the canals deepened and cleaned, the great wall of Palestrina of which I have spoken above, and the jetties in front of it, extended and maintained; that a canal of communication between the arsenal of Venice and the Pass of Mala-Mocco should be dug; and finally that this passage itself should be cleared and deepened sufficiently for vessels of the line of seventy-four tons burthen to pass in and out.

Other articles related to benevolent establishments, the administration of which was given to a kind of council called the Congregation of Charities, and the cession to the city from the royal domain of the island of Saint Christopher, to be used as a general cemetery; for until then here, as in the rest of Italy, they had the pernicious custom of interring the dead in churches. Finally the decree ordered the adoption of a new mode of lighting the beautiful square of Saint Mark, the construction of new quays, gateways, etc.

When we left Venice the Emperor was conducted to the shore by a crowd of the population fully as numerous as that which welcomed his arrival. Trevise, Undine, and Mantua rivalled each other in their eagerness to receive his Majesty in a becoming manner. King Joseph had left the Emperor to return to Naples; but Prince Murat and the vice-king accompanied his Majesty.

The Emperor stopped only two or three days at Milan, and continued his journey. On reaching the plains of Marengo, he found there the entire population of Alexandria awaiting him, and was received by the light of thousands of torches. We passed through Turin without stopping, and on the 30th of December again descended Mont Cenis, and on the evening of the 1st of January arrived at the Tuileries.

Chapter 38

We arrived in Paris on the 1st of January at nine o'clock in the evening; and as the theatre of the palace of the Tuileries was now completed, on the Sunday following his Majesty's return the Griselda of M. Paer was presented in this magnificent hall. Their Majesties' boxes were situated in front of the curtain, opposite each other, and presented a charming picture, with their hangings of crimson silk draped above, and forming a background to broad, movable mirrors, which reflected at will the audience or the play. The Emperor, still impressed with the recollections of the theatres of Italy, criticised unsparingly that of the Tuileries, saying that it was inconvenient, badly planned, and much too large for a palace theatre; but notwithstanding all these criticisms, when the day of inauguration came, and the Emperor was convinced of the very great ingenuity M. Fontaine had shown in distributing the boxes so as to make the splendid toilets appear to the utmost advantage, he appeared well satisfied, and charged the Duke of Frioul to present to M. Fontaine the congratulations he so well deserved.

A week after we saw the reverse of the medal. On that day Cinna was presented, and a comedy, the name of which I have forgotten. It was such extremely cold weather that we were obliged to leave the theatre immediately after the tragedy, in consequence of which the Emperor exhausted himself in invectives against the hall, which according to him was good for nothing but to be burnt. M. Fontaine[1] was summoned, and promised to do everything in his power to remedy the inconveniences pointed out to him; and in fact, by means of new furnaces placed under the theatre, with pipes through the ceiling, and steps placed under the benches of the second tier of boxes, in a week the hall was made warm and comfortable.

For several weeks the Emperor occupied himself almost exclusive-

---

1. Born at Pontoise, 1762; erected the arch of the Carrousel; died 1853.

ly with buildings and improvements. The arch of triumph of the Place du Carrousel, from which the scaffolding had been removed in order to allow the Imperial Guard to pass beneath it on their return from Prussia, first attracted his Majesty's attention. This monument was then almost completed, with the exception of a few bas-reliefs which were still to be put in position. The Emperor took a critical view of it from one of the palace windows, and said, after knitting his brows two or three times, that this mass resembled much more a pavilion than a gate, and that he would have much preferred one constructed in the style of the Porte Saint-Denis.

After visiting in detail the various works begun or carried on since his departure, his Majesty one morning sent for M. Fontaine, and having discoursed at length on what he thought worthy of praise or blame in all that he had seen, informed him of his intentions with regard to the plans which the architect had furnished for joining the Tuileries to the Louvre. It was agreed by the Emperor and M. Fontaine that these buildings should be united by two wings, the first of which should be finished in five years, a million to be granted each year for this purpose; and that a second wing should also be constructed on the opposite side, extending from the Louvre to the Tuileries, forming thus a perfect square, in the midst of which would be erected an opera house, isolated on all sides, and communicating with the palace by a subterranean gallery.

The gallery forming the court in front of the Louvre was to be opened to the public in winter, and decorated with statues, and also with all the shrubbery now in boxes in the garden of the Tuileries; and in this court he intended to erect an arch of triumph very similar to that of the Carrousel. Finally, all these beautiful buildings were to be used as lodgings for the grand officers of the crown, as stables, etc. The necessary expense was estimated as approximating forty-two millions.

The Emperor was occupied in succession with a palace of arts; with a new building for the Imperial library, to be placed on the spot now occupied by the Bourse; with a palace for the stock-exchange on the quay Desaix; with the restoration of the Sorbonne and the hotel Soubise; with a triumphal column at Neuilly; with a fountain on the Place Louis XV.; with tearing down the Hotel-Dieu to enlarge and beautify the Cathedral quarter; and with the construction of four hospitals at Mont-Parnasse, at Chaillot, at Montmartre, and in the Faubourg Saint-Antoine, etc. All these plans were very grand; and there is no doubt that he who had conceived them would have executed them; and it has often been said that had he lived, Paris would have had no rival in any department in the world.

At the same time his Majesty decided definitely on the form of the arch of triumph *de l'Etoile*, which had been long debated, and for which all the architects of the crown had submitted plans. It was M. Fontaine whose opinion prevailed; since among all the plans presented his was the simplest, and at the same time the most imposing.

The Emperor was also much interested in the restoration of the palace of Versailles. M. Fontaine had submitted to his Majesty a plan for the first repairs, by the terms of which, for the sum of six millions, the Emperor and Empress would have had a comfortable dwelling. His Majesty, who liked everything grand, handsome, superb, but at the same time economical, wrote at the bottom of this estimate the following note, which M. de Bausset reports thus in his Memoirs:

> The plans in regard to Versailles must be carefully considered. Those which M. Fontaine submits are very reasonable, the estimate being six millions; but this includes dwellings, with the restoration of the chapel and that of the theatre, only sufficiently comfortable for present use, not such as they should be one day. By this plan, the Emperor and Empress would have their apartments; but we must remember that this sum should also furnish lodgings for princes, grand and inferior officers.
>
> It is also necessary to know where will be placed the factory of arms, which will be needed at Versailles, since it puts silver in circulation.
>
> It will be necessary out of these six millions to find six lodgings for princes, twelve for grand officers, and fifty for inferior officers.
>
> Then only can we decide to make Versailles our residence, and pass the summers there. Before adopting these plans, it will be necessary that the architect who engages to execute them should certify that they can be executed for the proposed sum.

A few days after their arrival their Majesties, the Emperor and Empress, went to visit the celebrated David[2] at his studio in the Sorbonne, in order to see the magnificent picture of the coronation, which had just been finished. Their Majesties' suite was composed of Marshal Bessieres, an *aide-de-camp* of the Emperor, M. Lebrun, several ladies of the palace, and chamberlains. The Emperor and Empress contemplated

---

2. Jacques Louis David, born in Paris, 1748, celebrated historical painter, member of convention, 1792, and voted for the death of the king. Died in Brussels, 1825.

with admiration for a long while this beautiful painting, which comprised every species of merit; and the painter was in his glory while hearing his Majesty name, one by one, all the different personages of the picture, for the resemblance was really miraculous. "How grand that is!" said the Emperor; "how fine! how the figures are brought out in relief! how truthful! This is not a painting; the figures live in this picture!" First directing his attention to the grand tribune in the midst, the Emperor, recognized Madame his mother, General Beaumont, M. de Cosse, M. de La Ville, Madame de Fontanges, and Madame Soult. "I see in the distance," said he, "good M. Vien." M. David replied, "Yes, Sire; I wished to show my admiration for my illustrious master by placing him in this picture, which, on account of its subject, will be the most famous of my works." The Empress then took part in the conversation, and pointed out to the Emperor how happily M. David had seized upon and represented the interesting moment when the Emperor is on the point of being crowned. "Yes," said his Majesty, regarding it with a pleasure that he did not seek to disguise, "the moment is well chosen, and the scene perfectly represented; the two figures are very fine," and speaking thus, the Emperor looked at the Empress.

His Majesty continued the examination of the picture in all its details, and praised especially the group of the Italian clergy near the altar, which episode was invented by the painter. He seemed to wish only that the Pope had been represented in more direct action, appearing to give his blessing, and that the crown of the Empress had been borne by the cardinal legate. In regard to this group, Marshal Bessieres made the Emperor laugh heartily, by relating to him the very amusing discussion which had taken place between David and Cardinal Caprara.

It is well known that the artist had a great aversion to dressed figures, especially to those clothed in the modern style. In all his paintings, there may be remarked such a pronounced love for the antique that it even shows itself in his manner of draping living persons. Now, Cardinal Caprara, one of the assistants of the Pope at the ceremony of the coronation, wore a wig; and David, in giving him a place in his picture, thought it more suitable to take off his wig, and represent him with a bald head, the likeness being otherwise perfect. The Cardinal was much grieved, and begged the artist to restore his wig, but received from David a formal refusal. "Never," said he, "will I degrade my pencil so far as to paint a wig." His Eminence went away very angry, and complained to M. de Talleyrand, who was at this time

Minister of Foreign Affairs, giving, among other reasons, this, which seemed to him unanswerable, that, as no Pope had ever worn a wig, they would not fail to attribute to him, Cardinal Caprara, an intention of aspiring to the pontifical chair in case of a vacancy, which intention would be clearly shown by the suppression of his wig in the picture of the coronation. The entreaties of his Eminence were all in vain; for David would not consent to restore his precious wig, saying, that "he ought to be very glad he had taken off no more than that."

After hearing this story, the particulars of which were confirmed by the principal actor in the scene, his Majesty made some observations to M. David, with all possible delicacy. They were attentively noted by this admirable artist, who, with a bow, promised the Emperor to profit by his advice. Their Majesties' visit was long, and lasted until the fading light warned the Emperor that it was time to return. M. David escorted him to the door of his studio; and there, stopping short, the Emperor took off his hat, and, by a most graceful bow, testified to the honour he felt for such distinguished talent. The Empress added to the agitation by which M. David seemed almost overcome by a few of the charming words of appreciation she so well knew how to say, and said so opportunely.

Opposite the picture of the coronation was placed that of the Sabines. The Emperor, who perceived how anxious M. David was to dispose of this, gave orders to M. Lebrun, as he left, to see if this picture could not be placed to advantage in the grand gallery at the Tuileries. But he soon changed his mind when he reflected that most of the figures were represented in *naturalibus*, which would appear incongruous in an apartment used for grand diplomatic receptions, and in which the Council of Ministers usually sat.

Chapter 39

The last of January, Mademoiselle de Tascher, niece of her Majesty the Empress, was married to the Duke of Aremberg. The Emperor on this occasion raised Mademoiselle de Tascher to the dignity of a princess, and deigned, in company with the Empress, to honour with his presence the marriage, which took place at the residence of her Majesty the Queen of Holland, in the Rue de Ceriltti, and was celebrated with a splendour worthy of the august guests. The Empress remained some time after dinner, and opened the ball with the Duke of Aremberg. A few days after this the Prince of Hohenzollern married the niece of the Grand Duke of Berg and Cleves, Mademoiselle Antoinette Murat.

His Majesty honoured her as he had done Mademoiselle Tascher, and, in company with the Empress, also attended the ball which the Grand Duke of Berg gave on the occasion of this marriage, and at which Princess Caroline presided.

This was a brilliant winter at Paris, owing to the great number of fetes and balls which were given. The Emperor, as I have already said, had an aversion to balls, and especially masked balls, which he considered the most senseless things in the world, and this was a subject on which he was often at war with the Empress; but, notwithstanding this, on one occasion he yielded to the entreaties of M. de Marescalchi, the Italian ambassador, noted for his magnificent balls, which the most distinguished personages of the kingdom attended. These brilliant reunions took place in a hall which the ambassador had built for the purpose, and decorated with extraordinary luxury and splendour; and his Majesty, as I have said, consented to honour with his presence a masked ball given by this ambassador, which was to eclipse all others.

In the morning the Emperor called me, and said, "I have decided to dance this evening at the house of the ambassador of Italy; you will carry, during the day, ten complete costumes to the apartments he has prepared for me." I obeyed, and in the evening accompanied his Majesty to the residence of M. Marescalchi, and dressed him as best I could in a black domino, taking great pains to render him unrecognizable; and everything went well, in spite of numerous observations on the Emperor's part as to the absurdity of a disguise, the bad appearance a domino makes, etc. But, when it was proposed to change his shoes, he rebelled absolutely, in spite of all I could say on this point; and consequently he was recognized the moment he entered the ballroom. He went straight to a masker, his hands behind his back, as usual, and attempted to enter into an intrigue, and at the first question he asked was called Sire, in reply. Whereupon, much disappointed, he turned on his heel, and came back to me. "You are right, Constant; I am recognized. Bring me lace-boots and another costume." I put the boots on his feet, and disguised him anew, advising him to let his arms hang, if he did not wish to be recognized at once; and his Majesty promised to obey in every particular what he called my instructions. He had hardly entered the room in his new costume, however, before he was accosted by a lady, who, seeing him with his hands again crossed behind his back, said, "Sire, you are recognized!" The Emperor immediately let his arms fall; but it was too late, for already every one moved aside respectfully to make room for him. He then returned to his room, and took a third costume, promising me implicitly to pay attention to his gestures and his walk, and offering to bet that he would not be recognized. This time, in fact, he entered the hall as if it were a barrack, pushing and elbowing all around him; but, in spite of this, some one whispered in his ear, "Your Majesty is recognized." A new disappointment, new change of costume, and new advice on my part, with the same result; until at last his Majesty left the ambassador's ball, persuaded that he could not be disguised, and that the Emperor would be recognized whatever mask he might assume.

That evening at supper, the Prince de Neuchatel, the Duke de Trevise, the Duke de Frioul, and some other officers being present, the Emperor related the history of his disguises, and made many jests on his awkwardness. In speaking of the young lady who had recognized him the evening before, and who had, it appeared, puzzled him greatly, "Can you believe it, *Messieurs*," said he, "I never succeeded in recognizing the little wretch at all?" During the carnival the Empress expressed a wish to go once to the masked ball at the opera; and when she begged the Emperor to accompany her he refused, in spite of all the tender and enticing things the Empress could say, and all the grace with which, as is well known, she could surround a petition. She found that all was useless, as the Emperor said plainly that he would not go. "Well, I will go without you."

"As you please," and the Emperor went out.

That evening at the appointed hour the Empress went to the ball; and the Emperor, who wished to surprise her, had one of her femmes de *chambre* summoned, and obtained from her an exact description of the Empress's costume. He then told me to dress him in a domino, entered a carriage without decorations, and accompanied by the grand marshal of the palace, a superior officer, and myself, took the road to the opera. On reaching the private entrance of the Emperor's household, we encountered some difficulty, as the doorkeeper would not let us pass till I had told my name and rank. "These gentlemen are with you?"

"As you see."

"I beg your pardon, Monsieur Constant; but it is because in such times as these there are always persons who try to enter without paying."

"That is good! That is good!" and the Emperor laughed heartily at the doorkeeper's observations. At last we entered, and having got as far as the hall, promenaded in couples, I giving my arm to the Emperor, who said thou to me, and bade me reply in the same way. We gave each other fictitious names, the Emperor calling himself Auguste; the Duke de Frioul, Francois; the superior officer, whose name escapes me, Charles; while I was Joseph. As soon as his Majesty saw a domino similar to the one the femme de *chambre* had described, he pressed my arm and said, "Is that she?"

"No, Si—no, Auguste," replied I, constantly correcting myself; for it was impossible to accustom myself to calling the Emperor otherwise than Sire or your Majesty. He had, as I have said, expressly ordered me to *tutoy* him; but he was every moment compelled to repeat this order to me, for respect tied my tongue every time I tried to say *tu*. At last, after having gone in every direction, explored every corner and nook of the saloon, the green-room, the boxes, etc., in fact, examined everything, and looked each costume over in detail, his Majesty, who was no more successful in recognizing her Majesty than were we, began to feel great anxiety, which I, however, succeeded in allaying by telling him that doubtless the Empress had gone to change her costume. As I was speaking, a domino arrived who seemed enamoured of the Emperor, accosted him, mystified him, tormented him in every way, and with so much vivacity that Auguste was beside himself; and it is impossible to give even a faint idea of the comical sight the Emperor presented in his embarrassment. The domino, delighted at this, redoubled her wit and raillery until, thinking it time to cease, she disappeared in the crowd.

The Emperor was completely exasperated; he had seen enough, and we left the ball.

The next morning when he saw the Empress, he remarked, "Well, you did not go to the opera ball, after all!"

"Oh, yes, indeed I did."

"Nonsense!"

"I assure you that I went. And you, my dear, what did you do all the evening?"

"I worked."

"Why, that is very singular; for I saw at the ball last night a domino who had exactly your foot and boots. I took him for you, and consequently addressed him." The Emperor laughed heartily on learning that he had been thus duped; the Empress, just as she left for the ball, had changed her costume, not thinking the first sufficiently elegant.

The carnival was extremely brilliant this year, and there were in Paris all kinds of masquerades. The most amusing were those in which the theory advocated by the famous Doctor Gall[1] was illustrated. I saw a troop passing the Place du Carrousel, composed of clowns, harlequins, fishwives, etc., all rubbing their skulls, and making expressive grimaces; while a clown bore several skulls of different sizes, painted red, blue, or green, with these inscriptions: Skull of a robber, skull of an assassin, skull of a bankrupt, etc.; and a masked figure, representing Doctor Gall, was seated on an ass, his head turned to the animal's tail, and receiving from the hands of a woman who followed him, and was also seated on an ass, heads covered with wigs made of long grass.

Her Majesty Queen Caroline gave a masked ball, at which the Emperor and Empress were present, which was one of the most brilliant I have ever attended.

The opera of la Vestale was then new, and very much the fashion; it represented a quadrille of priests and vestals who entered to the sound of delicious music on the flute and harp, and in addition to this there were magicians, a Swiss marriage, Tyrolian betrothals, etc. All the costumes were wonderfully handsome and true to nature; and there had been arranged in the apartments at the palace a supply of costumes which enabled the dancers to change four or five times during the night, and which had the effect of renewing the ball as many times.

---

1. Franz Joseph Gall, founder of the system of phrenology. Born in Baden, 1758; died in Paris, 1825.

As I was dressing the Emperor for this ball, he said to me, "Constant, you must go with me in disguise. Take whatever costume you like, disguise yourself so that you cannot possibly be recognized, and I will give you instructions." I hastened to do as his Majesty ordered, donned a Swiss costume which suited me very well, and thus equipped awaited his Majesty's orders.

He had a plan for mystifying several great personages, and two or three ladies whom the Emperor designated to me with such minute details that it was impossible to mistake them, and told me some singular things in regard to them, which were not generally known, and were well calculated to embarrass them terribly. As I was starting, the Emperor called me back, saying, "Above all, Constant, take care to make no mistake, and do not confound Madame de M——with her sister; they have almost exactly the same costume, but Madame de M—is larger than she, so take care." On my arrival at the ball, I sought and easily found the persons whom his Majesty had designated, and the replies which they made afforded him much amusement when I narrated them as he was retiring.

There was at this time a third marriage at the court, that of the Prince de Neuchatel and the Princess of Bavaria, which was celebrated in the chapel of the Tuileries by Cardinal Fesch.

A traveller just returned from the Isle of France presented to the Empress a female monkey of the orang-utan species; and her Majesty gave orders that the animal should be placed in the menagerie at Malmaison. This baboon was extremely gentle and docile, and its master had given it an excellent education. It was wonderful to see her, when any one approached the chair on which she was seated, take a decent position, draw over her legs and thighs the fronts of a long redingote, and, when she rose to make a bow, hold the redingote carefully in front of her, acting, in fact, exactly as would a young girl who had been well reared. She ate at the table with a knife and fork more properly than many children who are thought to be carefully trained, and liked, while eating, to cover her face with her napkin, and then uncover it with a cry of joy. Turnips were her favourite food; and, when a lady of the palace showed her one, she began to run, caper, and cut somersaults, forgetting entirely the lessons of modesty and decency her professor had taught her. The Empress was much amused at seeing the baboon lose her dignity so completely under the influence of this lady.

This poor beast had inflammation of the stomach, and, according to the directions of the traveller who brought her, was placed in bed and a night-dress put on her. She took great care to keep the covering up to her chin, though unwilling to have anything on her head; and held her arms out of the bed, her hands hidden in the sleeves of the night-dress. When any one whom she knew entered the room, she nodded to them and took their hand, pressing it affectionately. She eagerly swallowed the medicines prescribed, as they were sweet; and one day, while a draught of manna was being prepared, which she thought too long delayed, she showed every sign of impatience, and threw herself from side to side like a fretful child; at last, throwing off the covering, she seized her physician by the coat with so much obstinacy that he was compelled to yield. The instant she obtained possession of the eagerly coveted cup she manifested the greatest delight, and began to drink, taking little sips, and smacking her lips with all the gratification of an epicure who tastes a glass of wine which he thinks very old and very delicious. At last the cup was emptied, she returned it, and lay down again. It is impossible to give an idea of the gratitude this poor animal showed whenever anything was done for her. The Empress was deeply attached to her.

Chapter 40

After remaining about a week at the chateau of Saint-Cloud, his Majesty set out, on the 2nd of April, at 11 o'clock in the morning, to visit the departments of the South; and as this journey was to begin at Bordeaux, the Emperor requested the Empress to meet him there. This publicly announced intention was simply a pretext, in order, to mislead the curious, for we knew that we were going to the frontier of Spain.

The Emperor remained barely ten days there, and then left for Bayonne alone, leaving the Empress at Bordeaux, and reaching Bayonne on the night of the 14-15th of April, where her Majesty the Empress rejoined him two or three days afterwards.

The Prince of Neuchatel and the grand marshal lodged at the chateau of Marrac, the rest of their Majesties' suite lodged at Bayonne and its suburbs, the guard camped in front of the chateau on a place called the Parterre, and in three days all were comfortably located.

On the morning of the 15th of April, the Emperor had hardly recovered from the fatigue of his journey, when he received the authorities of Bayonne, who came to congratulate him, and questioned them, as was his custom, most pointedly. His Majesty then set out to visit the fort and fortifications, which occupied him till the evening, when he returned to the Government palace, which he occupied temporarily while waiting till the chateau of Marrac should be ready to receive him.

On his return to the palace the Emperor expected to find the Infant Don Carlos, whom his brother Ferdinand, the Prince of the Asturias, had sent to Bayonne to present his compliments to the Emperor; but he was informed that the Infant was ill, and would not be able to come. The Emperor immediately gave orders to send one of his physicians to attend upon him, with a *valet de chambre* and several other persons; for the prince had come to Bayonne without attendants, and incognito, attended only by a military service composed of a few soldiers of the garrison. The Emperor also ordered that this

MACDONALD

service should be replaced by one more suitable, consisting of the Guard of Honour of Bayonne, and sent two or three times each day to inquire the condition of the Infant, who it was freely admitted in the palace was very ill.

On leaving the Government palace to take up his abode at Marrac, the Emperor gave all necessary orders that it should be in readiness to receive the King and Queen of Spain, who were expected at Bayonne the last of the month; and expressly recommended that everything should be done to render to the sovereigns of Spain all the honours due their position. Just as the Emperor entered the chateau the sound of music was heard, and the grand marshal entered to inform his Majesty that a large company of the inhabitants in the costume of the country were assembled before the gate of the chateau. The Emperor immediately went to the window; and, at sight of him, seventeen persons (seven men and ten women) began with inimitable grace a dance called *'la pamperruque'*, in which the women kept time on tambourines, and the men with castanets, to an orchestra composed of flutes and guitars. I went out of the castle to view this scene more closely. The women wore short skirts of blue silk, and pink stockings likewise embroidered in silver; their hair was tied with ribbons, and they wore very broad black bracelets, that set off to advantage the dazzling whiteness of their bare arms. The men wore tight-fitting white breeches, with silk stockings and large epaulettes, a loose vest of very fine woollen cloth ornamented with gold, and their hair caught up in a net like the Spaniards.

His Majesty took great pleasure in witnessing this dance, which is peculiar to the country and very ancient, which the custom of the country has consecrated as a means of rendering homage to great personages. The Emperor remained at the window until the *'pamperruque'* was finished, and then sent to compliment the dancers on their skill, and to express his thanks to the inhabitants assembled in crowds at the gate.

His Majesty a few days afterward received from his Royal Highness, the Prince of the Asturias, a letter, in which he announced that he intended setting out from Irun, where he then was, at an early day, in order to have the pleasure of making the acquaintance of his brother (it was thus Prince Ferdinand called the Emperor); a pleasure which he had long desired, and which he would at last enjoy if his good brother would allow him. This letter was brought to the Emperor by one of the *aides-de-camp* of the prince, who had accompanied him from Madrid, and preceded him to Bayonne by only ten days. His Majesty could hardly believe what he read and heard; and I, with several other persons, heard him exclaim, "What, he is coming here? but you must be mistaken; he must be deceiving us; that cannot be possible!" And I can certify that, in these words, the Emperor manifested no pleasure at the announcement.

It was necessary, however, to make preparations to receive the prince, since he was certainly coming; consequently the Prince of Neuchatel, the Duke of Frioul, and a chamberlain of honour, were selected by his Majesty. And the guard of honour received orders to accompany these gentlemen, and meet the Prince of Spain just outside the town of Bayonne; the rank which the Emperor recognized in Ferdinand not rendering it proper that the escort should go as far as the frontier of the two empires. The Prince made his entrance into Bayonne at noon, on the 20th of April. Lodgings which would have been considered very inferior in Paris, but which were elegant in Bayonne, had been prepared for him and his brother, the Infant Don Carlos, who was already installed there. Prince Ferdinand made a grimace on entering, but did not dare to complain aloud; and certainly it would have been most improper for him to have done so, since it was not the Emperor's fault that Bayonne possessed only one palace, which was at this time reserved for the king, and, besides, this house, the handsomest in the town, was large and perfectly new. Don Pedro de Cevallos, who accompanied the prince, thought it horrible, and unfit for a royal personage. It was the residence of the commissariat. An hour after Ferdinand's arrival, the Emperor visited him. He was awaiting the Emperor at the door, and held out his arms on his approach; they embraced, and ascended to his apartments, where they remained about half an hour, and when they separated the prince wore a somewhat anxious air. His Majesty on his return charged the grand marshal to convey to the prince and his brother, Don Carlos, the Duke of San-Carlos, the Duke of Infantado, Don Pedro de Cevallos, and two or three other persons of the suite, an invitation to dine with him; and the Emperor's carriages were sent for these illustrious guests at the appointed hour, and they were conveyed to the chateau. His Majesty descended to the foot of the staircase to receive the prince; but this was the limit of his deference, for not once during dinner did he give Prince Ferdinand, who was a king at Madrid, the title of your majesty, nor even that of highness; nor did he accompany him on his departure any farther than the first door of the saloon; and he afterwards informed him, by a message, that he would have no other rank than that of Prince of the Asturias until the arrival of his father, King Charles. Orders were given at the same time to place on duty at the house of the princes, the Bayonnaise guard of honour, with the Imperial Guard in addition to a detachment of picked police.

On the 27th of April the Empress arrived from Bordeaux at seven o'clock in the evening, having made no stay at Bayonne, where her arrival excited little enthusiasm, as they were perhaps displeased that she did not stop there. His Majesty received her with much tenderness, and showed much solicitude as to the fatigue she must have experienced, since the roads were so rough, and badly washed by the rains. In the evening the town and chateau were illuminated.

Three days after, on the 30th, the King and Queen of Spain arrived at Bayonne; and it is impossible to describe the homage which the Emperor paid them. The Duke Charles de Plaisance went as far as Irun, and the Prince de Neuchatel even to the banks of the Bidassoa, in order to pay marked respect to their Catholic Majesties on the part of their powerful friend; and the king and queen appeared to appreciate highly these marks of consideration. A detachment of picked troops, superbly uniformed, awaited them on the frontier, and served as their escort; the garrison of Bayonne was put under arms, all the buildings of the port were decorated, all the bells rang, and the batteries of both the citadel and the port saluted with great salvos. The Prince of the Asturias and his brother, hearing of the arrival of the king and queen, had left Bayonne in order to meet their parents, when they encountered, a short distance from the town, two or three grenadiers who had just left Vittoria, and related to them the following occurrence:

When their Spanish Majesties entered Vittoria, they found that a detachment of the Spanish body guards, who had accompanied the Prince of the Asturias and were stationed in this town, had taken possession of the palace which the king and queen were to occupy as they passed through, and on the arrival of their Majesties had put themselves under arms. As soon as the king perceived this, he said to them in a severe tone, "You will understand why I ask you to quit my palace. You have failed in your duty at Aranjuez. I have no need of your services, and I do not wish them. Go!" These words, pronounced with an energy far from habitual to Charles IV., met with no reply. The detachment of the guards retired; and the king begged General Verdier to give him a French guard, much grieved, he said, that he had not retained his brave riflemen, whose colonel he still kept near him as captain of the guards.

This news could not give the Prince of the Asturias a high opinion of the welcome his father had in store for him; and indeed he was very coolly received, as I shall now relate.

The King and Queen of Spain, on alighting at the governmental palace, found awaiting them the grand marshal, the Duke de Frioul, who escorted them to their apartments, and presented to them General Count Reille, the Emperor's *aide-de-camp*, performing the duties of governor of the palace; M. d'Audenarde, equerry, with M. Dumanoir and M. de Baral, chamberlains charged with the service of honour near their Majesties.

The grandees of Spain whom their Majesties found at Bayonne were the same who had followed the Prince of the Asturias, and the sight of them, as may well be imagined, was not pleasant to the king; and when the ceremony of the kissing of the hand took place, every one perceived the painful agitation of the unfortunate sovereigns. This ceremony, which consists of falling on your knees and kissing the hand of the king and queen, was performed in the deepest silence, as their Majesties spoke to no one but the Count of Fuentes, who by chance was at Bayonne.

The king hurried over this ceremony, which fatigued him greatly, and retired with the queen into his apartments, where the Prince of the Asturias wished to follow them; but his father stopped him at the door, and raising his arm as if to repulse him, said in a trembling tone, "Prince, do you wish still to insult my grey hairs?" These words had, it is said, the effect of a thunderbolt on the prince. He was overcome by his feelings for a moment, and withdrew without uttering a word.

Very different was the reception their Majesties gave to the Prince de la Paix[1] when he joined them at Bayonne, and he might have been taken for the nearest and dearest relative of their Majesties. All three wept freely on meeting again; at least, this is what I was told by a person in the service—the same, in fact, who gave me all the preceding details.

At five o'clock his Majesty the Emperor came to visit the King and Queen of Spain; and during this interview, which was very long, the two sovereigns informed his Majesty of the insults they had received, and the dangers they had encountered during the past month. They complained greatly of the ingratitude of so many men whom they had overwhelmed with kindness, and above all of the guard which had so basely betrayed them. "Your Majesty," said the king, "does not know what it is to be forced to commiserate yourself on account of

---

1. Manuel Godoi, born at Badajos, 1767. A common soldier, he became the queen's lover, and the virtual ruler of Spain; died in Paris, 1851.

your son. May Heaven forbid that such a misfortune should ever come to you! Mine is the cause of all that we have suffered."

The Prince de la Paix had come to Bayonne accompanied by Colonel Martes, *aide-de-camp* of Prince Murat, and a *valet de chambre*, the only servant who had remained faithful to him. I had occasion to talk with this devoted servant, who spoke very good French, having been reared near Toulouse; and he told me that he had not succeeded in obtaining permission to remain with his master during his captivity, and that this unfortunate prince had suffered indescribable torments; that not a day passed without some one entering his dungeon to tell him to prepare for death, as he was to be executed that very evening or the next morning. He also told me that the prisoners were left sometimes for thirty hours without food; that he had only a bed of straw, no linen, no books, and no communication with the outside world; and that when he came out of his dungeon to be sent to Colonel Marts, he presented a horrible appearance, with his long beard, and emaciated frame, the result of mental distress and insufficient food. He had worn the same shirt for a month, as he had never been able to prevail on his captors to give him others; and his eyes had been so long unaccustomed to the light that he was obliged to close them, and felt oppressed in the open air.

On the road from Bayonne, there was handed to the prince a letter from the king and queen which was stained with tears. The prince said to his *valet de chambre* after reading it, "These are the first consoling words I have received in a month, for every one has abandoned me except my excellent masters. The body guards, who have betrayed and sold their king, will also betray and sell his son; and as for myself, I hope for nothing, except to be permitted to find an asylum in France for my children and myself." M. Marts having shown him newspapers in which it was stated that the prince possessed a fortune of five hundred million, he exclaimed vehemently that it was an atrocious calumny, and he defied his most cruel enemies to prove that.

As we have seen, their Majesties had not a numerous suite; but they were, notwithstanding, followed by baggage-wagons filled with furniture, goods, and valuable articles, and though their carriages were old-fashioned, they found them very comfortable—especially the king, who was much embarrassed the day after his arrival at Bayonne, when, having been invited to dine with the Emperor, it was necessary to enter a modern carriage with two steps. He did not dare to put his foot on the frail things, which he feared would break under his weight; and the oscillating movement of the body of the carriage made him terribly afraid that it would upset.

At the table I had an opportunity of observing at my leisure the king and queen. The king was of medium height, and though not strictly handsome had a pleasant face. His nose was very long, his voice high-pitched and disagreeable; and he walked with a mincing air in which there was no majesty, but this, however, I attributed to the gout. He ate heartily of everything offered him, except vegetables, which he never ate, saying that grass was good only for cattle; and drank only water, having it served in two carafes, one containing ice, and poured from both at the same time. The Emperor gave orders that special attention should be paid to the dinner, knowing that the king was somewhat of an epicure. He praised in high terms the French cooking, which he seemed to find much to his taste; for as each dish was served him, he would say, "Louise, take some of that, it is good;" which greatly amused the Emperor, whose abstemiousness is well known.

The queen was fat and short, dressed very badly, and had no style or grace; her complexion was very florid, and her expression harsh and severe. She held her head high, spoke very loud, in tones still more brusque and piercing than those of her husband; but it is generally conceded that she had more character and better manners than he.

Before dinner that day there was some conversation on the subject of dress; and the Empress offered the services of M. Duplan, her hairdresser, in order to give her ladies some lessons in the French toilet. Her proposition was accepted; and the queen came out soon after from the hands of M. Duplan, better dressed, no doubt, and her hair better arranged, but not beautified, however, for the talent of the hairdresser could not go as far as that.

The Prince of the Asturias, now King Ferdinand VII., made an unpleasant impression on all, with his heavy step and careworn air, and rarely ever speaking.

Their Spanish Majesties as before brought with them the Prince de la Paix, who had not been invited by the Emperor, and whom for this reason the usher on duty detained outside of the dining-hall. But as they were about to be seated, the king perceived that the prince was absent. "And Manuel," said he quickly to the Emperor, "and Manuel, Sire!" Whereupon the Emperor, smiling, gave the signal, and Don Manuel Godoi was introduced. I was told that he had been a very handsome man; but he showed no signs of this, which was perhaps owing to the bad treatment he had undergone.

After the abdication of the princes, the king and queen, the Queen of Etruria, and the Infant Don Francisco, left Bayonne for Fontainebleau, which place the Emperor had selected as their residence while waiting until the chateau of Compiegne should be put in a condition to make them comfortable. The Prince of the Asturias left the same day, with his brother Don Carlos and his uncle Don Antonio, for the estates of Valencay belonging to the Prince of Benevento. They published, while passing through Bordeaux, a proclamation to the Spanish people, in which they confirmed the transmission of all their rights to the Emperor Napoleon.

Thus King Charles, freed from a throne which he had always regarded as a heavy burden, could hereafter give himself up unreservedly in retirement to his favourite pursuits. In all the world he cared only for the Prince de la Paix, confessors, watches, and music; and the throne was nothing to him. After what had passed, the Prince de la Paix could not return to Spain; and the king would never have consented to be separated from him, even if the remembrance of the insults which he had personally received had not been powerful enough to disgust him with his kingdom. He much preferred the life of a private individual, and could not be happier than when allowed without interruption to indulge his simple and tranquil tastes. On his arrival at the chateau of Fontainebleau, he found there M. Remusat, the first chamberlain; M. de Caqueray, officer of the hunt; M. de Lugay, *prefect* of the palace; and a household already installed. Mesdames de la Rochefoucault, Duchatel, and de Lugay had been selected by the Emperor for the service of honour near the queen.

The King of Spain remained at Fontainebleau only until the chateau of Compiegne could be repaired, and as he soon found the climate of this part of France too cold for his health, went, at the end of a few months, to Marseilles with the Queen of Etruria, the Infant Don Francisco, and the Prince de la Paix. In 1811 he left France for Italy, finding his health still bad at Marseilles, and chose Rome as his residence.

I spoke above of the fondness of the King of Spain for watches. I have been told that while at Fontainebleau, he had half a dozen of his watches worn by his *valet de chambre*, and wore as many himself, giving as a reason that pocket watches lose time by not being carried. I have also heard that he kept his confessor always near him, in the antechamber, or in the room in front of that in which he worked, and that when he wished to speak to him he whistled, exactly as one would whistle for a dog. The confessor never failed to respond promptly to this royal call, and followed his penitent into the embrasure of a window, in which improvised confessional the king divulged what he had on his conscience, received absolution, and sent back the priest until he felt himself obliged to whistle for him again.

When the health of the king, enfeebled by age and gout, no longer allowed him to devote himself to the pleasures of the chase, he began playing on the violin more than ever before, in order, he said, to perfect himself in it. This was beginning rather late. As is well known, he had for his first violin teacher the celebrated Alexander Boucher, with whom he greatly enjoyed playing; but he had a mania for beginning first without paying any attention to the measure; and if M. Boucher made any observation in regard to this, his Majesty would reply with the greatest coolness, "Monsieur, it seems to me that it is not my place to wait for you."

Between the departure of the royal family and the arrival of Joseph, King of Naples, the time was passed in reviews and military fetes, which the Emperor frequently honoured with his presence. The 7th of June, King Joseph arrived at Bayonne, where it had been known long in advance that his brother had summoned him to exchange his crown of Naples for that of Spain.

The evening of Joseph's arrival, the Emperor invited the members of the Spanish Junta, who for fifteen days had been arriving at Bayonne from all corners of the kingdom, to assemble at the chateau of Marrac, and congratulate the new king. The deputies accepted this somewhat sudden invitation without having time to concert together previously any course of action; and on their arrival at Marrac, the Emperor presented to them their sovereign, whom they acknowledged, with the exception of some opposition on the part of the Duke of Infantado, in the name of the grandees of Spain. The deputations from the Council of Castile, from the Inquisition, and from the army, etc., submitted most readily. A few days after, the king formed his ministry, in which all were astonished to find M. de Cevallos, who had accompanied the Prince of the Asturias to Bayonne, and had made such a parade of undying attachment to the person of the one whom he called his unfortunate master; while the Duke of Infantado, who had opposed to the utmost any recognition of the foreign monarch, was appointed Captain of the Guard. The king then left for Madrid, after appointing the Grand Duke of Berg lieutenant-general of the kingdom.

Chapter 41

At this time it was learned at Bayonne that M. de Belloy, Archbishop of Paris, had just died of a cold, contracted at the age of more than ninety-eight years. The day after this sad news arrived, the Emperor, who was sincerely grieved, was dilating upon the great and good qualities of this venerable prelate, and said that having one day thoughtlessly remarked to M. de Belloy, then already more than ninety-six years old, that he would live a century, the good old archbishop had exclaimed, smiling, "Why, does your Majesty think that I have no more than four years to live?"

I remember that one of the persons who was present at the Emperor's levee related the following anecdote concerning M. de Belloy, which seemed to excite the Emperor's respect and admiration.

The wife of the hangman of Genoa gave birth to a daughter, who could not be baptized because no one would act as godfather. In vain the father begged and entreated the few persons whom he knew, in vain he even offered money; that was an impossibility. The poor child had consequently remained unbaptized four or five months, though fortunately her health gave no cause for uneasiness. At last some one mentioned this singular condition of affairs to the archbishop, who listened to the story with much interest, inquired why he had not been informed earlier, and having given orders that the child should be instantly brought to him, baptized her in his palace, and was himself her godfather.

At the beginning of July the Grand Duke of Berg returned from Spain, fatigued, ill, and out of humour. He remained there only two or three days, and held each day an interview with his Majesty, who seemed little better satisfied with the grand duke than the grand duke was with him, and left afterwards for the springs of Bareges.

Their Majesties, the Emperor and Empress, left the chateau of Marrac the 20th of July, at six o'clock in the evening. This journey of the

Emperor was one of those which cost the largest number of snuff-boxes set in diamonds, for his Majesty was not economical with them.

Their Majesties arrived at Pau on the 22nd, at ten o'clock in the morning, and alighted at the chateau of Gelos, situated about a quarter of a league from the birthplace of the good Henry IV., on the bank of the river. The day was spent in receptions and horseback excursions, on one of which the Emperor visited the chateau in which the first king of the house of Bourbon was reared, and showed how much this visit interested him, by prolonging it until the dinner-hour.

On the border of the department of the Hautes-Pyrenees, and exactly in the most desolate and miserable part, was erected an arch of triumph, which seemed a miracle fallen from heaven in the midst of those plains uncultivated and burned up by the sun. A guard of honour awaited their Majesties, ranged around this rural monument, at their head an old marshal of the camp, M. de Noe, more than eighty years of age. This worthy old soldier immediately took his place by the side of the carriage, and as cavalry escort remained on horseback for a day and two nights without showing the least fatigue.

As we continued our journey, we saw, on the plateau of a small mountain, a stone pyramid forty or fifty feet high, its four sides covered with inscriptions to the praise of their Majesties. About thirty children dressed as Mamelukes seemed to guard this monument, which recalled to the Emperor glorious memories. The moment their Majesties appeared, balladeers, or dancers, of the country emerged from a neighbouring wood, dressed in the most picturesque costumes, bearing banners of different colours, and reproducing with remarkable agility and vigour the traditional dance of the mountaineers of the south.

Near the town of Tarbes was a sham mountain planted with firs, which opened to let the cortege pass through, surmounted by an imperial eagle suspended in the air, and holding a banner on which was inscribed—"He will open our Pyrenees."

On his arrival at Tarbes, the Emperor immediately mounted his horse to pay a visit to the Grand Duke of Berg, who was ill in one of the suburbs. We left next day without visiting Bareges and Bagneres, where the most brilliant preparations had been made to receive their Majesties.

As the Emperor passed through Agen, there was presented to him a brave fellow named Printemps, over a hundred years old, who had served under Louis XIV., XV., and XVI., and who, although bending beneath the weight of many years and burdens, finding himself in the presence of the Emperor, gently pushed aside two of his grandsons by whom he had been supported, and exclaimed almost angrily that he could go very well alone. His Majesty, who was much touched, met him half-way, and most kindly bent over the old centenarian, who on his knees, his white head uncovered, and his eyes full of tears, said in trembling tones, "Ah, Sire, I was afraid I should die without seeing you." The Emperor assisted him to rise, and conducted him to a chair, in which he placed him with his own hands, and seated himself beside him on another, which he made signs to hand him. "I am glad to see you, my dear Printemps, very glad. You have heard from me lately?" (His Majesty had given this brave man a pension, which his wife was to inherit after his death.) Printemps put his hand on his heart, "Yes, I have heard from you." The Emperor took pleasure in making him speak of his campaigns, and bade him farewell after a long conversation, handing him at the same time a gift of fifty napoleons.

There was also presented to his Majesty a soldier born at Agen, who had lost his sight in consequence of the campaign in Egypt. The Emperor gave him three hundred *francs*, and promised him a pension, which was afterwards sent him.

The day after their arrival at Saint-Cloud, the Emperor and Empress went to Paris in order to be present at the fetes of the 15th of August, which it is useless to say were magnificent. As soon as he entered the Tuileries, the Emperor hastened through the chateau to examine the repairs and improvements which had been made during his absence, and, as was his habit, criticised more than he praised all that he saw. Looking out of the hall of the marshals, he demanded of M. de Fleurieu, governor of the palace, why the top of the arch of triumph on the Carrousel was covered with a cloth; and his Majesty was told that it was because all the arrangements had not yet been made for placing his statue in the chariot to which were attached the Corinthian horses, and also because the two Victories who were to guide the four horses were not yet completed. "What!" vehemently exclaimed the Emperor; "but I will not allow that! I said nothing about it! I did not order it!" Then turning to M. Fontaine, he continued, "Monsieur Fontaine, was my statue in the design which was presented to you?"

"No, Sire, it was that of the god Mars."

"Well, why have you put me in the place of the god of war?"

"Sire, it was not I, but M. the director-general of the museum."

"The director-general was wrong," interrupted the Emperor impatiently. "I wish this statue removed; do you hear, Monsieur Fontaine? I wish it taken away; it is most unsuitable. What! shall I erect statues to myself! Let the chariot and the Victories be finished; but let the chariot let the chariot remain empty." The order was executed; and the statue of the Emperor was taken down and placed in the orangery, and is perhaps still there. It was made of gilded lead, was a fine piece of work, and a most excellent likeness.

The Sunday following the Emperor's arrival, his Majesty received at the Tuileries the Persian ambassador, Asker-Khan; M. Jaubert accompanied him, and acted as interpreter. This savant, learned in Oriental matters, had by the Emperor's orders received His Excellency on the frontiers of France, in company with M. Outrey, vice-consul of France at Bagdad. Later His Excellency had a second audience, which took place in state at the palace of Saint-Cloud.

The ambassador was a very handsome man, tall, with regular features, and a noble and attractive countenance; his manners were polished and elegant, especially towards ladies, with even something of French gallantry. His suite, composed of select personages all magnificently dressed, comprised, on his departure from Erzeroum, more than three hundred persons; but the innumerable difficulties encountered on the journey compelled His Excellency to dismiss a large part of his retinue, and, though thus reduced, this suite was notwithstanding one of the most numerous ever brought by an ambassador into France. The ambassador and suite were lodged in the Rue de Frejus, in the residence formerly occupied by Mademoiselle de Conti.

The presents which he brought to the Emperor in the name of his sovereign were of great value, comprising more than eighty cashmere shawls of all kinds; a great quantity of fine pearls of various sizes, a few of them very large; an Eastern bridle, the curb adorned with pearls, turquoise, emeralds, etc.; and finally the sword of Tamerlane, and that of Thamas-Kouli-Khan, the former covered with pearls and precious stones, the second very simply mounted, both having Indian blades of fabulous value with arabesques of embossed gold.

I took pleasure at the time in inquiring some particulars about this ambassador. His character was very attractive; and he showed much consideration and regard for every one who visited him, giving the ladies attar of roses, the men tobacco, perfumes, and pipes. He took much pleasure in comparing French jewels with those he had brought from his own country, and even carried his gallantry so far as to propose to the ladies certain exchanges, always greatly to their advantage; and a refusal of these proposals wounded him deeply. When a pretty woman entered his residence he smiled at first, and heard her speak in a kind of silent ecstasy; he then devoted his attention to seating her, placed under her feet cushions and carpets of cashmere (for he had only this material about him). Even his clothing and bed-coverings were of an exceedingly fine quality of cashmere. Asker-Khan did not scruple to wash his face, his beard, and hands in the presence of everybody, seating himself for this operation in front of a slave, who presented to him on his knees a porcelain ewer.

The ambassador had a decided taste for the sciences and arts, and was himself a very learned man. Messieurs Dubois and Loyseau conducted near his residence an institution which he often visited, especially preferring to be present at the classes in experimental physics; and the questions which he propounded by means of his interpreter evinced on his part a very extensive knowledge of the phenomena of electricity. Those who traded in curiosities and objects of art liked him exceedingly, since he bought their wares without much bargaining. However, on one occasion he wished to purchase a telescope, and sent for a famous optician, who seized the opportunity to charge him an enormous price. But Asker-Khan having examined the instrument, with which he was much pleased, said to the optician, "You have given me your long price, now give me your short one."

He admired above all the printed calicoes of the manufactures of Jouy, the texture, designs, and colours of which he thought even superior to cashmere; and bought several robes to send to Persia as models.

On the day of the Emperor's fete, His Excellency gave in the garden of his residence an entertainment in the Eastern style, at which the Persian musicians attached to the embassy executed warlike pieces, astonishing both for vigour and originality. There were also artificial fireworks, conspicuous among which were the arms of the Sufi, on which were represented most ingeniously the cipher of Napoleon.

His Excellency visited the Imperial library, M. Jaubert serving as interpreter; and the ambassador was overcome with admiration on seeing the order in which this immense collection of books was kept. He remained half an hour in the hall of the manuscripts, which he thought very handsome, and recognized several as being copied by writers of much renown in Persia. A copy of the Koran struck him most of all; and he said, while admiring it, that there was not a man in Persia who would not sell his children to acquire such a treasure.

On leaving, the library, Asker-Khan presented his compliments to the librarians, and promised to enrich the collection by several precious manuscripts which he had brought from his own country.

A few days after his presentation, the ambassador went to visit the Museum, and was much impressed by a portrait of his master, the King of Persia; and could not sufficiently express his joy and gratitude when several copies of this picture were presented to him. The historical pictures, especially the battle-scenes, then engrossed his attention completely; and he remained at least a quarter of an hour in front of the one representing the surrender of the city of Vienna.

Having arrived at the end of the gallery of Apollo, Asker-Khan seated himself to rest, asked for a pipe, and indulged in a smoke; and when he had finished, rose, and seeing around him many ladies whom curiosity had attracted, paid them, through M. Jaubert, exceedingly flattering compliments. Then leaving the Museum, His Excellency went to promenade in the garden of the Tuileries, where he was soon followed by an immense crowd. On that day His Excellency bestowed on Prince de Benevento, in the name of his sovereign, the Grand Order of the Sun, a magnificent decoration consisting of a diamond sun attached to a cordon of red cloth covered with pearls.

Asker-Khan made a greater impression at Paris than the Turkish ambassador. He was generous and more gallant, paid his court with more address, and conformed more readily to French customs and manners. The Turk was irascible, austere, and irritable, while the Persian was fond of and well understood a joke. One day, however, he became red with anger, and it must be admitted not without good reason.

At a concert given in the apartments of the Empress Josephine, Asker-Khan, whom the music evidently did not entertain very highly, at first applauded by ecstatic gestures and rolling his eyes in admiration, until at last nature overcame politeness, and the ambassador fell sound asleep. His Excellency's position was not the best for sleeping, however, as he was standing with his back against the wall, with his feet braced against a sofa on which a lady was seated. It occurred to some of the officers of the palace that it would be a good joke to take away suddenly this point of support, which they accomplished with all ease by simply beginning a conversation with the lady on the sofa, who rising suddenly, the seat slipped over the floor; His Excellency's feet followed this movement, and the ambassador, suddenly deprived of the weight which had balanced him, extended his length on the floor. On this rude awakening, he tried to stop himself in his fall by clutching at his neighbours, the furniture, and the curtains, uttering at the same time frightful screams. The officers who had played this cruel joke upon him begged him, with the most ridiculously serious air, to place himself on a stationary chair in order to avoid the recurrence of such an accident; while the lady who had been made the accomplice in this practical joke, with much difficulty stifled her laughter, and His Excellency was consumed with an anger which he could express only in looks and gestures.

Another adventure of Asker-Khan's was long a subject of conversation, and furnished much amusement. Having felt unwell for several days, he thought that French medicine might cure him more quickly than Persian; so he sent for M. Bourdois, a most skilful physician whose name he well knew, having taken care to acquaint himself with all our celebrities of every kind. The ambassador's orders were promptly executed; but by a singular mistake it was not Dr. Bourdois who was requested to visit Asker-Khan, but the president of the Court of Accounts, M. Marbois, who was much astonished at the honour the Persian ambassador did him, not being able to comprehend what connection there could be between them. Nevertheless, he repaired promptly to Asker-Khan, who could scarcely believe that the severe costume of the president of the Court of Accounts was that of a physician. No sooner had M. Marbois entered than the ambassador held out his hand and stuck out his tongue, regarding him very attentively. M. Marbois was a little surprised at this welcome; but thinking it was doubtless the Oriental manner of saluting magistrates, he bowed profoundly, and timidly pressed the hand presented to him, and he was in this respectful position when four of the servants of the ambassador brought a vessel with unequivocal signs. M. Marbois recognized the use of it with a surprise and indignation that could not be expressed, and drew back angrily, inquiring what all this meant. Hearing himself called doctor, "What!" cried he, *"M. le Docteur!"*

"Why; yes; *le Docteur Bourdois!"* M. Marbois was enlightened. The similarity between the sound of his name and that of the doctor had exposed him to this disagreeable visit.

Chapter 42

The day preceding the Emperor's fete, or the day following, the colossal bronze statue which was to be placed on the monument in the Place Vendome was removed from the studio of M. Launay. The brewers of the Faubourg Saint-Antoine offered their handsomest horses to draw the chariot on which the statue was carried, and twelve were selected, one from each brewer; and as their masters requested the privilege of riding them, nothing could be more singular than this cortege, which arrived on the Place Vendome at five o'clock in the evening, followed by an immense crowd, amid cries of "*Vive l'Empereur.*" A few days before his Majesty's departure for Erfurt, the Emperor with the Empress and their households played prisoner's base for the last time. It was in the evening; and footmen bore lighted torches, and followed the players when they went beyond the reach of the light. The Emperor fell once while trying to catch the Empress, and was taken prisoner; but he soon broke bounds and began to run again, and when he was free, carried off Josephine in spite of the protests of the players; and thus ended the last game of prisoner's base that I ever saw the Emperor play.

It had been decided that the Emperor Alexander and the Emperor Napoleon should meet at Erfurt on the 27th of September; and most of the sovereigns forming the Confederation of the Rhine had been invited to be present at this interview, which it was intended should be both magnificent and imposing. Consequently the Duke of Frioul, grand marshal of the palace, sent M. de Canouville, marshal of lodgings of the palace, M. de Beausset, *prefect* of the palace, and two quartermasters to prepare at Erfurt lodgings for all these illustrious visitors, and to organize the grand marshal's service.

The government palace was chosen for the Emperor Napoleon's lodgings, as on account of its size it perfectly suited the Emperor's intention of holding his court there; for the Emperor Alexander, the residence of M. Triebel was prepared, the handsomest in the town; and for S. A. L, the Grand Duke Constantine, that of Senator Remann. Other residences were reserved for the Princes of the Confederation and the persons of their suite; and a detachment of all branches of the service of the Imperial household was established in each of these different lodgings.

There had been sent from the storehouse of the crown a large quantity of magnificent furniture, carpets and tapestry, both Gobelin and la Savonnerie; bronzes, lustres, candelabras, girandoles, Sevres china; in fine, everything which could contribute to the luxurious furnishing of the two Imperial palaces, and those which were to be occupied by the other sovereigns; and a crowd of workmen came from Paris. General Oudinot was appointed Governor of Erfurt, and had under his orders the First regiment of hussars, the Sixth of cuirassiers, and the Seventeenth of light infantry, which the major-general had appointed to compose the garrison. Twenty select police, with a battalion chosen from the finest grenadiers of the guard, were put on duty at the Imperial palaces.

The Emperor, who sought by every means to render this interview at Erfurt as agreeable as possible to the sovereigns for whom he had conceived an affection at Tilsit, wished to have the masterpieces of the French stage played in their honour. This was the amusement most worthy of them that he could procure, so he gave orders that the theatre should be embellished and repaired. M. Dazincourt was appointed director of the theatre, and set out from Paris with Messieurs Talma, Lafon, Saint-Prix, Damas, Despres, Varennes, Lacave; Mesdames Duchesnoir, Raucourt, Talma, Bourgoin, Rose Dupuis, Grosand, and Patrat; and everything was in order before the arrival of the sovereigns.

Napoleon disliked Madame Talma exceedingly, although she displayed most remarkable talent, and this aversion was well known, although I could never discover the cause; and no one was willing to be first to place her name on the list of those selected to go to Erfurt, but M. Talma made so many entreaties that at last consent was given. And then occurred what everybody except M. Talma and his wife had foreseen, that the Emperor, having seen her play once, was much provoked that she had been allowed to come, and had her name struck from the list.

Mademoiselle Bourgoin, who was at that time young and extremely pretty, had at first more success; but it was necessary, in order to accomplish this, that she should conduct herself differently from Madame Talma. As soon as she appeared at the theatre of Erfurt she excited the admiration, and became the object of the attentions, of all the illustrious spectators; and this marked preference gave rise to jealousies, which delighted her greatly, and which she increased to the utmost of her ability by every means in her power. When she was not playing, she took her seat in the theatre magnificently dressed, whereupon all looks were bent on her, and distracted from the stage, to the very great displeasure of the actors, until the Emperor at last perceived these frequent distractions, and put an end to them by forbidding Mademoiselle Bourgoin to appear in the theatre except on the stage.

This measure, which was very wisely taken by his Majesty, put him in the bad graces of Mademoiselle Bourgoin; and another incident added still more to the displeasure of the actress. The two sovereigns attended the theatre together almost every evening, and the Emperor Alexander thought Mademoiselle Bourgoin charming. She was aware of this, and tried by every means to increase the monarch's devotion. One day at last the amorous Czar confided to the Emperor his feelings for Mademoiselle Bourgoin. "I do not advise you to make any advances," said the Emperor Napoleon. "You think that she would refuse me?"

"Oh, no; but tomorrow is the day for the post, and in five days all Paris would know all about your Majesty from head to foot." These words singularly cooled the ardour of the autocrat, who thanked the Emperor for his advice, and said to him, "But from the manner in which your Majesty speaks, I should be tempted to believe that you bear this charming actress some ill-will."

"No, in truth," replied the Emperor, "I do not know anything about her." This conversation took place in his bedroom during the toilet. Alexander left his Majesty perfectly convinced, and Mademoiselle Bourgoin ceased her ogling and her assurance.

His Majesty made his entrance into Erfurt on the morning of the 27th of September, 1808. The King of Saxony, who had arrived first, followed by the Count de Marcolini, the Count de Haag, and the Count de Boze, awaited the Emperor at the foot of the stairs in the governor's palace; after them came the members of the Regency and the municipality of Erfurt, who congratulated him in the usual form. After a short rest, the Emperor mounted his horse, and left Erfurt by the gate of Weimar, making, in passing, a visit to the King of Saxony, and found outside the city the whole garrison arranged in line of battle,—the grenadiers of the guard commanded by M. d'Arquies; the First regiment of hussars by M. de Juniac; the Seventeenth infantry by M. de Cabannes-Puymisson; and the Sixth cuirassiers, the finest body of men imaginable, by Colonel d'Haugeranville. The Emperor reviewed these troops, ordered a change in some dispositions, and then continued on his way to meet the Emperor Alexander.

The latter had set out from Saint Petersburg on the 17th of September; and the King and Queen of Prussia awaited him at Koenigsberg, where he arrived on the 18th. The Duke of Montebello had the honour of receiving him at Bromberg amid a salute of twenty-one cannon. Alighting from his carriage, the Emperor Alexander mounted his horse, accompanied by the Marshals of the Empire, Soult, Duke of Dalmatia, and Lannes, Duke of Montebello, and set off at a gallop to meet the Nansouty division, which awaited him arranged in line of battle. He was welcomed by a new salute, and by oft repeated cries of "Long live the Emperor Alexander." The monarch, while reviewing the different corps which formed this fine division, said to the officers, "I think it a great honour, messieurs, to be amongst such brave men and splendid soldiers."

By orders of Marshal Soult, who simply executed those given by Napoleon, relays of the post had been arranged on all the roads which the Monarch of the North would pass over, and they were forbidden to receive any compensation. At each relay were escorts of dragoons or light cavalry, who rendered military honours to the Czar as he passed.

After having dined with the generals of the Nansouty division, the Emperor of Russia re-entered his carriage, a barouche with two seats, and seated the Duke of Montebello beside him, who afterwards told me with how many marks of esteem and kind feeling the Emperor overwhelmed him during the journey, even arranging the marshal's cloak around his shoulders while he was asleep.

His Imperial Russian Majesty arrived at Weimar the evening of the 26th, and next day continued his journey to Erfurt, escorted by Marshal Soult, his staff, and the superior officers of the Nansouty division, who had not left him since he had started from Bromberg, and met Napoleon a league and a half from Erfurt, to which place the latter had come on horseback for this purpose.

The moment the Czar perceived the Emperor, he left his carriage, and advanced towards his Majesty, who had also alighted from his horse. They embraced each other with the affection of two college friends who meet again after a long absence; then both mounted their horses, as did also the Grand Duke Constantine, and passing at a gallop in front of the regiments, all of which presented arms at their approach, entered the town, while the troops, with an immense crowd collected from twenty leagues around, made the air resound with their acclamations. The Emperor of Russia wore on entering Erfurt the grand decoration of the Legion of Honour, and the Emperor of the French that of Saint Andrew of Russia; and the two sovereigns during their stay continued to show each other these marks of mutual deference, and it was also remarked that in his palace the Emperor always gave the right to Alexander. On the evening of his arrival, by his Majesty's invitation, Alexander gave the countersign to the grand marshal, and it was afterwards given alternately by the two sovereigns.

They went first to the palace of Russia, where they remained an hour; and later, when Alexander came to return the visit of the Emperor, he received him at the foot of the staircase, and accompanied him when he left as far as the entrance of the grand hall. At six o'clock the two sovereigns dined at his Majesty's residence, and it was the same each day. At nine o'clock the Emperor escorted the Emperor of Russia to his palace; and they then held a private conversation, which continued more than an hour, and in the evening the whole city was illuminated. The day after his arrival the Emperor received at his levee the officers of the Czar's household, and granted them the grand entry during the rest of their Stay.

The two sovereigns gave to each other proofs of the most sincere friendship and most confidential intimacy. The Emperor Alexander almost every morning entered his Majesty's bedroom, and conversed freely with him. One day he was examining the Emperor's dressing-case in silver gilt, which cost six thousand *francs*, and was most conveniently arranged and beautifully carved by the goldsmith Biennais, and admired it exceedingly. As soon as he had gone, the Emperor ordered me to have a dressing-case sent to the Czar's palace exactly similar to that which had just been received from Paris.

Another time the Emperor Alexander remarked on the elegance and durability of his Majesty's iron bedstead; and the very next day by his Majesty's orders, conveyed by me, an exactly similar bed was set up in the room of the Emperor of Russia, who was delighted with these polite attentions, and two days after, as an evidence of his satisfaction, ordered M. de Remusat to hand me two handsome diamond rings.

The Czar one day made his toilet in the Emperor's room, and I assisted. I took from the Emperor's linen a white cravat and cambric handkerchief, which I handed him, and for which he thanked me most graciously; he was an exceedingly gentle, good, amiable prince, and extremely polite.

There was an exchange of presents between these illustrious sovereigns. Alexander made the Emperor a present of three superb pelisses of martin-sable, one of which the Emperor gave to his sister Pauline, another to the Princess de Ponte-Corvo; and the third he had lined with green velvet and ornamented with gold lace, and it was this cloak which he constantly wore in Russia. The history of the one which I carried from him to the Princess Pauline is singular enough to be related here, although it may have been already told.

The Princess Pauline showed much pleasure in receiving the Emperor's present, and enjoyed displaying her cloak for the admiration of the household. One day, when she was in the midst of a circle of ladies, to whom she was dilating on the quality and excellence of this fur, M. de Canouville arrived, and the princess asked his opinion of the present she had received from the Emperor. The handsome colonel not appearing as much struck with admiration as she expected, she was somewhat piqued, and exclaimed, "What, *monsieur*, you do not think it exquisite?"

"No, *madame*."

"In order to punish you I wish you to keep this cloak; I give it to you, and require you to wear it; I wish it, you understand." It is probable that there had been some disagreement between her Imperial highness and her *protégé*, and the princess had seized the first means of establishing peace; but however that may be, M. de Canouville needed little entreaty, and the rich fur was carried to his house. A few days after, while the Emperor was holding a review on the Place du Carrousel, M, de Canouville appeared on an unruly horse, which he had great difficulty in controlling. This caused some confusion, and attracted his Majesty's attention, who, glancing at M. de Canouville, saw the cloak which he had given his sister metamorphosed into a hussar's cape. The Emperor had great difficulty in controlling his anger. "M. de Canouville," he cried, in a voice of thunder, "your horse is young, and his blood is too warm; you will go and cool it in Russia." Three days after M. de Canouville had left Paris.

Chapter 43

The Emperor Alexander never tired of showing his regard for actors by presents and compliments; and as for actresses, I have told before how far he would have gone with one of them if Napoleon had not deterred him. Each day the Grand Duke Constantine got up parties of pleasure with Murat and other distinguished persons, at which no expense was spared, and some of these ladies did the honours. And what furs and diamonds they carried away from Erfurt! The two Emperors were not ignorant of all this, and were much amused thereby; and it was the favourite subject of conversation in the morning. Constantine had conceived an especial affection for King Jerome; the king even carried his affection so far as to '*tutoy*' him, and wished him to do the same. "Is it because I am a king," he said one day, "that you are afraid to say thou to me? Come, now, is there any need of formality between friends?" They performed all sorts of college pranks together, even running through the streets at night, knocking and ringing at every door, much delighted when they had waked up some honest bourgeois. As the Emperor was leaving, King Jerome said to the grand duke: "Come, tell me what you wish me to send you from Paris."

"Nothing whatever," replied the grand duke; "your brother has presented me with a magnificent sword; I am satisfied, and desire nothing more."

"But I wish to send you something, so tell me what would give you pleasure."

"Well, send me six *demoiselles* from the Palais Royal."

The play at Erfurt usually began at seven o'clock; but the two Emperors, who always came together, never arrived till half-past seven. At their entrance, all the pit of kings rose to do them honour, and the first piece immediately commenced.

At the representation of Cinna, the Emperor feared that the Czar, who was placed by his side in a box facing the stage, and on the first tier, might not hear very well, as he was somewhat deaf; and consequently gave orders to M. de Remusat, first chamberlain, that a platform should be raised on the floor of the orchestra, and armchairs placed there for Alexander and himself; and on the right and left four handsomely decorated chairs for the King of Saxony and the other sovereigns of the Confederation, while the princes took possession of the box abandoned by their Majesties. By this arrangement the two Emperors found themselves in such a conspicuous position that it was impossible for them to make a movement without being seen by every one. On the 3rd of October *Oedipus* was presented. "All the sovereigns," as the Emperor called them, were present at this representation; and just as the actor pronounced these words in the first scene:

"The friendship of a great man is a gift from the gods:"

The Czar arose, and held out his hand with much grace to the Emperor; and immediately acclamations, which the presence of the sovereigns could not restrain, burst forth from every part of the hall.

On the evening of this same day I prepared the Emperor for bed as usual. All the doors which opened into his sleeping-room were carefully closed, as well as the shutters and windows; and there was consequently no means of entering his Majesty's room except through the chamber in which I slept with Roustan, and a sentinel was also stationed at the foot of the staircase. Every night I slept very calmly, knowing that it was impossible any one could reach Napoleon without waking me; but that night, about two o'clock, while I was sleeping soundly, a strange noise woke me with a start. I rubbed my eyes, and listened with the greatest attention, and, hearing nothing whatever, thought this noise the illusion of a dream, and was just dropping to sleep again, when my ear was struck by low, smothered screams, such as a man might utter who was being strangled. I heard them repeated twice, and in an instant was sitting up straight in bed, my hair on end, and my limbs covered with a cold sweat. Suddenly it occurred to me that the Emperor was being assassinated, and I sprang out of bed and woke Roustan; and as the cries now recommenced with added intensity, I opened the door as cautiously as my agitation allowed, and entered the sleeping-room, and with a hasty glance assured myself that no one could have entered. On advancing towards the bed, I perceived his Majesty extended across it, in a position denoting great agony, the drapery and bed-covering thrown off, and his whole body in a frightful condition of nervous contraction. From his open mouth escaped inarticulate sounds, his breathing appeared greatly oppressed, and one of his hands, tightly clinched, lay on the pit of his stomach. I was terrified at the sight, and called him. He did not reply; again, once, twice even, still no reply. At last I concluded to shake him gently; and at this the Emperor awoke with a loud cry, saying, "What is it? What is it?" then sat up and opened his eyes wide; upon which I told him that, seeing him tormented with a horrible nightmare, I had taken the liberty of waking him. "And you did well, my dear Constant," interrupted his Majesty. "Ah, my friend, I have had a frightful dream; a bear was tearing open my breast, and devouring my heart!" Thereupon the Emperor rose, and, while I put his bed in order, walked about the room. He was obliged to change his shirt, which was wet with perspiration, and at length again retired.

The next day, when he woke, he told me that it was long before he could fall to sleep again, so vivid and terrible was the impression made on him. He long retained the memory of this dream, and often spoke of it, each time trying to draw from it different conclusions, according to circumstances.

As to myself, I avow I was struck with the coincidence of the compliment of Alexander at the theatre and this frightful nightmare, especially as the Emperor was not subject to disturbances of this kind. I do not know whether his Majesty related his dream to the Emperor of Russia.

On the 6th of October their Majesties attended a hunting-party which the Grand Duke of Weimar prepared for them in the forest of Ettersbourg. The Emperor set out from Erfurt at noon, with the Emperor of Russia in the same coach. They arrived in the forest at one o'clock, and found prepared for them a hunting-pavilion, which had been erected expressly for this occasion, and was very handsomely decorated. This pavilion was divided into three parts, separated by open columns; that in the middle, raised higher than the others, formed a pretty room, arranged and furnished for the two Emperors. Around the pavilion were placed numerous orchestras, which played inspiriting airs, with which were mingled the acclamations of an immense crowd, who had been attracted by a desire to see the Emperor.

The two sovereigns were received on their descent from their carriage by the Grand Duke of Weimar and his son, the hereditary prince, Charles Frederic; while the King of Bavaria, King of Saxony, King of Wurtemberg, Prince William of Prussia, the Princes of Mecklenburg, the Prince Primate, and the Duke of Oldenburg awaited them at the entrance to the saloon.

The Emperor had in his suite the Prince of Neuchatel; the Prince of Benevento; the grand marshal of the palace, Duke de Frioul; General Caulaincourt, Duke of Vicenza; the Duke of Rovigo; General Lauriston, his Majesty's *aide-de-camp*; General Nansouty, first equerry; the chamberlain, Eugene de Montesquiou; the Count de Beausset, *prefect* of the palace; and M. Cavaletti.

The Emperor of Russia was accompanied by the Grand Duke Constantine; the Count Tolstoi, grand marshal; and Count Oggeroski, *aide-de-camp* to his Majesty.

The hunt lasted nearly two hours, during which time about sixty stags and roebucks were killed. The space in which these poor animals had to run was enclosed by netting, in order that the monarchs might shoot them at pleasure, without disturbing themselves while seated in the windows of the pavilion. I have never seen anything more absurd than hunts of this sort, which, nevertheless, give those who engage in them a reputation as fine shots. What skill is there in killing an animal which the gamekeepers, so to speak, take by the ears and place in front of your gun.

The Emperor of Russia was near-sighted, and this infirmity had deterred him from an amusement which he would have enjoyed very much; but that day, however, he wished to make the attempt, and, having expressed this. wish, the Duke of Montebello handed him a gun, and M. de Beauterne had the honour of giving the Emperor his first lesson. A stag was driven so as to pass within about eight steps of Alexander, who brought him down at the first shot.

After the hunt their Majesties repaired to the palace of Weimar; and the reigning duchess received them, as they alighted from their carriages, accompanied by her whole court. The Emperor saluted the duchess affectionately, remembering that he had seen her two years before under very different circumstances, which I mentioned in its place.

The Duke of Weimar had requested from the grand marshal French cooks to prepare the Emperor's dinner, but the Emperor preferred being served in the German style.

Their Majesties invited to dine with them the Duke and Duchess of Weimar, the Queen of Westphalia, the King of Wurtemberg, the King of Saxony, the Grand Duke Constantine, Prince William of Prussia, the Prince Primate, the Prince of Neuchatel, Prince Talleyrand, the Duke of Oldenburg, the hereditary Prince of Weimar, and the Prince of Mecklenburg-Schwerin.

After this dinner there was a play, followed by a ball, the play being at the town theatre, where the ordinary comedians of his Majesty presented the death of Caesar; and the ball, at the ducal palace. The Emperor Alexander opened the ball with the Queen of Westphalia, to the great astonishment of every one; for it was well known that this monarch had never danced since his accession to the throne, conduct which the older men of the court thought very praiseworthy, holding the opinion that a sovereign occupies too high a place to share in the tastes and take pleasure in amusements common to the rest of mankind. Except this, however, there was nothing in the ball of Weimar to scandalize them, as they did not dance, but promenaded in couples, whilst the orchestra played marches.

The morning of the next day their Majesties entered carriages to visit Mount Napoleon, near Jena, where a splendid breakfast was prepared for them under a tent which the Duke of Weimar had erected on the identical spot where the Emperor's bivouac stood on the day of the battle of Jena. After breakfast the two Emperors ascended a temporary pavilion which had been erected on Mount Napoleon; this pavilion, which was very large, had been decorated with plans of the battle. A deputation from the town and university of Jena arrived, and were received by their Majesties; and the Emperor inquired of the deputies the most minute particulars relating to their town, its resources, and the manners and character of its inhabitants; questioned them on the approximate damages which the military hospital, which had been so long left with them, had caused the inhabitants of Jena; inquired the names of those who had suffered most from fire and war, and gave orders that a gratuity should be distributed among them, and the small proprietors entirely indemnified. His Majesty informed himself with much interest of the condition of the Catholic worship, and promised to endow the vicarage in perpetuity, granting three hundred thousand *francs* for immediate necessities, and promising to give still more.

After having visited, on horseback, the positions which the two armies had held the evening before, and on the day of, the battle of Jena, as well as the plain of Aspolda, on which the duke had prepared a hunt with guns, the two Emperors returned to Erfurt, which they reached at five o'clock in the evening, almost at the very moment the grand hereditary duke of Baden and the Princess Stephanie arrived.

During the entire visit of the sovereigns to the battlefield, the Emperor most graciously made explanations to the young Czar, to which he listened with the greatest interest. His Majesty seemed to take pleasure in explaining at length, first, the plan which he had formed and carried out at Jena, and afterwards the various plans of his other campaigns, the manoeuvres which he had executed, his usual tactics, and, in fine, his whole ideas on the art of war. The Emperor thus, for several hours, carried on the whole conversation alone; and his royal audience paid him as much attention as scholars, eager to learn, pay to the instructions of their teacher.

When his Majesty returned to his apartment, I heard Marshal Berthier say to him, "Sire, are you not afraid that the sovereigns may some day use to advantage against you all that you have just taught them? Your Majesty just now seemed to forget what you formerly told us, that it is necessary to act with our allies as if they were afterwards to be our enemies."

"Berthier," replied the Emperor, smiling, "that is a good observation on your part, and I thank you for it; I really believe I have made you think I was an idiot. You think, then," continued his Majesty, pinching sharply one of the Prince de Neuchatel's ears, "that I committed the indiscretion of giving them whips with which to return and flog us? Calm yourself, I did not tell them all."

The Emperor's table at Erfurt was in the form of a half-moon; and at the upper end, and consequently at the rounded part, of this table their Majesties were seated, and on the right and left the sovereigns of the Confederation according to their rank. The side facing their Majesties was always empty; and there stood M. de Beausset, the *prefect* of the palace, who relates in his Memoirs that one day he overheard the following conversation:

"On that day the subject of conversation was the Golden Bull, which, until the establishment of the Confederation of the Rhine, had served as a constitution, and had regulated the law for the election of emperors, the number and rank of the electors, etc. The Prince Primate entered into some details regarding this Golden Bull, which he said was made in 1409; whereupon the Emperor Napoleon pointed out to him that the date which was assigned to the Golden Bull was not correct, and that it was proclaimed in 1336, during the reign of the Emperor Charles IV. 'That is true, Sire,' replied the Prince Primate I was mistaken; but how does it happen that your Majesty is so well acquainted with these matters?'—'When I was a mere sub-lieutenant in the artillery, said Napoleon,—at this beginning, there was on the part of the guests a marked movement of interest, and he continued, smiling,—when I had the honour to be simply sub-lieutenant in the artillery I remained three years in the garrison at Valence, and, as I cared little for society, led a very retired life. By fortunate chance I had lodgings with a kind and intelligent bookseller. I read and re-read his library during the three years I remained in the garrison and have forgotten nothing, even matters which have had no connection with my position. Nature, besides, has given me a good memory for figures, and it often happens with my ministers that I can give them details and the sum total of accounts they presented long since.'"

A few days before his departure from Erfurt, the Emperor bestowed the cross of the Legion of Honour on M. de Bigi, commandant of arms at this place; M. Vegel, burgomaster of Jena; Messrs. Weiland and Goethe; M. Starlk, senior physician at Jena. He gave to General Count Tolstoi, ambassador from Russia, who had been recalled from this post by his sovereign to take a command in the army, the grand decoration of the Legion of Honour; to M. the dean Meimung, who had said mass twice at the palace, a ring of brilliants, with the cipher N surmounted by a crown; and a hundred napoleons to the two priests who had assisted him; finally, to the grand marshal of the palace, Count Tolstoi, the beautiful Gobelin tapestry, Savonnerie carpets, and Sevres porcelain, which had been brought from Paris to furnish the palace of Erfurt. The minister's grand officers, and officers of Alexander's suite, received from his Majesty magnificent presents; and the Emperor Alexander did likewise in regard to the persons attached to his Majesty. He gave the Duke of Vicenza the grand cordon of Saint Andrew, and a badge of the same order set in diamonds to the Princes of Benevento and Neuchatel.

Charmed by the talent of the French comedians, especially that of Talma, the Emperor Alexander sent very handsome presents to her as well as all her companions; he sent compliments to the actresses, and to the director, M. Dazincourt, whom he did not forget in his distribution of gifts. This interview at Erfurt, which was so brilliant with illuminations, splendour, and luxury, ended on the 14th of October; and all the great personages whom it had attracted left between the 8th and the 14th of October.

The day of his departure the Emperor gave an audience, after his toilet, to Baron Vincent, envoy extraordinary of Austria, and sent by him a letter to his sovereign. At eleven o'clock the Emperor of Russia came to his Majesty, who received him, and reconducted him to his residence with great ceremony; and soon after his Majesty repaired to the Russian palace, followed by his whole suite. After mutual compliments they entered the carriage together, and did not part till they reached the spot on the road from Weimar where they had met on their arrival. There they embraced each other affectionately and separated; and the 18th of October, at half-past nine in the evening, the Emperor was at Saint-Cloud, having made the whole trip incognito.

Chapter 44

His Majesty remained only ten days at Saint-Cloud, passed two or three of these in Paris at the opening of the session of the Corps Legislatif, and at noon on the 29th set out a second time for Bayonne.

The Empress, who to her great chagrin could not accompany the Emperor, sent for me on the morning of his departure, and renewed in most touching accents the same recommendations which she made on all his journeys, for the character of the Spaniards made her timid and fearful as to his safety.

Their parting was sad and painful; for the Empress was exceedingly anxious to accompany him, and the Emperor had the greatest difficulty in satisfying her, and making her understand that this was impossible. Just as he was setting out he returned to his dressing-room a moment, and told me to unbutton his coat and vest; and I saw the Emperor pass around his neck between his vest and shirt a black silk ribbon on which was hung a kind of little bag about the size of a large hazel-nut, covered with black silk. Though I did not then know what this bag contained, when he returned to Paris he gave it to me to keep; and I found that this bag had a pleasant feeling, as under the silk covering was another of skin. I shall hereafter tell for what purpose the Emperor wore this bag.

I set out with a sad heart. The recommendations of her Majesty the Empress, and fears which I could not throw off, added to the fatigue of these repeated journeys, all conspired to produce feelings of intense sadness, which was reflected on almost all the countenances of the Imperial household; while the officers said among themselves that the combats in the North were trifling compared with those which awaited us in Spain.

We arrived on the 3rd of November at the chateau of Marrac, and four days after were at Vittoria in the midst of the French army, where the Emperor found his brother and a few grandees of Spain who had not yet deserted his cause.

The arrival of his Majesty electrified the troops; and a part of the enthusiasm manifested, a very small part it is true, penetrated into the heart of the king, and somewhat renewed his courage. They set out almost immediately, in order to at once establish themselves temporarily at Burgos, which had been seized by main force and pillaged in a few hours, since the inhabitants had abandoned it, and left to the garrison the task of stopping the French as long as possible.

The Emperor occupied the archiepiscopal palace, a magnificent building situated in a large square on which the grenadiers of the Imperial Guard bivouacked. This bivouac presented a singular scene. Immense kettles, which had been found in the convents, hung, full of mutton, poultry, rabbits, etc., above a fire which was replenished from time to time with furniture, guitars, or mandolins, and around which grenadiers, with pipes in their mouths, were gravely seated in gilded chairs covered with crimson damask, while they intently watched the kettles as they simmered, and communicated to each other their conjectures on the campaign which had just opened.

The Emperor remained ten or twelve days at Burgos, and then gave orders to march on Madrid, which place could have been reached by way of Valladolid, and the road was indeed safer and better; but the Emperor wished to seize the Pass of Somo-Sierra, an imposing position with natural fortifications which had always been regarded as impregnable. This pass, between two mountain peaks, defended the capital, and was guarded by twelve thousand insurgents, and twelve pieces of cannon placed so advantageously that they could do as much injury as thirty or forty elsewhere, and were, in fact, a sufficient obstacle to delay even the most formidable army; but who could then oppose any hindrance to the march of the Emperor?

On the evening of the 29th of November we arrived within three leagues of this formidable defile, at a village called Basaguillas; and though the weather was very cold, the Emperor did not lie down, but passed the night in his tent, writing, wrapped in the pelisse which the Emperor Alexander had given him. About three o'clock in the morning he came to warm himself by the bivouac fire where I had seated myself, as I could no longer endure the cold and dampness of a cellar which had been assigned as my lodging, and where my bed was only a few handfuls of straw, filled with manure.

At eight o'clock in the morning the position was attacked and carried, and the next day we arrived before Madrid.

The Emperor established his headquarters at the chateau of Champ-Martin, a pleasure house situated a quarter of a league from the town, and belonging to the mother of the Duke of Infantado; and the army camped around this house. The day after our arrival, the owner came in tears to entreat of his Majesty a revocation of the fatal decree which put her son outside the protection of the law; the Emperor did all he could to reassure her, but he could promise her nothing, as the order was general.

We had some trouble in capturing this town; in the first place, because his Majesty recommended the greatest moderation in making the attack, not wishing, as he said, to present to his brother a burned-up city; in the second place, because the Grand Duke of Berg during his stay at Madrid had fortified the palace of Retiro, and the Spanish insurgents had entrenched themselves there, and defended it most courageously. The town had no other defence, and was surrounded only by an old wall, almost exactly similar to that of Paris, consequently at the end of three days it was taken; but the Emperor preferred not to enter, and still resided at Champ-Martin, with the exception of one day when he came incognito and in disguise, to visit the queen's palace and the principal districts.

One striking peculiarity of the Spaniards is the respect they have always shown for everything relating to royalty, whether they regard it as legitimate or not. When King Joseph left Madrid the palace was closed, and the government established itself in a passably good building which had been used as the post-office. From this time no one entered the palace except the servants, who had orders to clean it from time to time; not a piece of furniture even, not a book, was moved. The portrait of Napoleon on Mont St. Bernard, David's masterpiece, remained hanging in the grand reception hall, and the queen's portrait opposite, exactly as the king had placed them; and even the cellars were religiously respected. The apartments of King Charles had also remained untouched, and not one of the watches in his immense collection had been removed.

The act of clemency which his Majesty showed toward the Marquis of Saint-Simon, a grandee of Spain, marked in an especial manner the entrance of the French troops into Madrid. The Marquis of Saint-Simon, a French emigrant, had been in the service of Spain since the emigration, and had the command of a part of the capital. The post which he defended was exactly in front of that which the Emperor commanded at the gates of Madrid, and he had held out long after all the other leaders had surrendered.

The Emperor, impatient at being so long withstood at this point, gave orders to make a still more vigorous charge; and in this the marquis was taken prisoner. In his extreme anger the Emperor sent him to be tried before a military commission, who ordered him to be shot; and this order was on the point of being executed, when Mademoiselle de Saint-Simon, a charming young person, threw herself at his Majesty's feet, and her father's pardon was quickly granted.

The king immediately re-entered his capital; and with him returned the noble families of Madrid, who had withdrawn from the stirring scenes enacted at the centre of the insurrection; and soon balls, fetes, festivities, and plays were resumed as of yore.

The Emperor left Champ-Martin on the 22nd of December, and directed his march towards Astorga, with the intention of meeting the English, who had just landed at Corunna; but dispatches sent to Astorga by a courier from Paris decided him to return to France, and he consequently gave orders to set out for Valladolid.

We found the road from Benavente to Astorga covered with corpses, slain horses, artillery carriages, and broken wagons, and at every step met detachments of soldiers with torn clothing, without shoes, and, indeed, in a most deplorable condition. These unfortunates were all fleeing towards Astorga, which they regarded as a port of safety, but which soon could not contain them all. It was terrible weather, the snow falling so fast that it was almost blinding; and, added to this, I was ill, and suffered greatly during this painful journey.

The Emperor while at Tordesillas had established his headquarters in the buildings outside the convent of Saint-Claire, and the abbess of this convent was presented to his Majesty. She was then more than sixty-five years old, and from the age of ten years back never left this place. Her intelligent and refined conversation made a most agreeable impression on the Emperor, who inquired what were her wishes, and granted each one.

We arrived at Valladolid the 6th of January, 1809, and found it in a state of great disorder. Two or three days after our arrival, a cavalry officer was assassinated by Dominican monks; and as Hubert, one of our comrades, was passing in the evening through a secluded street, three men threw themselves on him and wounded him severely; and he would doubtless have been killed if the grenadiers of the guard had not hastened to his assistance, and delivered him from their hands. It was the monks again. At length the Emperor, much incensed, gave orders that the convent of the Dominicans should be searched; and in a well was found the corpse of the aforesaid officer, in the midst of a considerable mass of bones, and the convent was immediately suppressed by his Majesty's orders; he even thought at one time of issuing the same rigorous orders against all the convents of the city. He took time for reflection, however, and contented himself by appointing an audience, at which all the monks of Valladolid were to appear before him. On the appointed day they came; not all, however, but deputations from each convent, who prostrated themselves at the Emperor's feet, while he showered reproaches upon them, called them assassins and brigands, and said they all deserved to be hung. These poor men listened in silence and humility to the terrible language of the irritated conqueror whom their patience alone could appease; and finally, the Emperor's anger having exhausted itself, he grew calmer, and at last, struck by the reflection that it was hardly just to heap abuse on men thus prostrate on their knees and uttering not a word in their own defence, he left the group of officers who surrounded him, and advanced into the midst of the monks, making them a sign to rise from their supplicating posture; and as these good men obeyed him, they kissed the skirts of his coat, and pressed around him with an eagerness most alarming to the persons of his Majesty's suite; for had there been among these devotees any Dominican, nothing surely could have been easier than an assassination.

During the Emperor's stay at Valladolid, I had with the grand marshal a disagreement of which I retain most vivid recollections, as also of the Emperor's intervention wherein he displayed both justice and good-will towards me. These are the facts of the case: one morning the Duke de Frioul, encountering me in his Majesty's apartments, inquired in a very brusque tone (he was very much excited) if I had ordered the carriage to be ready, to which I replied in a most respectful manner that they were always ready. Three times the duke repeated the same question, raising his voice still more each time; and three times I made him the same reply, always in the same respectful manner. "Oh, you fool!" said he at last, "you do not understand, then."

"That arises evidently, *Monseigneur*, from your Excellency's imperfect explanations!" Upon which he explained that he was speaking of a new carriage which had come from Paris that very day, a fact of which I was entirely ignorant. I was on the point of explaining this to His Excellency; but without deigning to listen, the grand marshal rushed out of the room exclaiming, swearing, and addressing me in terms to which I was totally unaccustomed. I followed him as far as his own room in order to make an explanation; but when he reached his door he entered, and slammed it in my face.

In spite of all this I entered a few moments later; but His Excellency had forbidden his *valet de chambre* to introduce me, saying that he had nothing to say to me, nor to hear from me, all of which was repeated to me in a very harsh and contemptuous manner.

Little accustomed to such experiences, and entirely unnerved, I went to the Emperor's room; and when his Majesty entered I was still so agitated that my face was wet with tears. His Majesty wished to know what had happened, and I related to him the attack which had just been made upon me by the grand marshal. "You are very foolish to cry," said the Emperor; "calm yourself, and say to the grand marshal that I wish to speak to him."

His Excellency came at once in response to the Emperor's invitation, and I announced him. "See," said he, pointing to me, "see into what a state you have thrown this fellow! What has he done to be thus treated?" The grand marshal bowed without replying, but with a very dissatisfied air; and the Emperor went on to say that he should have given me his orders more clearly, and that any one was excusable for not executing an order not plainly given. Then turning toward me, his Majesty said, "Monsieur Constant, you may be certain this will not occur again."

This simple affair furnishes a reply to many false accusations against the Emperor. There was an immense distance between the grand marshal of the palace and the simple *valet de chambre* of his Majesty, and yet the marshal was reprimanded for a wrong done to the *valet de chambre*.

The Emperor showed the utmost impartiality in meting out justice in his domestic affairs; and never was the interior of a palace better governed than his, owing to the fact that in his household he alone was master.

The grand marshal felt unkindly toward me for sometime after; but, as I have already said, he was an excellent man, his bad humour soon passed away, and so completely, that on my return to Paris he requested me to stand for him at the baptism of the child of my father-in-law, who had begged him to be its godfather; the godmother was Josephine, who was kind enough to choose my wife to represent her. M. le Duke de Frioul did things with as much nobility and magnanimity as grace; and afterwards I am glad to be able to state in justice to his memory, he eagerly seized every occasion to be useful to me, and to make me forget the discomfort his temporary excitement had caused me.

I fell ill at Valladolid with a violent fever a few days before his Majesty's departure. On the day appointed for leaving, my illness was at its height; aid as the Emperor feared that the journey might increase, or at any rate prolong, my illness, he forbade my going, and set out without me, recommending to the persons whom he left at Valladolid to take care of my health. When I had gotten somewhat better I was told that his Majesty had left, whereupon I could no longer be controlled, and against my physician's orders, and in spite of my feebleness, in spite of everything, in fact, had myself placed in a carriage and set out. This was wise; for hardly had I put Valladolid two leagues behind me, than I felt better, and the fever left me. I arrived at Paris five or six days after the Emperor, just after his Majesty had appointed the Count Montesquiou grand chamberlain in place of Prince Talleyrand, whom I met that very day, and who seemed in no wise affected by this disgrace, perhaps he was consoled by the dignity of vice-grand elector which was bestowed on him in exchange.

Chapter 45

The Emperor arrived at Paris on the 23rd of January, and passed the remainder of the winter there, with the exception of a few days spent at Rambouillet and Saint-Cloud.

On the very day of his arrival in Paris, although he must have been much fatigued by an almost uninterrupted ride from Valladolid, the Emperor visited the buildings of the Louvre and the Rue de Rivoli.

His mind was full of what he had seen at Madrid, and repeated suggestions to M. Fontaine and the other architects showed plainly his desire to make the Louvre the finest palace in the world. His Majesty then had a report made him as to the chateau of Chambord, which he wished to present to the Prince of Neuchatel. M. Fontaine found that repairs sufficient to make this place a comfortable residence would amount to 1,700,000 *francs*, as the buildings were in a state of decay, and it had hardly been touched since the death of Marshal Sage.

His Majesty passed the two months and a half of his stay working in his cabinet, which he rarely left, and always unwillingly; his amusements being, as always, the theatre and concerts. He loved music passionately, especially Italian music, and like all great amateurs was hard to please. He would have much liked to sing had he been able, but he had no voice, though this did not prevent his humming now and then pieces which struck his fancy; and as these little reminiscences usually recurred to him in the mornings, he regaled me with them while he was being dressed. The air that I have heard him thus mutilate most frequently was that of The Marseillaise. The Emperor also whistled sometimes, but very rarely; and the air, *'Malbrook s'en va-t-en guerre'*, whistled by his Majesty was an unerring announcement to me of his approaching departure for the army. I remember that he never whistled so much, and was never so gay, as just before he set out for the Russian campaign.

His Majesty's, favourite singer were Crescentini and Madame

Grassini. I saw Crescentini's debut at Paris in the role of Romeo, in Romeo and Juliet. He came preceded by a reputation as the first singer of Italy; and this reputation was found to be well deserved, notwithstanding all the prejudices he had to overcome, for I remember well the disparaging statements made concerning him before his debut at the court theatre. According to these self-appointed connoisseurs, he was a bawler without taste, without method, a maker of absurd trills, an unimpassioned actor of little intelligence, and many other things besides. He knew, when he appeared on the stage, how little disposed in his favour his audience were, yet he showed not the slightest embarrassment; this, and his noble, dignified mien, agreeably surprised those who expected from what they had been told to behold an awkward man with an ungainly figure. A murmur of approbation ran through the hall on his appearance; and electrified by this welcome, he gained all hearts from the first act. His movements were full of grace and dignity; he had a perfect knowledge of the scene, modest gestures perfectly in harmony with the dialogue, and a countenance on which all shades of passion were depicted with the most astonishing accuracy; and all these rare and precious qualities combined to give to the enchanting accents of this artist a charm of which it is impossible to give an idea.

At each scene the interest he inspired became more marked, until in the third act the emotion and delight of the spectator were carried almost to frenzy. In this act, played almost solely by Crescentini, this admirable singer communicated to the hearts of his audience all that is touching and, pathetic in a love expressed by means of delicious melody, and by all that grief and despair can find sublime in song.

The Emperor was enraptured, and sent Crescentini a considerable compensation, accompanied by most flattering testimonials of the pleasure he had felt in hearing him.

On this day, as always when they played together afterwards, Crescentini was admirably supported by Madame Grassini, a woman of superior talent, and who possessed the most astonishing voice ever heard in the theatre. She and Madame Barilli then divided the admiration of the public.

The very evening or the day after the debut of Crescentini, the French stage suffered an irreparable loss in the death of Dazincourt, only sixty years of age. The illness of which he died had begun on his return from Erfurt, and was long and painful; and yet the public, to whom this great comedian had so long given such pleasure, took no notice of him after it was found his sickness was incurable and his death certain. Formerly when a highly esteemed actor was kept from his place for some time by illness (and who deserved more esteem than Dazincourt?), the pit was accustomed to testify its regret by inquiring every day as to the condition of the afflicted one, and at the end of each representation the actor whose duty it was to announce the play for the next day gave the audience news of his comrade. This was not done for Dazincourt, and the pit thus showed ingratitude to him.

I liked and esteemed sincerely Dazincourt, whose acquaintance I had made several years before his death; and few men better deserved or so well knew how to gain esteem and affection. I will not speak of his genius, which rendered him a worthy successor of Preville, whose pupil and friend he was, for all his contemporaries remember Figaro as played by Dazincourt; but I will speak of the nobility of his character, of his generosity, and his well-tested honour. It would seem that his birth and education should have kept him from the theatre, where circumstances alone placed him; but he was able to protect himself against the seductions of his situation, and in the greenroom, and in the midst of domestic intrigues, remained a man of good character and pure manners. He was welcomed in the best society, where he soon became a favourite by his piquant sallies, as much as by his good manners and urbanity, for he amused without reminding that he was a comedian.

At the end of February his Majesty went to stay for some time at the palace of the Elysee; and there I think was signed the marriage contract of one of his best lieutenants, Marshal Augereau, recently made Duke of Castiglione, with Mademoiselle Bourlon de Chavanges, the daughter of an old superior officer; and there also was rendered the imperial decree which gave to the Princess Eliza the grand duchy of Tuscany, with the title of grand duchess.

About the middle of March, the Emperor passed several days at Rambouillet; there were held some exciting hunts, in one of which his Majesty himself brought to bay and killed a stag near the pool of Saint-Hubert. There was also a ball and concert, in which appeared Crescentini, Mesdames Grassini, Barelli, and several celebrated virtuosos, and lastly Talma recited.

On the 13th of April, at four o'clock in the morning, the Emperor having received news of another invasion of Bavaria by the Austrians, set out for Strasburg with the Empress, whom he left in that city; and on the 15th, at eleven o'clock in the morning, he passed the Rhine at the head of his army. The Empress did not long remain alone, as the Queen of Holland and her sons, the Grand Duchess of Baden and her husband, soon joined her.

The splendid campaign of 1809 at once began. It is known how glorious it was, and that one of its least glorious victories was the capture of Vienna.

At Ratisbon, on the 23rd of April, the Emperor received in his right foot a spent ball, which gave him quite a severe bruise. I was with the service when several grenadiers hastened to tell me that his Majesty was wounded, upon which I hastened to him, and arrived while M. Yvan was dressing the contusion. The Emperor's boot was cut open, and laced up, and he remounted his horse immediately; and, though several of the generals insisted on his resting, he only replied: "My friends, do you not know that it is necessary for me to see everything?" The enthusiasm of the soldiers cannot be expressed when they learned that their chief had been wounded, though his wound was not dangerous. "The Emperor is exposed like us," they said; "he is not a coward, not he." The papers did not mention this occurrence.

Before entering a battle, the Emperor always ordered that, in case he was wounded, every possible measure should be taken to conceal it from his troops. "Who knows," said he, "what terrible confusion might be produced by such news? To my life is attached the destiny of a great Empire. Remember this, gentlemen; and if I am wounded, let no one know it, if possible. If I am slain, try to win the battle without me; there will be time enough to tell it afterwards."

Two weeks after the capture of Ratisbon, I was in advance of his Majesty on the road to Vienna, alone in a carriage with an officer of the household, when we suddenly heard frightful screams in a house on the edge of the road. I gave orders to stop at once, and we alighted; and, on entering the house, found several soldiers, or rather stragglers, as there are in all armies, who, paying no attention to the alliance between France and Bavaria, were treating most cruelly a family which lived in this house, and consisted of an old grandmother, a young man, three children, and a young girl.

Our embroidered coats had a happy effect on these madmen, whom we threatened with the Emperor's anger; and we succeeded in driving them out of the house, and soon after took our departure, overwhelmed with thanks. In the evening I spoke to the Emperor of what I had done; and he approved highly, saying, "It cannot be helped. There are always some cowardly fellows in the army; and they are the ones who do the mischief. A brave and good soldier would blush to do such things!"

I had occasion, in the beginning of these Memoirs, to speak of the steward, M. Pfister, one of his Majesty's most faithful servants, and

Augereau

also one of those to whom his Majesty was most attached. M. Pfister had followed him to Egypt, and had faced countless dangers in his service. The day of the battle of Landshut, which either preceded or followed very closely the taking of Ratisbon this poor man became insane, rushed out of his tent, and concealed himself in a wood near the field of battle, after taking off all his clothing. At the end of a few hours his Majesty asked for M. Pfister. He was sought for, and every one was questioned; but no one could tell what had become of him. The Emperor, fearing that he might have been taken prisoner, sent an orderly officer to the Austrians to recover his steward, and propose an exchange; but the officer returned, saying that the Austrians had not seen M. Pfister. The Emperor, much disquieted, ordered a search to be made in the neighbourhood; and by this means the poor fellow was discovered entirely naked, as I have said, cowering behind a tree, in a frightful condition, his body torn by thorns. He was brought back, and having become perfectly quiet, was thought to be well, and resumed his duties; but a short time after our return to Paris he had a new attack. The character of his malady was exceedingly obscene; and he presented himself before the Empress Josephine in such a state of disorder, and with such indecent gestures, that it was necessary to take precautions in regard to him. He was confided to the care of the wise Doctor Esquirol, who, in spite of his great skill, could not effect a cure. I went to see him often. He had no more violent attacks; but his brain was diseased, and though he heard and understood perfectly, his replies were those of a real madman. He never lost his devotion to the Emperor, spoke of him incessantly, and imagined himself on duty near him. One day he told me with a most mysterious air that he wished to confide to me a terrible secret, the plot of a conspiracy against his Majesty's life, handing me at the same time a note for his Majesty, with a package of about twenty scraps of paper, which he had scribbled off himself, and thought were the details of the plot. Another time he handed me, for the Emperor, a handful of little stones, which he called diamonds of great value. "There is more than a million in what I hand you," said he. The Emperor, whom I told of my visits, was exceedingly touched by the continued monomania of this poor unfortunate, whose every thought, every act, related to his old master, and who died without regaining his reason.

On the 10th of May, at nine o'clock in the morning, the first line of defence of the Austrian capital was attacked and taken by Marshal Oudinot the *faubourgs* surrendering at discretion. The Duke of Montebello then advanced on the esplanade at the head of his division; but the gates having been closed, the garrison poured a frightful discharge from the top of the ramparts, which fortunately however killed only a very small number. The Duke of Montebello summoned the garrison to surrender the town, but the response of the Archduke Maximilian was that he would defend Vienna with his last breath; which reply was conveyed to the Emperor.

After taking counsel with his generals, his Majesty charged Colonel Lagrange to bear a new demand to the archduke; but the poor colonel had hardly entered the town than he was attacked by the infuriated populace. General O'Reilly saved his life by having him carried away by his soldiers; but the Archduke Maximilian, in order to defy the Emperor still further, paraded in triumph in the midst of the national guard the individual who has struck the first blow at the bearer of the French summons. This attempt, which had excited the indignation of many of the Viennese themselves, did not change his Majesty's intentions, as he wished to carry his moderation and kindness as far as possible; and he wrote to the archduke by the Prince of Neuchatel the following letter, a copy of which accidentally fell into my hands:

> The Prince de Neuchatel to his Highness the Archduke Maximilian, commanding the town of Vienna,
>
> His Majesty the Emperor and King desires to spare this large and worthy population the calamities with which it is threatened, and charges me to represent to your Highness, that if he continues the attempt to defend this place, it will cause the destruction of one of the finest cities of Europe. In every country where he has waged war, my sovereign has manifested his anxiety to avoid the disasters which armies bring on the population. Your Highness must be persuaded that his Majesty is much grieved to see this town, which he has the glory of having already saved, on the point of being destroyed. Nevertheless, contrary to the established usage of fortresses, your Highness has fired your cannon from the city walls, and these cannon may kill, not an enemy of your sovereign, but the wives or children of his most devoted servants. If your Highness prolongs the attempt to defend the place, his Majesty will be compelled to begin his preparations for attack; and the ruin of this immense capital will be consummated in thirty-six hours, by the shells and bombs from our batteries, as the outskirts of the town will be destroyed by the effect of yours. His Majesty does not

doubt that these considerations will influence your Highness to renounce a determination which will only delay for a short while the capture of the place. If, however, your Highness has decided not to pursue a course which will save the town from destruction, its population plunged by your fault into such terrible misfortunes will become, instead of faithful subjects, the enemies of your house."

This letter did not deter the grand duke from persisting in his defence; and this obstinacy exasperated the Emperor to such a degree that he at last gave orders to place two batteries in position, and within an hour cannonballs and shells rained upon the town. The inhabitants, with true German indifference, assembled on the hillsides to watch the effect of the fires of attack and defence, and appeared much interested in the sight. A few cannonballs had already fallen in the court of the Imperial palace when a flag of truce came out of the town to announce that the Archduchess Marie Louise had been unable to accompany her father, and was ill in the palace, and consequently exposed to danger from the artillery; and the Emperor immediately gave orders to change the direction of the firing so that the bombs and balls would pass over the palace. The archduke did not long hold out against such a sharp and energetic attack, but fled, abandoning Vienna to the conquerors.

On the 12th of May the Emperor made his entrance into Vienna, one month after the occupation of Munich by the Austrians. This circumstance made a deep impression, and did much to foster the superstitious ideas which many of the troops held in regard to the person of their chief. "See," said one, "he needed only the time necessary for the journey. That man must be a god."

"He is a devil rather," said the Austrians, whose stupefaction was indescribable. They had reached a point when many allowed the arms to be taken out of their hands without making the least resistance, or without even attempting to fly, so deep was their conviction that the Emperor and his guard were not men, and that sooner or later they must fall into the power of these supernatural enemies.

Chapter 46

The Emperor did not remain in Vienna, but established his headquarters at the chateau of Schoenbrunn, an imperial residence situated about half a league from the town; and the ground in front of the chateau was arranged for the encampment of the guard. The chateau of Schoenbrunn, erected by the Empress Maria Theresa in 1754, and situated in a commanding position, is built in a very irregular, and defective, but at the same time majestic, style of architecture. In order to reach it, there has been thrown over the little river, la Vienne, a broad and well-constructed bridge, ornamented with four stone sphinxes; and in front of the bridge is a large iron gate, opening on an immense court, in which seven or eight thousand men could be drilled. This court is square, surrounded by covered galleries, and ornamented with two large basins with marble statues; and on each side of the gateway are two large obelisks in rose-colored stone, surmounted by eagles of gilded lead.

'*Schoenbrunn*', in German, signifies beautiful fountain; and this name comes from a clear and limpid spring, which rises in a grove in the park, on a slight elevation, around which has been built a little pavilion, carved on the inside to imitate stalactites. In this pavilion lies a sleeping Naiad, holding in her hand a shell, from which the water gushes and falls into a marble basin. This is a delicious retreat in summer.

We can speak only in terms of admiration regarding the interior of the palace, the furniture of which was handsome and of an original and elegant style. The Emperor's sleeping-room, the only part of the building in which there was a fireplace, was ornamented with wainscoting in Chinese lacquer work, then very old, though the painting and gilding were still fresh, and the cabinet was decorated like the bedroom; and all the apartments, except this, were warmed in winter by immense stoves, which greatly injured the effect of the interior architecture. Between the study and the Emperor's room was a very curious machine, called the flying chariot, a kind of mechanical contrivance, which had been made for the Empress Maria Theresa, and was used in conveying her from one story to the other, so that she might not be obliged to ascend and descend staircases like the rest of the world. This machine was operated by means of cords, pulleys, and weights, like those at the theatre.

The beautiful grove which serves as park and garden to the palace of Schoenbrunn is much too small to belong to an imperial residence; but, on the other hand, it would be hard to find one more beautiful or better arranged. The park of Versailles is grander and more imposing; but it has not the picturesque irregularity, the fantastic and unexpected beauties, of the park of Schoenbrunn, and more closely resembles the park at Malmaison. In front of the interior facade of the palace was a magnificent lawn, sloping down to a broad lake, decorated with a group of statuary representing the triumph of Neptune. This group is very fine; but French amateurs (every Frenchman, as you are aware, desires to be considered a connoisseur) insisted that the women were more Austrian than Grecian, and that they did not possess the slender grace belonging to antique forms; and, for my part, I must confess that these statues did not appear to me very remarkable.

At the end of the grand avenue, and bounding the horizon, rose a hill, which overlooked the park, and was crowned by a handsome building, which bore the name of La Gloriette. This building was a circular gallery, enclosed with glass, supported by a charming colonnade, between the arches of which hung various trophies. On entering the avenue from the direction of Vienna, La Gloriette rose at the farther end, seeming almost to form a part of the palace; and the effect was very fine.

What the Austrians especially admired in the palace of Schoenbrunn was a grove, containing what they called the Ruins, and a lake with a fountain springing from the midst, and several small cascades flowing from it; by this lake were the ruins of an aqueduct and a temple, fallen vases, tombs, broken bas-reliefs, statues without heads, arms, or limbs, while limbs, arms, and heads lay thickly scattered around; columns mutilated and half-buried, others standing and supporting the remains of pediments and entablatures; all combining to form a scene of beautiful disorder, and representing a genuine ancient ruin when viewed from a short distance. Viewed more closely, it is quite another thing: the hand of the modern sculptor is seen; it is evident that all these fragments are made from the same kind of stone; and the weeds which grow in the hollows of these columns appear what they really are, that is to say, made of stone, and painted to imitate verdure.

But if the productions of art scattered through the park of Schoenbrunn were not all irreproachable, those of nature fully made up the deficiency. What magnificent trees! What thick hedges! What dense and refreshing shade! The avenues were remarkably high and broad, and bordered with trees, which formed a vault impenetrable to the sun, while the eye lost itself in their many windings; from these other smaller walks diverged, where fresh surprises were in store at every step. At the end of the broadest of these was placed the menagerie, which was one of the most extensive and varied in Europe, and its construction, which was very ingenious, might well serve as a model; it was shaped like a star, and in the round centre of this star had been erected a small but very elegant kiosk, placed there by the Empress Maria Theresa as a resting-place for herself, and from which the whole menagerie could be viewed at leisure.

Each point of this star formed a separate garden, where there could be seen elephants, buffaloes, camels, dromedaries, stags, and kangaroos grazing; handsome and substantial cages held tigers, bears, leopards, lions, hyenas, etc; and swans and rare aquatic birds and amphibious animals sported in basins surrounded by iron gratings. In this menagerie I specially remarked a very extraordinary animal, which his Majesty had ordered brought to France, but which had died the day before it was to have started. This animal was from Poland, and was called a *'curus'*; it was a kind of ox, though much larger than an ordinary ox, with a mane like a lion, horns rather short and somewhat curved, and enormously large at the base.

Every morning, at six o'clock, the drums beat, and two or three hours after the troops were ordered to parade in the court of honour; and at precisely ten o'clock his Majesty descended, and put himself at the head of his generals.

It is impossible to give an idea of these parades, which in no particular resembled reviews in Paris. The Emperor, during these reviews, investigated the smallest details, and examined the soldiers one by one, so to speak, looked into the eyes of each to see whether there was pleasure or work in his head, questioned the officers, sometimes also the soldiers themselves; and it was usually on these occasions that the Emperor made his promotions. During one of these reviews, if he asked a colonel who was the bravest officer in his regiment, there was no hesitation in his answer; and it was always prompt, for he knew that the Emperor was already well informed on this point. After the colonel had replied, he addressed himself to all the other officers, saying, "Who is the bravest among you?"

"Sire, it is such an one;" and the two answers were almost always the same. "Then," said the Emperor, "I make him a baron; and I reward in him, not only his own personal bravery, but that of the corps of which he forms a part. He does not owe this favour to me alone, but also to the esteem of his comrades." It was the same case with the soldiers; and those most distinguished for courage or good conduct were promoted or received rewards, and sometimes pensions, the Emperor giving one of twelve hundred *francs* to a soldier, who, on his first campaign, had passed through the enemy's squadron, bearing on his shoulders his wounded general, protecting him as he would his own father.

On these reviews the Emperor could be seen personally inspecting the haversacks of the soldiers, examining their certificates, or taking a gun from the shoulders of a young man who was weak, pale, and suffering, and saying to him, in a sympathetic tone, "That is too heavy for you." He often drilled them himself; and when he did not, the drilling was directed by Generals Dorsenne, Curial, or Mouton. Sometimes he was seized with a sudden whim; for example, one morning, after reviewing a regiment of the Confederation, he turned to the ordnance officers, and addressing Prince Salm, who was among them, remarked "M. de Salm, the soldiers ought to get acquainted with you; approach, and order them to make a charge in twelve movements." The young prince turned crimson, without being disconcerted, however, bowed, and drawing his sword most gracefully, executed the orders of the Emperor with an ease and precision which charmed him.

Another day, as the engineer corps passed with about forty wagons, the Emperor cried, "Halt!" and pointing out a wagon to General Bertrand, ordered him to summon one of the officers. "What does that wagon contain?"

"Sire, bolts, bags of nails, ropes, hatchets, and saws."

"How much of each?" The officer gave the exact account. His Majesty, to verify this report, had the wagon emptied, counted the pieces, and found the number correct; and in order to assure himself that nothing was left in the wagon, climbed up into it by means of the wheel, holding on to the spokes. There was a murmur of approbation and cries of joy all along the line. "Bravo!" they said; "well and good! that is the way to make sure of not being deceived." All these things conspired to make the soldiers adore the Emperor.

Chapter 47

At one of the reviews which I have just described, and which usually attracted a crowd of curious people from Vienna and its suburbs, the Emperor came near being assassinated. It was on the 13th of October, his Majesty had just alighted from his horse, and was crossing the court on foot with the Prince de Neuchatel and General Rapp beside him, when a young man with a passably good countenance pushed his way rudely through the crowd, and asked in bad French if he could speak to the Emperor. His Majesty received him kindly, but not understanding his language, asked General Rapp to see what the young man wanted, and the general asked him a few questions; and not satisfied apparently with his answers, ordered the police-officer on duty to remove him. A sub-officer conducted the young man out of the circle formed by the staff, and drove him back into the crowd. This circumstance had been forgotten, when suddenly the Emperor, on turning, found again near him the pretended suppliant, who had returned holding his right hand in his breast, as if to draw a petition from the pocket of his coat. General Rapp seized the man by the arm, and said to him, "Monsieur, you have already been ordered away; what do you want?" As he was about to retire a second time the general, thinking his appearance suspicious, gave orders to the police-officer to arrest him, and he accordingly made a sign to his subalterns. One of them seizing him by the collar shook him slightly, when his coat became partly unbuttoned, and something fell out resembling a package of papers; on examination it was found to be a large carving knife, with several folds of grey paper wrapped around it as a sheath; thereupon he was conducted to General Savary.

This young man was a student, and the son of a Protestant minister of Naumbourg; he was called Frederic Stabs, and was about eighteen or nineteen years old, with a pallid face and effeminate features. He did not deny for an instant that it was his intention to kill the Emperor; but on the contrary boasted of it, and expressed his intense regret that circumstances had prevented the accomplishment of his design.

He had left his father's house on a horse which the want of money had compelled him to sell on the way, and none of his relatives or friends had any knowledge of his plan. The day after his departure he had written to his father that he need not be anxious about him nor the horse; that he had long since promised some one to visit Vienna, and his family would soon hear of him with pride. He had arrived at Vienna only two days before, and had occupied himself first in obtaining information as to the Emperor's habits, and finding that he held a review every morning in the court of the chateau, had been there once in order to acquaint himself with the locality. The next day he had undertaken to make the attack, and had been arrested.

The Duke of Rovigo, after questioning Stabs, sought the Emperor, who had returned to his apartments, and acquainted him with the danger he had just escaped. The Emperor at first shrugged his shoulders, but having been shown the knife which had been taken from Stabs, said, "Ah, ha! send for the young man; I should like very much to talk with him." The duke went out, and returned in a few moments with Stabs. When the latter entered, the Emperor made a gesture of pity, and said to the Prince de Neuchatel, "Why, really, he is nothing more than a child!" An interpreter was summoned and the interrogation begun.

His Majesty first asked the assassin if he had seen him, anywhere before this. "Yes; I saw you," replied Stabbs, "at Erfurt last year."

"It seems that a crime is nothing in your eyes. Why did you wish to kill me?"

"To kill you is not a crime; on the contrary, it is the duty of every good German. I wished to kill you because you are the oppressor of Germany."

"It is not I who commenced the war; it is your nation. Whose picture is this?" (the Emperor held in his hands the picture of a woman that had been found on Stabs). "It is that of my best friend, my father's adopted daughter."

"What! and you are an assassin! and have no fear of afflicting and destroying beings who are so dear to you?"

"I wished to do my duty, and nothing could have deterred me from it."

"But how would you have succeeded in, striking me?"

"I would first have asked you if we were soon to have peace; and if you had answered no, I should have stabbed you."

"He is mad!" said the Emperor; "he is evidently mad! And how could you have hoped to escape, after you had struck me thus in the midst of my soldiers?"

"I knew well to what I was exposing myself, and am astonished to be still alive." This boldness made such a deep impression on the Emperor that he remained silent for several moments, intently regarding Stabs, who remained entirely unmoved under this scrutiny. Then the Emperor continued, "The one you love will be much distressed."

"Oh, she will no doubt be distressed because I did not succeed, for she hates you at least as much as I hate you myself."

"Suppose I pardoned you?"

"You would be wrong, for I would again try to kill you." The Emperor summoned M. Corvisart and said to him, "This young man is either sick or insane, it cannot be otherwise."

"I am neither the one nor the other," replied the assassin quickly. M. Corvisart felt Stabs's pulse. "This gentleman is well," he said. "I have already told you so," replied Stabs with a triumphant air.

"Well, doctor," said his Majesty, "this young man who is in such good health has travelled a hundred miles to assassinate me."

Notwithstanding this declaration of the physician and the avowal of Stabs, the Emperor, touched by the coolness and assurance of the unfortunate fellow, again offered him his pardon, upon the sole condition of expressing some repentance for his crime; but as Stabs again asserted that his only regret was that he had not succeeded in his undertaking, the Emperor reluctantly gave him up to punishment.

After he was conducted to prison, as he still persisted in his assertions, he was immediately brought before a military commission, which condemned him to death. He did not undergo his punishment till the 17th; and after the 13th, the day on which he was arrested, took no food, saying that he would have strength enough to go to his death. The Emperor had ordered that the execution should be delayed as long as possible, in the hope that sooner or later Stabs would repent; but he remained unshaken. As he was being conducted to the place where he was to be shot, some one having told him that peace had just been concluded, he cried in a loud voice, "Long live liberty! Long live Germany!" These were his last words.

Chapter 48

During his stay at Schoenbrunn the Emperor was constantly engaged in gallant adventures. He was one day promenading on the Prater in Vienna, with a very numerous suite (the Prater is a handsome promenade situated in the Faubourg Leopold), when a young German, widow of a rich merchant, saw him, and exclaimed involuntarily to the ladies promenading with her, "It is he!" This exclamation was overheard by his Majesty, who stopped short, and bowed to the ladies with a smile, while the one who had spoken blushed crimson; the Emperor comprehended this unequivocal sign, looked at her steadfastly, and then continued his walk.

For sovereigns there are neither long attacks nor great difficulties, and this new conquest of his Majesty was not less rapid than the others. In order not to be separated from her illustrious lover, Madame B—— followed the army to Bavaria, and afterwards came to him at Paris, where she died in 1812.

His Majesty's attention was attracted by a charming young person one morning in the suburbs of Schoenbrunn; and some one was ordered to see this young lady, and arrange for a rendezvous at the chateau the following evening. Fortune favoured his Majesty on this occasion. The *éclat* of so illustrious a name, and the renown of his victories, had produced a deep impression on the mind of the young girl, and had disposed her to listen favourably to the propositions made to her. She therefore eagerly consented to meet him at the chateau; and at the appointed hour the person of whom I have spoken came for her, and I received her on her arrival, and introduced her to his Majesty. She did not speak French, but she knew Italian well, and it was consequently easy for the Emperor to converse with her; and he soon learned with astonishment that this charming young lady belonged to a very honourable family of Vienna, and that in coming to him that evening she was inspired alone by a desire to express to him her sincere admiration. The Emperor respected the innocence of the young girl, had her reconducted to her parents' residence, and gave orders that a marriage should be arranged for her, and that it should be rendered more advantageous by means of a considerable dowry.

At Schoenbrunn, as at Paris, his Majesty dined habitually at six o'clock; but since he worked sometimes very far into the night, care was taken to prepare every evening a light supper, which was placed in a little locked basket covered with oil-cloth. There were two keys to this basket; one of which the steward kept, and I the other. The care of this basket belonged to me alone; and as his Majesty was extremely busy, he hardly ever asked for supper. One evening Roustan, who had been busily occupied all day in his master's service, was in a little room next to the Emperor's, and meeting me just after I had assisted in putting his Majesty to bed, said to me in his bad French, looking at the basket with an envious eye, "I could eat a chicken wing myself; I am very hungry." I refused at first; but finally, as I knew that the Emperor had gone to bed, and had no idea he would take a fancy to ask me for supper that evening, I let Roustan have it. He, much delighted, began with a leg, and next took a wing; and I do not know if any of the chicken would have been left had I not suddenly heard the bell ring sharply. I entered the room, and was shocked to hear the Emperor say to me, "Constant, my chicken." My embarrassment may be imagined. I had no other chicken; and by what means, at such an hour, could I procure one! At last I decided what to do. It was best to cut up the fowl, as thus I would be able to conceal the absence of the two limbs Roustan had eaten; so I entered proudly with the chicken replaced on the dish Roustan following me, for I was very willing, if there were any reproaches, to share them with him. I picked up the remaining wing, and presented it to the Emperor; but he refused it, saying to me, "Give me the chicken; I will choose for myself." This time there was no means of saving ourselves, for the dismembered chicken must pass under his Majesty's eyes. "See here," said he, "since when did chickens begin to have only one wing and one leg? That is fine; it seems that I must eat what others leave. Who, then, eats half of my supper?" I looked at Roustan, who in confusion replied, "I was very hungry, Sire, and I ate a wing and leg."

"What, you idiot! so it was you, was it?"

"Ah, I will punish you for it." And without another word the Emperor ate the remaining leg and wing.

The next day at his toilet he summoned the grand marshal for some purpose, and during the conversation said, "I leave you to guess what I ate last night for my supper. The scraps which M. Roustan left. Yes, the wretch took a notion to eat half of my chicken." Roustan entered at that moment. "Come here, you idiot," continued the Emperor; "and the next time this happens, be sure you will pay for it." Saying this, he seized him by the ears and laughed heartily.

(Continued in Volume 2)

ALSO FROM LEONAUR
AVAILABLE IN SOFTCOVER OR HARDCOVER WITH DUST JACKET

LIGHT BOB by *Robert Blakeney*—The experiences of a young officer in H.M 28th & 36th regiments of the British Infantry during the Peninsular Campaign of the Napoleonic Wars 1804 - 1814.

NAPOLEON'S RUSSIAN CAMPAIGN by *Philippe Henri de Segur*—The Invasion, Battles and Retreat by an Aide-de-Camp on the Emperor's Staff

SWORDS OF HONOUR by *Henry Newbolt & Stanley L. Wood*—The Careers of Six Outstanding Officers from the Napoleonic Wars, the Wars for India and the American Civil War. Illustrated.

HUSSAR IN WINTER by *Alexander Gordon*—A British Cavalry Officer during the retreat to Corunna in the Peninsular campaign of the Napoleonic Wars.

THE LIFE OF THE REAL BRIGADIER GERARD VOLUME 1 THE YOUNG HUSSAR 1782 - 1807 by *Jean-Baptiste De Marbot*—A French Cavalryman Of the Napoleonic Wars at Marengo, Austerlitz, Jena, Eylau & Friedland.

THE LIFE OF THE REAL BRIGADIER GERARD VOLUME 2 IMPERIAL AIDE-DE-CAMP 1807 - 1811 by *Jean-Baptiste De Marbot*—A French Cavalryman of the Napoleonic Wars at Saragossa, Landshut, Eckmuhl, Ratisbon, Aspern-Essling, Wagram, Busaco & Torres Vedras.

THE LIFE OF THE REAL BRIGADIER GERARD VOLUME 3 COLONEL OF CHASSEURS 1811 - 1815 by *Jean-Baptiste De Marbot*—A French Cavalryman in the retreat from Moscow, Lutzen, Bautzen, Katzbach, Leipzig, Hanau & Waterloo.

RIFLEMAN COSTELLO by *Edward Costello*—The adventures of a soldier of the 95th (Rifles) in the Peninsular & Waterloo Campaigns of the Napoleonic wars.

WITH THE LIGHT DIVISION by *John H. Cooke*—The Experiences of an Officer of the 43rd Light Infantry in the Peninsula and South of France During the Napoleonic Wars.

COLBORNE: A SINGULAR TALENT FOR WAR by *John Colborne*—The Napoleonic Wars Career of One of Wellington's Most Highly Valued Officers in Egypt, Holland, Italy, the Peninsula and at Waterloo.

A VOICE FROM WATERLOO by *Edward Cotton*—The Personal Experiences of a British Cavalryman Who Became a Battlefield Guide and Authority on the Campaign of 1815.

AVAILABLE ONLINE AT
www.leonaur.com
AND OTHER GOOD BOOK STORES

ALSO FROM LEONAUR
AVAILABLE IN SOFTCOVER OR HARDCOVER WITH DUST JACKET

WELLINGTON AND THE PYRENEES CAMPAIGN VOLUME I: FROM VITORIA TO THE BIDASSOA by *F. C. Beatson*—The final phase of the campaign in the Iberian Peninsula.

WELLINGTON AND THE INVASION OF FRANCE VOLUME II: THE BIDASSOA TO THE BATTLE OF THE NIVELLE by *F. C. Beatson*—The second of Beatson's series on the fall of Revolutionary France published by Leonaur, the reader is once again taken into the centre of Wellington's strategic and tactical genius.

WELLINGTON AND THE FALL OF FRANCE VOLUME III: THE GAVES AND THE BATTLE OF ORTHEZ by *F. C. Beatson*—This final chapter of F. C. Beatson's brilliant trilogy shows the 'captain of the age' at his most inspired and makes all three books essential additions to any Peninsular War library.

NAVAL BATTLES OF THE NAPOLEONIC WARS by *W. H. Fitchett*—Cape St. Vincent, the Nile, Cadiz, Copenhagen, Trafalgar & Others

SERGEANT GUILLEMARD: THE MAN WHO SHOT NELSON? by *Robert Guillemard*—A Soldier of the Infantry of the French Army of Napoleon on Campaign Throughout Europe

WITH THE GUARDS ACROSS THE PYRENEES by *Robert Batty*—The Experiences of a British Officer of Wellington's Army During the Battles for the Fall of Napoleonic France, 1813.

A STAFF OFFICER IN THE PENINSULA by *E. W. Buckham*—An Officer of the British Staff Corps Cavalry During the Peninsula Campaign of the Napoleonic Wars

THE LEIPZIG CAMPAIGN: 1813—NAPOLEON AND THE "BATTLE OF THE NATIONS" by *F. N. Maude*—Colonel Maude's analysis of Napoleon's campaign of 1813.

BUGEAUD: A PACK WITH A BATON by *Thomas Robert Bugeaud*—The Early Campaigns of a Soldier of Napoleon's Army Who Would Become a Marshal of France.

TWO LEONAUR ORIGINALS

SERGEANT NICOL by *Daniel Nicol*—The Experiences of a Gordon Highlander During the Napoleonic Wars in Egypt, the Peninsula and France.

WATERLOO RECOLLECTIONS by *Frederick Llewellyn*—Rare First Hand Accounts, Letters, Reports and Retellings from the Campaign of 1815.

AVAILABLE ONLINE AT **www.leonaur.com**
AND OTHER GOOD BOOK STORES

ALSO FROM LEONAUR
AVAILABLE IN SOFTCOVER OR HARDCOVER WITH DUST JACKET

THE JENA CAMPAIGN: 1806 by *F. N. Maude*—The Twin Battles of Jena & Auerstadt Between Napoleon's French and the Prussian Army.

PRIVATE O'NEIL by *Charles O'Neil*—The recollections of an Irish Rogue of H. M. 28th Regt.—The Slashers— during the Peninsula & Waterloo campaigns of the Napoleonic wars.

ROYAL HIGHLANDER by *James Anton*—A soldier of H.M 42nd (Royal) Highlanders during the Peninsular, South of France & Waterloo Campaigns of the Napoleonic Wars.

CAPTAIN BLAZE by *Elzéar Blaze*—Elzéar Blaze recounts his life and experiences in Napoleon's army in a well written, articulate and companionable style.

LEJEUNE VOLUME 1 by *Louis-François Lejeune*—The Napoleonic Wars through the Experiences of an Officer on Berthier's Staff.

LEJEUNE VOLUME 2 by *Louis-François Lejeune*—The Napoleonic Wars through the Experiences of an Officer on Berthier's Staff.

FUSILIER COOPER by *John S. Cooper*—Experiences in the 7th (Royal) Fusiliers During the Peninsular Campaign of the Napoleonic Wars and the American Campaign to New Orleans.

CAPTAIN COIGNET by *Jean-Roch Coignet*—A Soldier of Napoleon's Imperial Guard from the Italian Campaign to Russia and Waterloo.

FIGHTING NAPOLEON'S EMPIRE by *Joseph Anderson*—The Campaigns of a British Infantryman in Italy, Egypt, the Peninsular & the West Indies During the Napoleonic Wars.

CHASSEUR BARRES by *Jean-Baptiste Barres*—The experiences of a French Infantryman of the Imperial Guard at Austerlitz, Jena, Eylau, Friedland, in the Peninsular, Lutzen, Bautzen, Zinnwald and Hanau during the Napoleonic Wars.

MARINES TO 95TH (RIFLES) by *Thomas Fernyhough*—The military experiences of Robert Fernyhough during the Napoleonic Wars.

HUSSAR ROCCA by *Albert Jean Michel de Rocca*—A French cavalry officer's experiences of the Napoleonic Wars and his views on the Peninsular Campaigns against the Spanish, British And Guerilla Armies.

SERGEANT BOURGOGNE by *Adrien Bourgogne*—With Napoleon's Imperial Guard in the Russian Campaign and on the Retreat from Moscow 1812 - 13.

AVAILABLE ONLINE AT **www.leonaur.com**
AND OTHER GOOD BOOK STORES

ALSO FROM LEONAUR
AVAILABLE IN SOFTCOVER OR HARDCOVER WITH DUST JACKET

CAPTAIN OF THE 95th (Rifles) *by Jonathan Leach*—An officer of Wellington's Sharpshooters during the Peninsular, South of France and Waterloo Campaigns of the Napoleonic Wars.

BUGLER AND OFFICER OF THE RIFLES *by William Green & Harry Smith* With the 95th (Rifles) during the Peninsular & Waterloo Campaigns of the Napoleonic Wars

BAYONETS, BUGLES AND BONNETS *by James 'Thomas' Todd*—Experiences of hard soldiering with the 71st Foot - the Highland Light Infantry - through many battles of the Napoleonic wars including the Peninsular & Waterloo Campaigns

THE ADVENTURES OF A LIGHT DRAGOON *by George Farmer & G.R. Gleig*—A cavalryman during the Peninsular & Waterloo Campaigns, in captivity & at the siege of Bhurtpore, India

THE COMPLEAT RIFLEMAN HARRIS *by Benjamin Harris as told to & transcribed by Captain Henry Curling*—The adventures of a soldier of the 95th (Rifles) during the Peninsular Campaign of the Napoleonic Wars

WITH WELLINGTON'S LIGHT CAVALRY *by William Tomkinson*—The Experiences of an officer of the 16th Light Dragoons in the Peninsular and Waterloo campaigns of the Napoleonic Wars.

SURTEES OF THE RIFLES *by William Surtees*—A Soldier of the 95th (Rifles) in the Peninsular campaign of the Napoleonic Wars.

ENSIGN BELL IN THE PENINSULAR WAR *by George Bell*—The Experiences of a young British Soldier of the 34th Regiment 'The Cumberland Gentlemen' in the Napoleonic wars.

WITH THE LIGHT DIVISION *by John H. Cooke*—The Experiences of an Officer of the 43rd Light Infantry in the Peninsula and South of France During the Napoleonic Wars

NAPOLEON'S IMPERIAL GUARD: FROM MARENGO TO WATERLOO *by J. T. Headley*—This is the story of Napoleon's Imperial Guard from the bearskin caps of the grenadiers to the flamboyance of their mounted chasseurs, their principal characters and the men who commanded them.

BATTLES & SIEGES OF THE PENINSULAR WAR *by W. H. Fitchett*—Corunna, Busaco, Albuera, Ciudad Rodrigo, Badajos, Salamanca, San Sebastian & Others

AVAILABLE ONLINE AT **www.leonaur.com**
AND OTHER GOOD BOOK STORES

NAP-1

www.ingramcontent.com/pod-product-compliance
Lightning Source LLC
Chambersburg PA
CBHW030216170426
43201CB00006B/111